HEROMAN 2

Original/Stan Lee + BONES TAMON OHTA

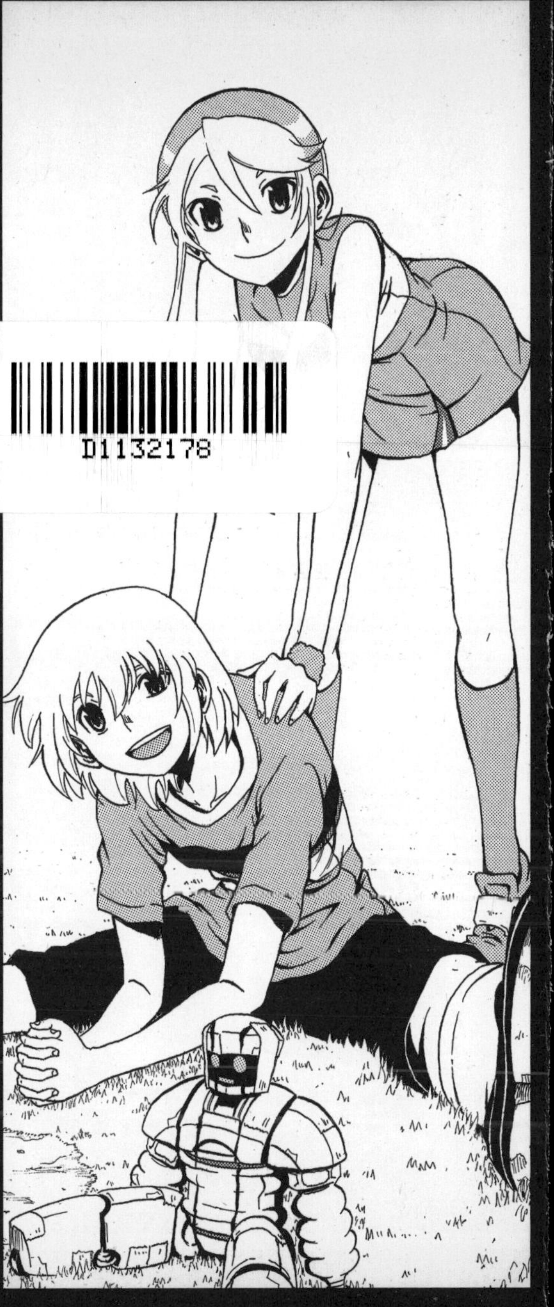

HEROMAN 02 ▸ contents

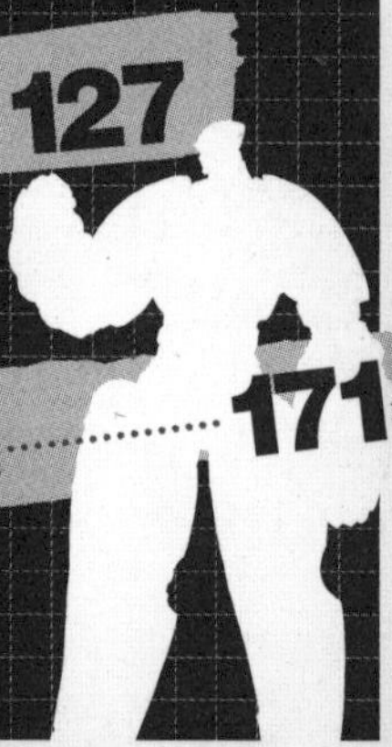

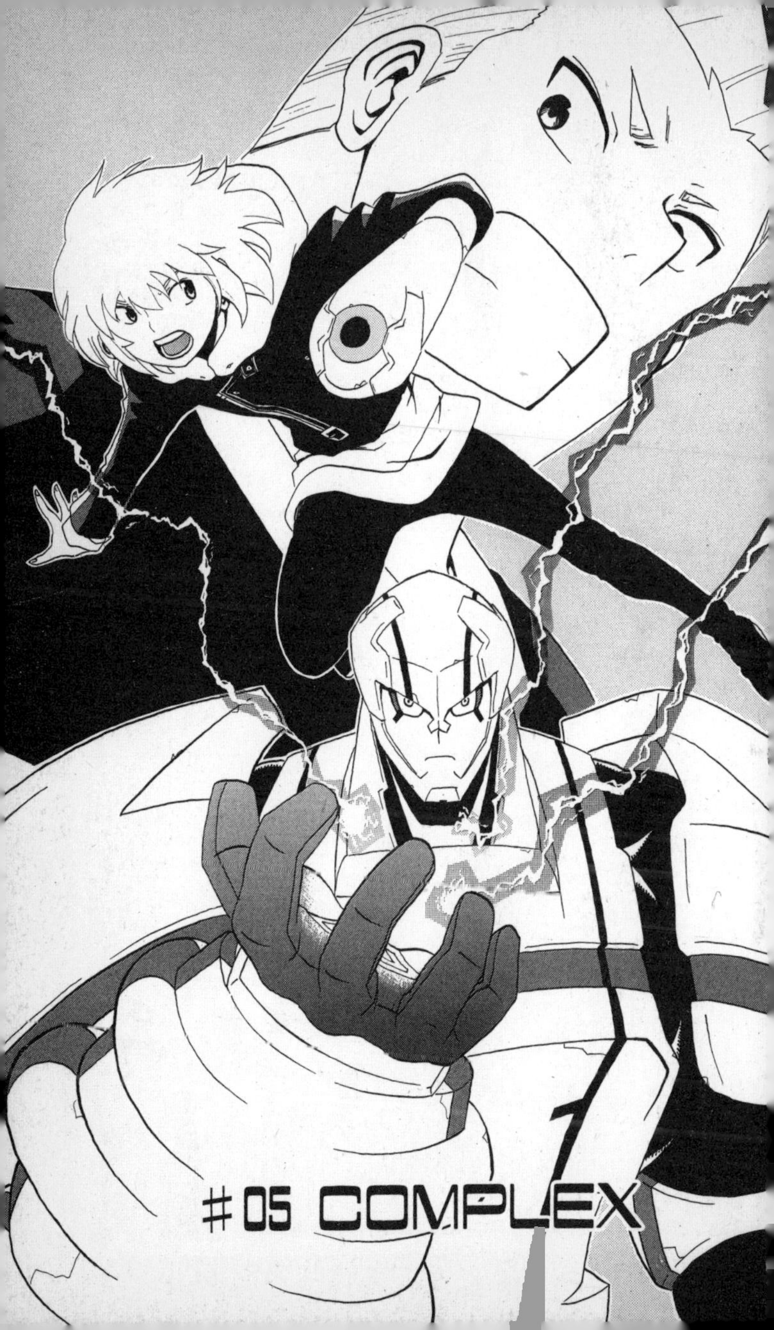
#05 COMPLEX

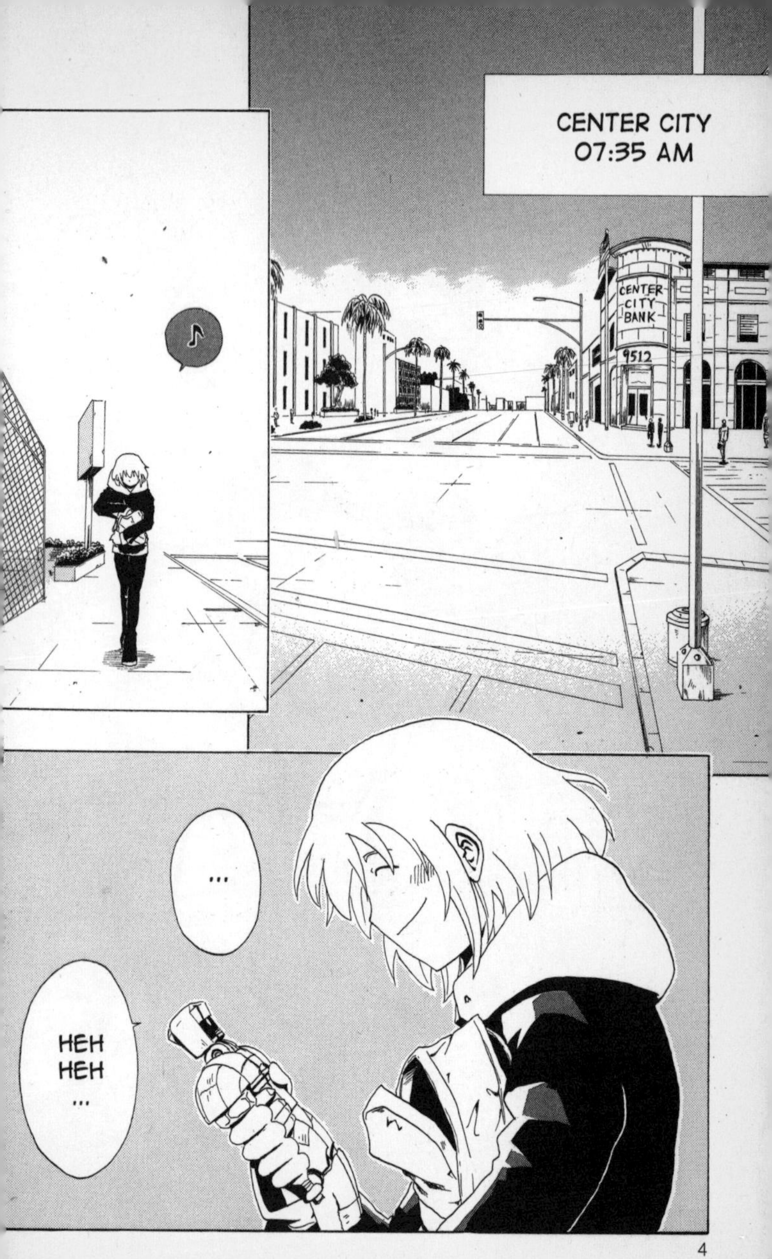
CENTER CITY 07:35 AM
CENTER CITY BANK
9512
♪
...
HEH HEH ...

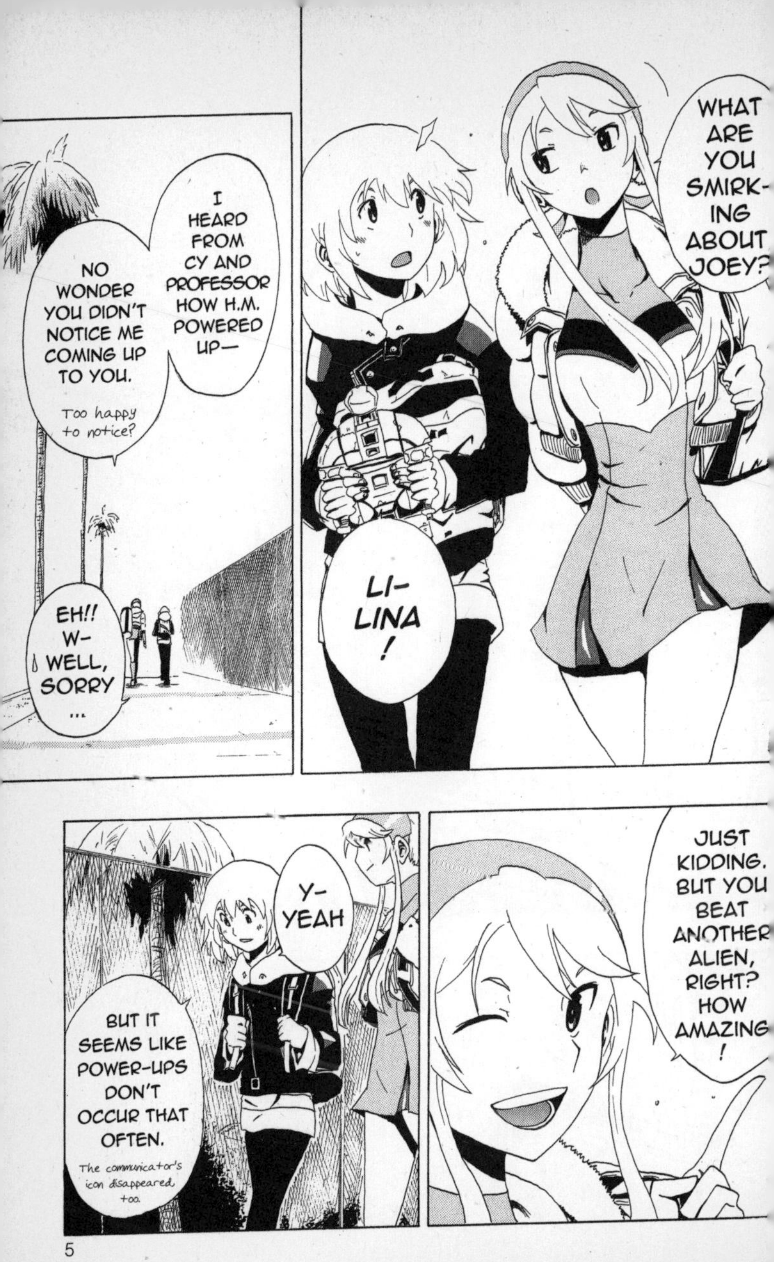
WHAT ARE YOU SMIRKING ABOUT JOEY?
LI-LINA!
I HEARD FROM CY AND PROFESSOR HOW H.M. POWERED UP—
NO WONDER YOU DIDN'T NOTICE ME COMING UP TO YOU.
Too happy to notice?
EH!! W-WELL, SORRY...
JUST KIDDING. BUT YOU BEAT ANOTHER ALIEN, RIGHT? HOW AMAZING!
Y-YEAH
BUT IT SEEMS LIKE POWER-UPS DON'T OCCUR THAT OFTEN.
The communicator's icon disappeared too.

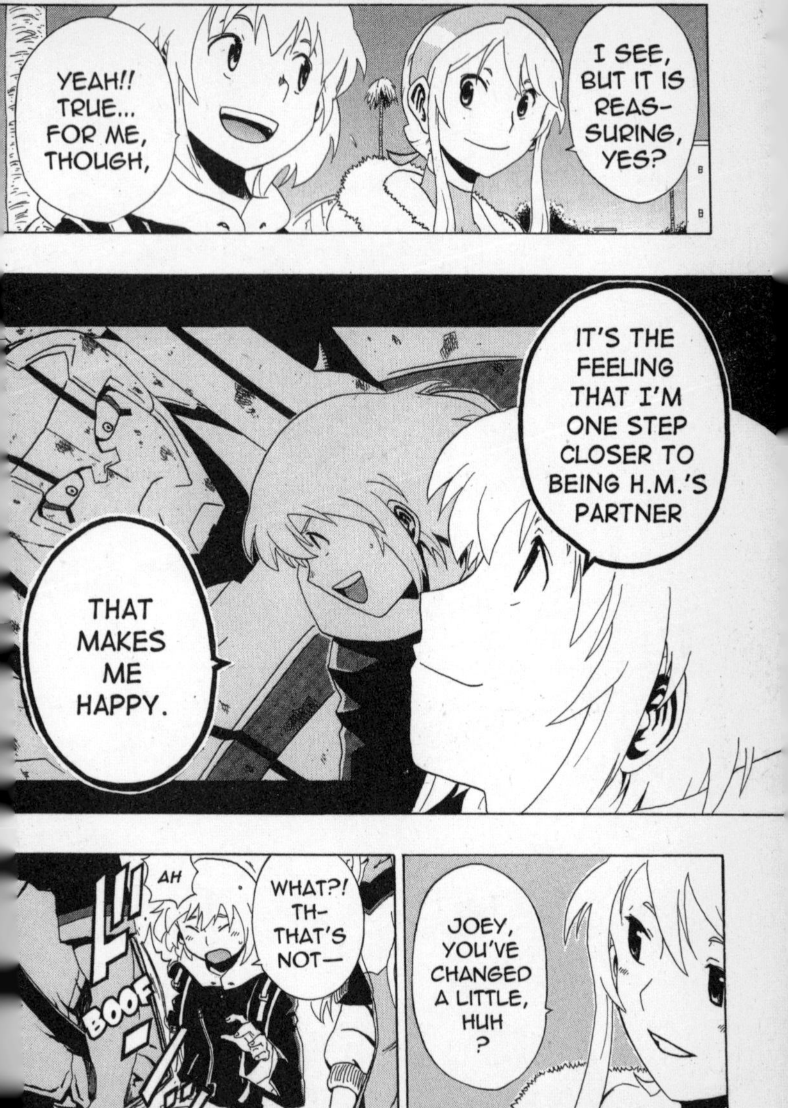
I SEE, BUT IT IS REAS- SURING, YES?
YEAH!! TRUE... FOR ME, THOUGH,
IT'S THE FEELING THAT I'M ONE STEP CLOSER TO BEING H.M.'S PARTNER
THAT MAKES ME HAPPY.
JOEY, YOU'VE CHANGED A LITTLE, HUH ?
WHAT?! TH- THAT'S NOT—
AH
BOOF

W- WILL...

and Nick

BROTHER!

I-I'M SORR—

!

OH ...

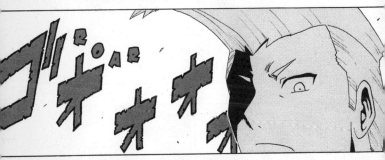

ROAR

L-LINA...

WH-WHAT?! WHY SHOULD YOU CARE WHO YOUR SISTER WALKS WITH?!

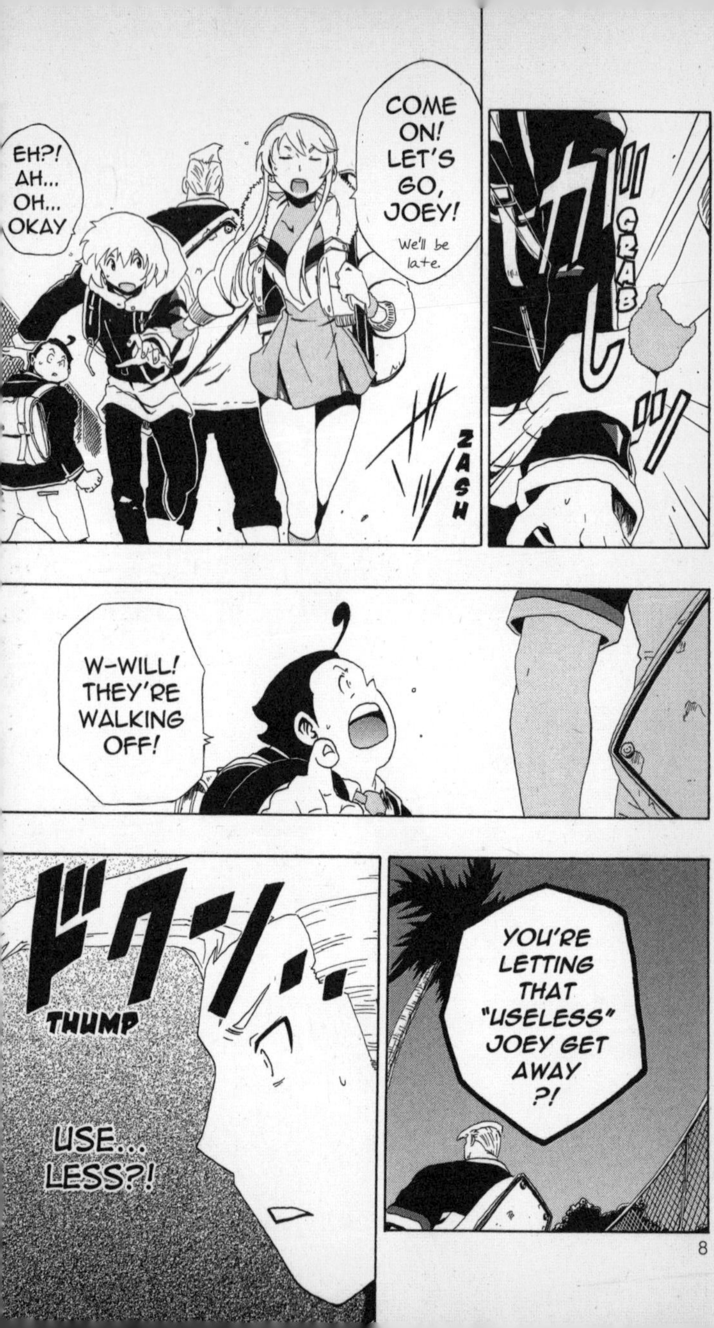
GRAB
COME ON! LET'S GO, JOEY!
We'll be late.
ZASH
EH?! AH... OH... OKAY
W-WILL! THEY'RE WALKING OFF!
YOU'RE LETTING THAT "USELESS" JOEY GET AWAY?!
THUMP
USE... LESS?!

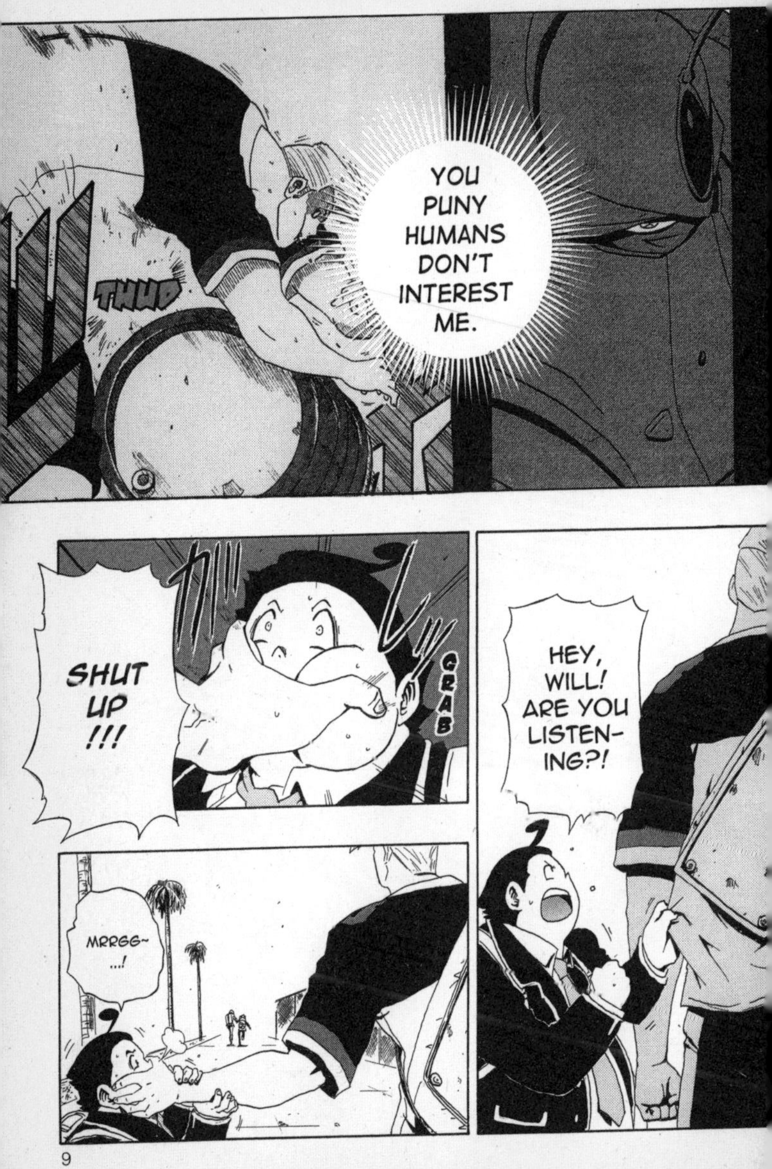
YOU PUNY HUMANS DON'T INTEREST ME.
THUD
HEY, WILL! ARE YOU LISTEN-ING?!
GRAB
SHUT UP !!!
MRRGG~ ...!

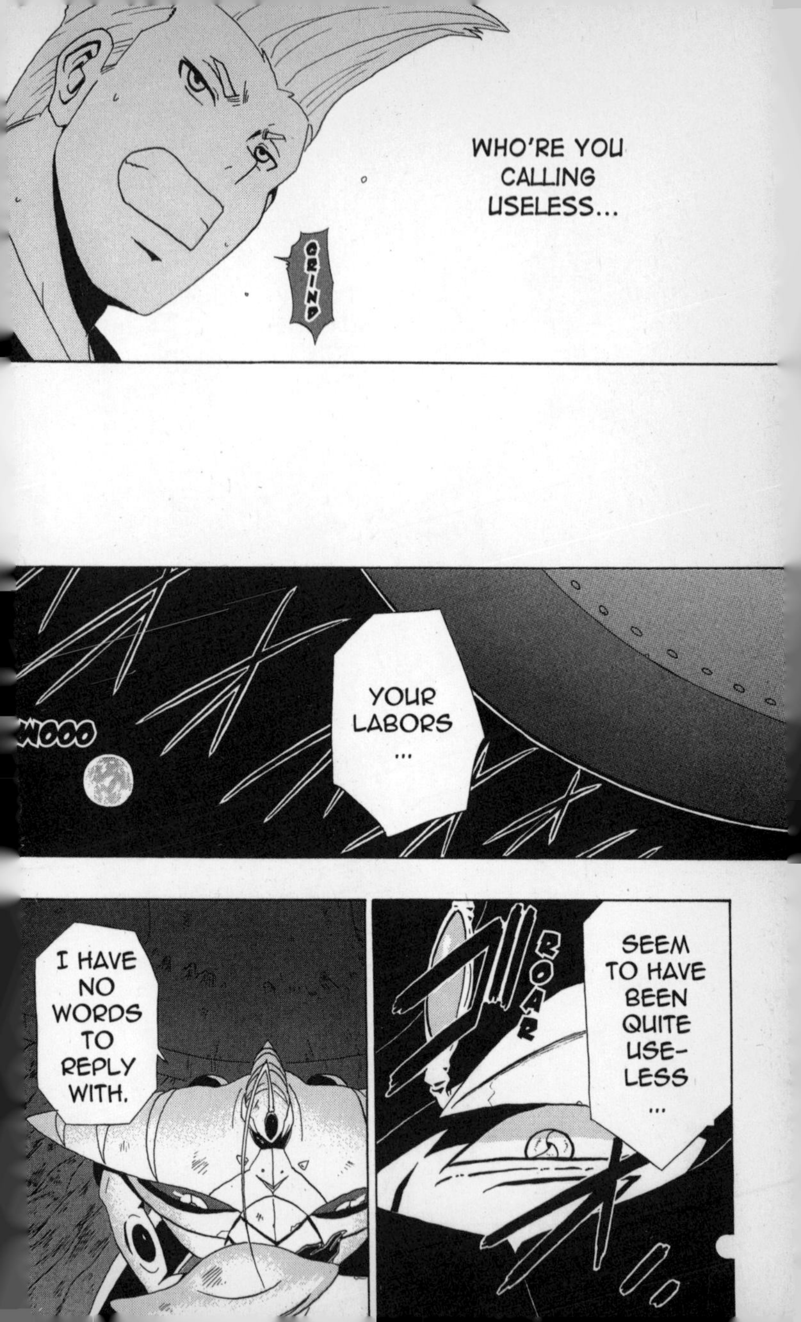
WHO'RE YOU CALLING USELESS...
GRIND
YOUR LABORS ...
WOOO
SEEM TO HAVE BEEN QUITE USE-LESS ...
ROAR
I HAVE NO WORDS TO REPLY WITH.

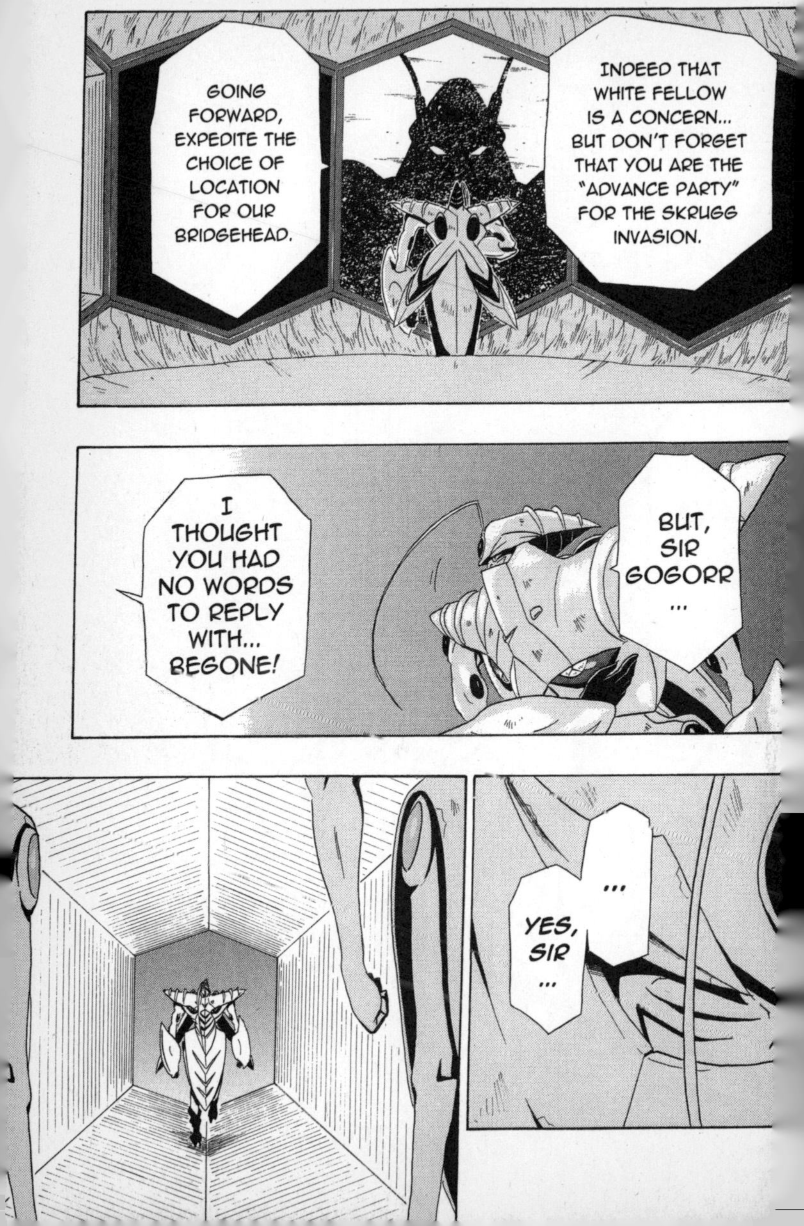
INDEED THAT WHITE FELLOW IS A CONCERN... BUT DON'T FORGET THAT YOU ARE THE "ADVANCE PARTY" FOR THE SKRUGG INVASION.
GOING FORWARD, EXPEDITE THE CHOICE OF LOCATION FOR OUR BRIDGEHEAD.
BUT, SIR GOGORR ...
I THOUGHT YOU HAD NO WORDS TO REPLY WITH... BEGONE!
...
YES, SIR ...

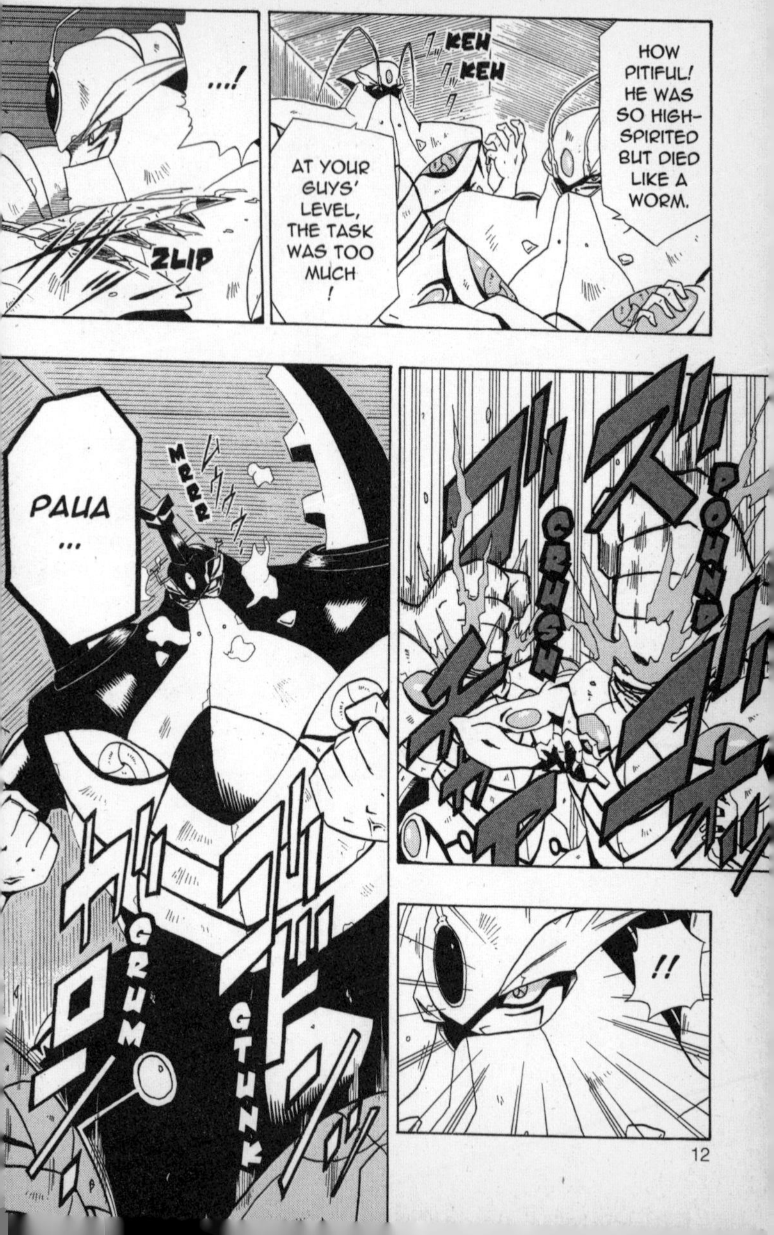
HOW PITIFUL! HE WAS SO HIGH-SPIRITED BUT DIED LIKE A WORM.
KEH KEH
AT YOUR GUYS' LEVEL, THE TASK WAS TOO MUCH !
...!
ZLIP
POUND
CRUSH
!!
PAUA ...
MRRR
GTUNK
GRUM

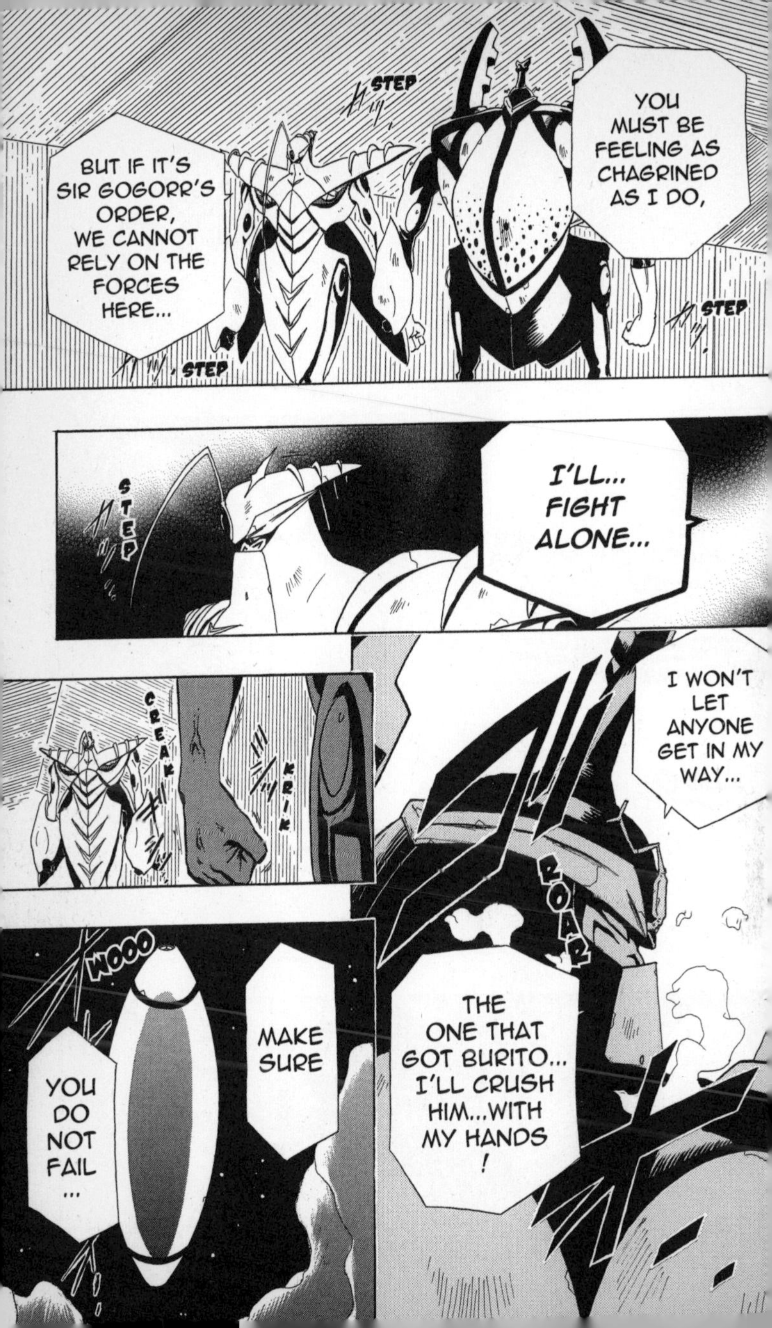
YOU MUST BE FEELING AS CHAGRINED AS I DO,
STEP
BUT IF IT'S SIR GOGORR'S ORDER, WE CANNOT RELY ON THE FORCES HERE...
STEP
STEP
I'LL... FIGHT ALONE...
STEP
I WON'T LET ANYONE GET IN MY WAY...
ROAR
THE ONE THAT GOT BURITO... I'LL CRUSH HIM...WITH MY HANDS!
CREAK
KRIK
WOOO
MAKE SURE
YOU DO NOT FAIL...

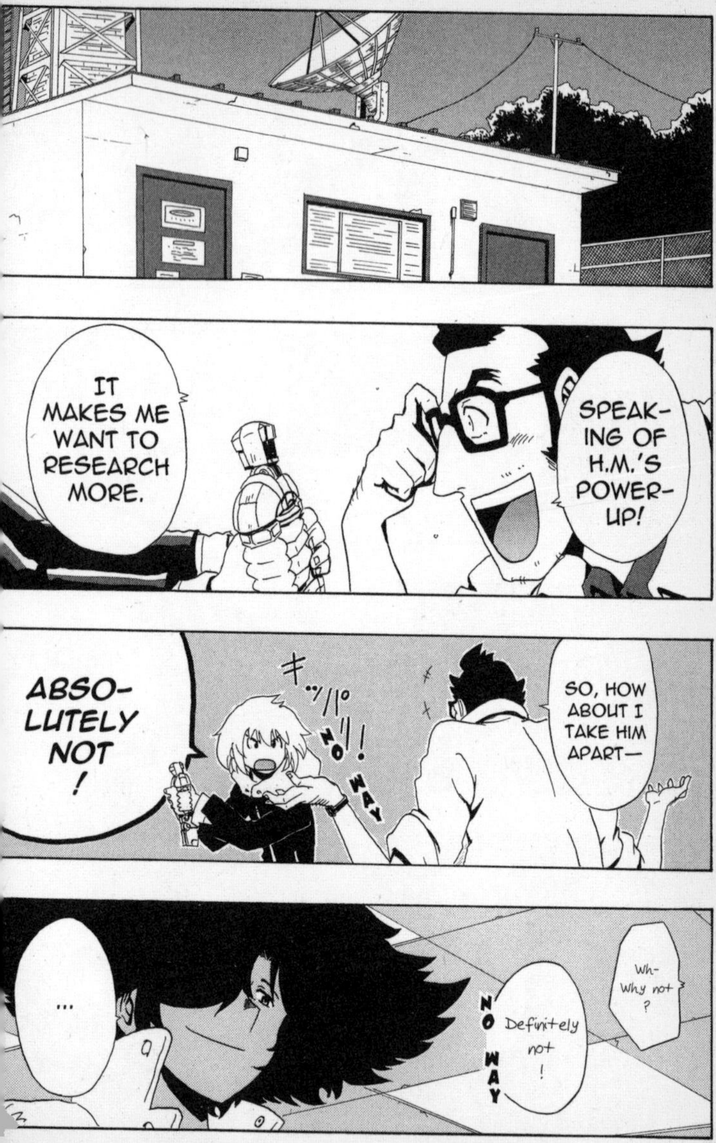
SPEAKING OF H.M.'S POWER-UP!
IT MAKES ME WANT TO RESEARCH MORE.
SO, HOW ABOUT I TAKE HIM APART—
キッパリ!!
NO WAY
ABSOLUTELY NOT!
Wh- Why not?
Definitely not!
NO WAY
...

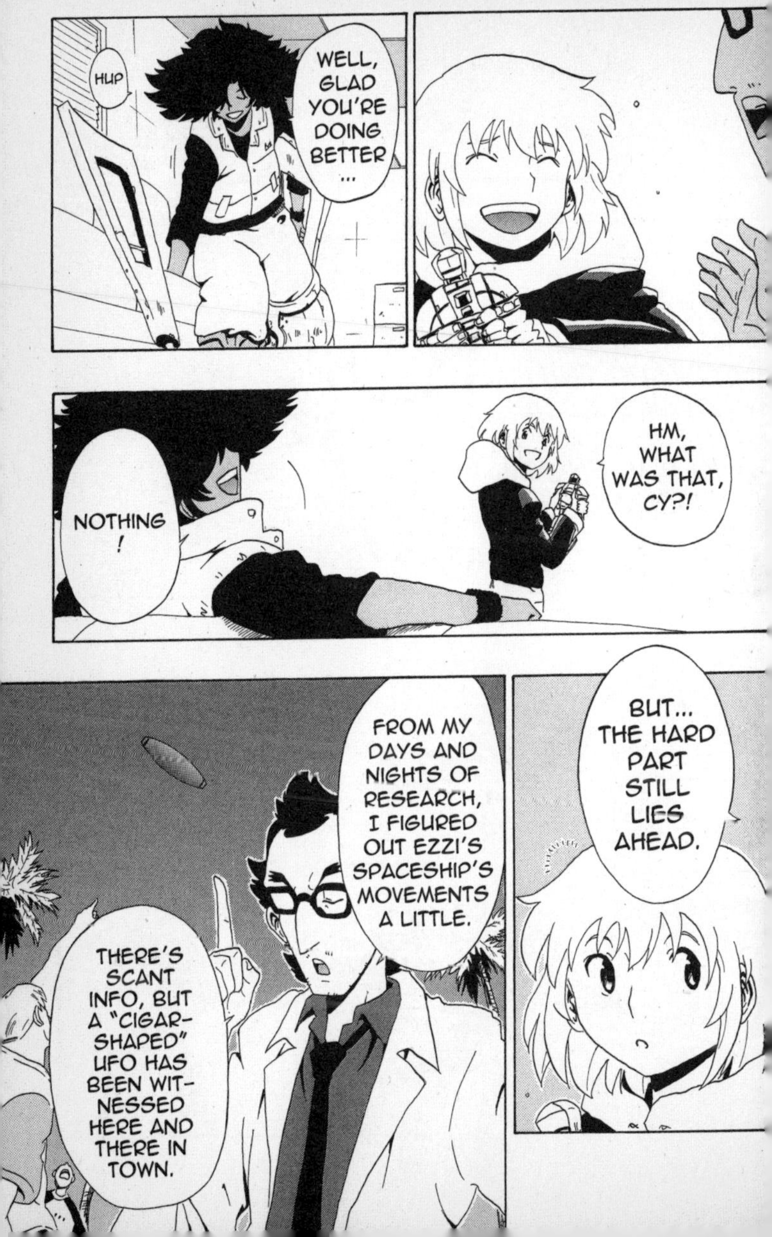

WELL, GLAD YOU'RE DOING BETTER ...
HUP
HM, WHAT WAS THAT, CY?!
NOTHING !
BUT... THE HARD PART STILL LIES AHEAD.
FROM MY DAYS AND NIGHTS OF RESEARCH, I FIGURED OUT EZZI'S SPACESHIP'S MOVEMENTS A LITTLE.
THERE'S SCANT INFO, BUT A "CIGAR-SHAPED" UFO HAS BEEN WIT-NESSED HERE AND THERE IN TOWN.

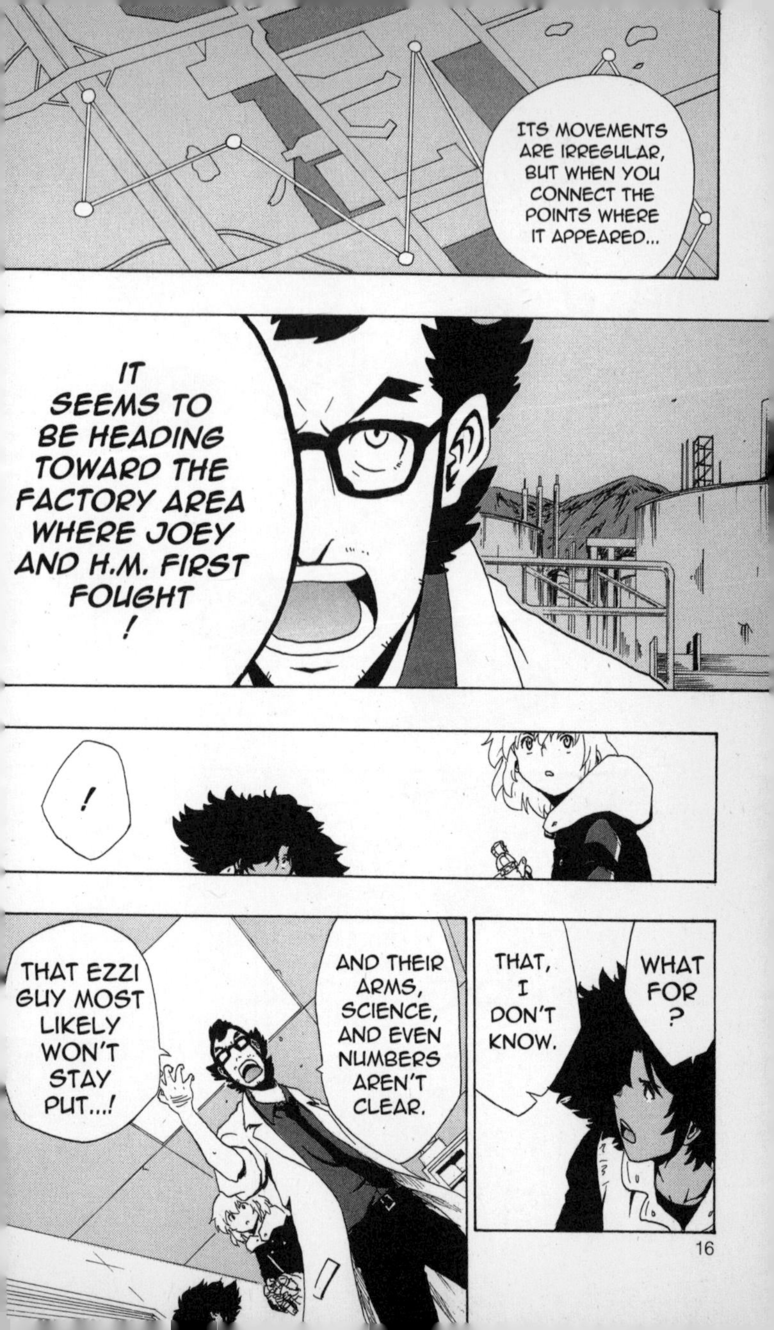
ITS MOVEMENTS ARE IRREGULAR, BUT WHEN YOU CONNECT THE POINTS WHERE IT APPEARED...
IT SEEMS TO BE HEADING TOWARD THE FACTORY AREA WHERE JOEY AND H.M. FIRST FOUGHT !
!
WHAT FOR ?
THAT, I DON'T KNOW.
AND THEIR ARMS, SCIENCE, AND EVEN NUMBERS AREN'T CLEAR.
THAT EZZI GUY MOST LIKELY WON'T STAY PUT...!
!

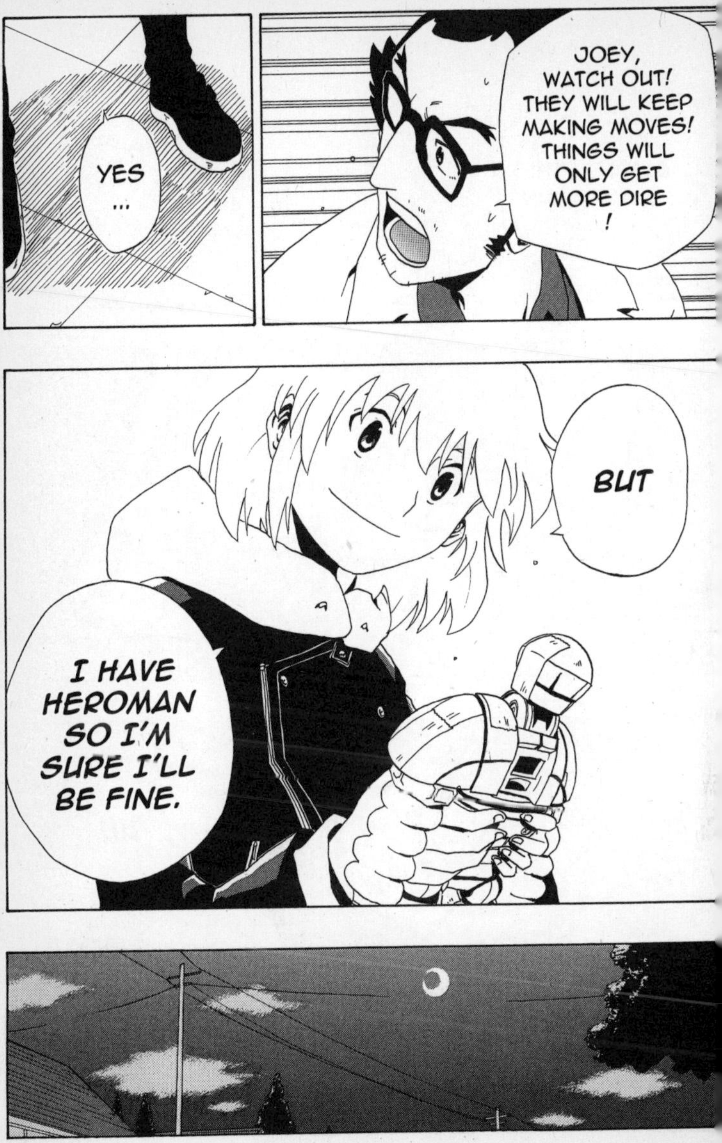
JOEY, WATCH OUT! THEY WILL KEEP MAKING MOVES! THINGS WILL ONLY GET MORE DIRE !
YES ...
BUT
I HAVE HEROMAN SO I'M SURE I'LL BE FINE.

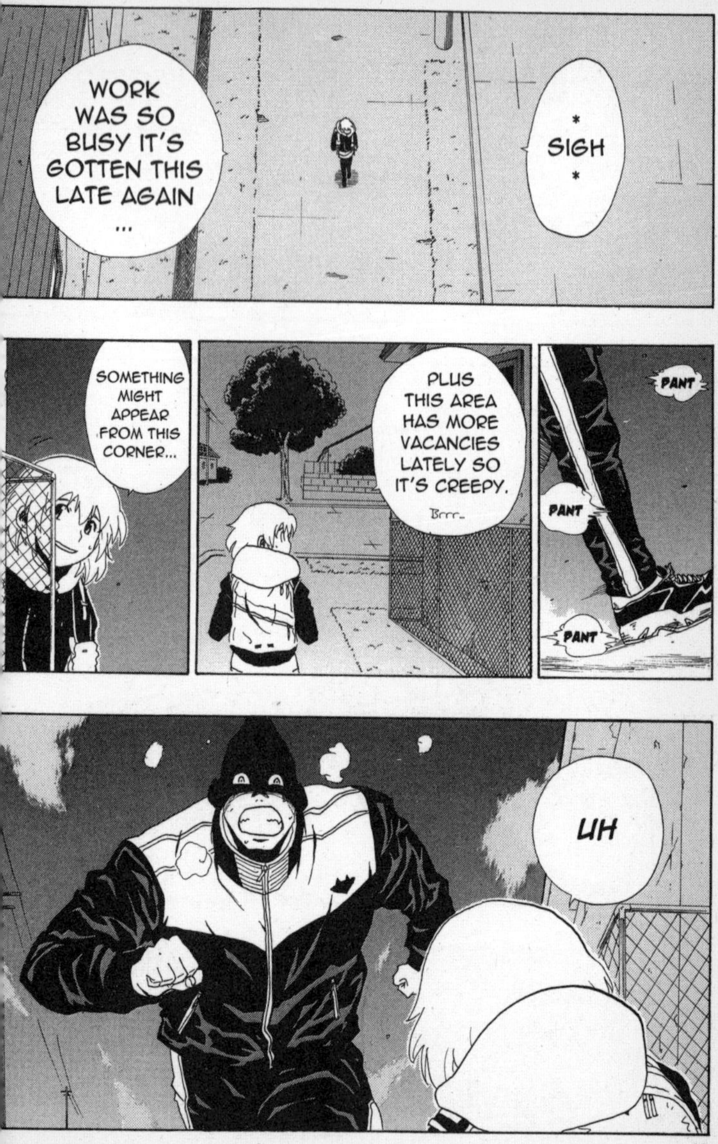
* SIGH *
WORK WAS SO BUSY IT'S GOTTEN THIS LATE AGAIN ...
PANT
PANT
PANT
PLUS THIS AREA HAS MORE VACANCIES LATELY SO IT'S CREEPY.
Brrr..
SOMETHING MIGHT APPEAR FROM THIS CORNER...
UH

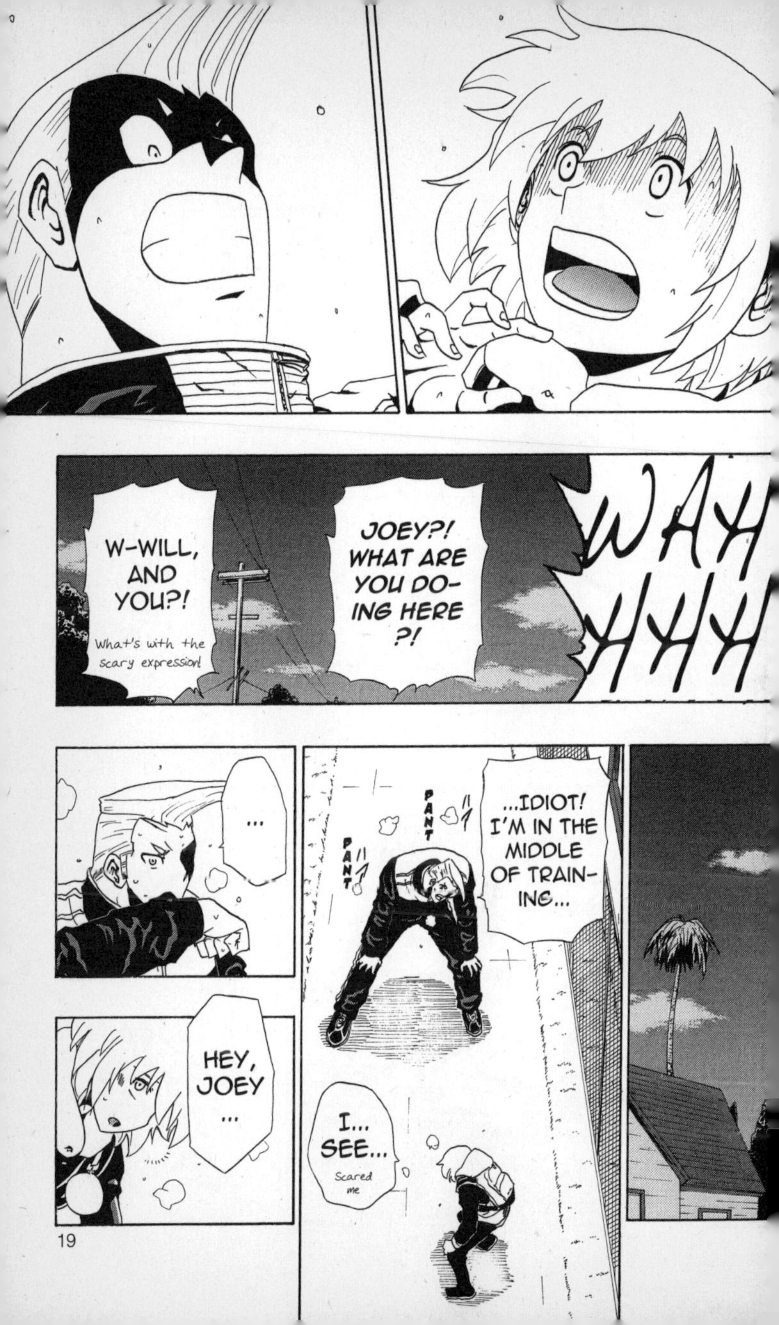
WAHHHHH
JOEY?! WHAT ARE YOU DO-ING HERE?!
W-WILL, AND YOU?!
What's with the scary expression!
PANT PANT
...IDIOT! I'M IN THE MIDDLE OF TRAIN-ING...
I... SEE...
Scared me
...
HEY, JOEY ...

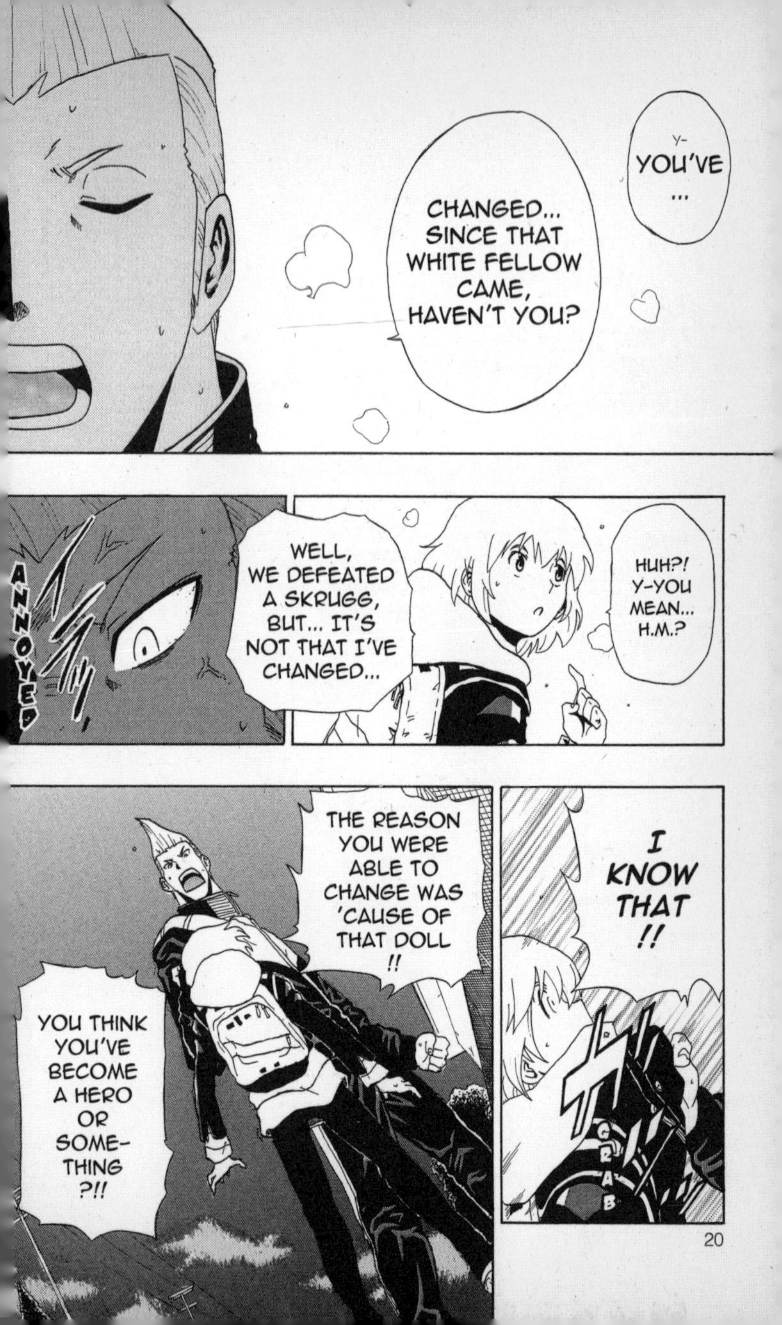
Y- YOU'VE ...
CHANGED... SINCE THAT WHITE FELLOW CAME, HAVEN'T YOU?
HUH?! Y-YOU MEAN... H.M.?
WELL, WE DEFEATED A SKRUGG, BUT... IT'S NOT THAT I'VE CHANGED...
ANNOYED
I KNOW THAT !!
GRAB
THE REASON YOU WERE ABLE TO CHANGE WAS 'CAUSE OF THAT DOLL !!
YOU THINK YOU'VE BECOME A HERO OR SOMETHING ?!!

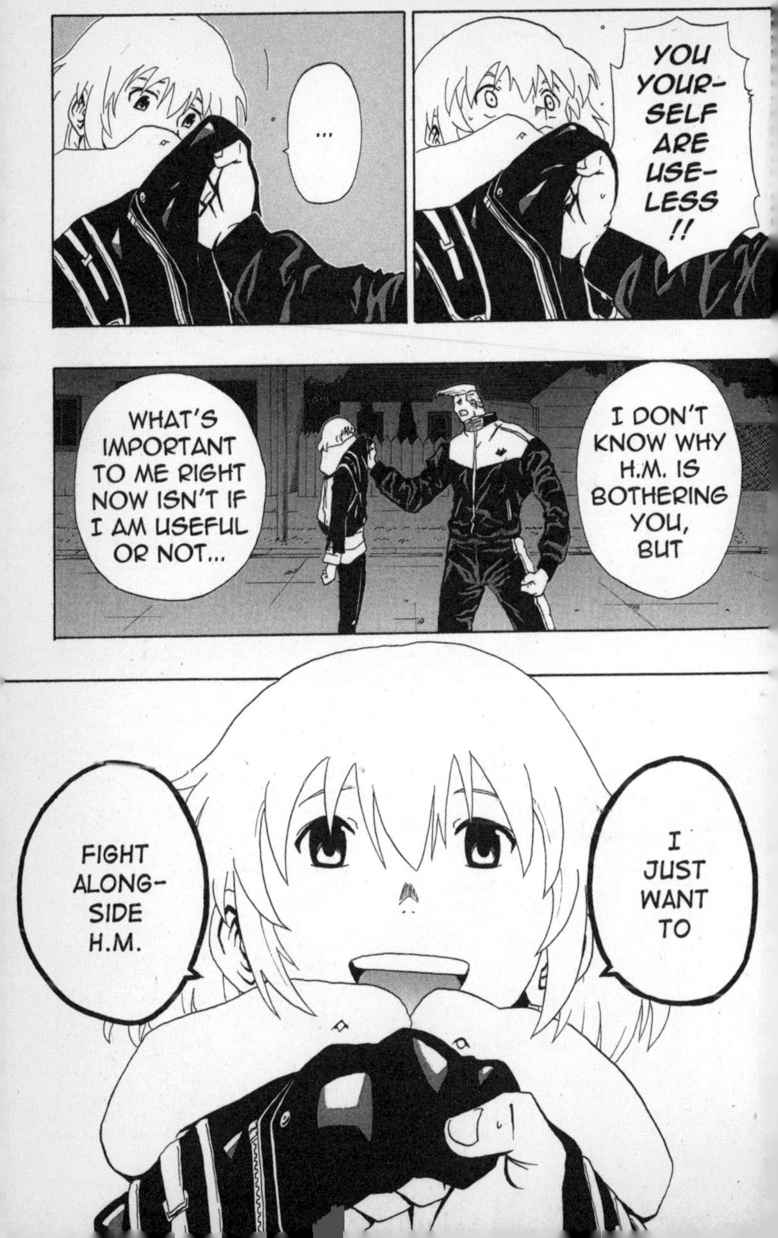
YOU YOURSELF ARE USELESS!!
...
I DON'T KNOW WHY H.M. IS BOTHERING YOU, BUT
WHAT'S IMPORTANT TO ME RIGHT NOW ISN'T IF I AM USEFUL OR NOT...
I JUST WANT TO
FIGHT ALONGSIDE H.M.

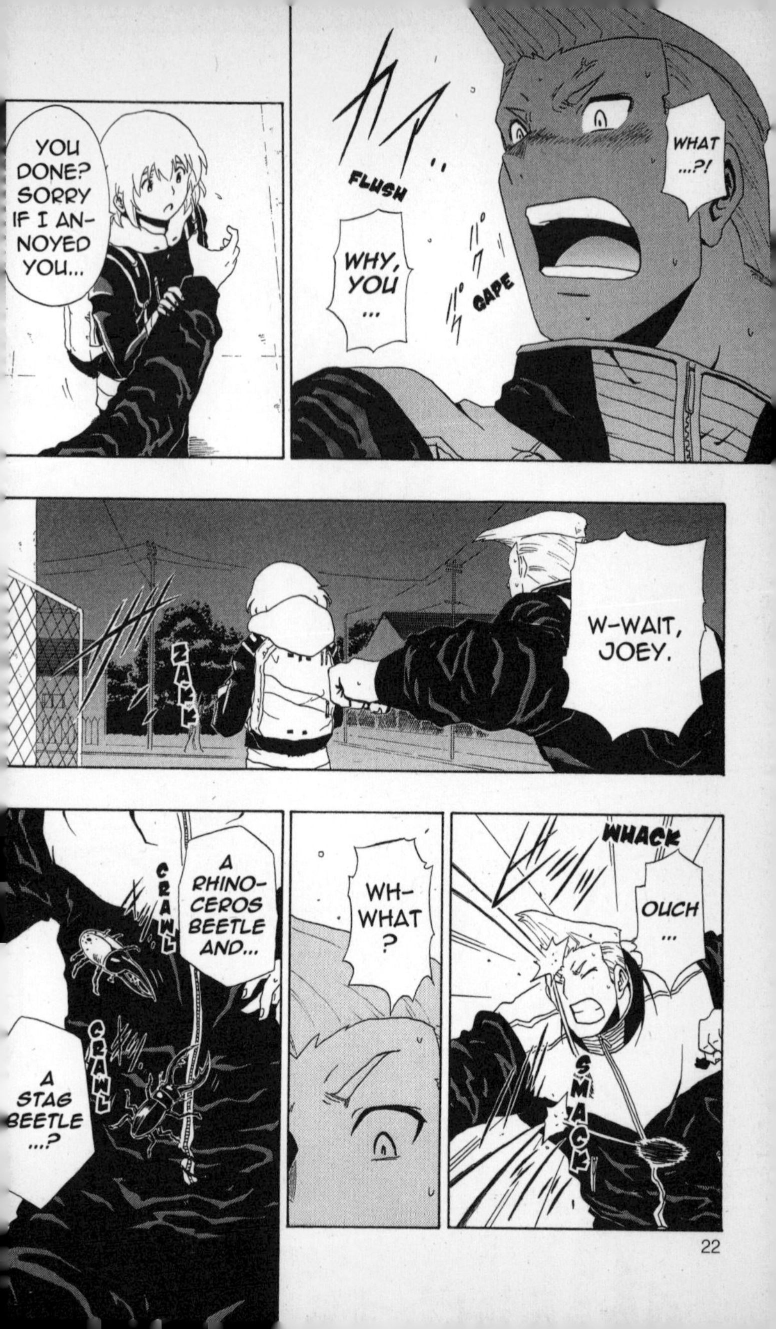
WHAT ...?!
FLUSH
WHY, YOU ...
GAPE
YOU DONE? SORRY IF I AN-NOYED YOU...
W-WAIT, JOEY.
ZAKK
WHACK
OUCH ...
SMACK
WH-WHAT ?
A RHINO-CEROS BEETLE AND...
CRAWL
A STAG BEETLE ...?
CRAWL

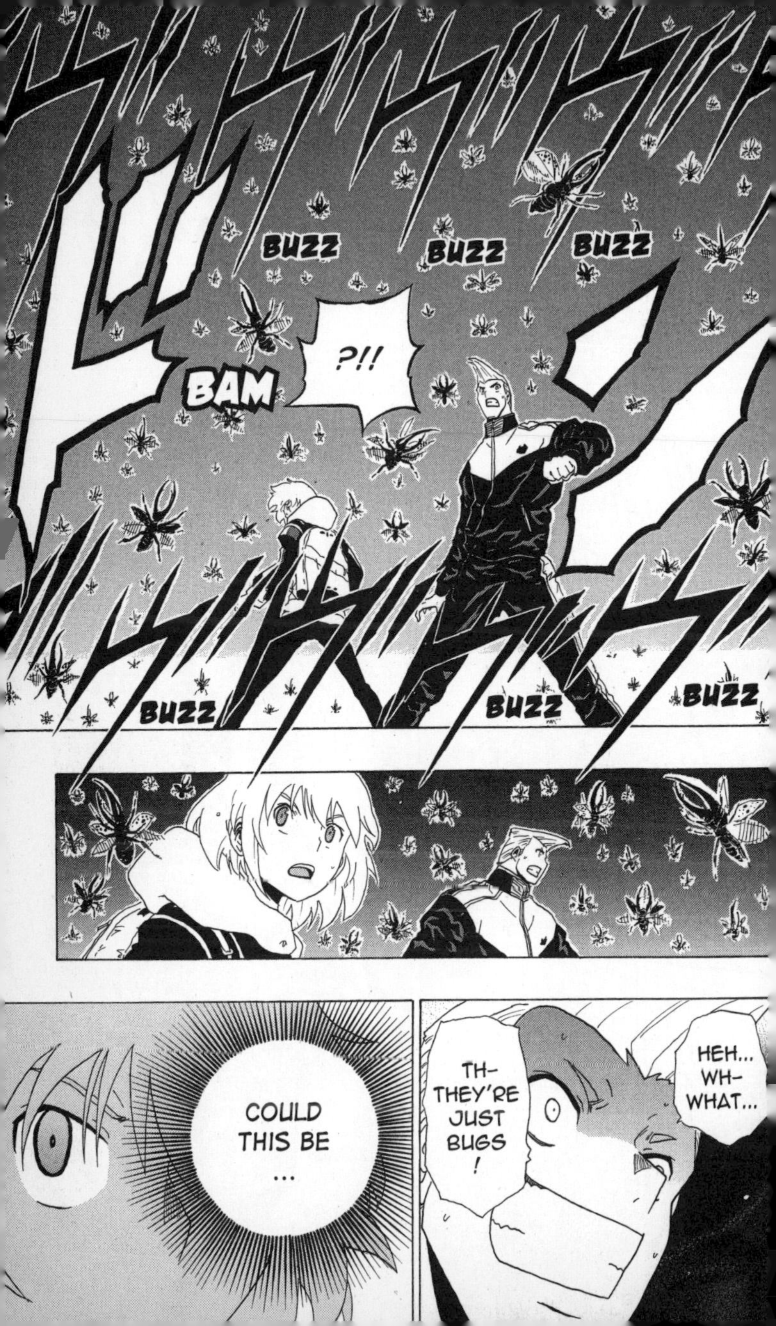
BUZZ
BUZZ
BUZZ
?!!
BAM
BUZZ
BUZZ
BUZZ
HEH... WH- WHAT...
TH- THEY'RE JUST BUGS!
COULD THIS BE ...

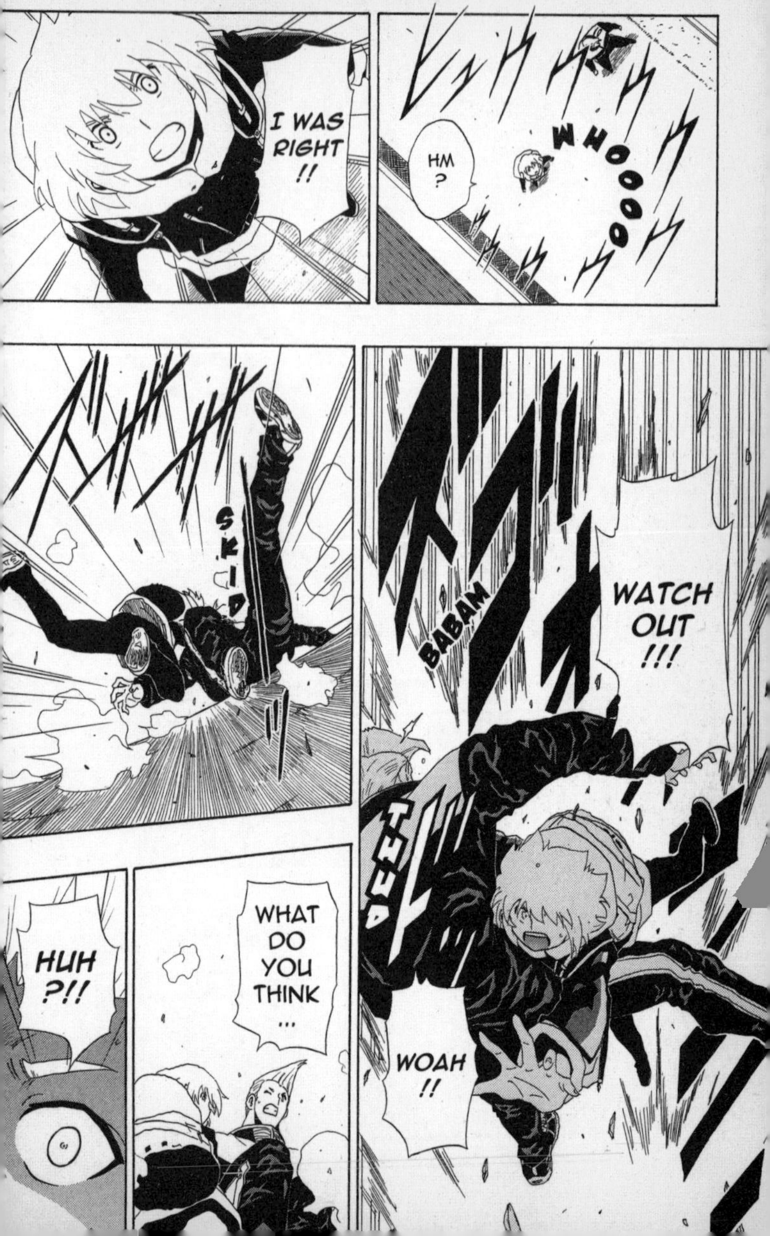
HM ?
WHOOOO
I WAS RIGHT !!
WATCH OUT !!!
BABAM
THUD
WOAH !!
SKID
WHAT DO YOU THINK ...
HUH ?!!

SO YOU'RE HERE!

A-ALIEN...

BAM

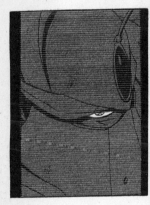

GRR

25

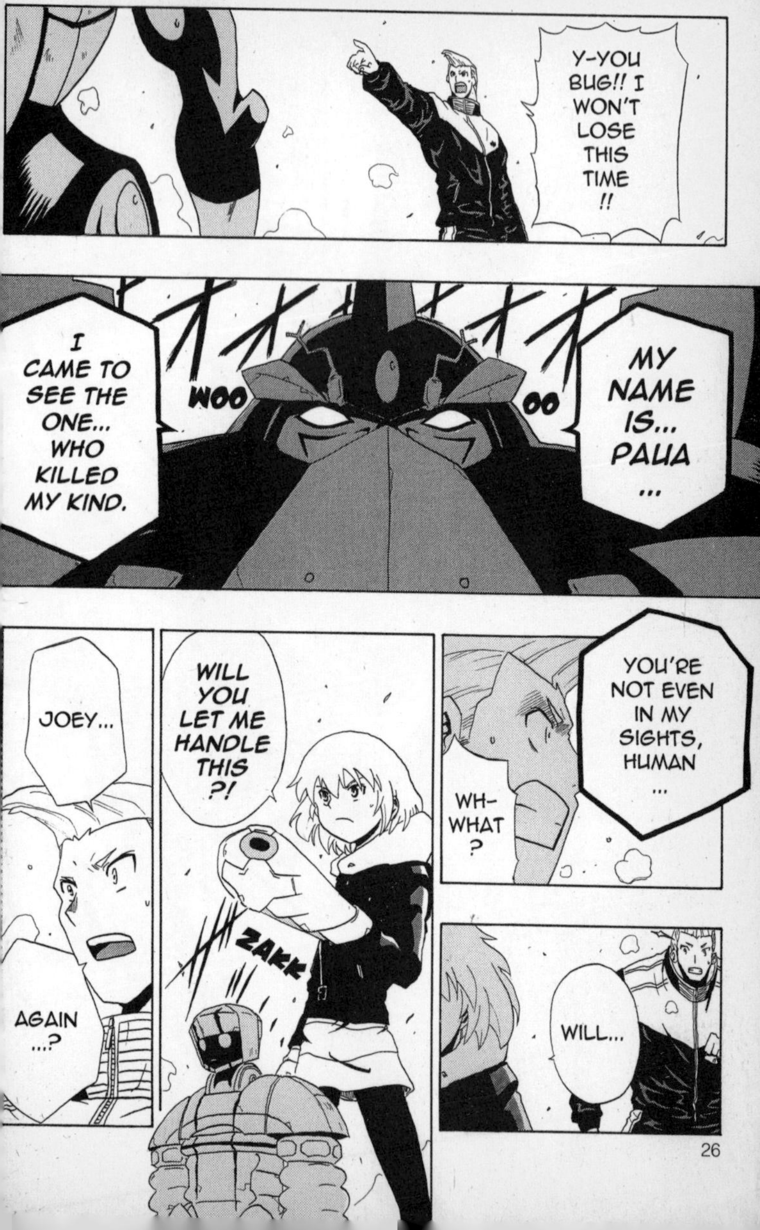
Y-YOU BUG!! I WON'T LOSE THIS TIME !!
MY NAME IS... PAUA ...
WOO OO
I CAME TO SEE THE ONE... WHO KILLED MY KIND.
YOU'RE NOT EVEN IN MY SIGHTS, HUMAN ...
WH- WHAT ?
WILL...
WILL YOU LET ME HANDLE THIS ?!
ZAKK
JOEY...
AGAIN ...?

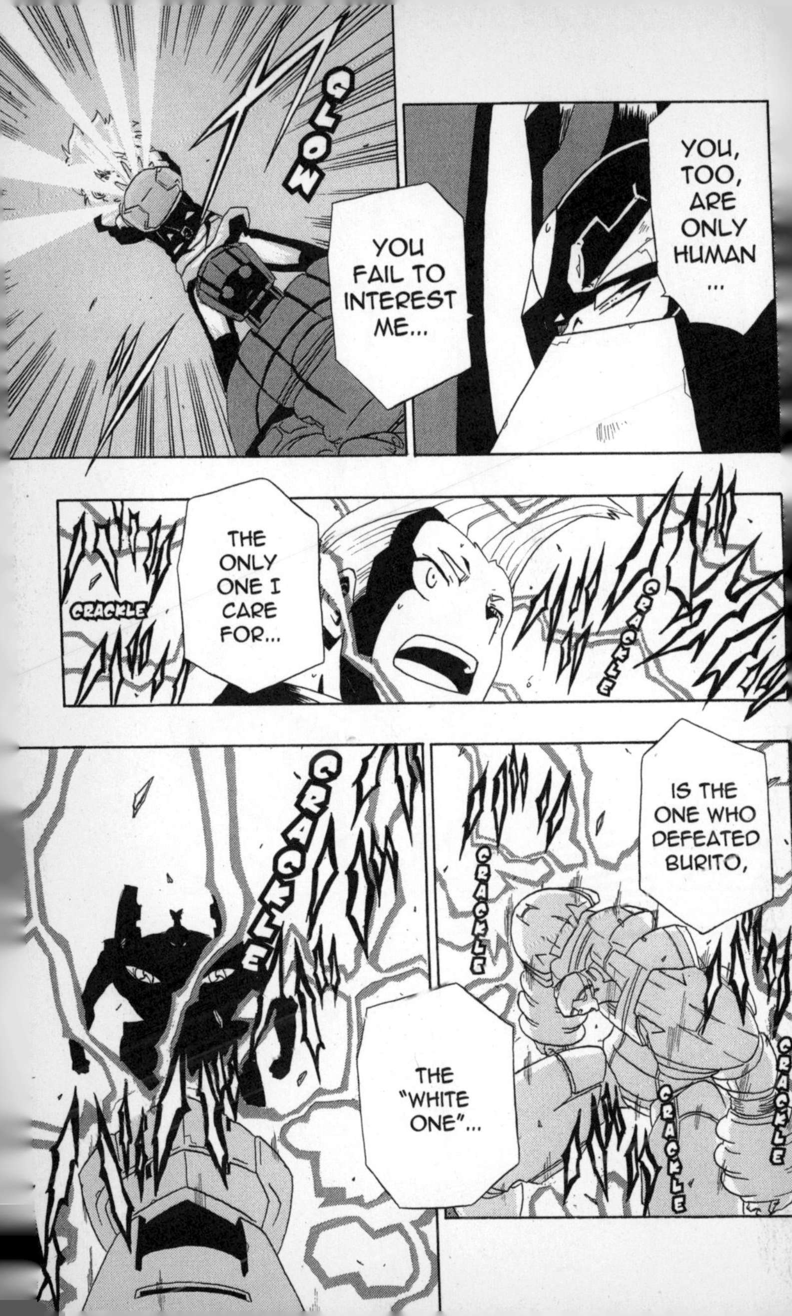
YOU, TOO, ARE ONLY HUMAN...
GLOW
YOU FAIL TO INTEREST ME...
CRACKLE
THE ONLY ONE I CARE FOR...
CRACKLE
IS THE ONE WHO DEFEATED BURITO,
CRACKLE
CRACKLE
CRACKLE
THE "WHITE ONE"...
CRACKLE

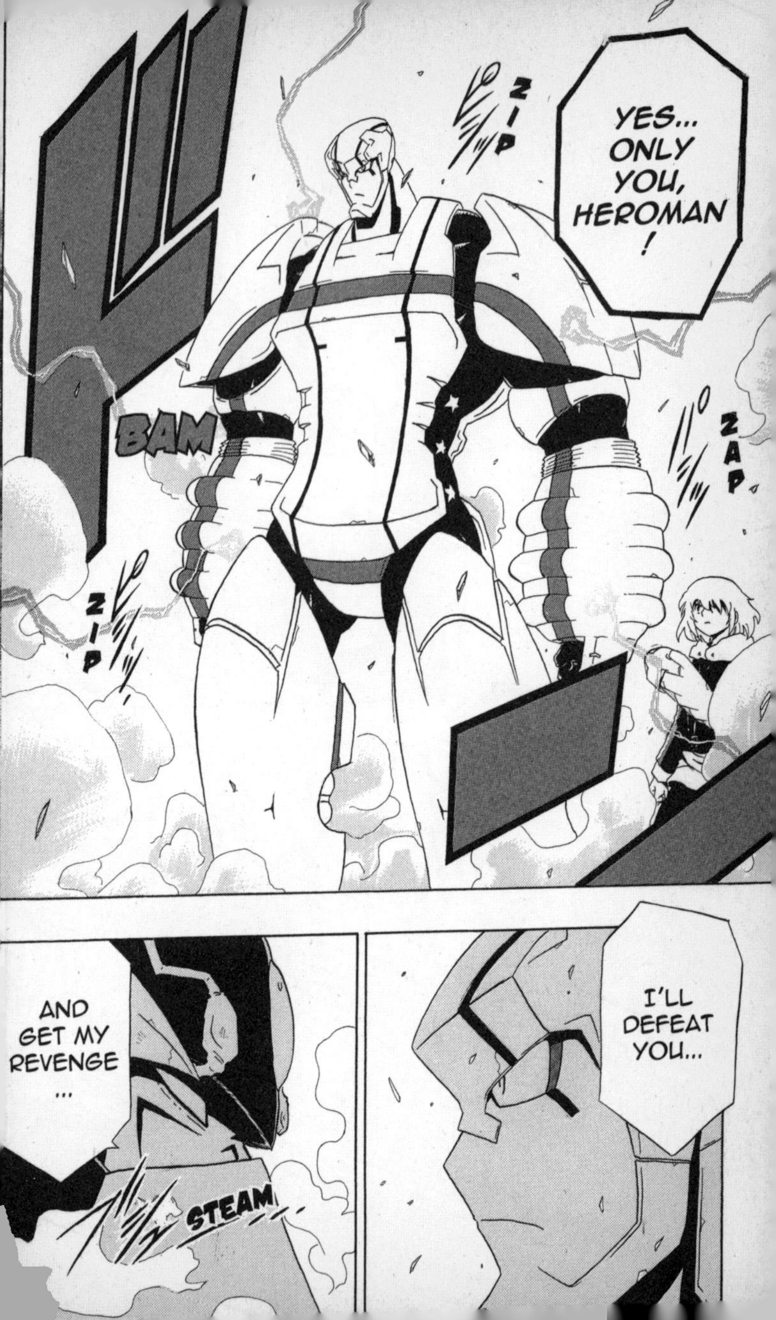
YES... ONLY YOU, HEROMAN!
ZIP
ZAP
BAM
ZIP
I'LL DEFEAT YOU...
AND GET MY REVENGE ...
STEAM

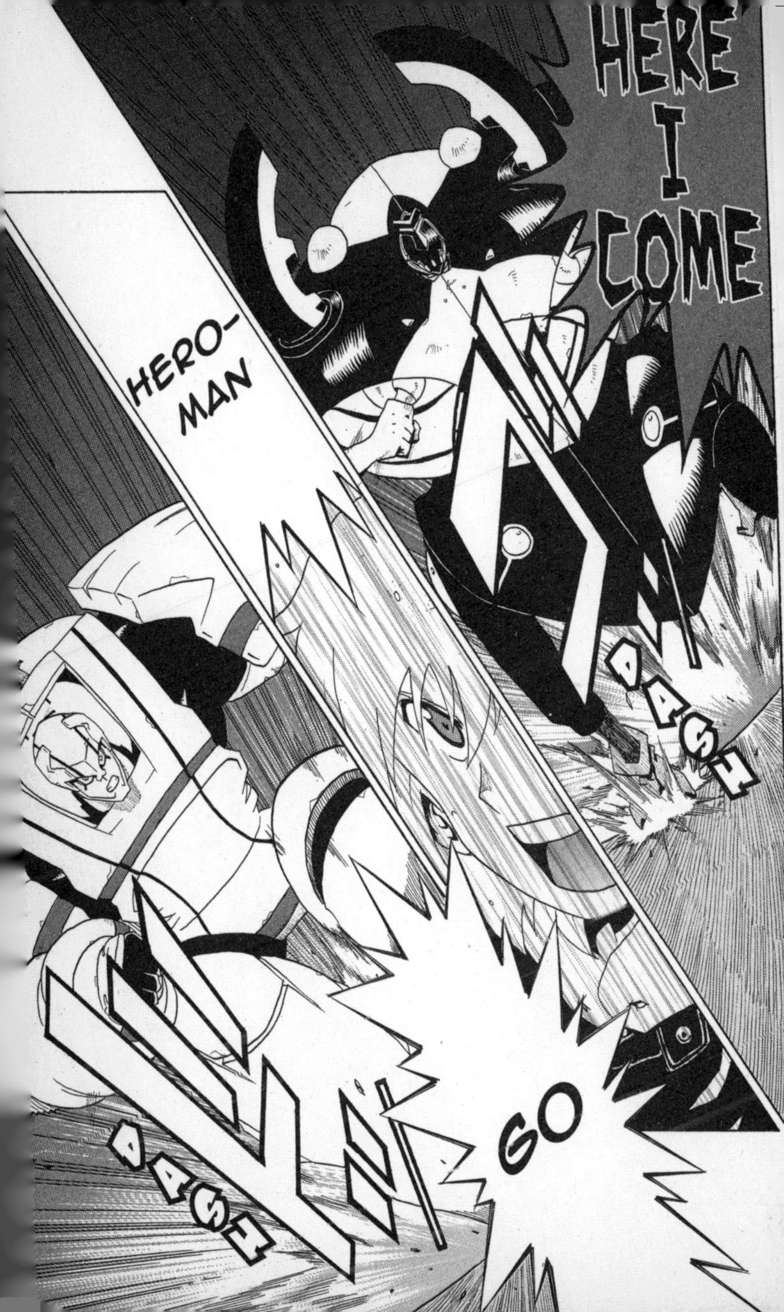
HERE I COME
DASH
HERO-MAN
GO
DASH

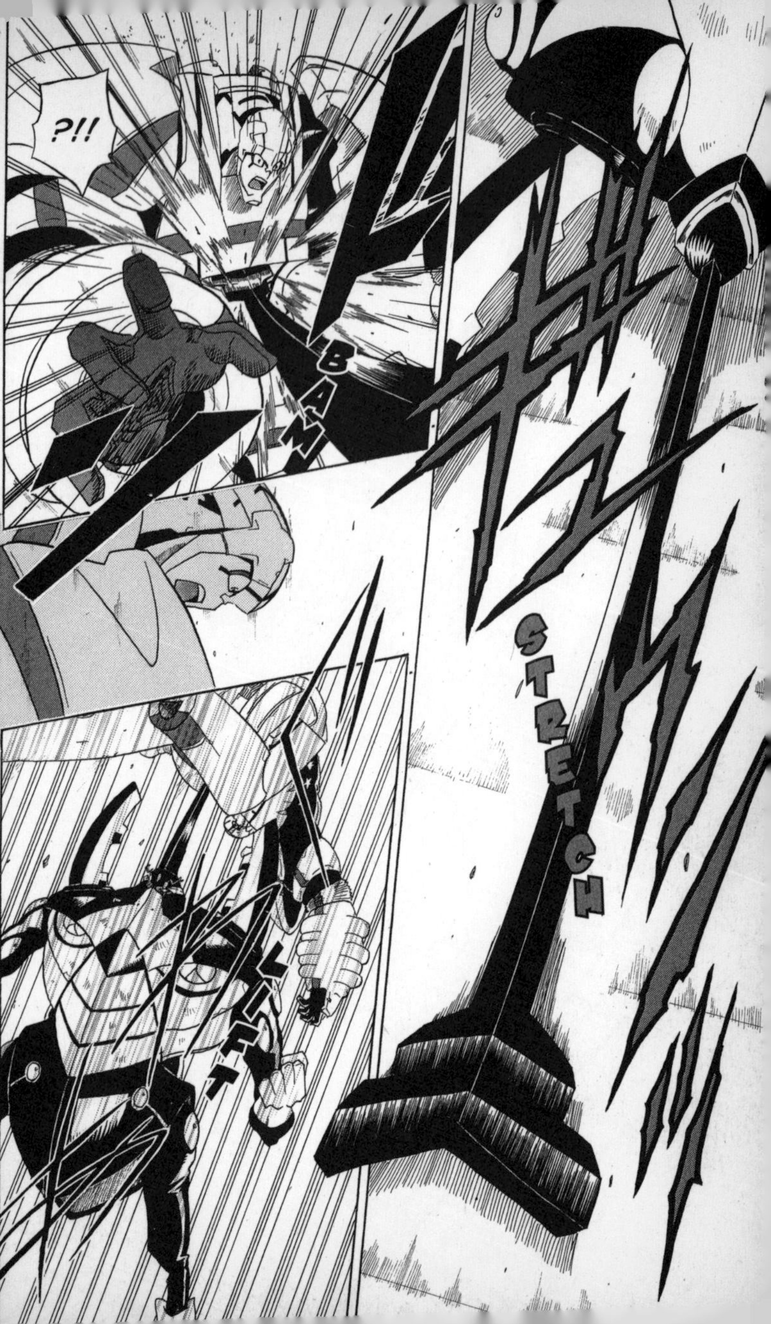
STRETCH
?!!
BAM
LIFT

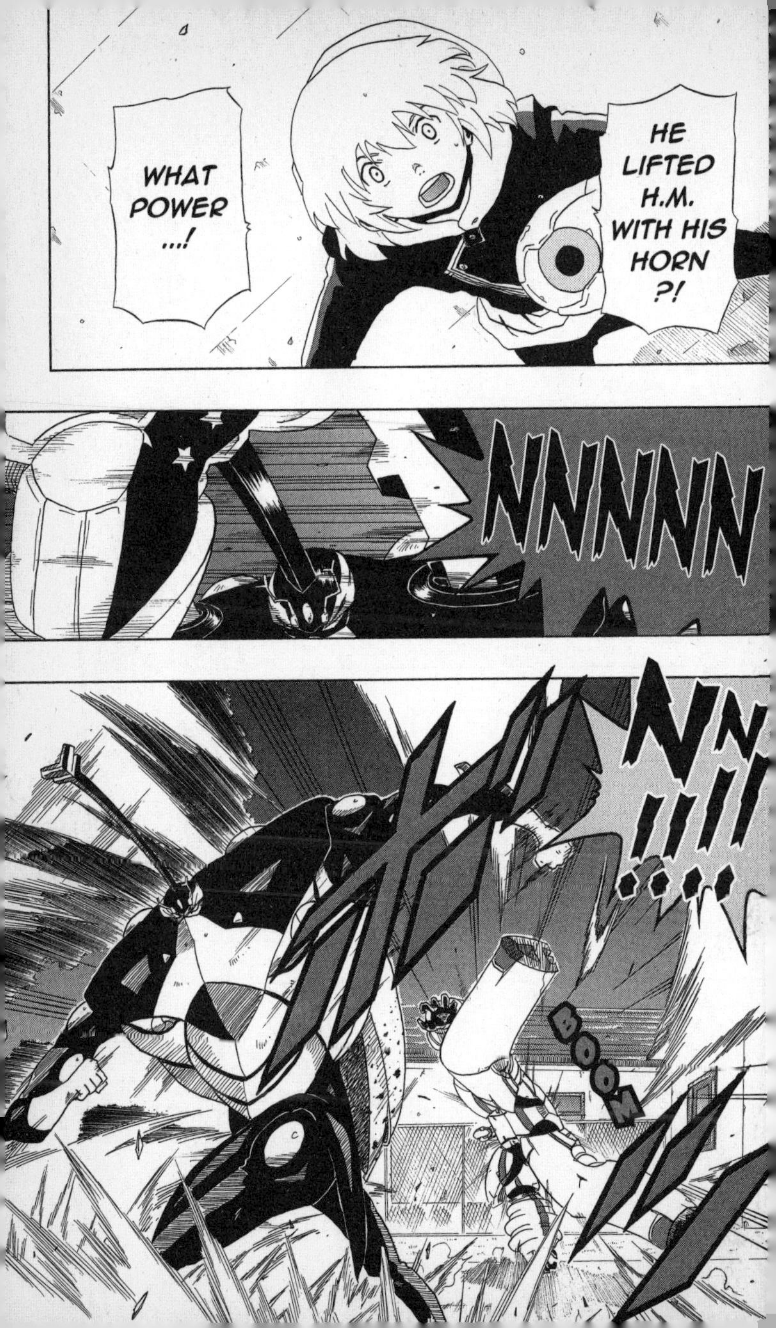
HE LIFTED H.M. WITH HIS HORN ?!
WHAT POWER ...!
NNNNNN
NN !!!!....
BOOM

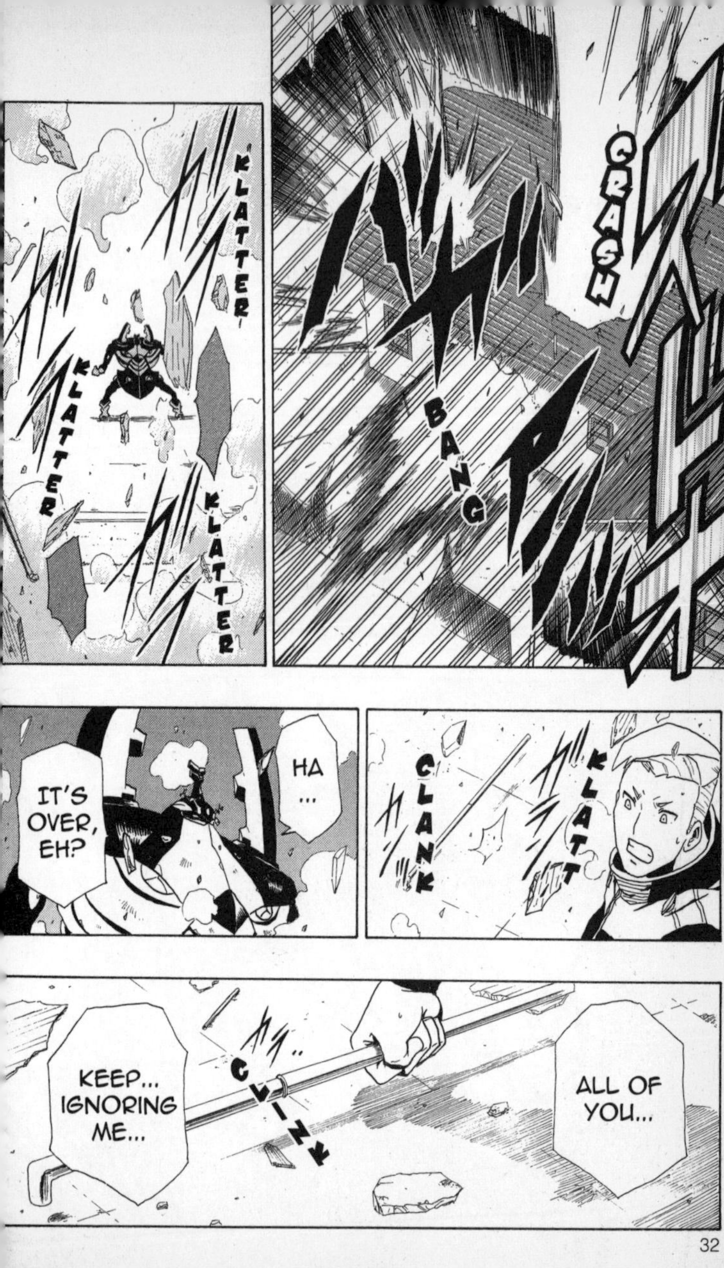
CRASH
BANG
KLATTER
KLATTER
KLATTER
KLATT
CLANK
HA ...
IT'S OVER, EH?
ALL OF YOU...
CLINK
KEEP... IGNORING ME...

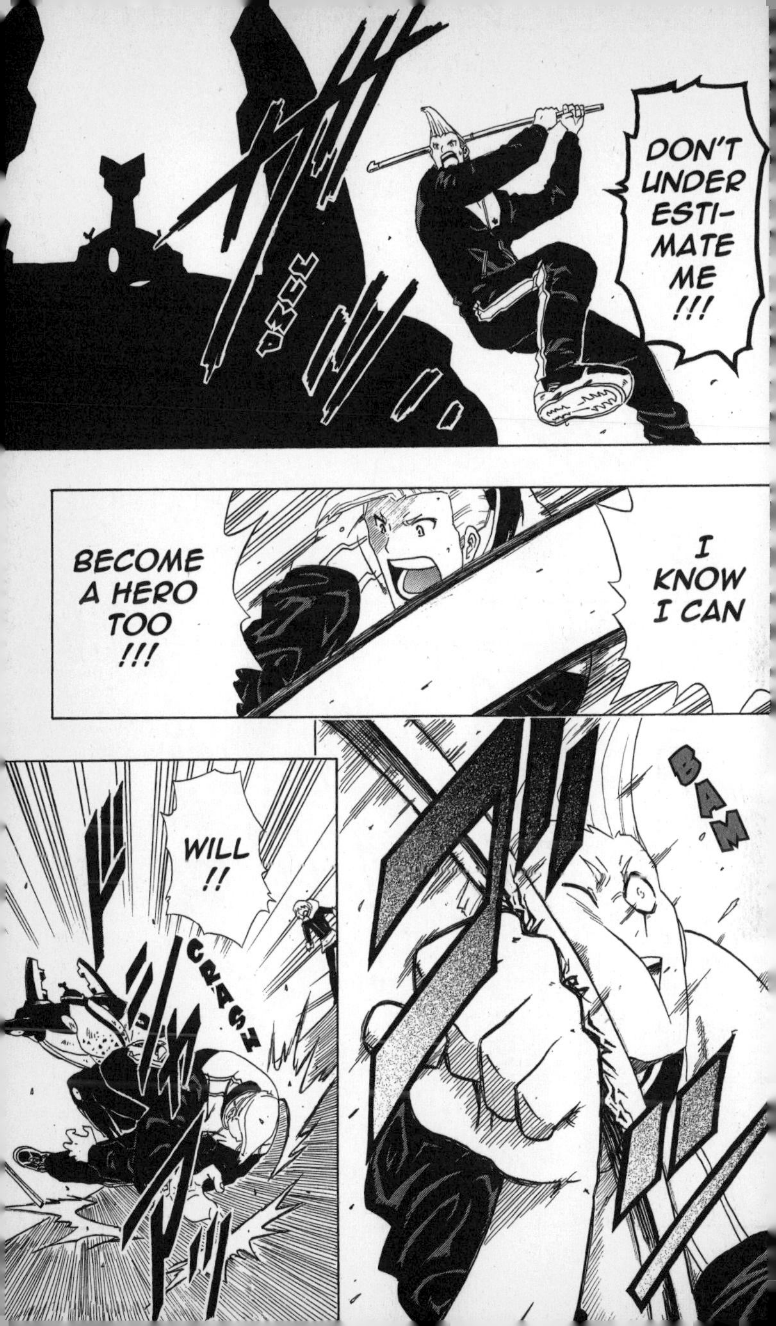
DON'T UNDER ESTI-MATE ME !!!
I KNOW I CAN
BECOME A HERO TOO !!!
BAM
WILL !!
CRASH

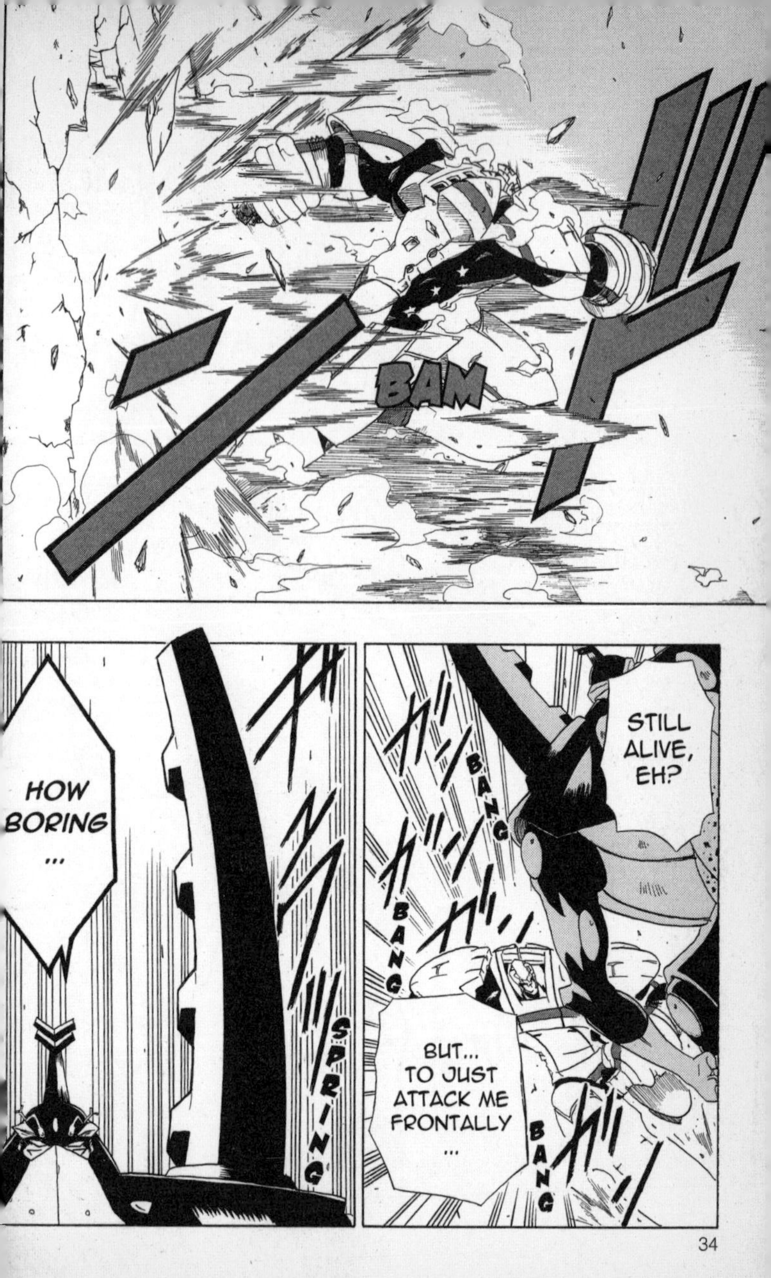
BAM
STILL ALIVE, EH?
BANG
BANG
BUT... TO JUST ATTACK ME FRONTALLY ...
BANG
SPRING
HOW BORING ...

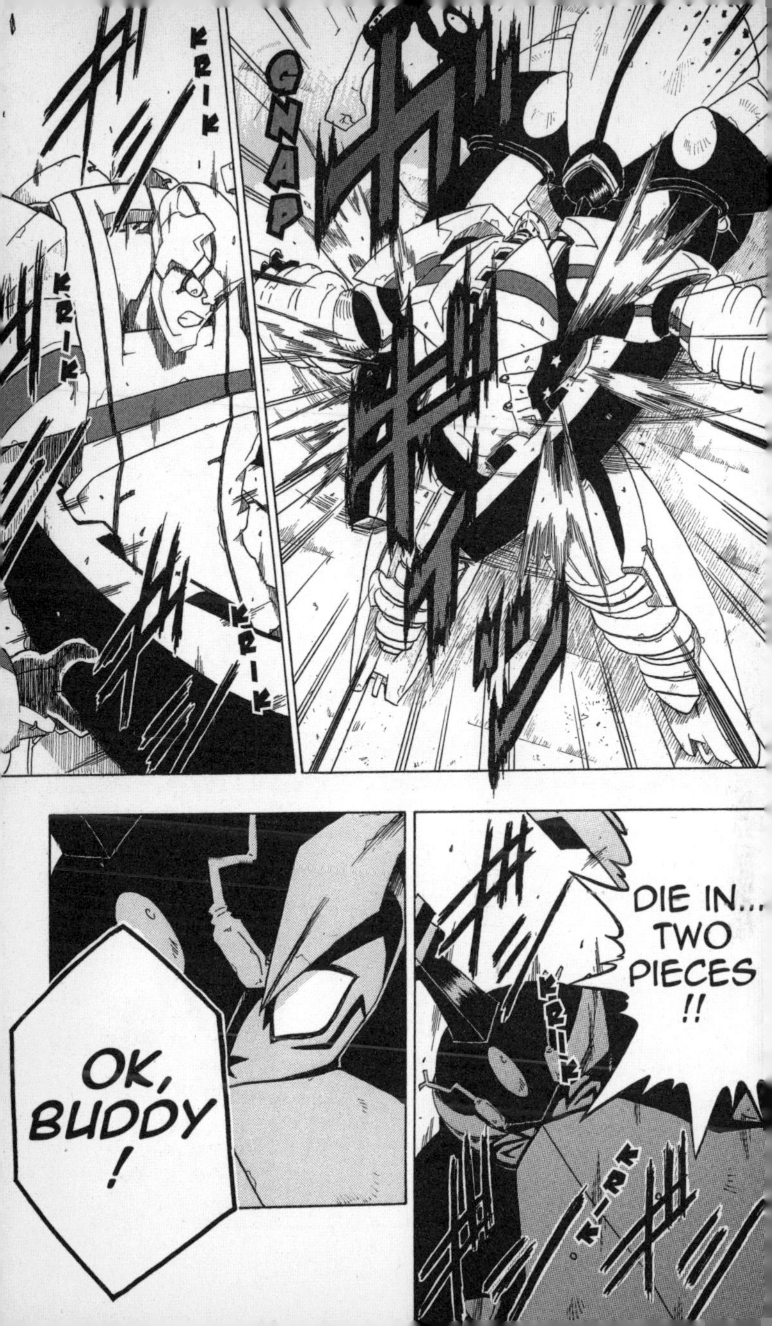
GNAP
KRIK
KRIK
KRIK
DIE IN... TWO PIECES !!
KRIK
KRIK
OK, BUDDY !

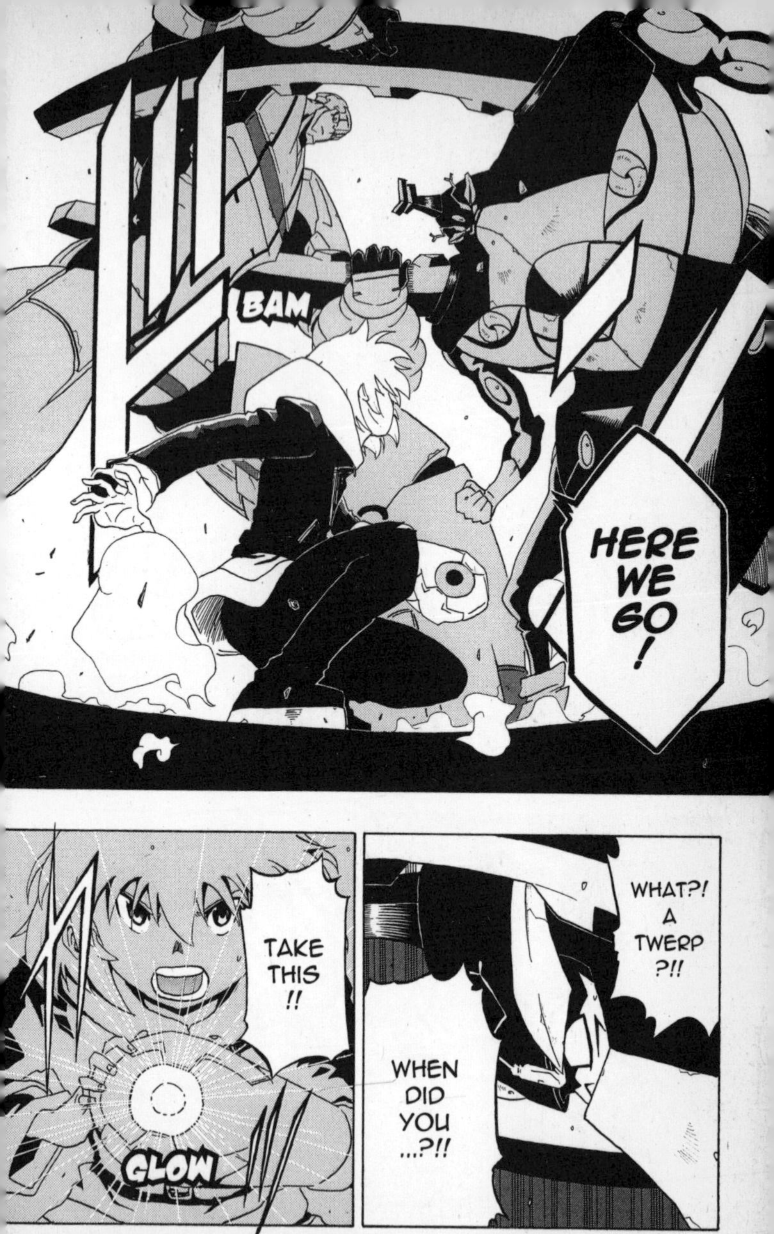
BAM
HERE WE GO!
WHAT?! A TWERP?!!
WHEN DID YOU ...?!!
TAKE THIS!!
GLOW

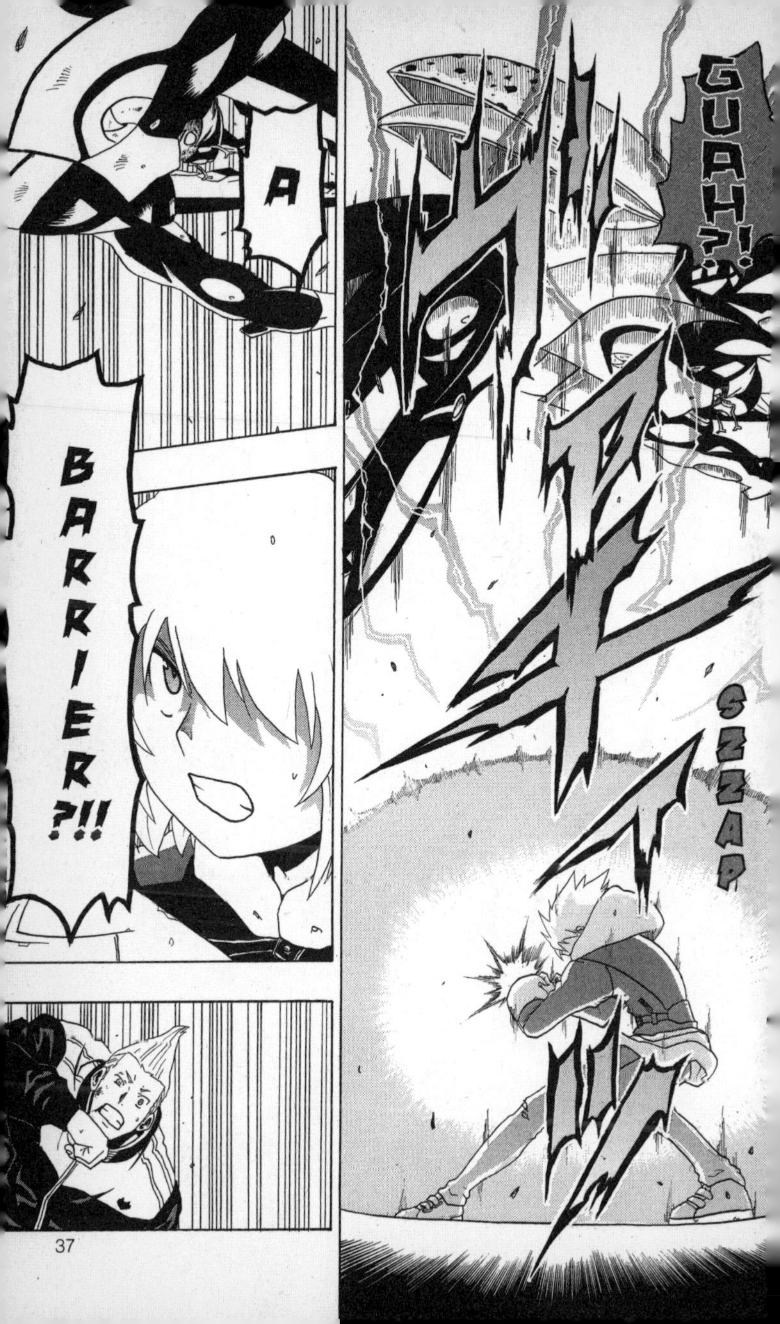
GUAH?!
SZZAP
A
BARRIER?!!

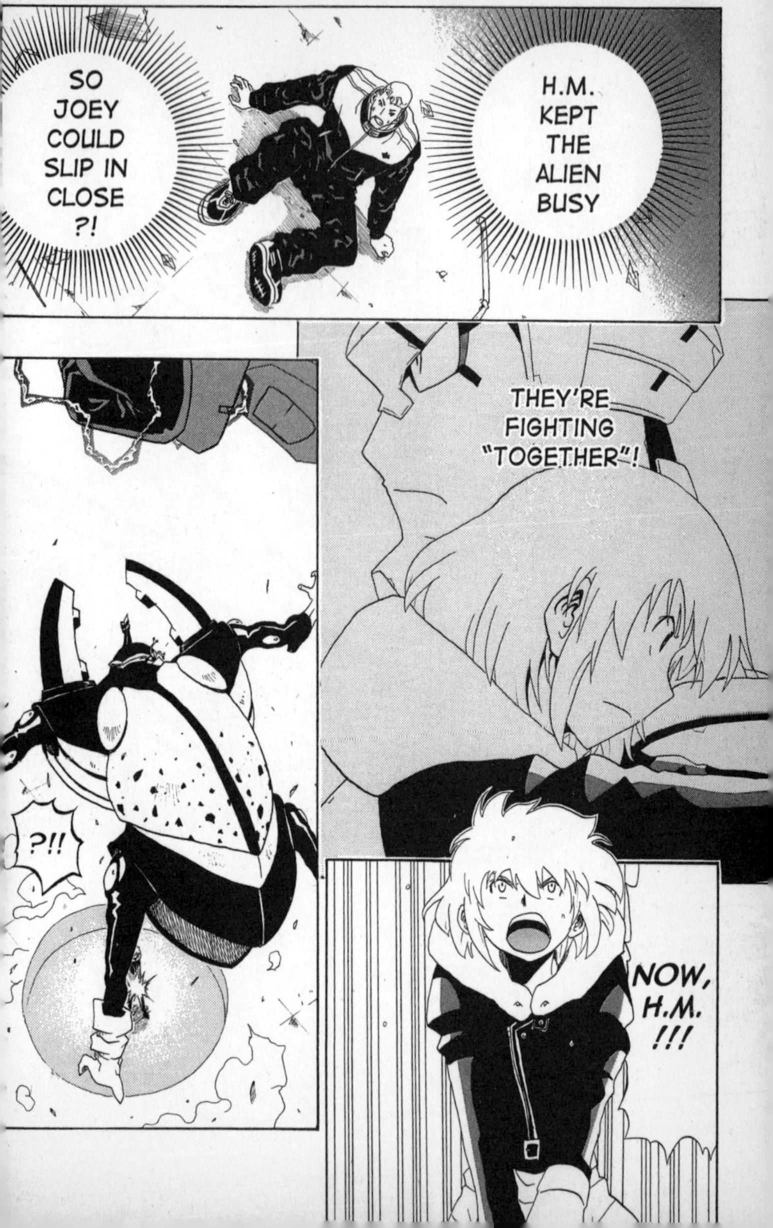
H.M. KEPT THE ALIEN BUSY
SO JOEY COULD SLIP IN CLOSE ?!
THEY'RE FIGHTING "TOGETHER"!
NOW, H.M. !!!
?!!

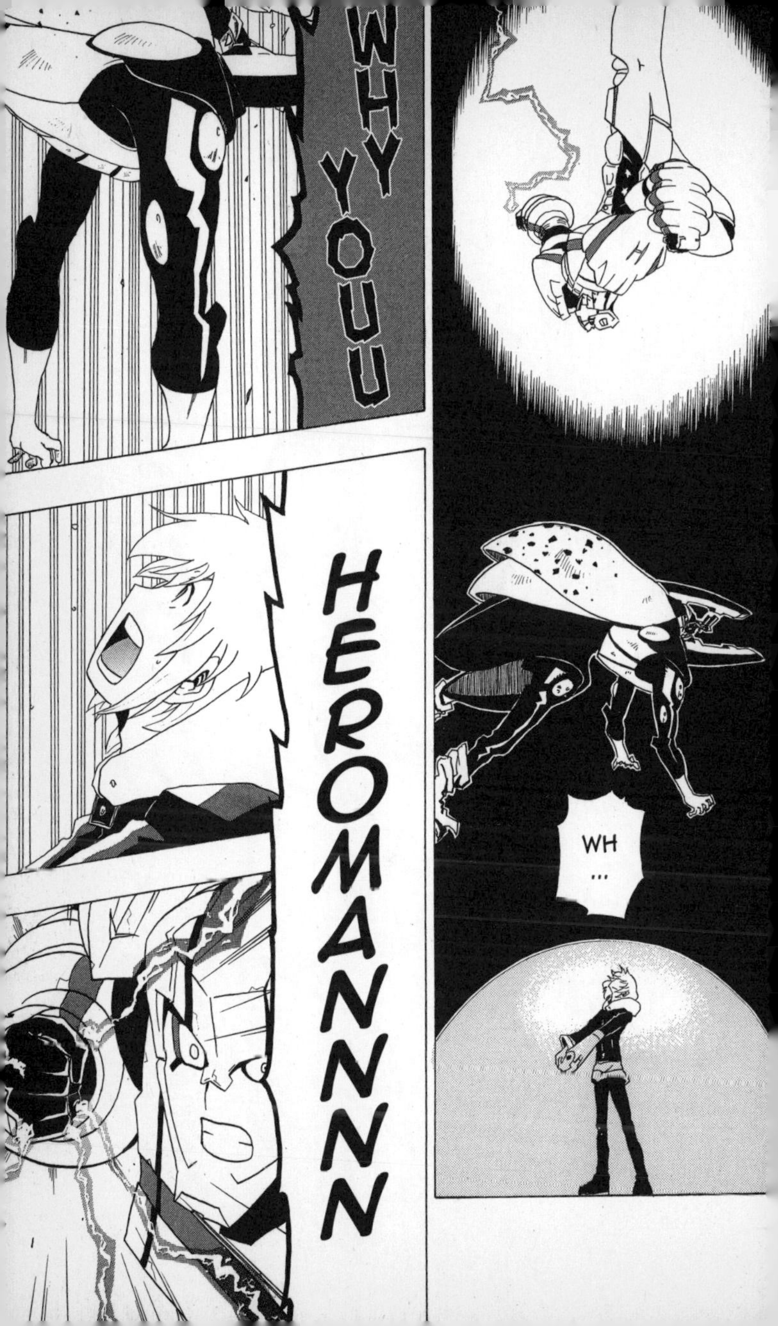
WH ...
HEROMANNNN
WHY YOUUU

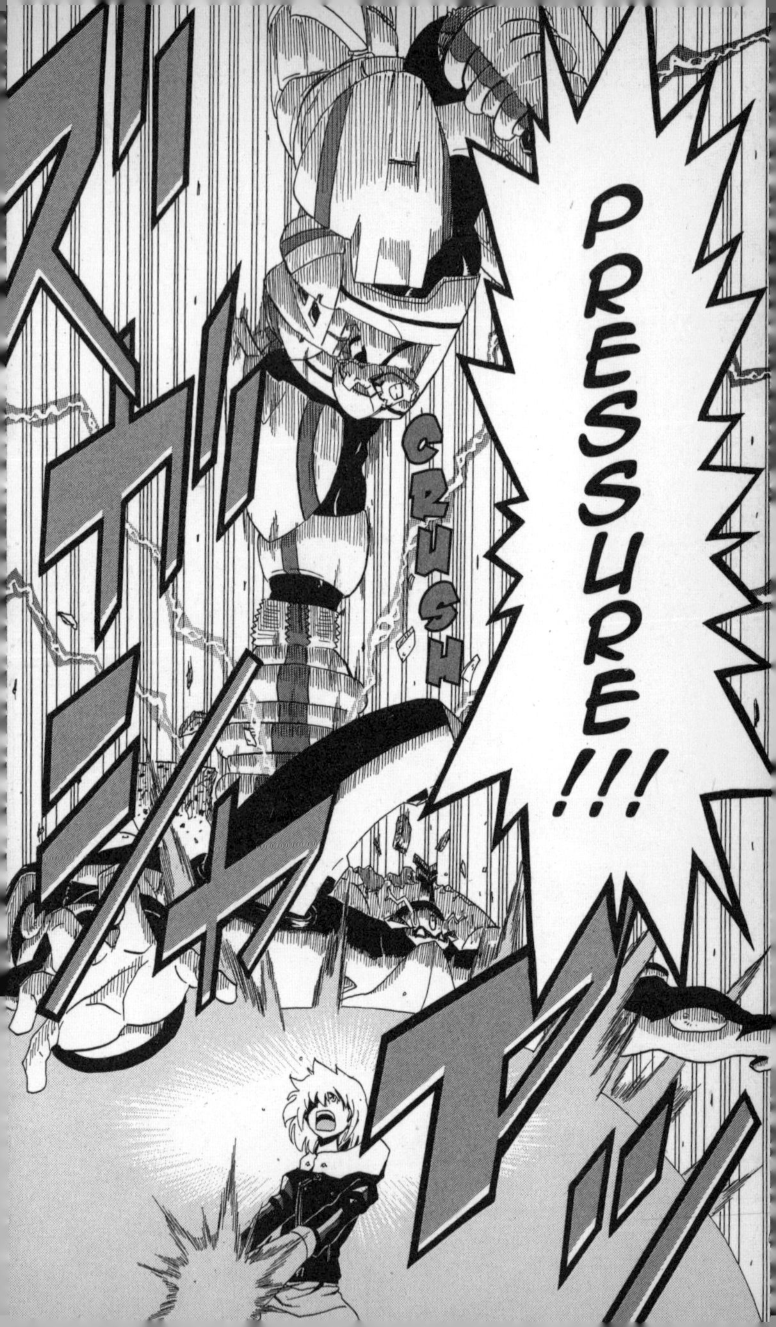
PRESSURE!!!
CRUSH

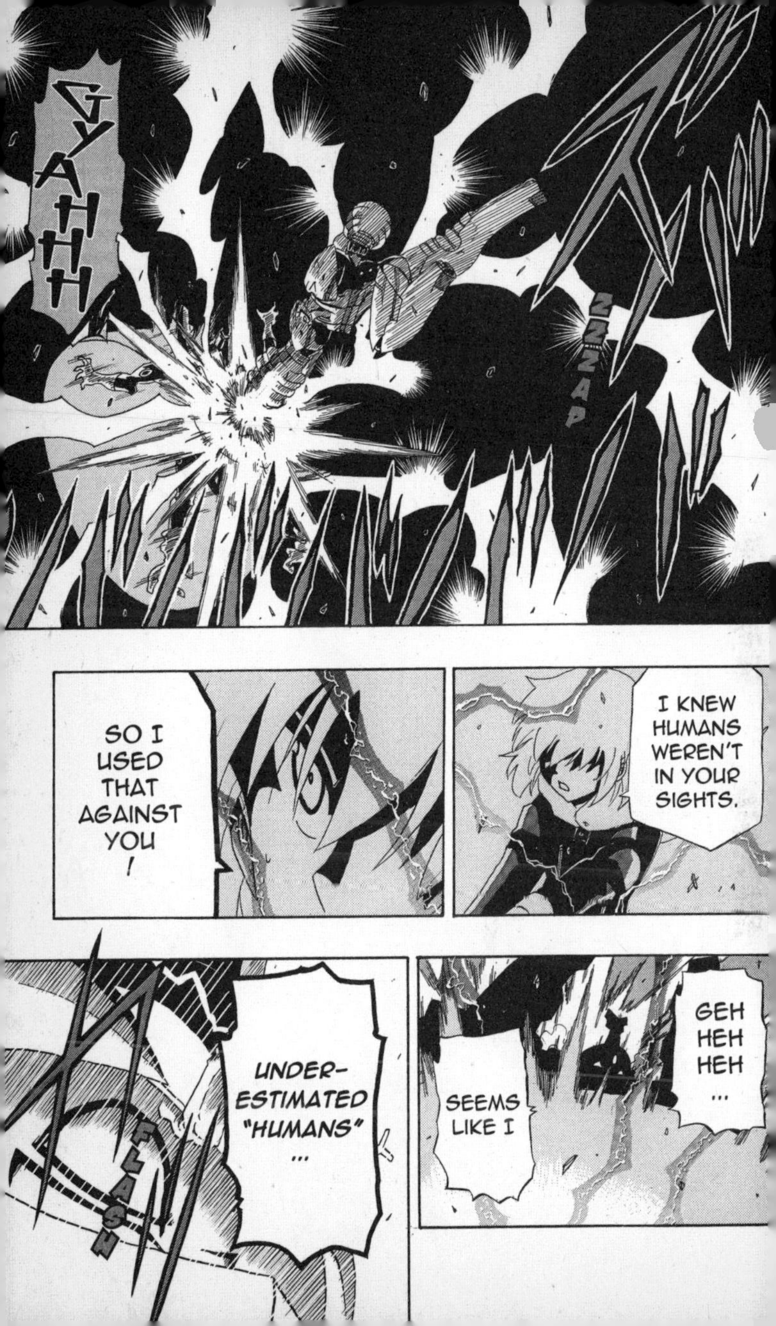
ZZZAP
GYAHHH
I KNEW HUMANS WEREN'T IN YOUR SIGHTS.
SO I USED THAT AGAINST YOU!
GEH HEH HEH...
SEEMS LIKE I
UNDER-ESTIMATED "HUMANS"...
FLASH

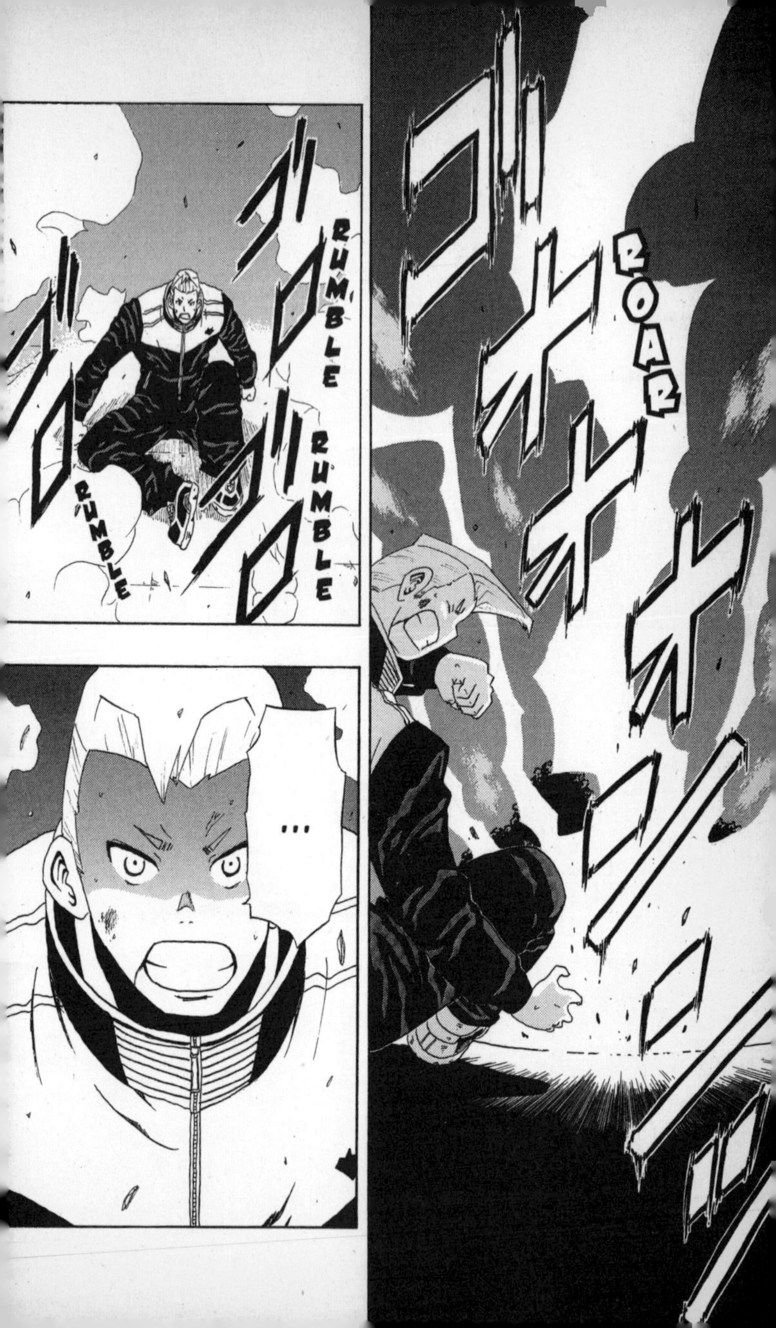
ROAR
RUMBLE
RUMBLE
RUMBLE
...

BAM

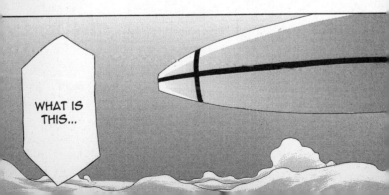

WHAT IS
THIS...

NOW
PAUA, TOO...
SO I'M THE ONLY ONE LEFT...
...
HA!
THAT'S FINE...
ZLIP
NEXT TIME, I WON'T STAY MY BLADE,
"WHITE ONE"... NO, "HERO-MAN."
ZMM

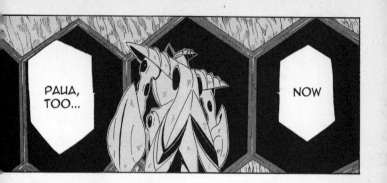

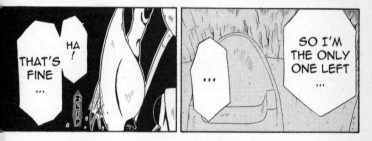

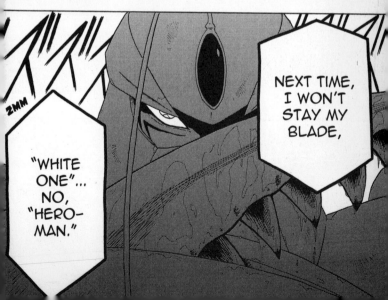

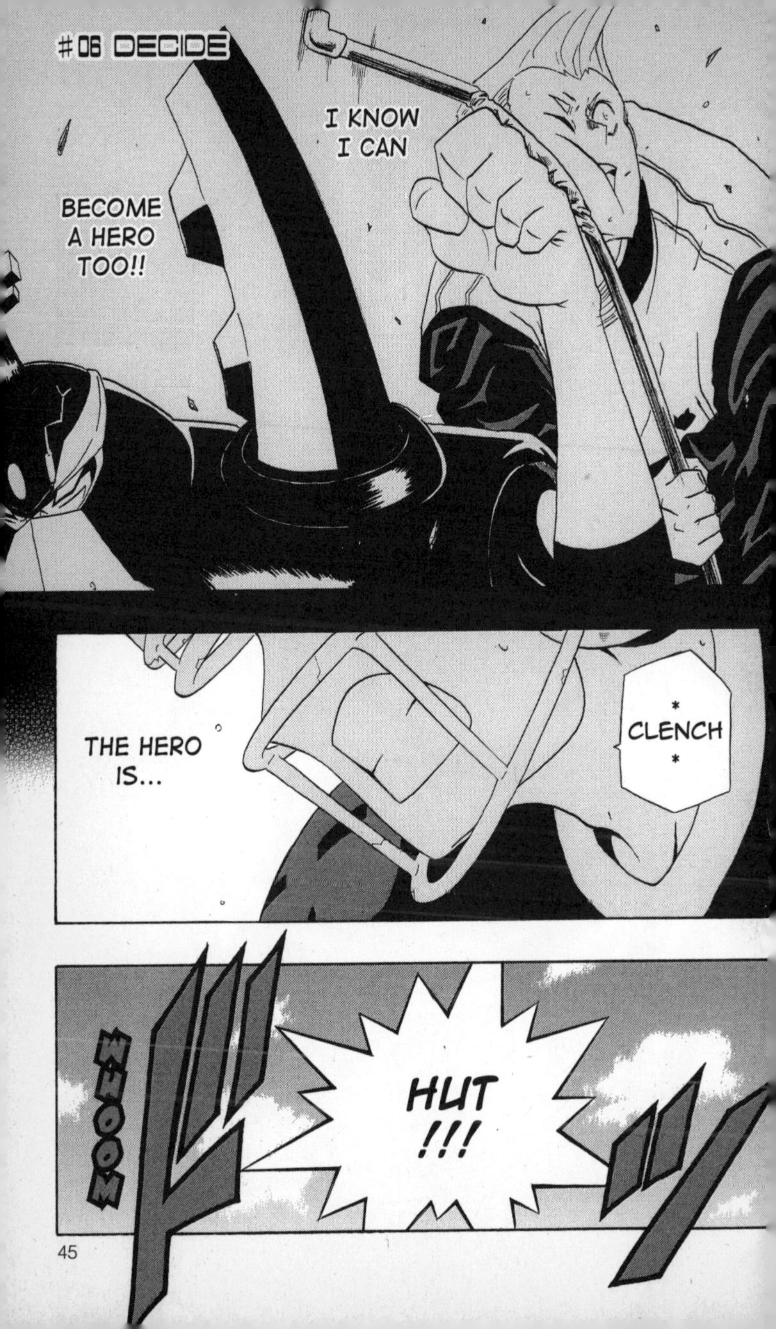
#06 DECIDE
I KNOW I CAN
BECOME A HERO TOO!!
* CLENCH *
THE HERO IS...
HUT !!!
WHOOM

#06 DECIDE

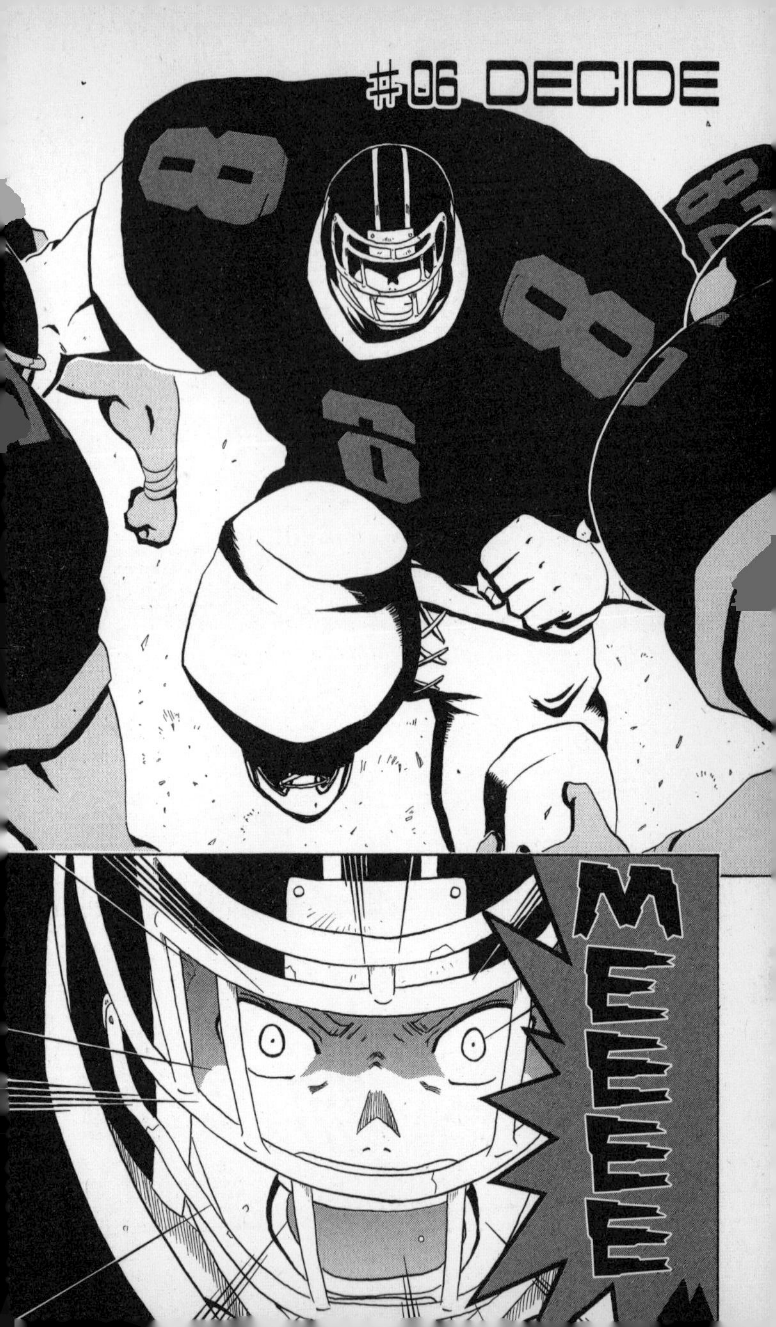
MEEEE

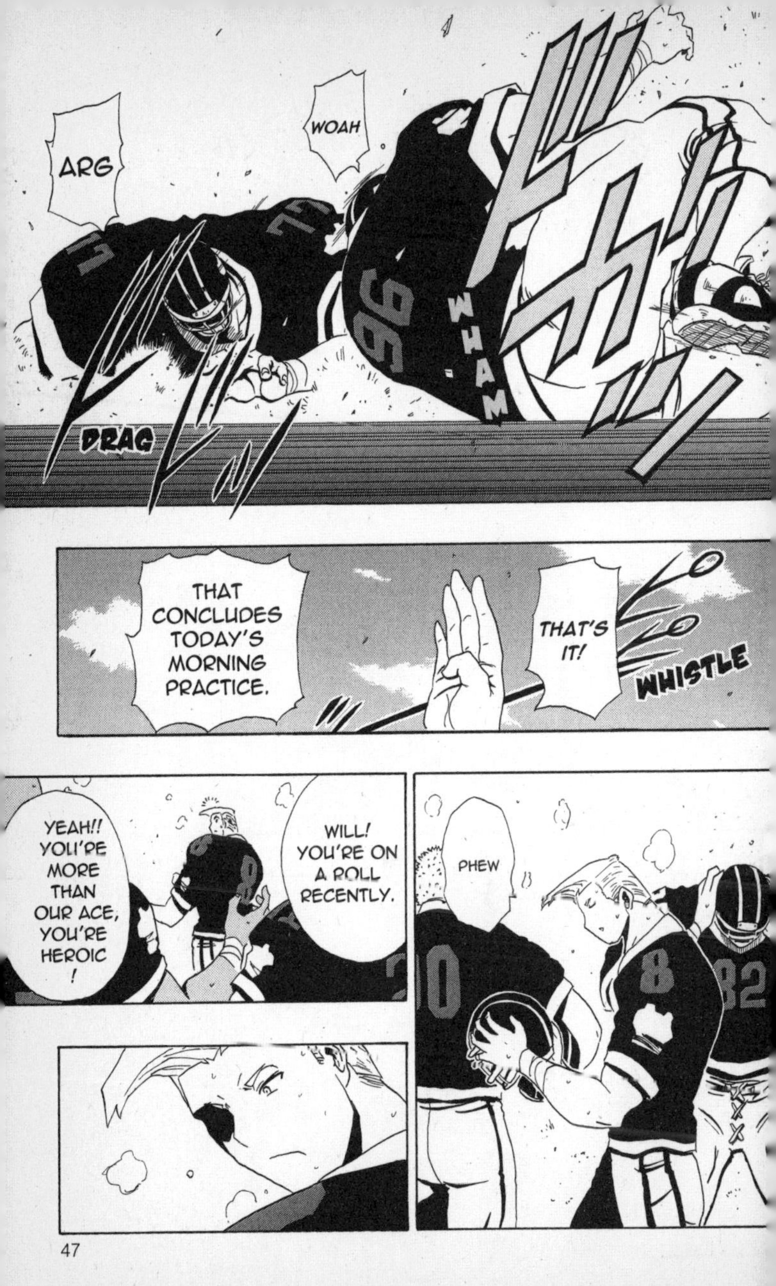
WOAH
ARG
WHAM
DRAG
THAT'S IT!
WHISTLE
THAT CONCLUDES TODAY'S MORNING PRACTICE.
PHEW
WILL! YOU'RE ON A ROLL RECENTLY.
YEAH!! YOU'RE MORE THAN OUR ACE, YOU'RE HEROIC!

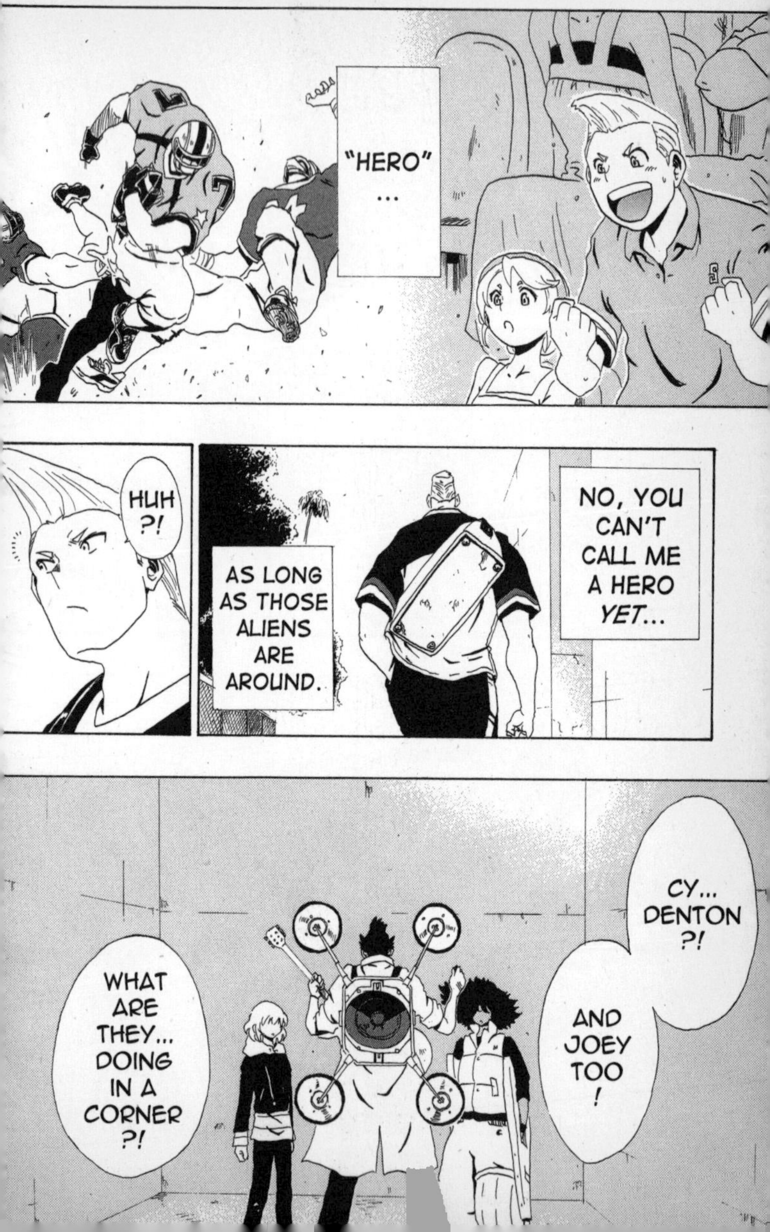

"HERO" ...
NO, YOU CAN'T CALL ME A HERO *YET*...
AS LONG AS THOSE ALIENS ARE AROUND.
HUH?!
CY... DENTON?!
AND JOEY TOO!
WHAT ARE THEY... DOING IN A CORNER?!

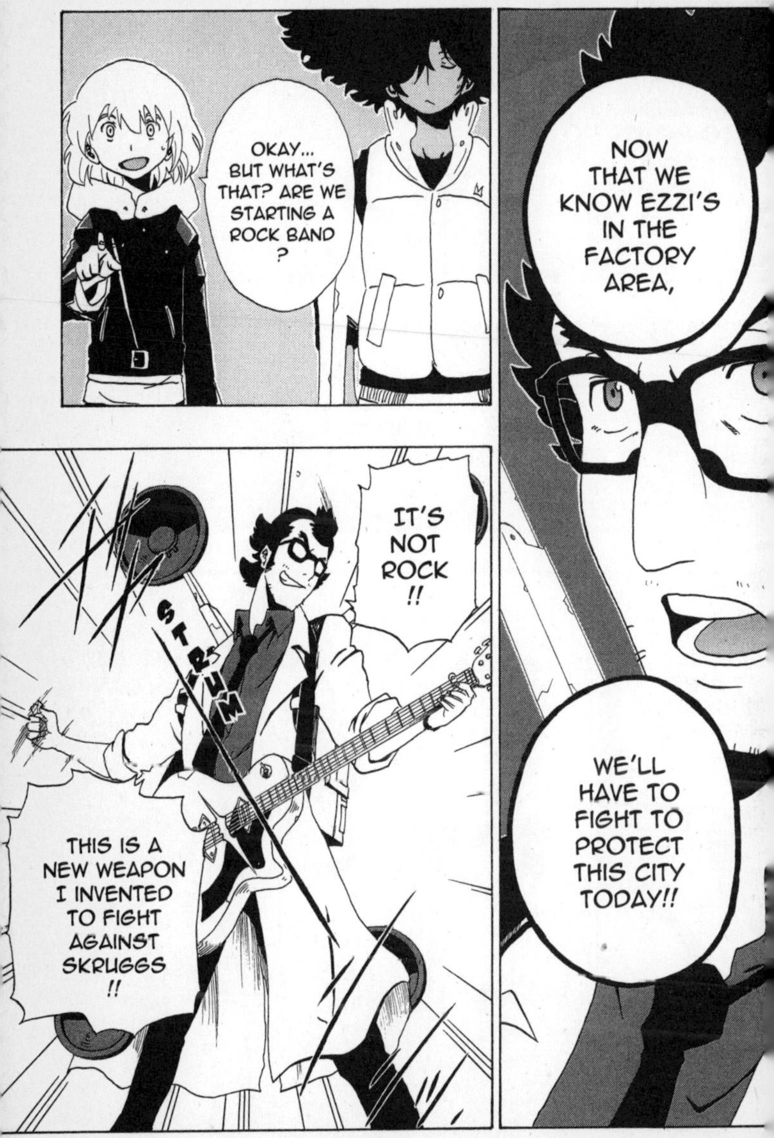
NOW THAT WE KNOW EZZI'S IN THE FACTORY AREA,
WE'LL HAVE TO FIGHT TO PROTECT THIS CITY TODAY!!
OKAY... BUT WHAT'S THAT? ARE WE STARTING A ROCK BAND ?
IT'S NOT ROCK !!
STRUM
THIS IS A NEW WEAPON I INVENTED TO FIGHT AGAINST SKRUGGS !!

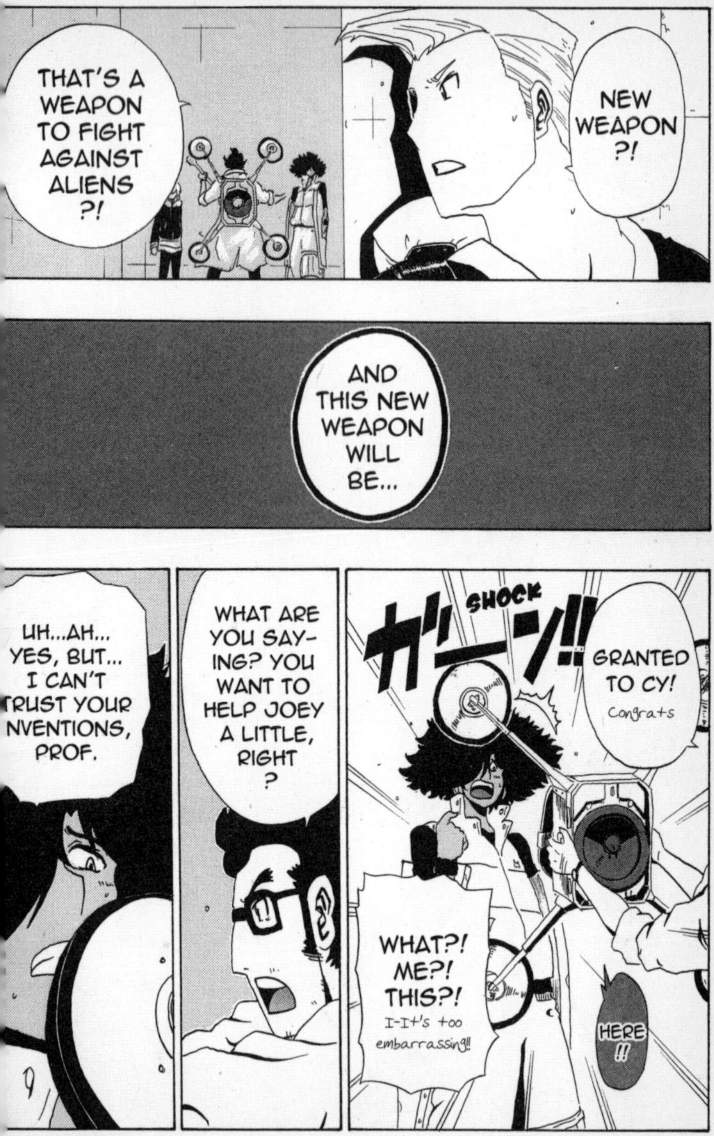
NEW WEAPON ?!
THAT'S A WEAPON TO FIGHT AGAINST ALIENS ?!
AND THIS NEW WEAPON WILL BE...
GRANTED TO CY! Congrats
SHOCK
HERE !!
WHAT?! ME?! THIS?! I-It's too embarrassing!!
WHAT ARE YOU SAYING? YOU WANT TO HELP JOEY A LITTLE, RIGHT ?
UH...AH... YES, BUT... I CAN'T TRUST YOUR NVENTIONS, PROF.

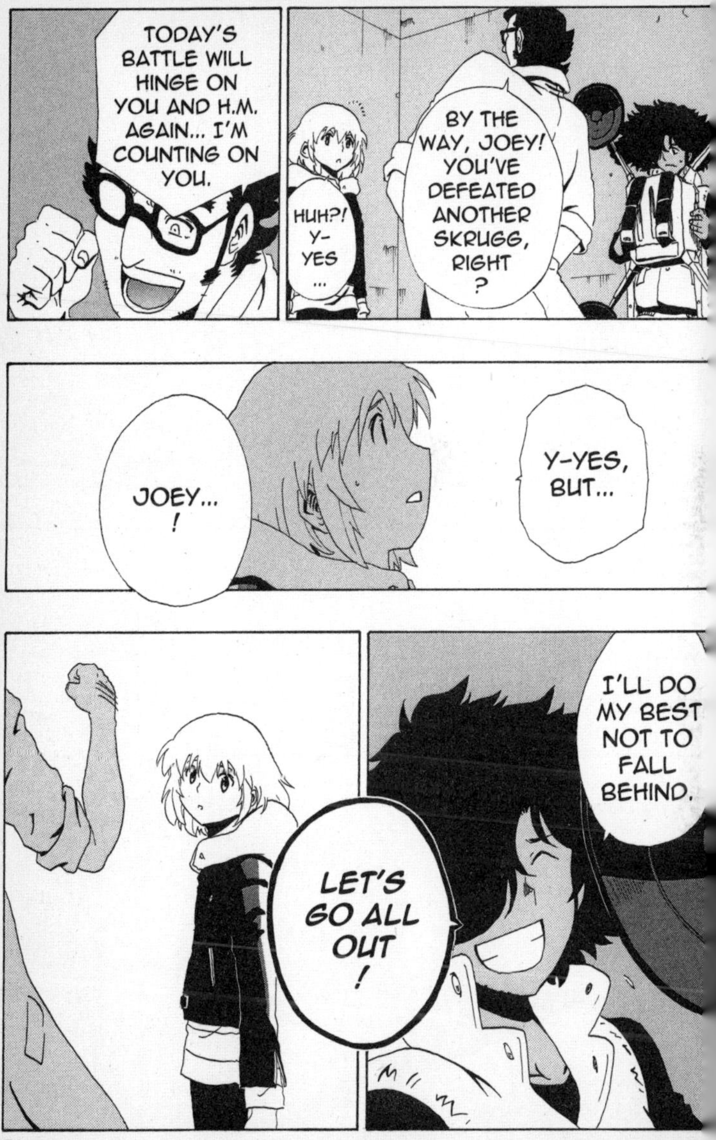
BY THE WAY, JOEY! YOU'VE DEFEATED ANOTHER SKRUGG, RIGHT?
HUH?! Y-YES...
TODAY'S BATTLE WILL HINGE ON YOU AND H.M. AGAIN... I'M COUNTING ON YOU.
Y-YES, BUT...
JOEY...!
I'LL DO MY BEST NOT TO FALL BEHIND.
LET'S GO ALL OUT!

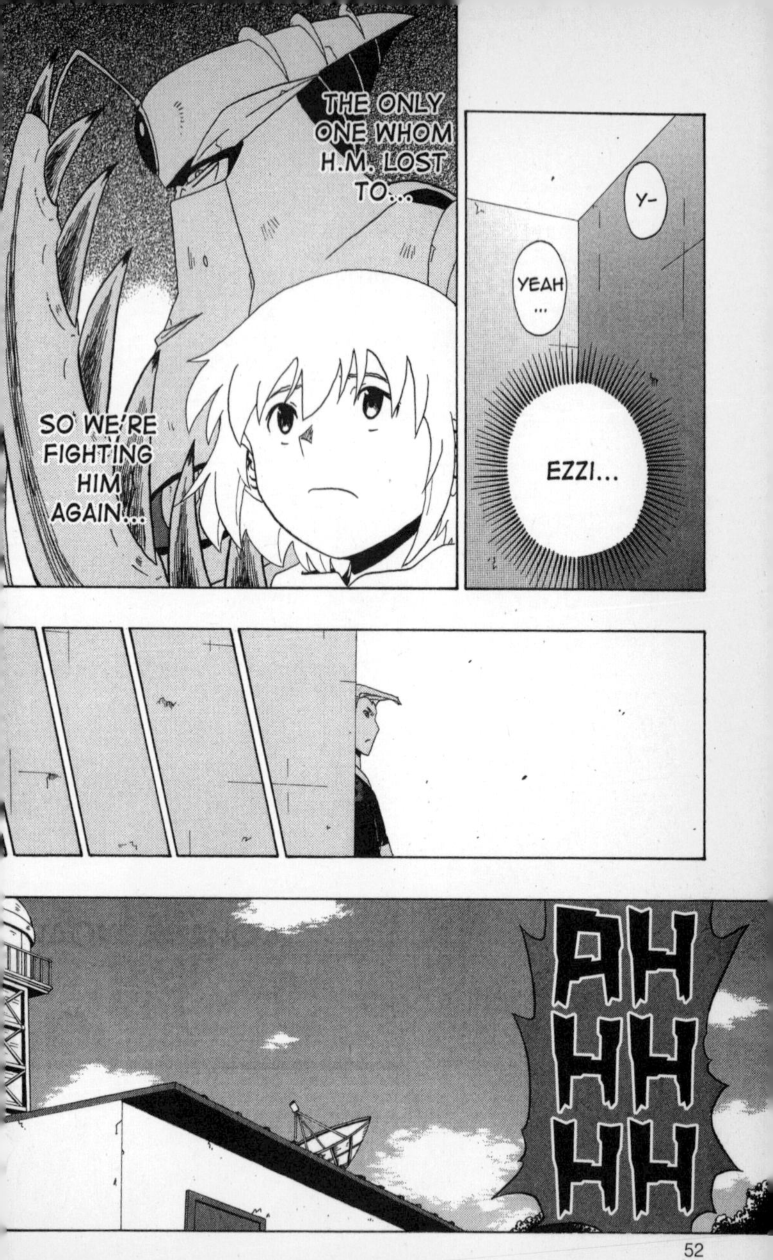
Y-
YEAH ...
EZZI...
THE ONLY ONE WHOM H.M. LOST TO...
SO WE'RE FIGHTING HIM AGAIN...
AHHHHH

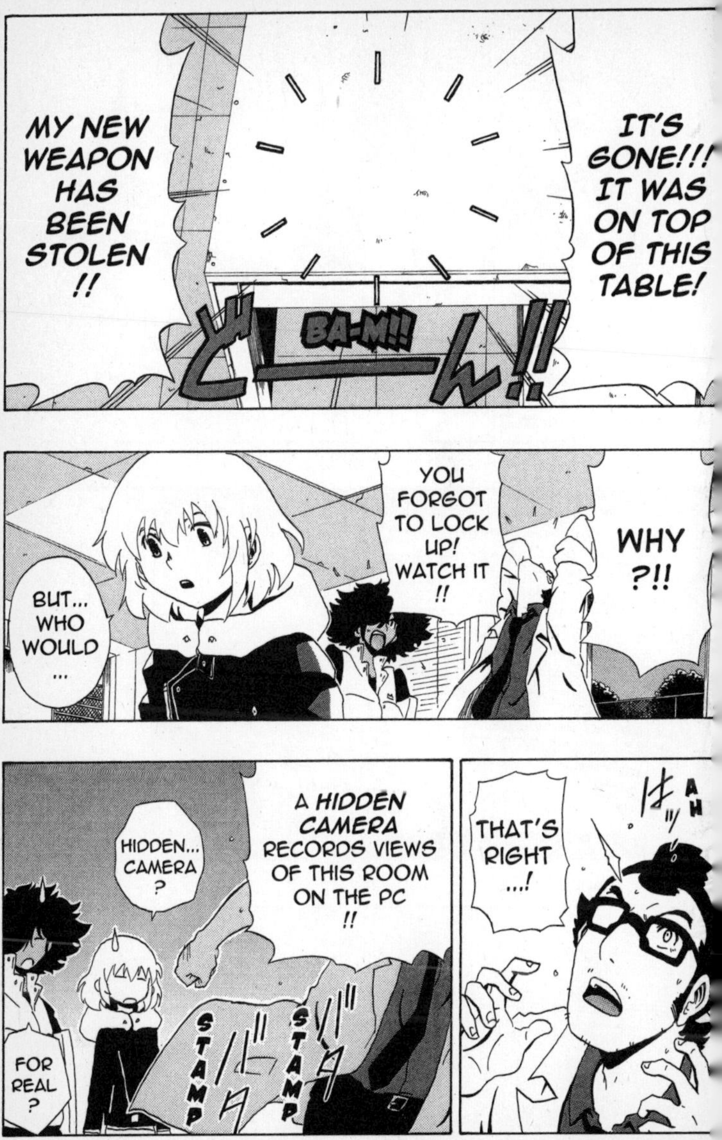
IT'S GONE!!! IT WAS ON TOP OF THIS TABLE!
MY NEW WEAPON HAS BEEN STOLEN!!
BA-M!!
WHY?!!
YOU FORGOT TO LOCK UP! WATCH IT!!
BUT... WHO WOULD...
AH
THAT'S RIGHT...!
A HIDDEN CAMERA RECORDS VIEWS OF THIS ROOM ON THE PC!!
HIDDEN... CAMERA?
STAMP
STAMP
FOR REAL?

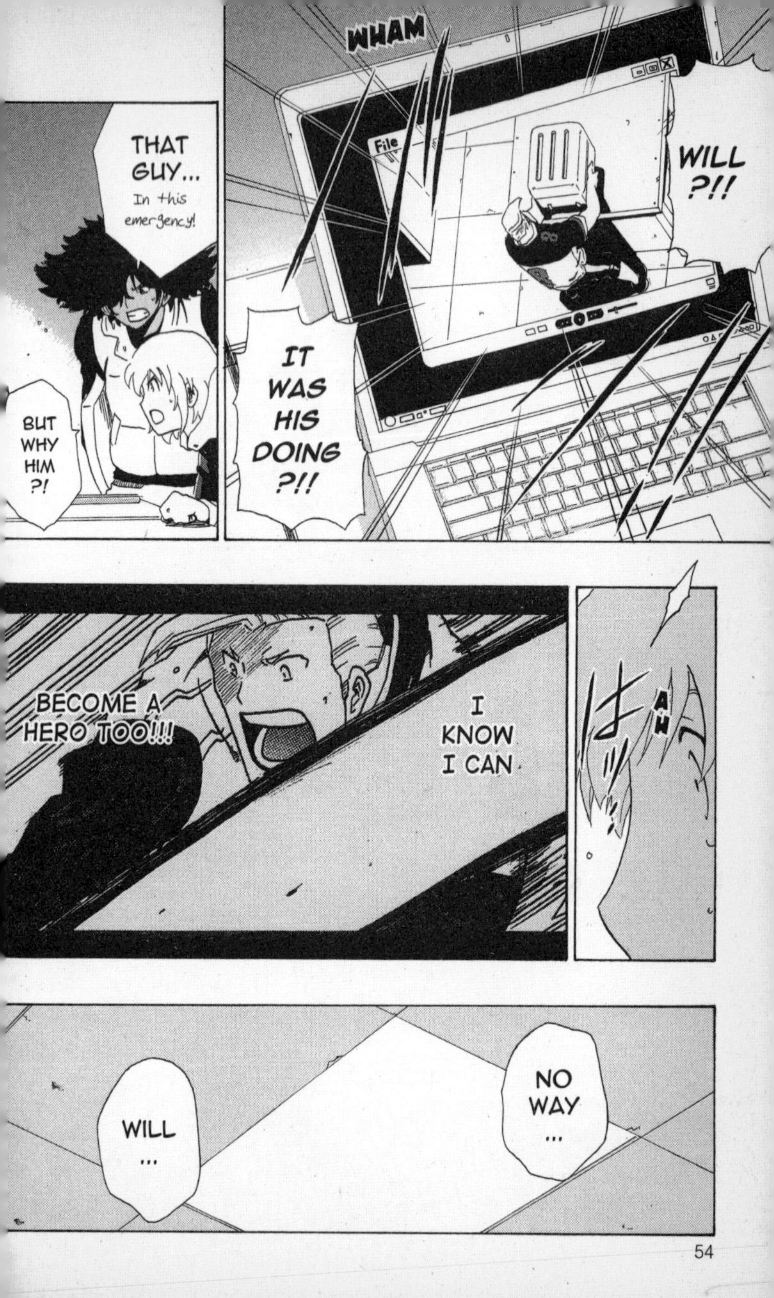
WHAM
WILL ?!!
IT WAS HIS DOING ?!!
THAT GUY... In this emergency!
BUT WHY HIM ?!
はッ
AH
I KNOW I CAN
BECOME A HERO TOO!!!
NO WAY ...
WILL ...

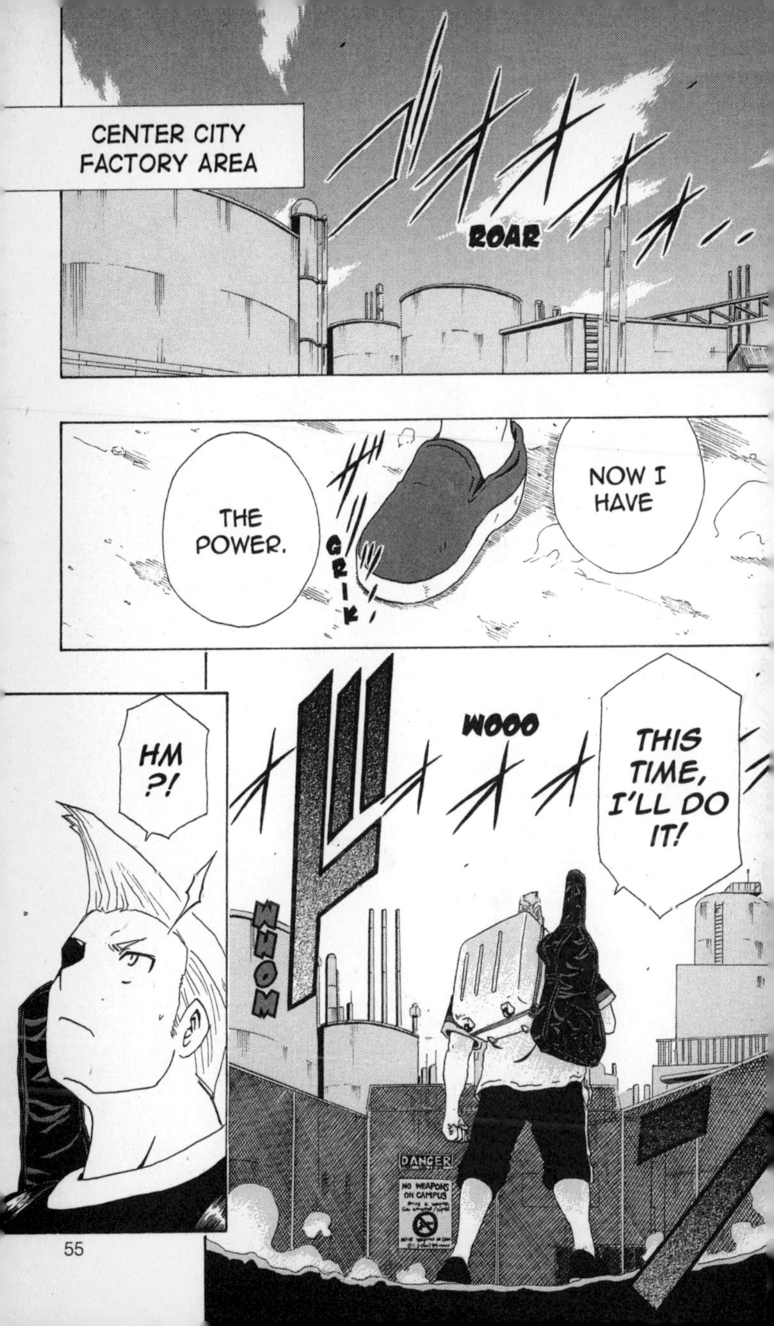

CENTER CITY FACTORY AREA
ROAR
NOW I HAVE
THE POWER.
GRIK
THIS TIME, I'LL DO IT!
WOOO
WHOM
DANGER
NO WEAPONS ON CAMPUS
HM ?!

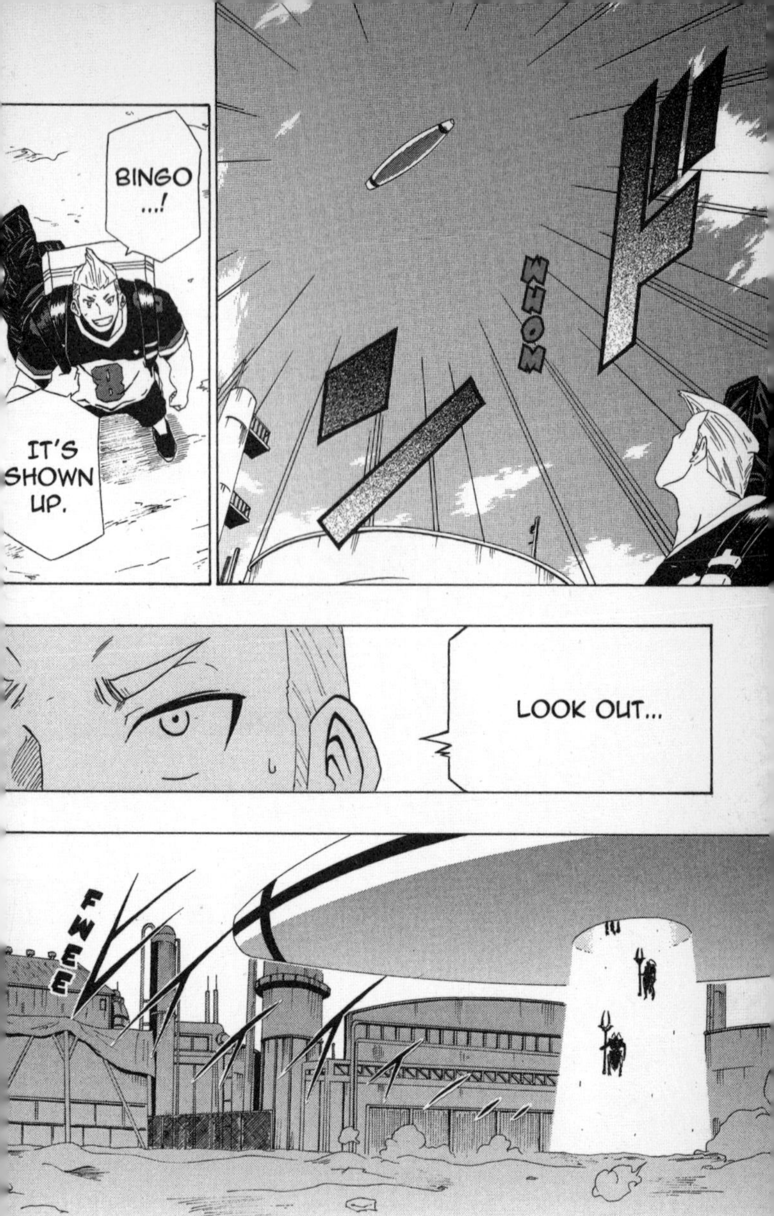
WHOM
BINGO ...!
IT'S SHOWN UP.
LOOK OUT...
FWEE

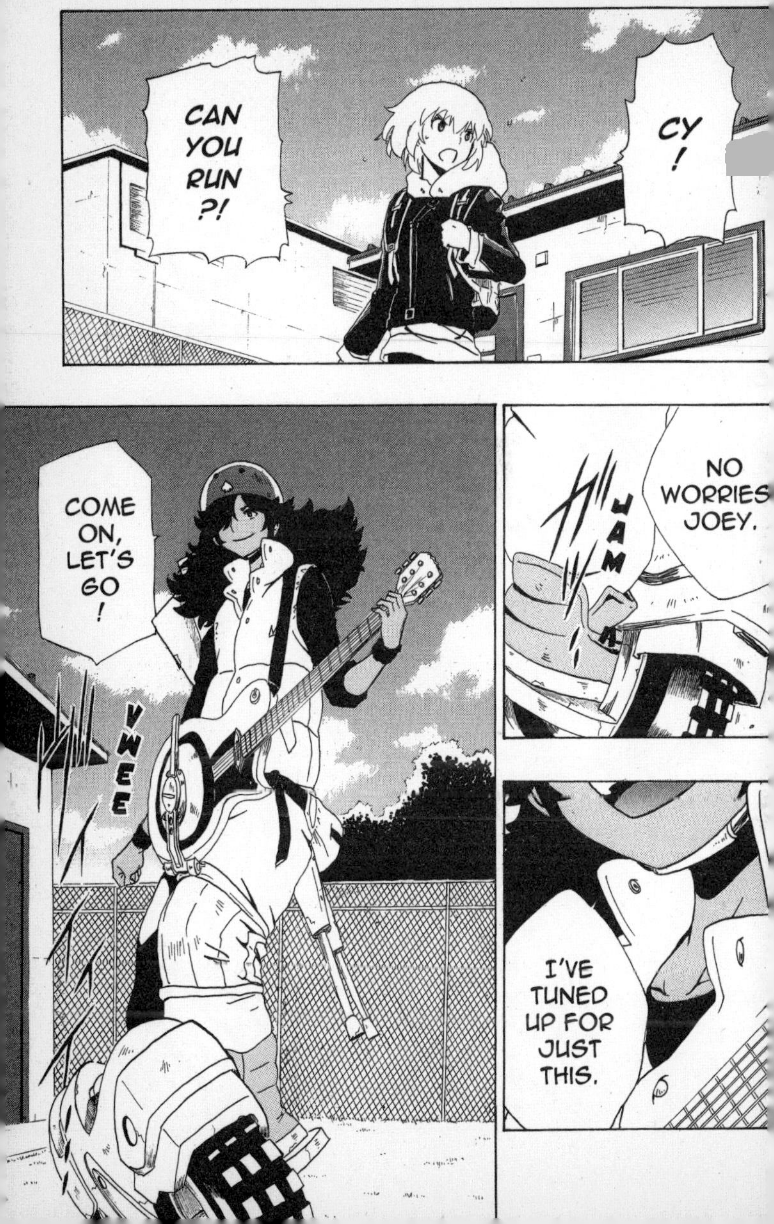
CY!
CAN YOU RUN?!
NO WORRIES JOEY.
JAM
I'VE TUNED UP FOR JUST THIS.
COME ON, LET'S GO!
VWEE

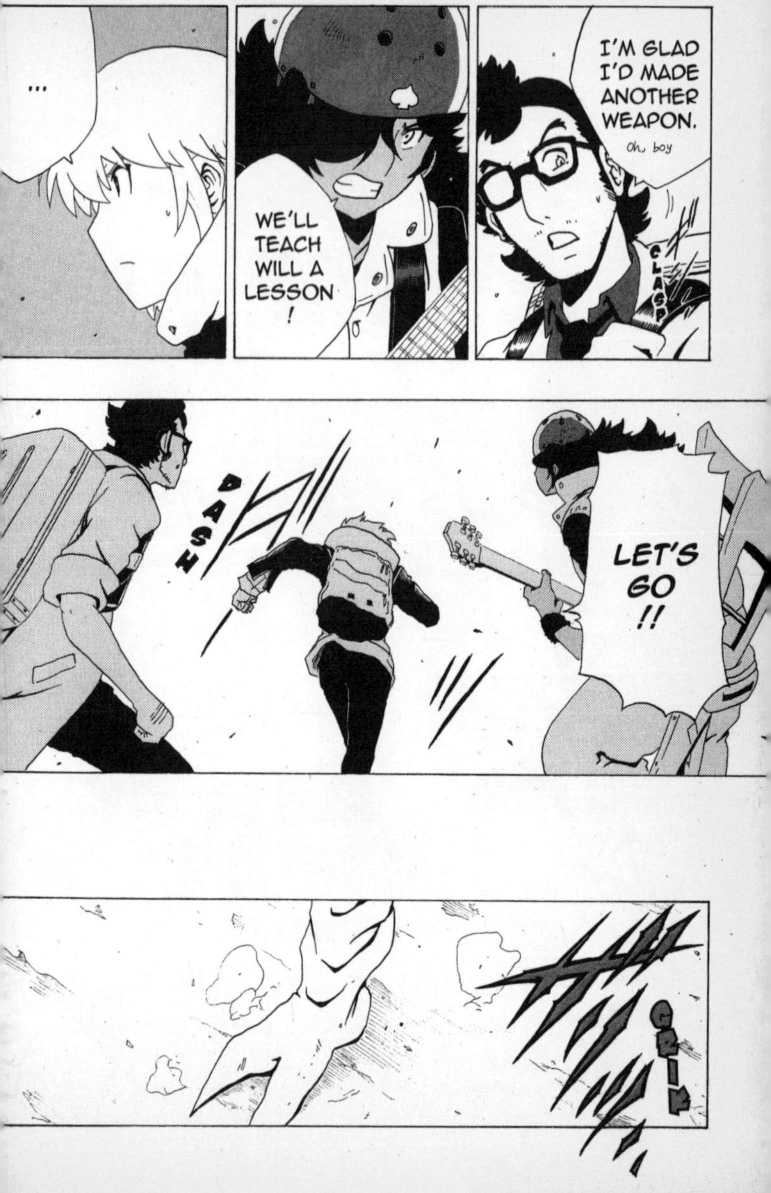
I'M GLAD I'D MADE ANOTHER WEAPON.
oh, boy
CLASP
WE'LL TEACH WILL A LESSON!
...
LET'S GO!!
DASH
GZIK

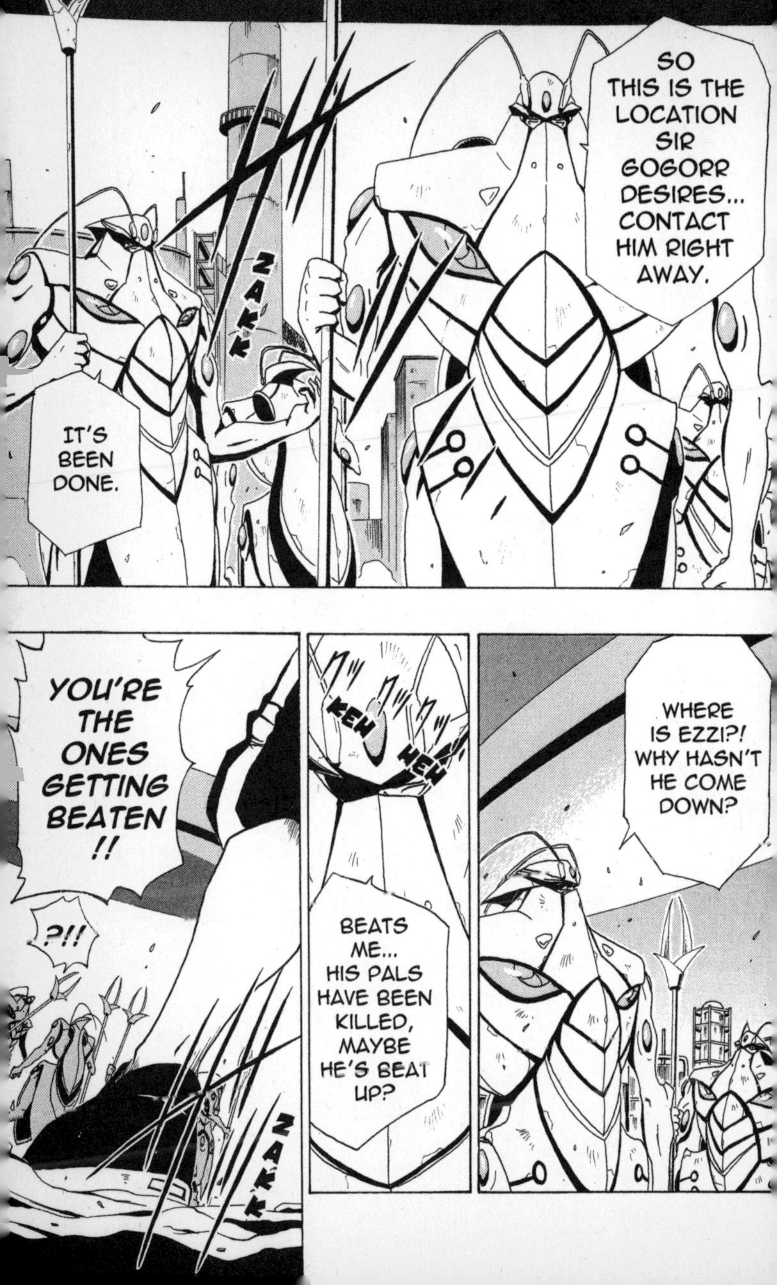
SO THIS IS THE LOCATION SIR GOGORR DESIRES... CONTACT HIM RIGHT AWAY.
ZAKK
IT'S BEEN DONE.
WHERE IS EZZI?! WHY HASN'T HE COME DOWN?
KEH HEH
BEATS ME... HIS PALS HAVE BEEN KILLED, MAYBE HE'S BEAT UP?
YOU'RE THE ONES GETTING BEATEN !!
?!!
ZAKK

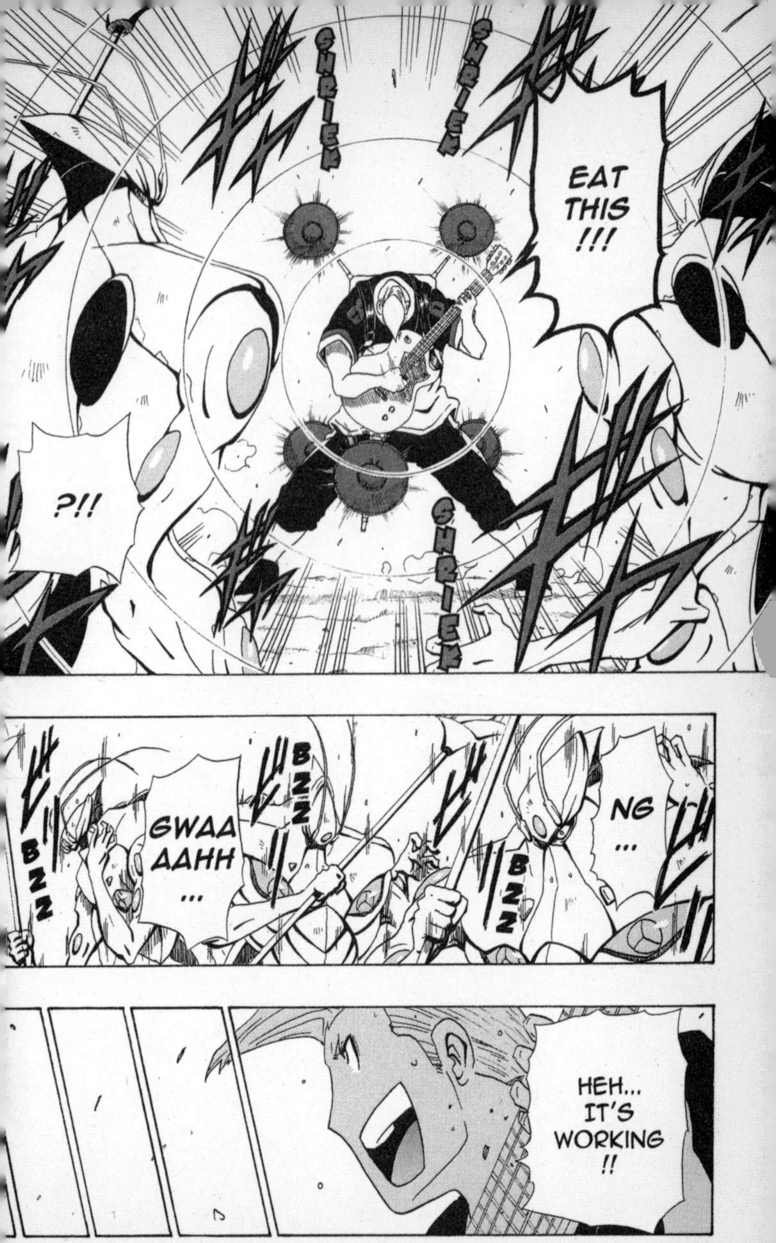
SHRIEK
SHRIEK
EAT THIS !!!
SHRIEK
?!!
NG ...
BZZ
BZZ
GWAA AAHH ...
BZZ
HEH... IT'S WORKING !!

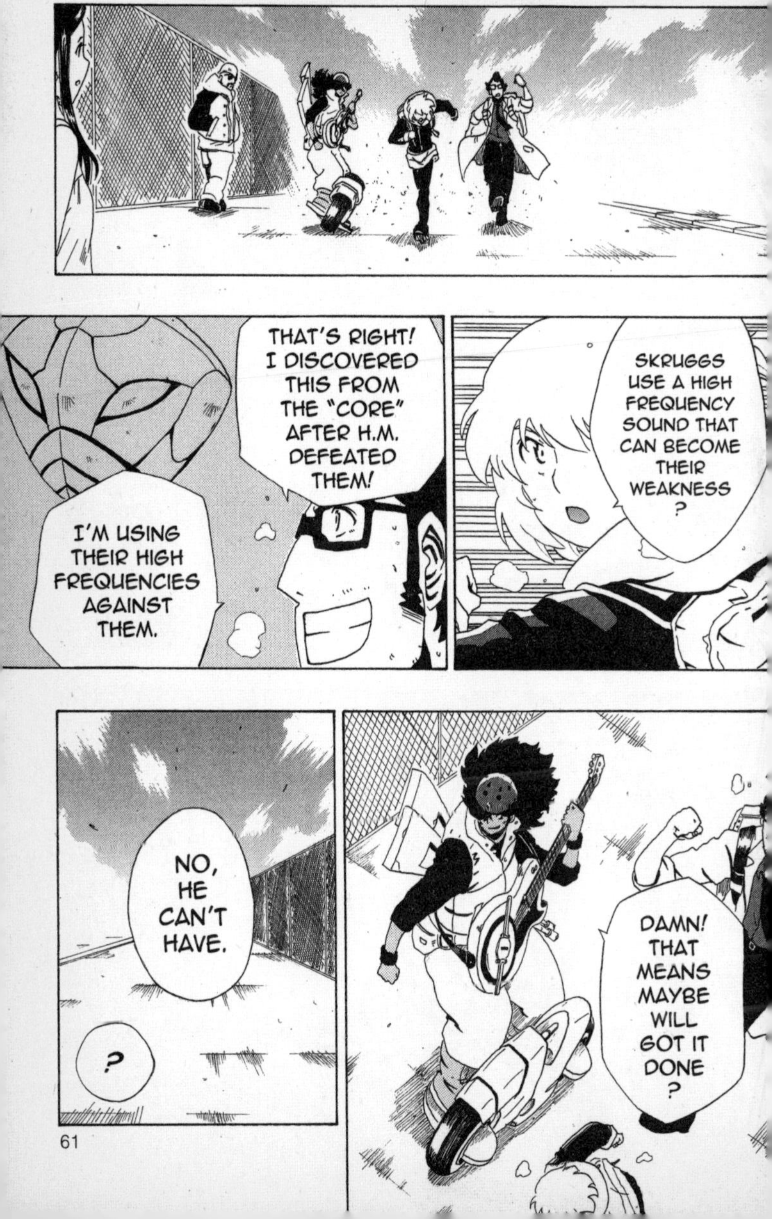
SKRUGGS USE A HIGH FREQUENCY SOUND THAT CAN BECOME THEIR WEAKNESS ?
THAT'S RIGHT! I DISCOVERED THIS FROM THE "CORE" AFTER H.M. DEFEATED THEM!
I'M USING THEIR HIGH FREQUENCIES AGAINST THEM.
DAMN! THAT MEANS MAYBE WILL GOT IT DONE ?
NO, HE CAN'T HAVE.
?

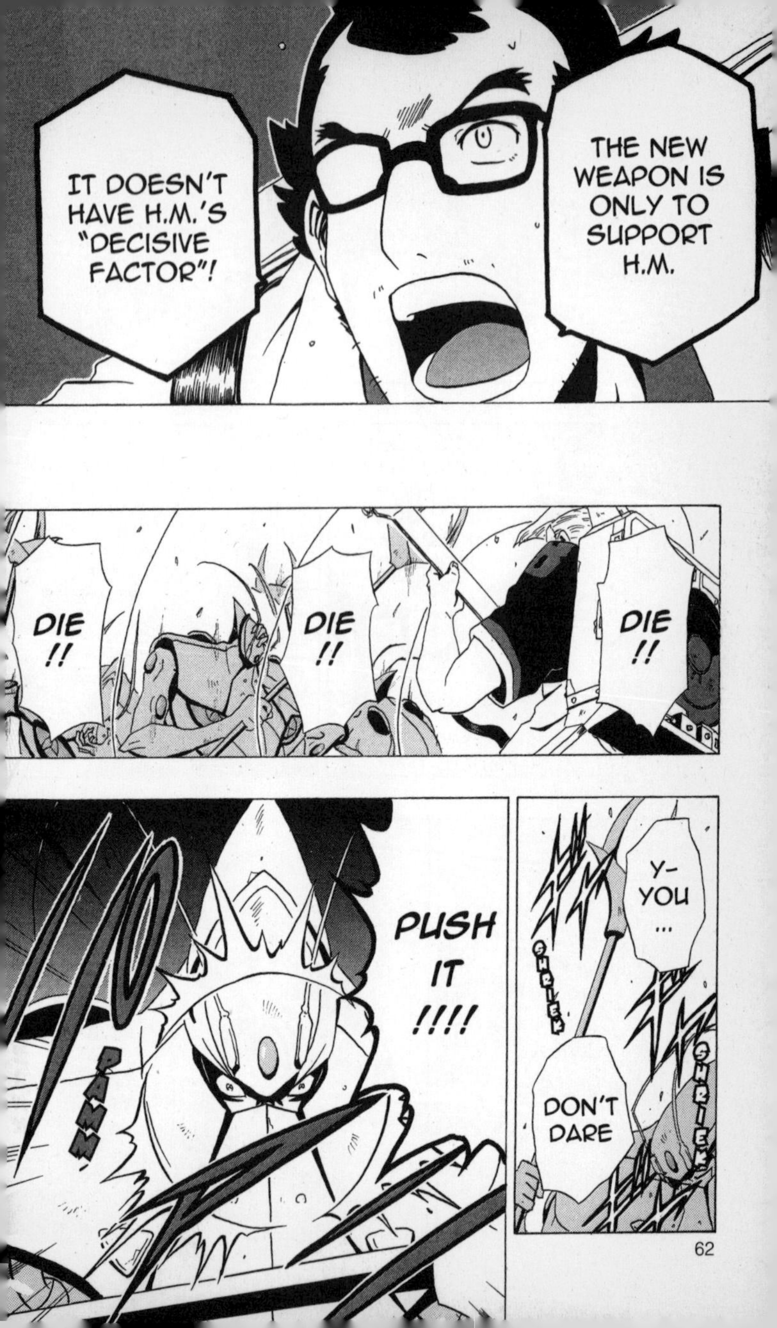
THE NEW WEAPON IS ONLY TO SUPPORT H.M.
IT DOESN'T HAVE H.M.'S "DECISIVE FACTOR"!
DIE !!
DIE !!
DIE !!
Y-YOU ...
SHRIEK
DON'T DARE
SHRIEK
PUSH IT !!!!
PAMM

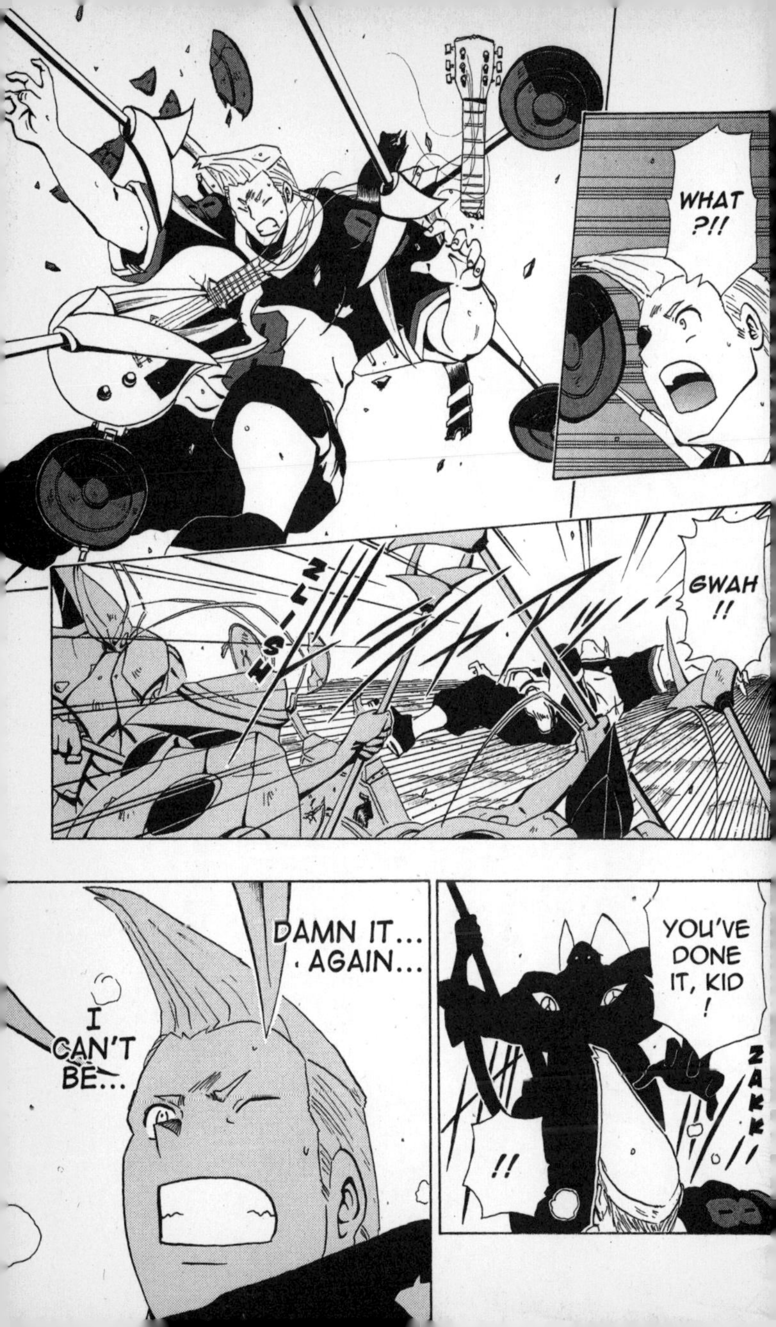
WHAT ?!!
GWAH !!
ZLISH
YOU'VE DONE IT, KID !
ZAKK !!
!!
DAMN IT... ...AGAIN...
I CAN'T BE...

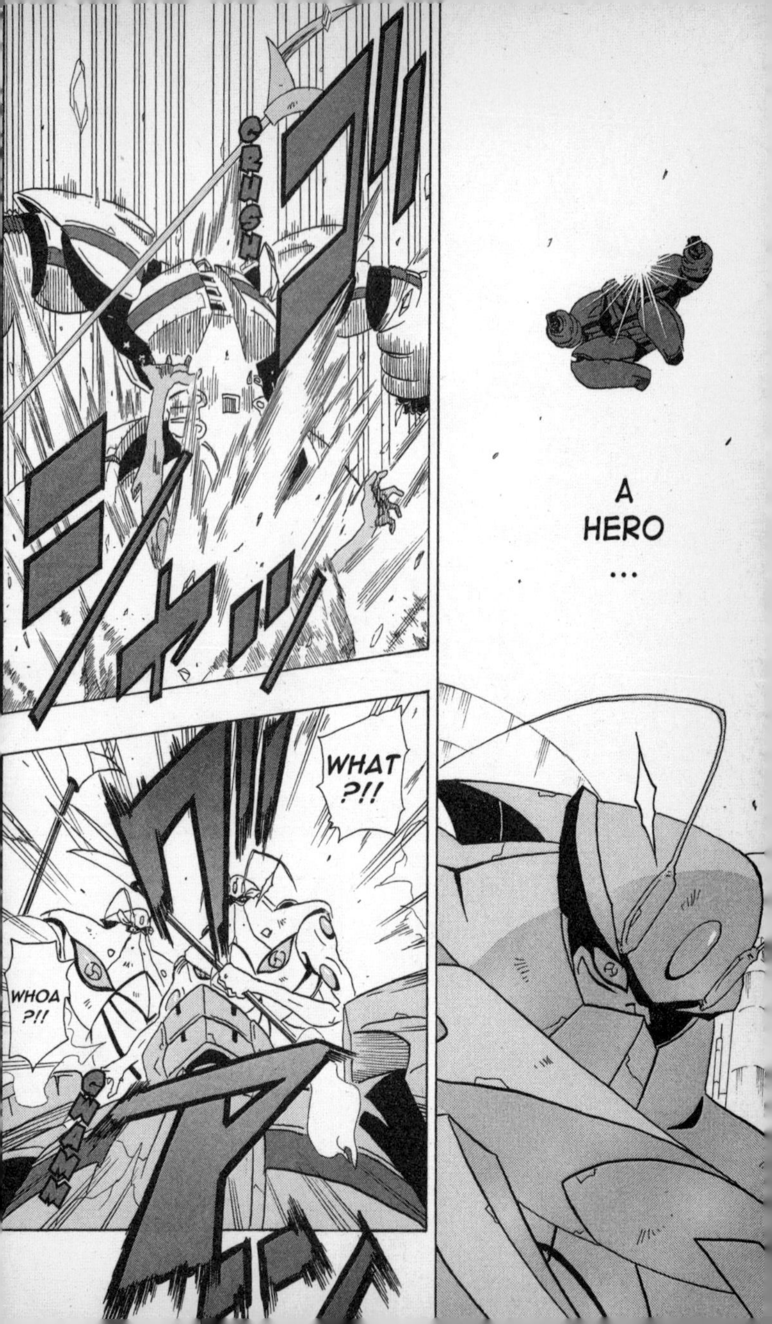
A HERO
...
CRUSH
WHAT ?!!
WHOA ?!!
GWAMM

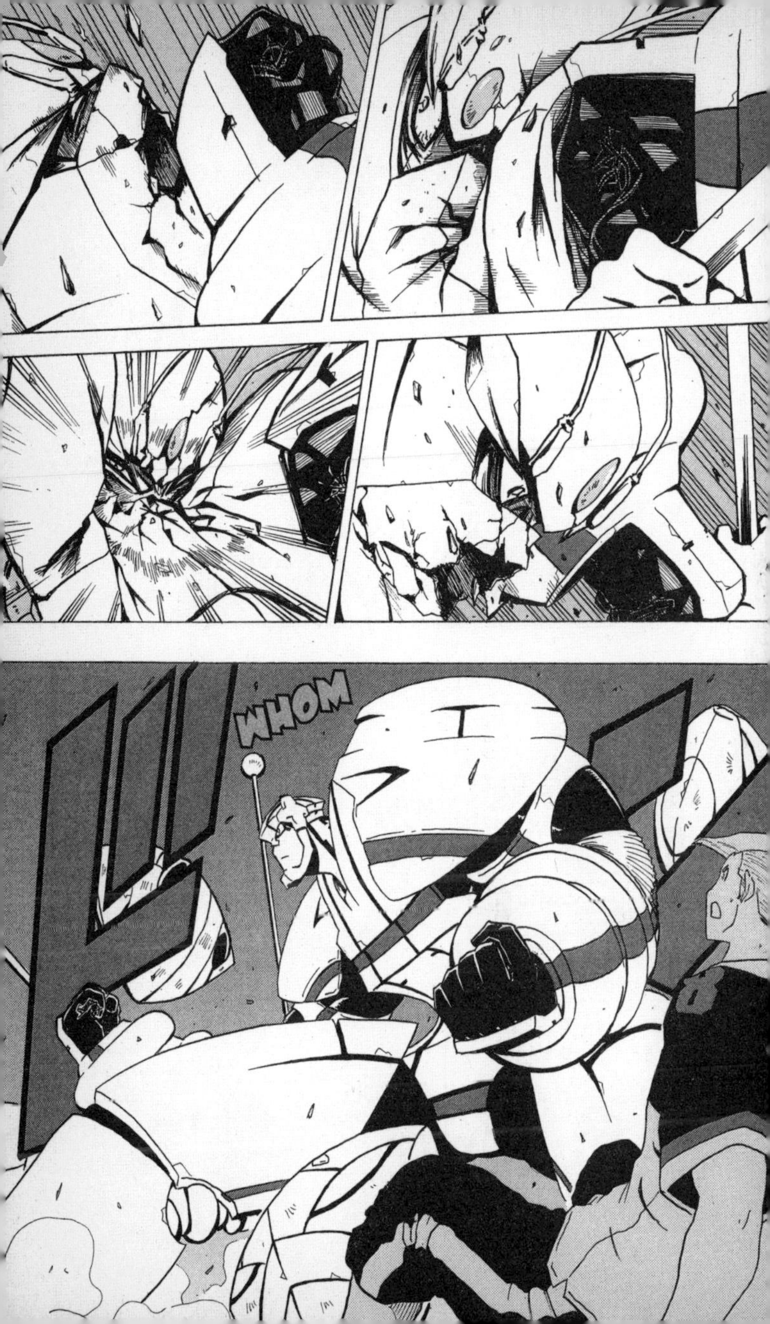
WHOM

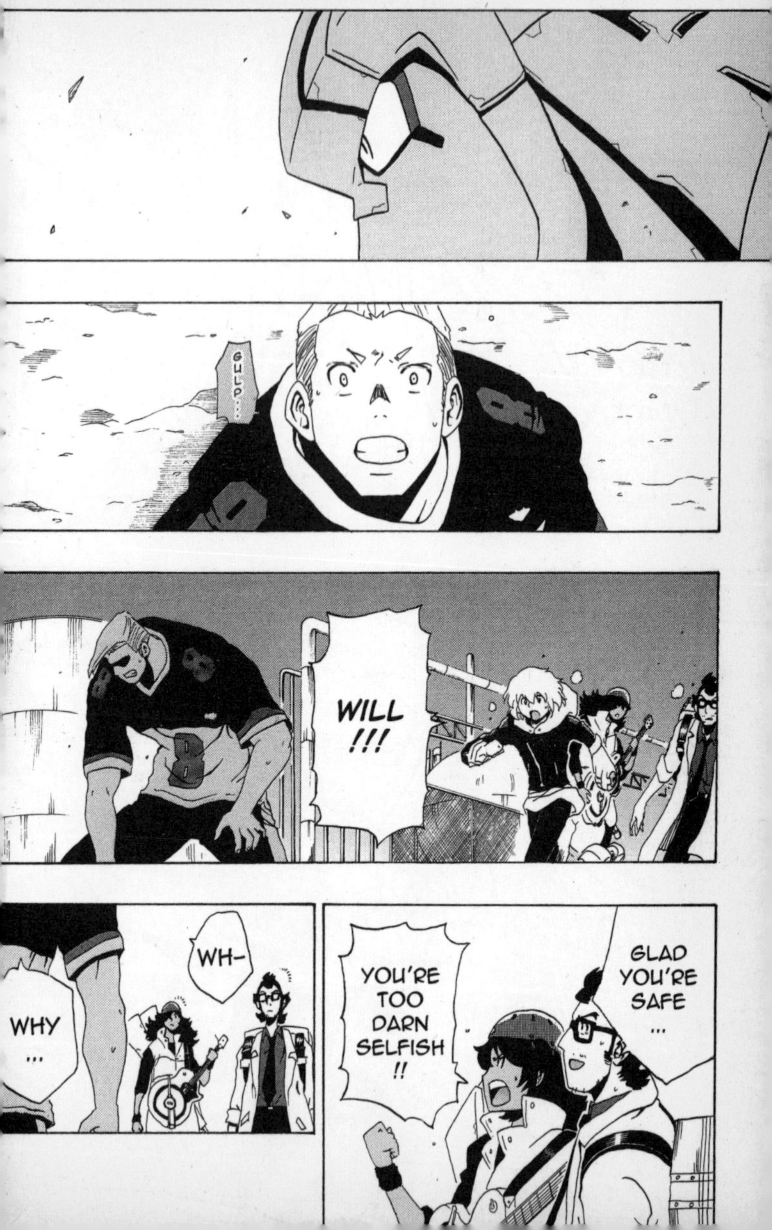
GULP...
WILL!!!
GLAD YOU'RE SAFE...
YOU'RE TOO DARN SELFISH!!
WH-
WHY...

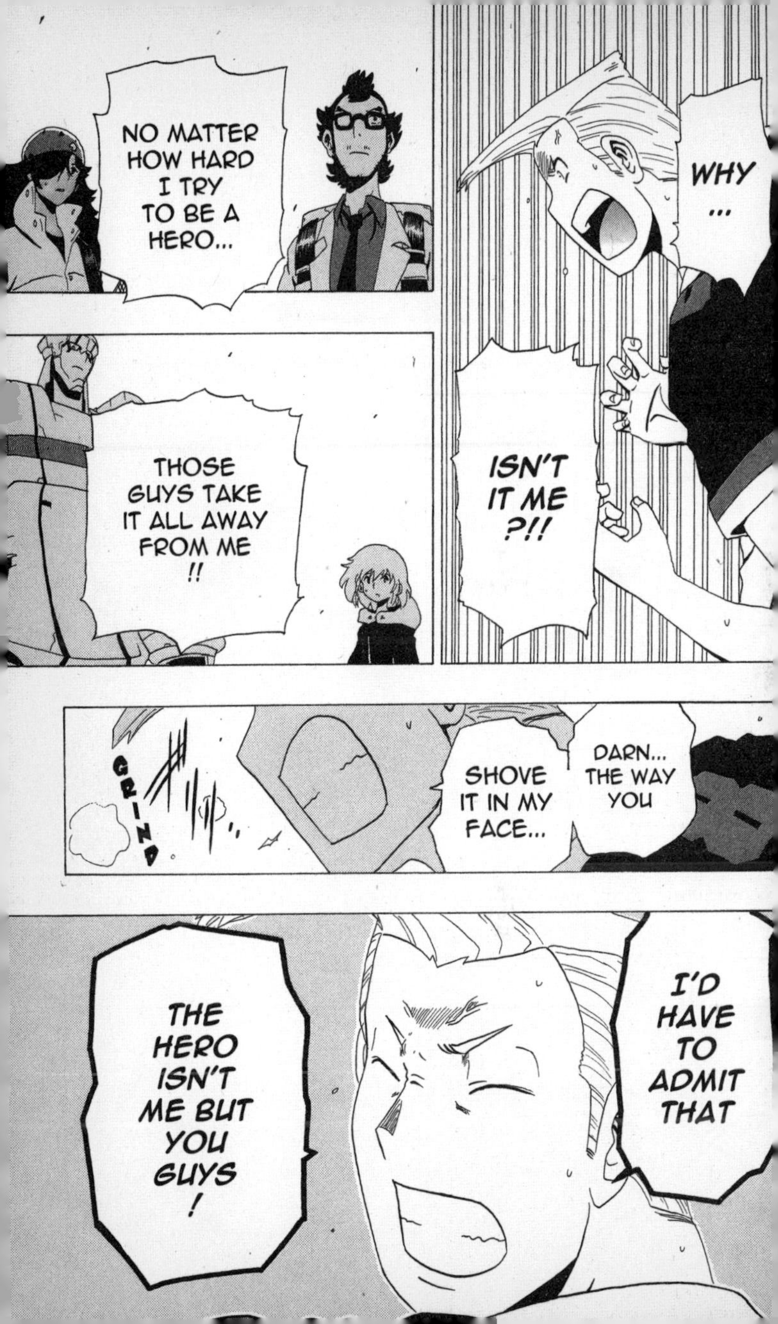
WHY...
ISN'T IT ME?!!
NO MATTER HOW HARD I TRY TO BE A HERO...
THOSE GUYS TAKE IT ALL AWAY FROM ME!!
DARN... THE WAY YOU
SHOVE IT IN MY FACE...
GRIND
I'D HAVE TO ADMIT THAT
THE HERO ISN'T ME BUT YOU GUYS!

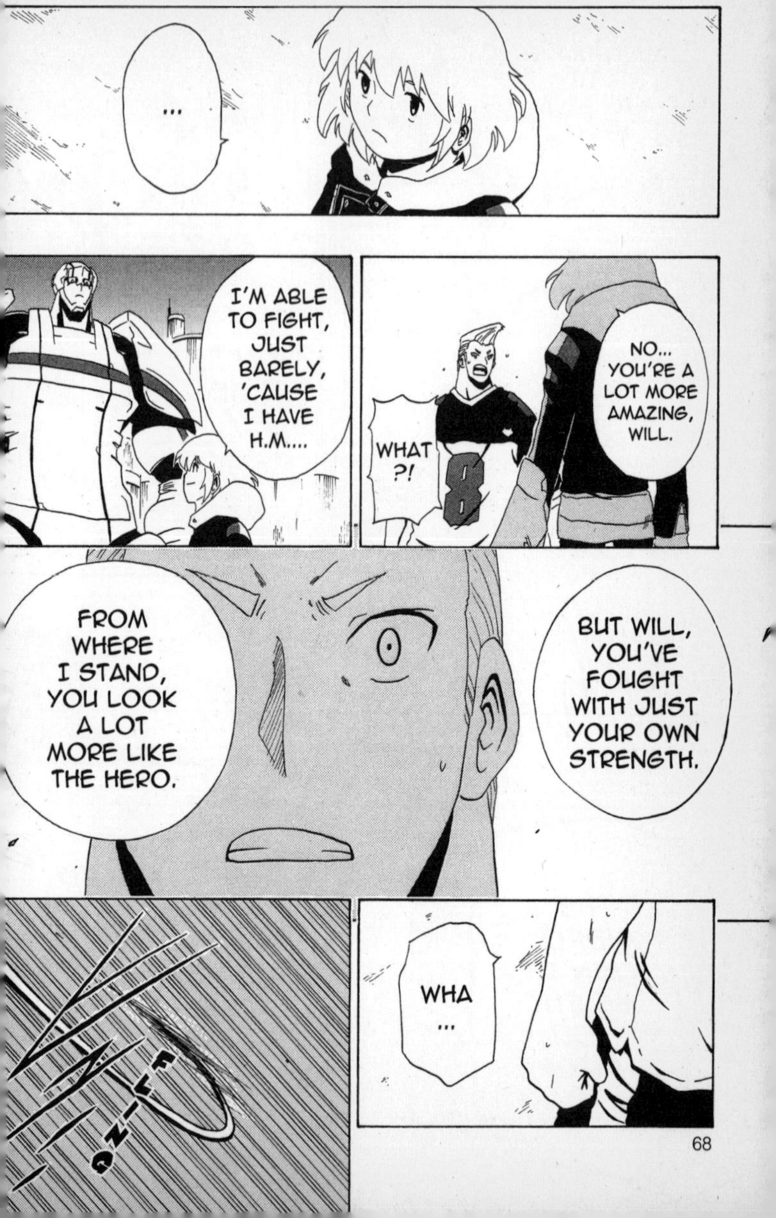
...
NO... YOU'RE A LOT MORE AMAZING, WILL.
WHAT ?!
I'M ABLE TO FIGHT, JUST BARELY, 'CAUSE I HAVE H.M....
BUT WILL, YOU'VE FOUGHT WITH JUST YOUR OWN STRENGTH.
FROM WHERE I STAND, YOU LOOK A LOT MORE LIKE THE HERO.
WHA ...
FLING

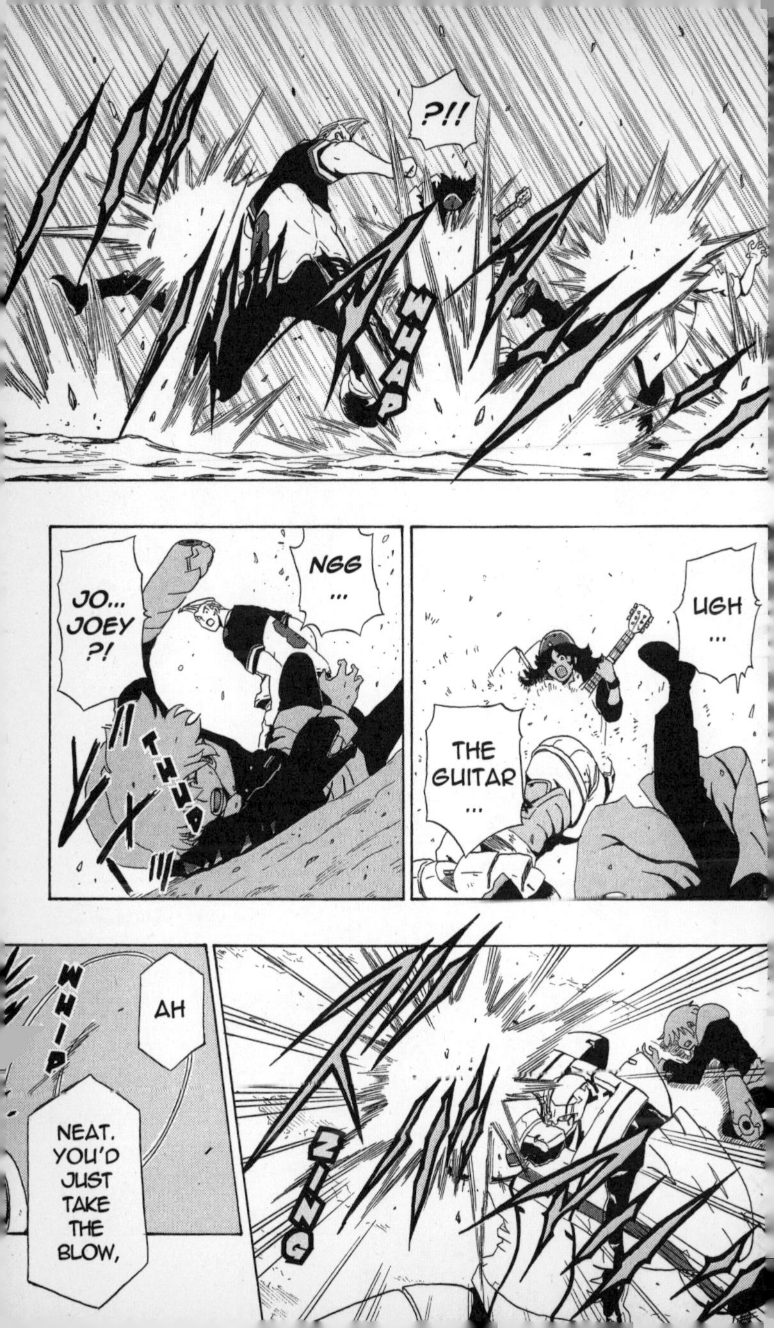
?!!
WHAP
UGH ...
THE GUITAR ...
NGG ...
JO... JOEY ?!
THUD
ZING
AH
WHIP
NEAT. YOU'D JUST TAKE THE BLOW,

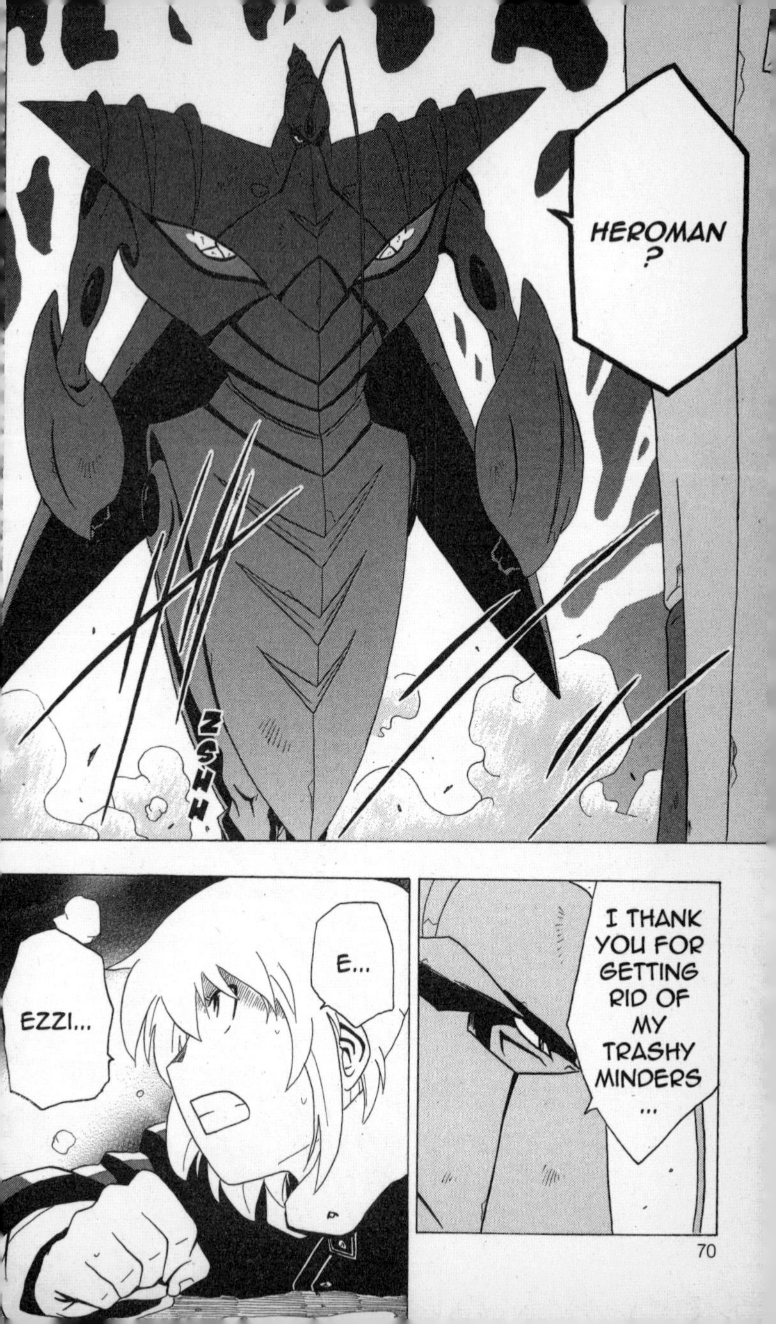
HEROMAN ?
ZSHH
I THANK YOU FOR GETTING RID OF MY TRASHY MINDERS ...
E...
EZZI...

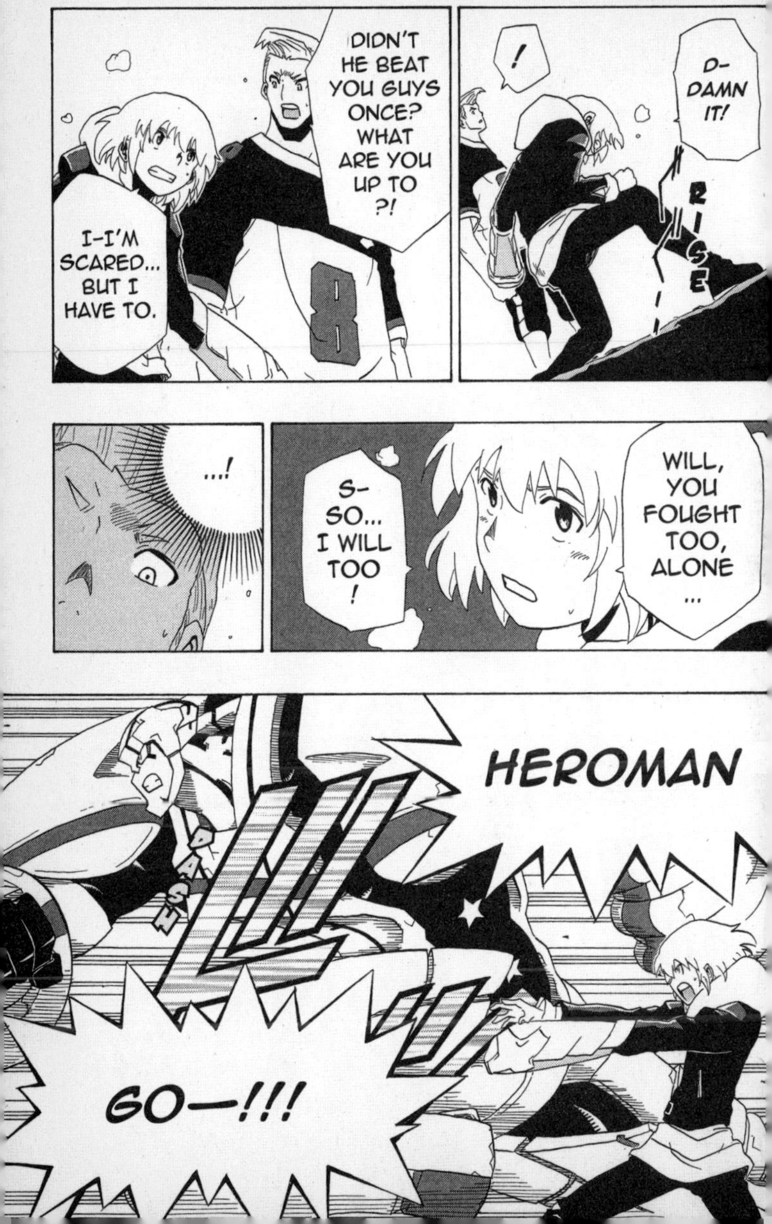
D-DAMN IT!
!
RISE
DIDN'T HE BEAT YOU GUYS ONCE? WHAT ARE YOU UP TO ?!
I-I'M SCARED... BUT I HAVE TO.
WILL, YOU FOUGHT TOO, ALONE ...
S-SO... I WILL TOO !
...!
HEROMAN
DASH
GO—!!!

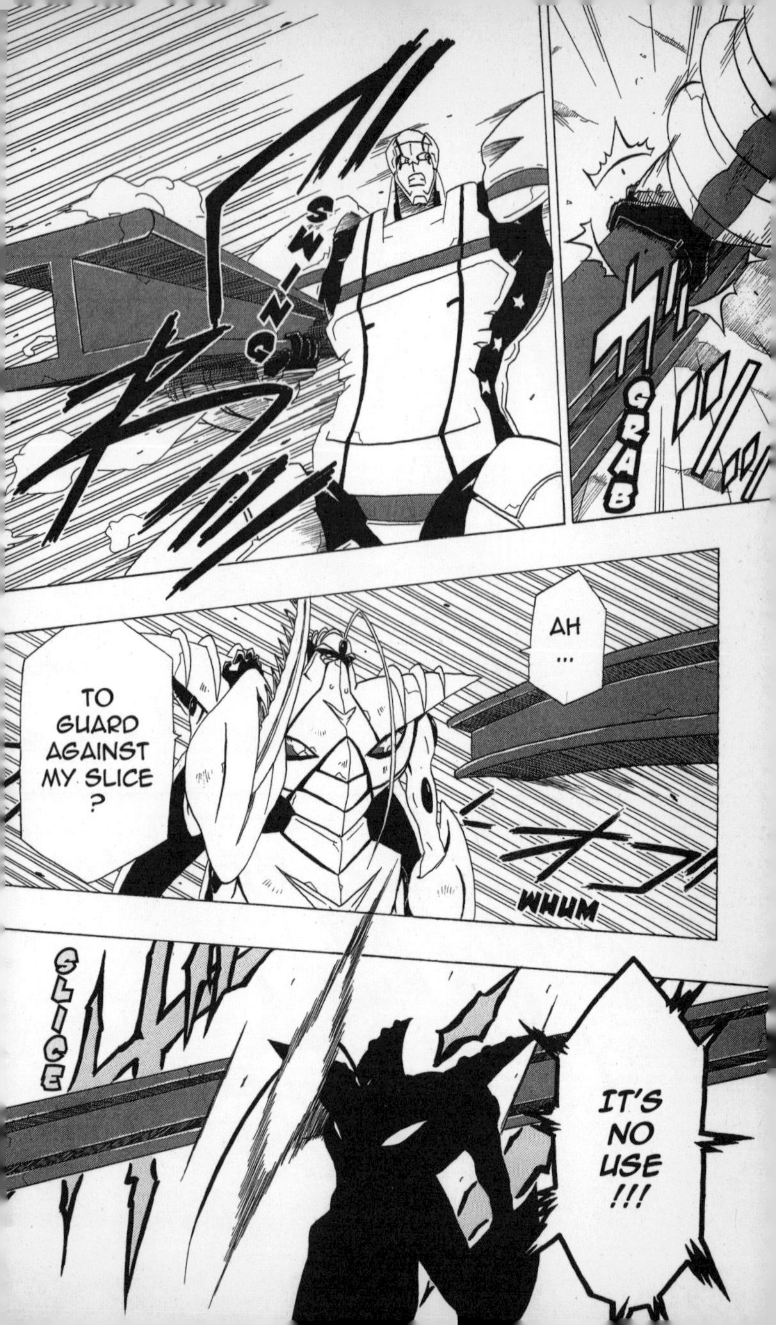
GRAB
SWING
AH ...
TO GUARD AGAINST MY SLICE ?
WHUM
IT'S NO USE !!!
SLICE

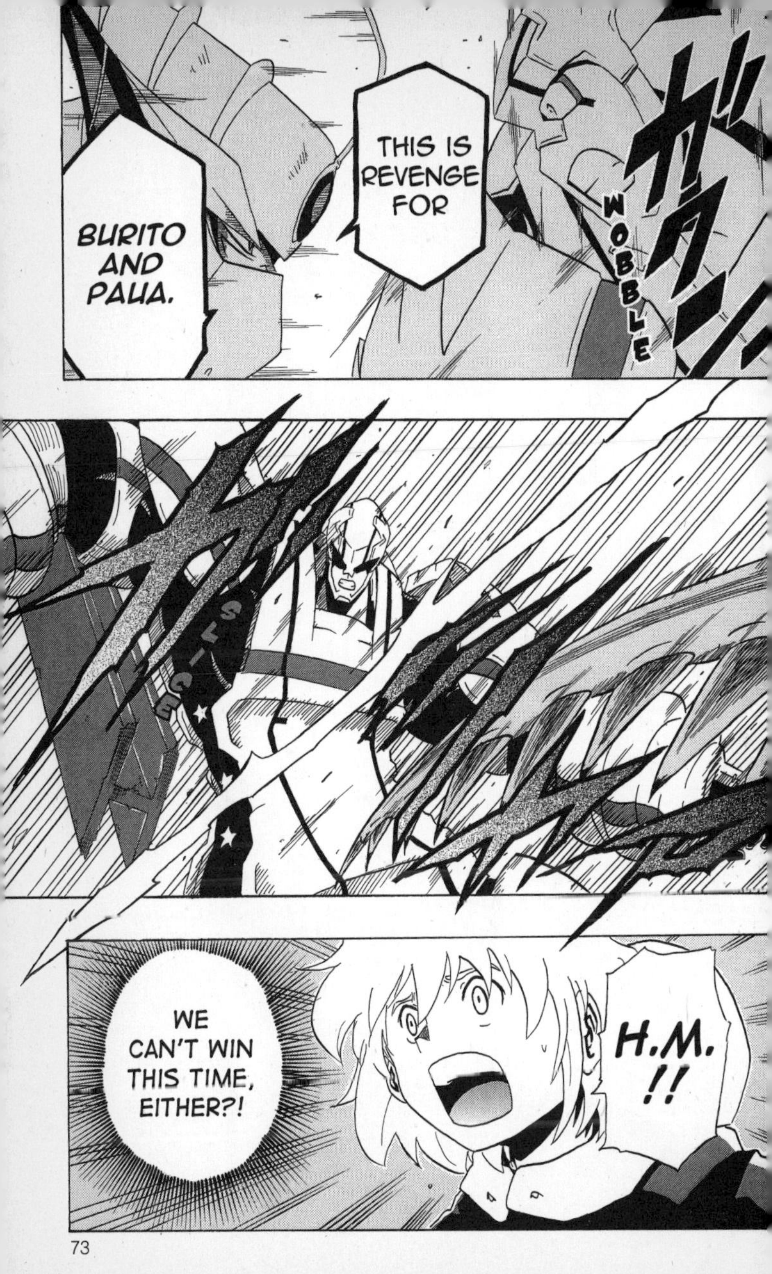
WOBBLE
THIS IS REVENGE FOR
BURITO AND PAUA.
SLICE
H.M. !!
WE CAN'T WIN THIS TIME, EITHER?!

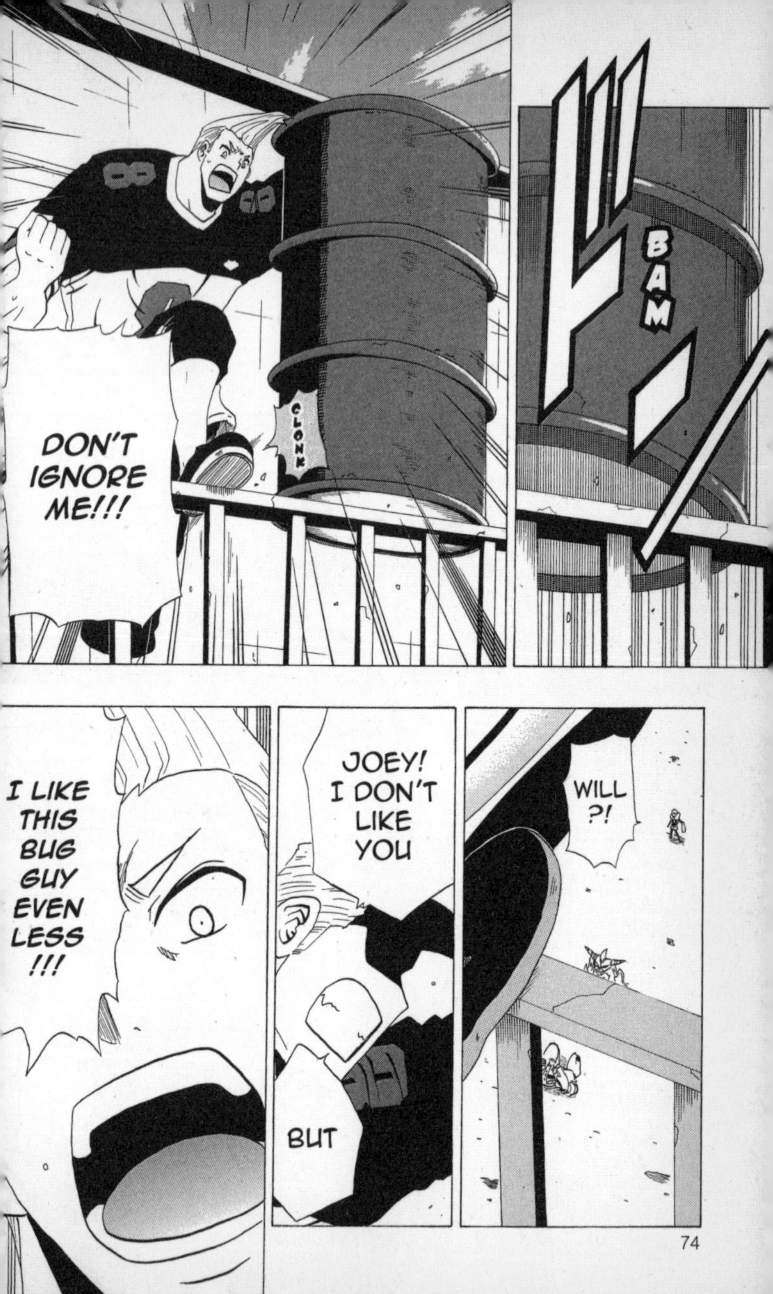
BAM
CLONK
DON'T IGNORE ME!!!
WILL ?!
JOEY! I DON'T LIKE YOU
BUT
I LIKE THIS BUG GUY EVEN LESS!!!

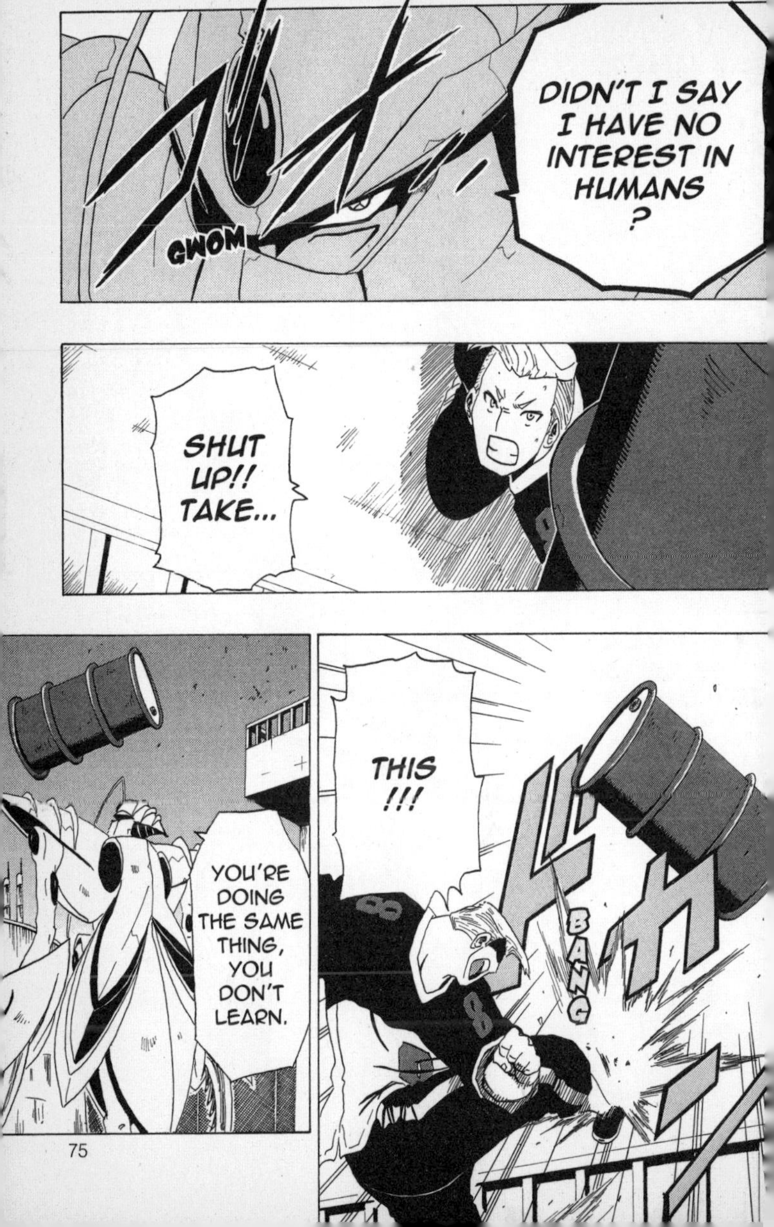
GWOM
DIDN'T I SAY I HAVE NO INTEREST IN HUMANS ?
SHUT UP!! TAKE...
THIS !!!
BANG
YOU'RE DOING THE SAME THING, YOU DON'T LEARN.

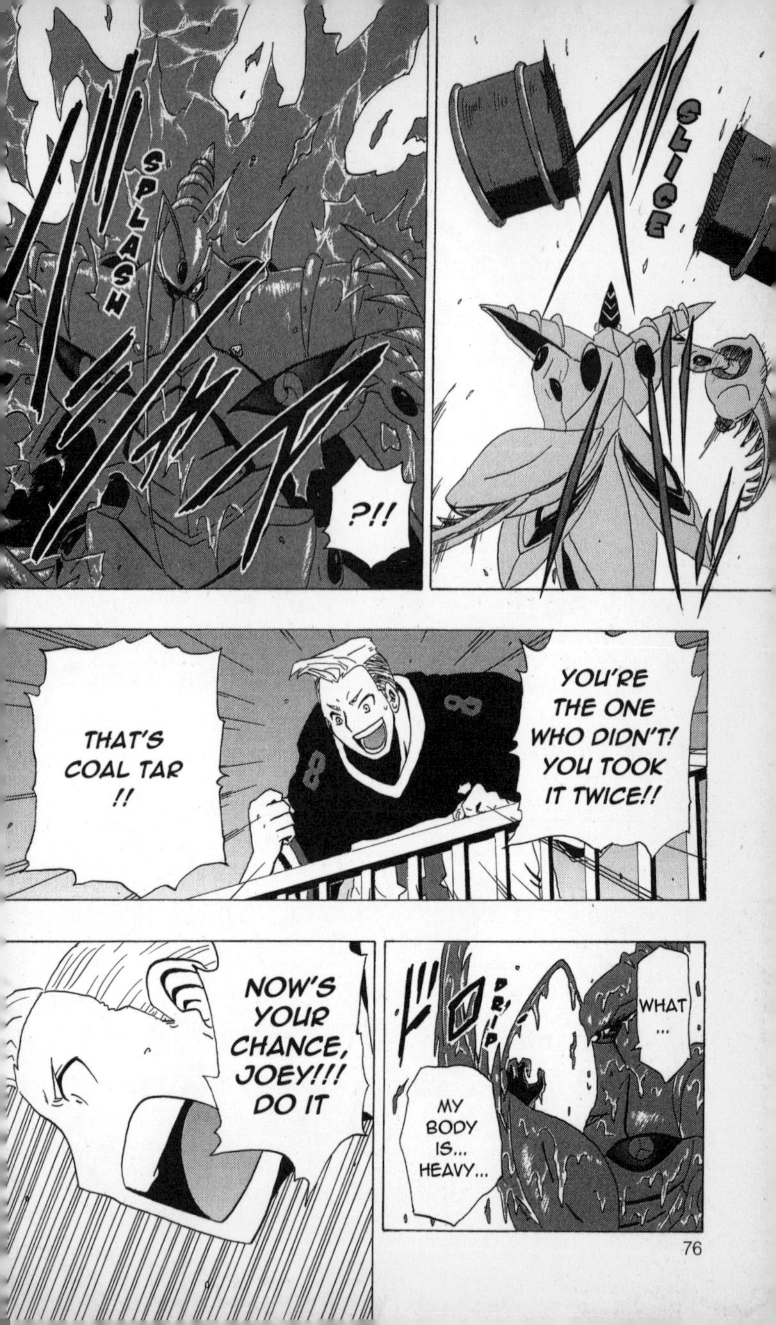

SLICE
SPLASH
?!!
YOU'RE THE ONE WHO DIDN'T! YOU TOOK IT TWICE!!
THAT'S COAL TAR !!
DRIP
WHAT ...
MY BODY IS... HEAVY...
NOW'S YOUR CHANCE, JOEY!!! DO IT

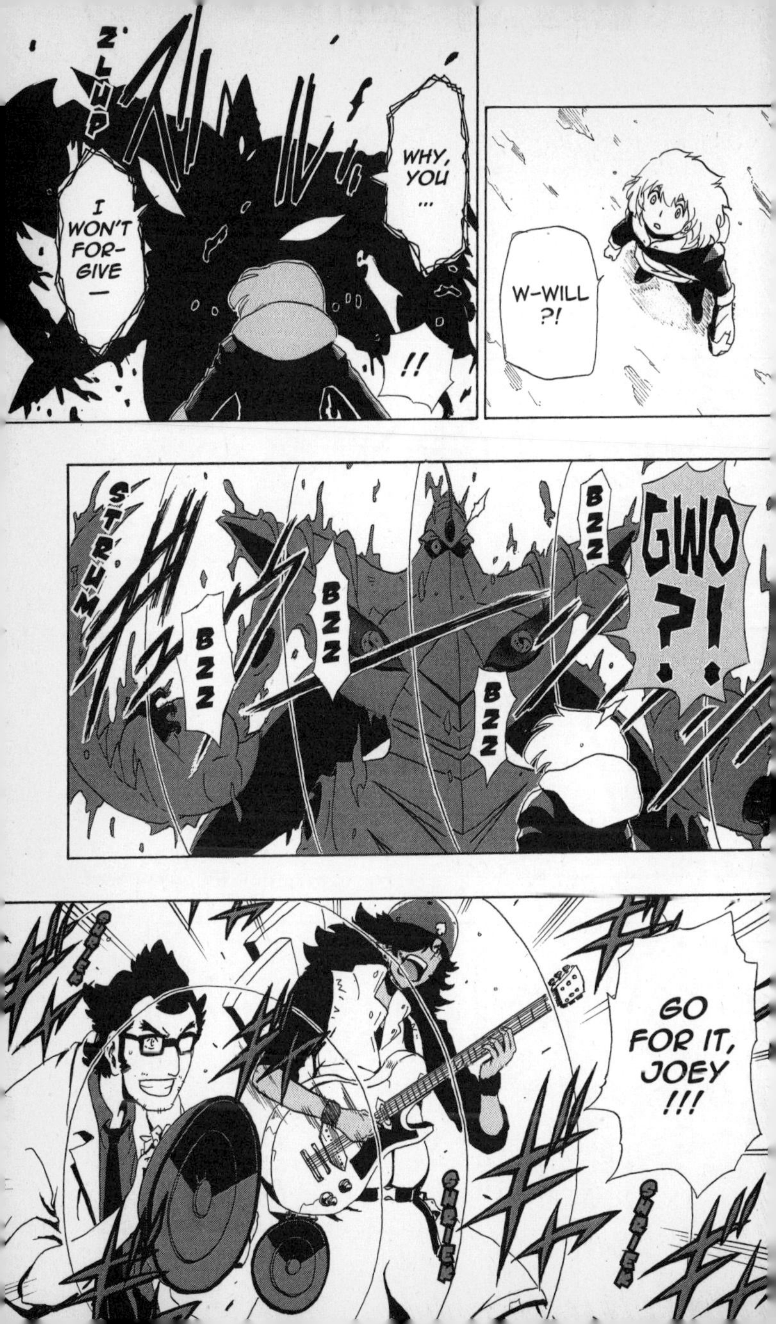
W-WILL ?!
WHY, YOU ...
ZLUP
I WON'T FOR-GIVE —
!!
GWO ?!
BZZ
BZZ
BZZ
BZZ
STRUM
GO FOR IT, JOEY !!!
SHRIEK
SHRIEK
SHRIEK

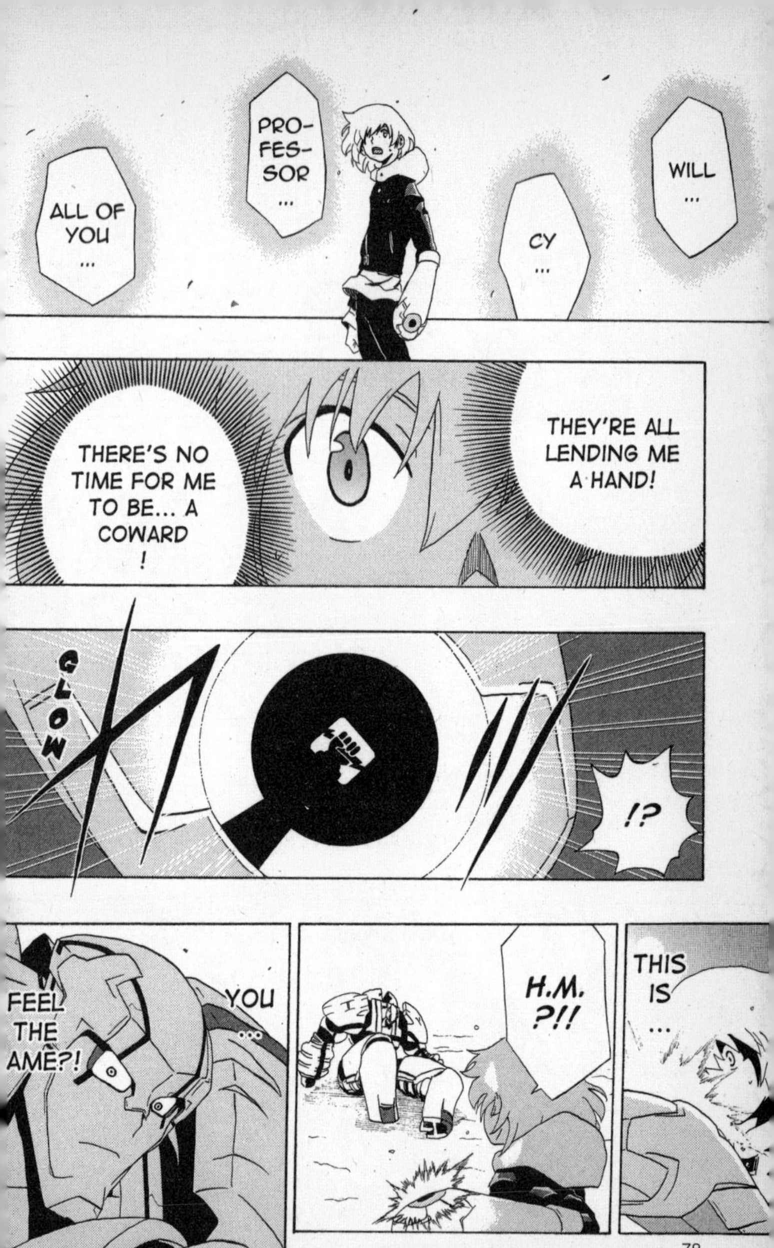
WILL ...
CY ...
PRO-FES-SOR ...
ALL OF YOU ...
THEY'RE ALL LENDING ME A HAND!
THERE'S NO TIME FOR ME TO BE... A COWARD !
!?
GLOW
THIS IS ...
H.M. ?!!
YOU ...
FEEL THE AME?!

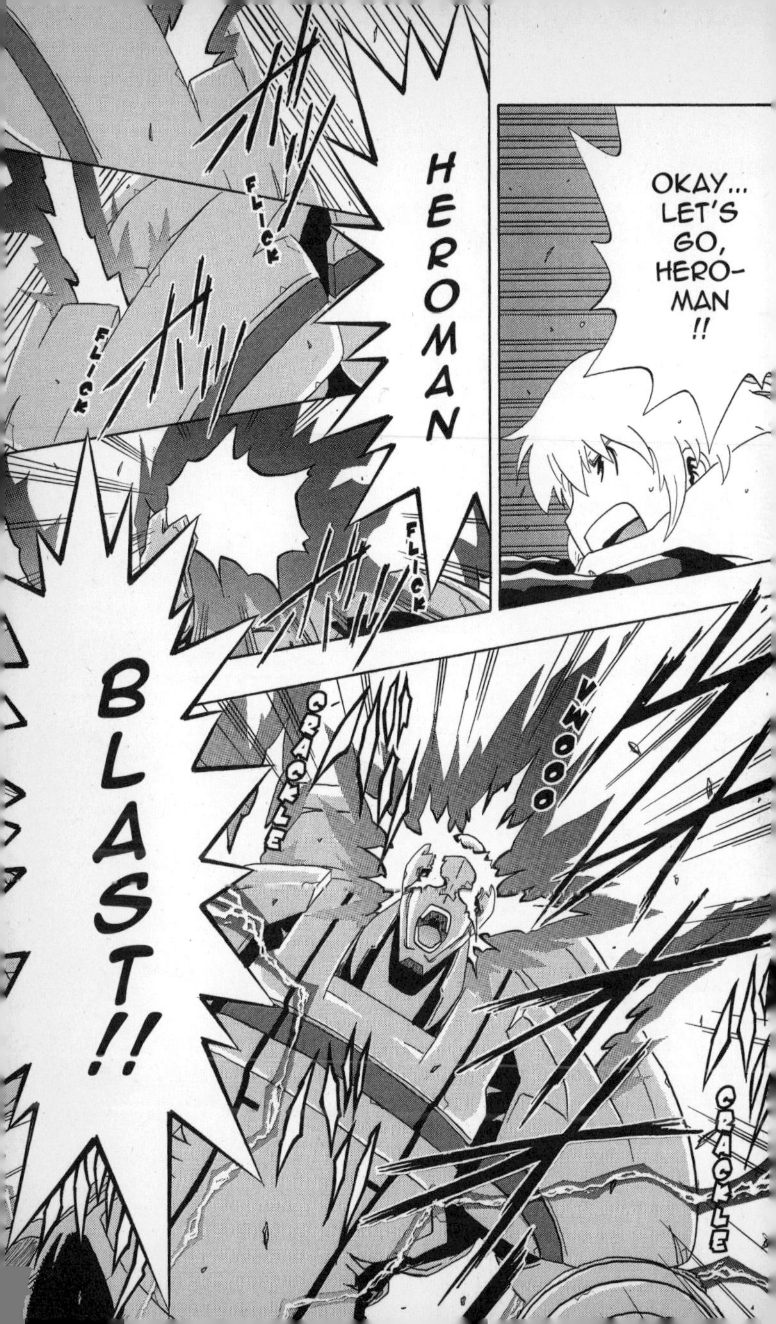
OKAY... LET'S GO, HERO-MAN!!
HEROMAN
FLICK
FLICK
FLICK
VWOOOO
CRACKLE
BLAST!!
CRACKLE

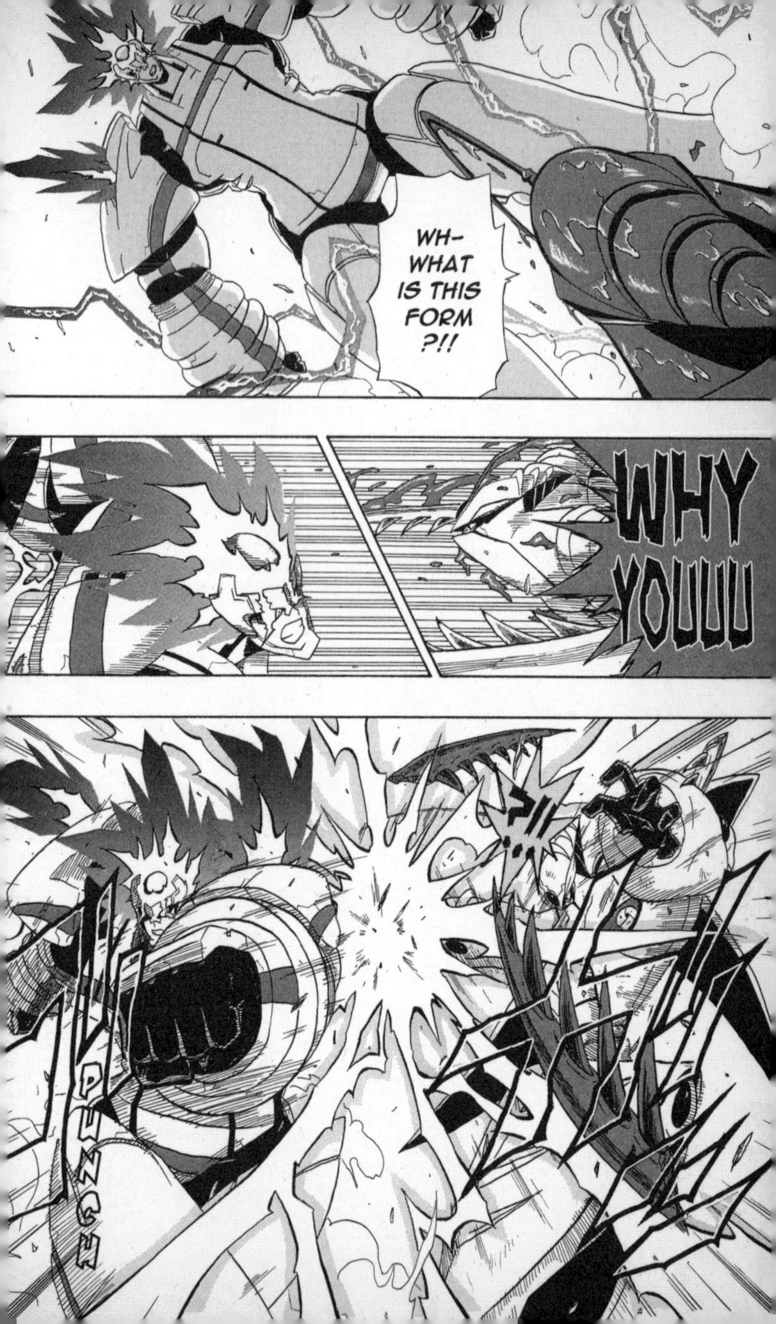
WH- WHAT IS THIS FORM ?!!
WHY YOUUU
?!
PUNCH

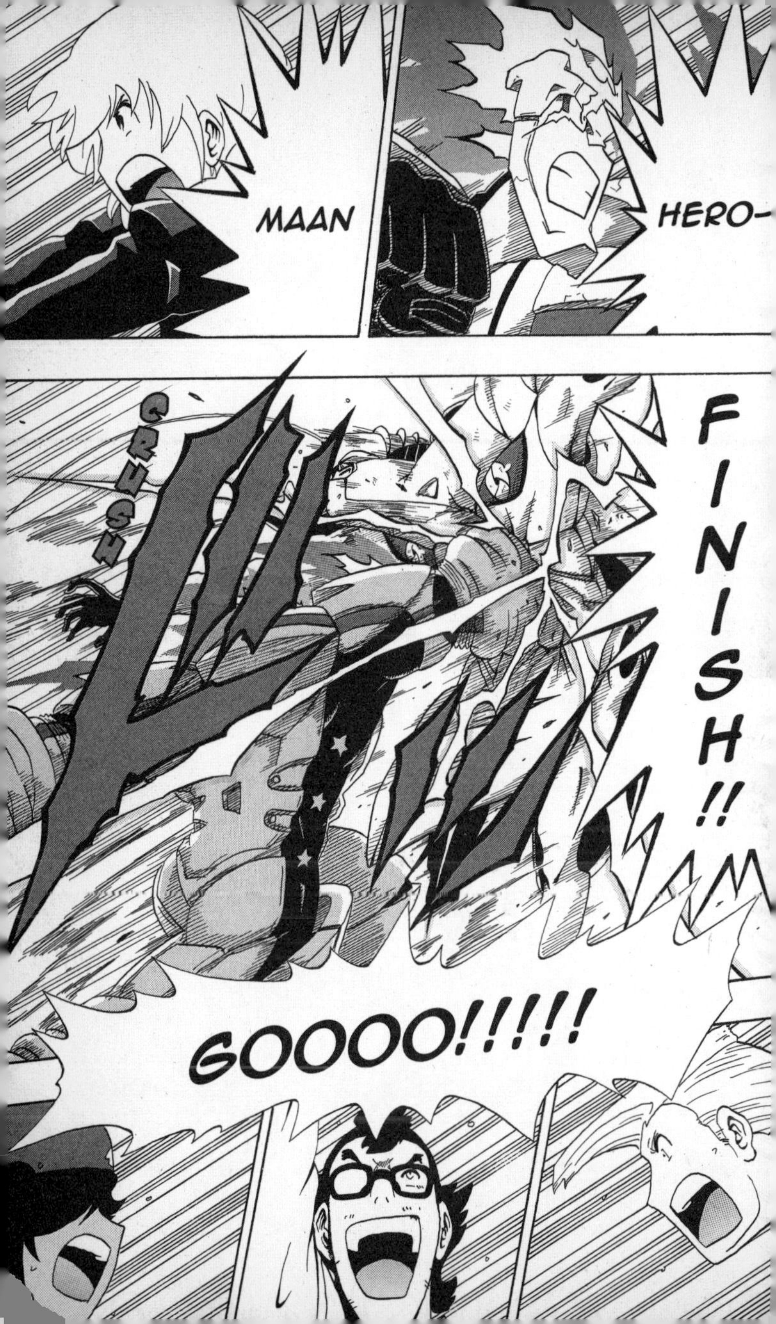
HERO-
MAAN
FINISH!!
CRUSH
GOOOOO!!!!!

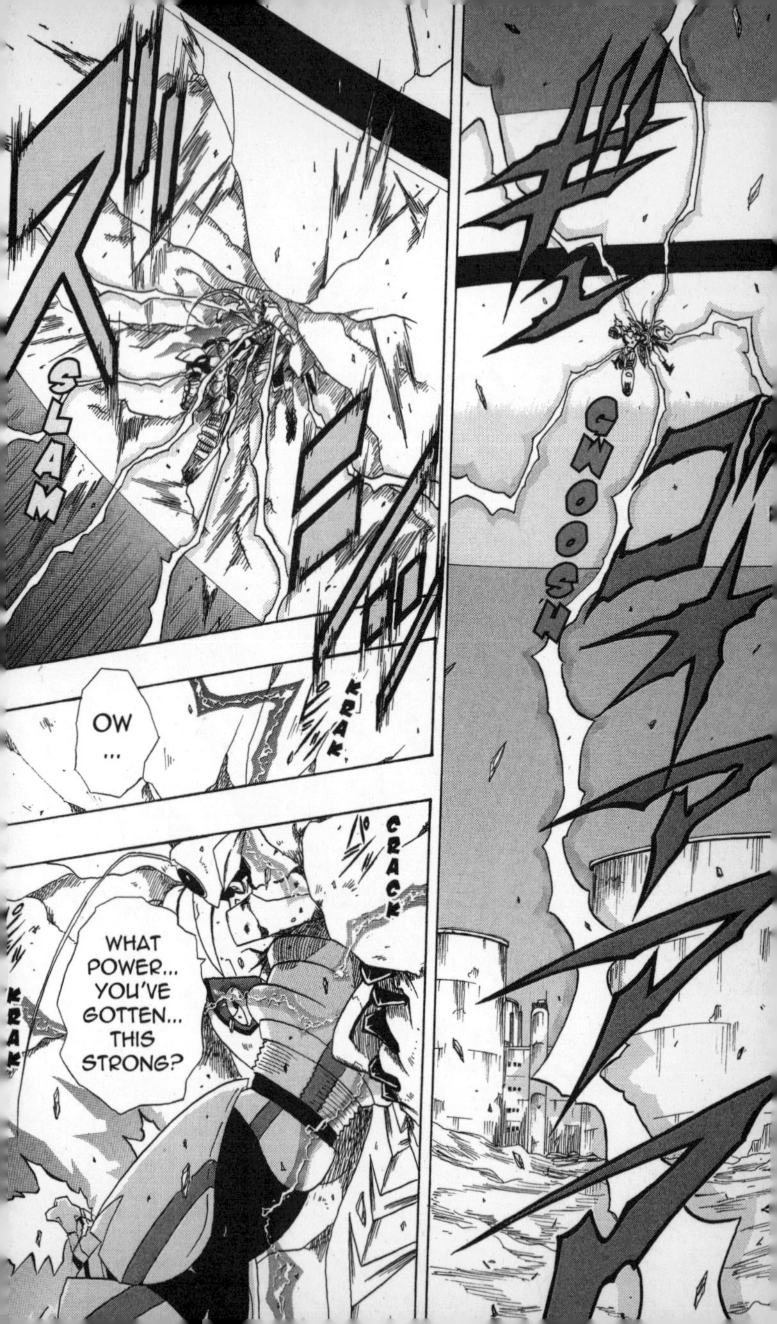
GWOOSH
SLAM
KRAK
OW ...
CRACK
WHAT POWER... YOU'VE GOTTEN... THIS STRONG?
KRAK

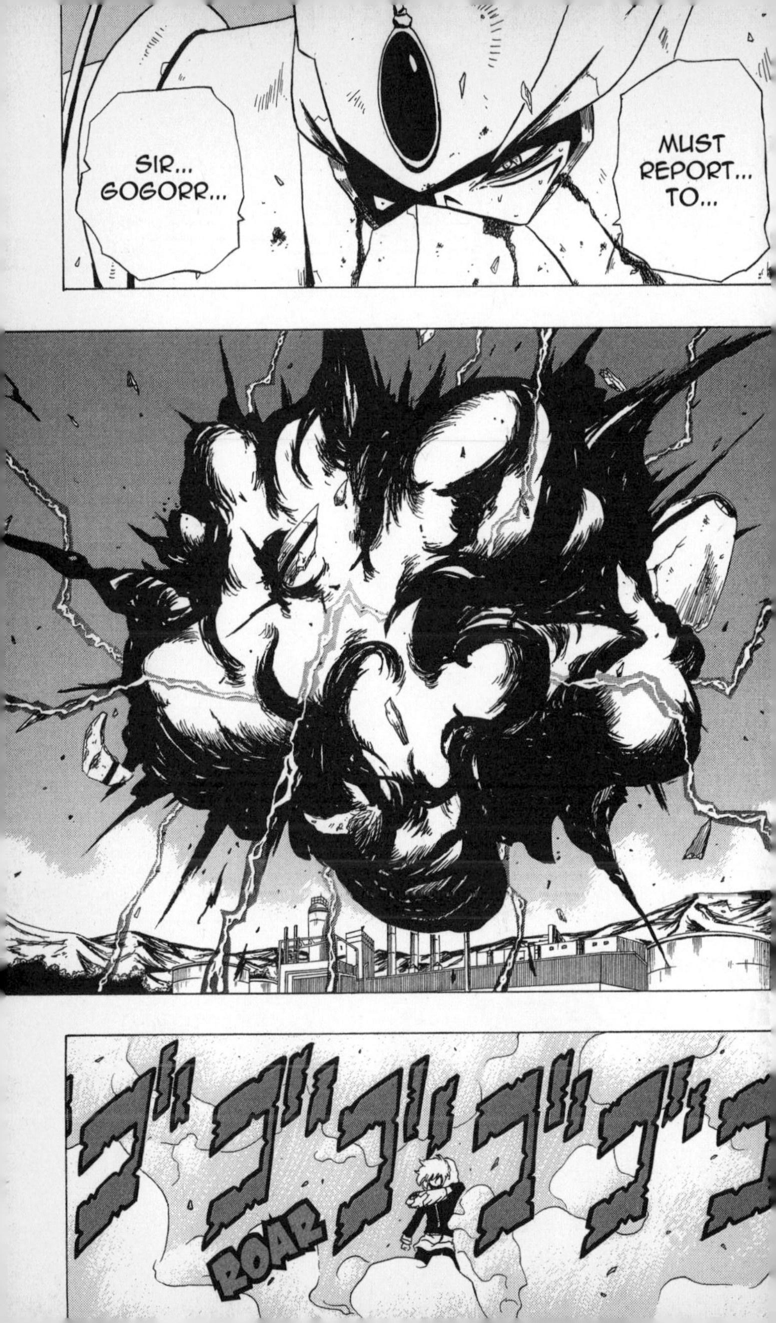
MUST REPORT... TO...
SIR... GOGORR...
ROAR

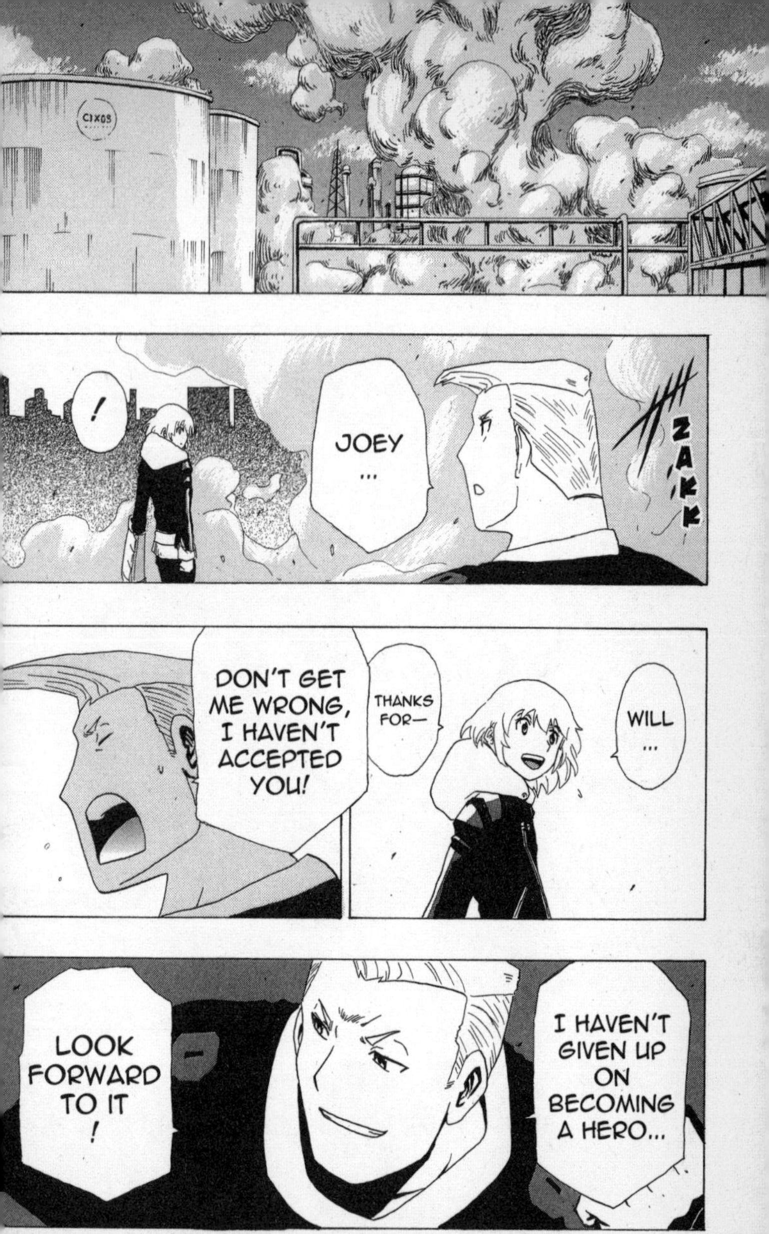
CIXOS
ZAKK
JOEY ...
!
WILL ...
THANKS FOR—
DON'T GET ME WRONG, I HAVEN'T ACCEPTED YOU!
I HAVEN'T GIVEN UP ON BECOMING A HERO...
LOOK FORWARD TO IT !

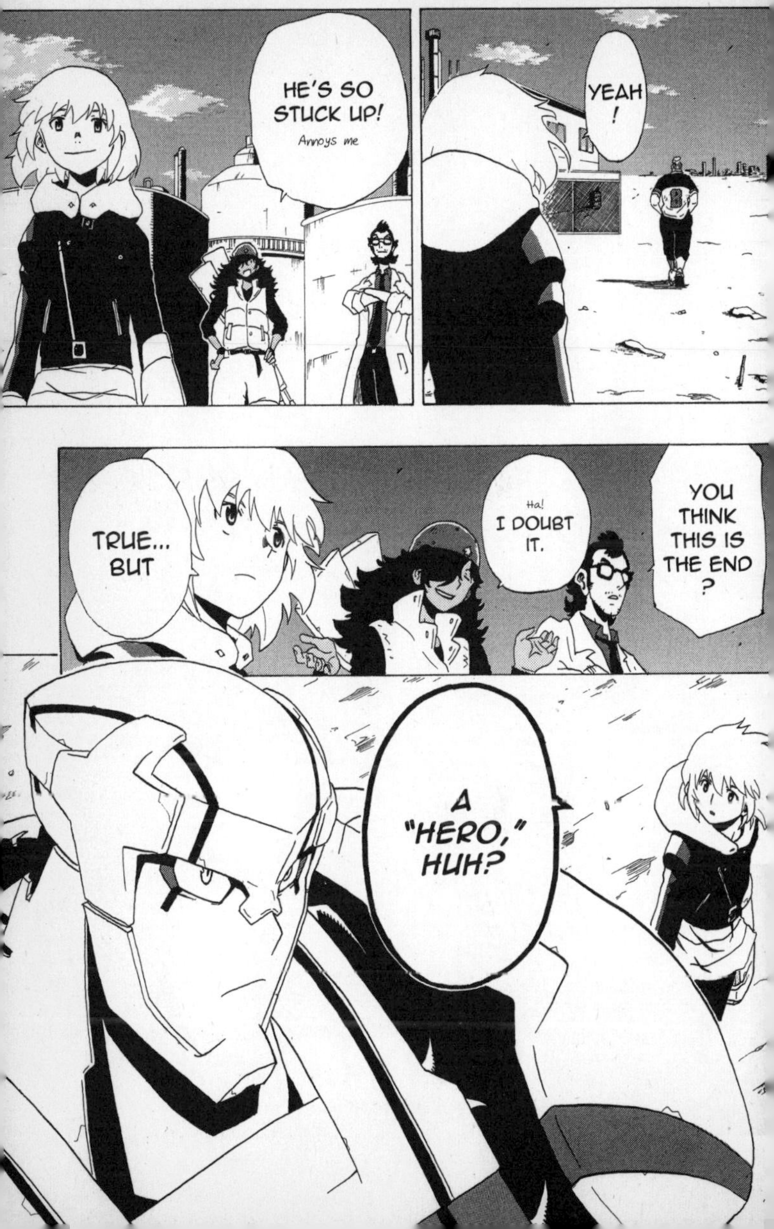
YEAH!
HE'S SO STUCK UP!
Annoys me
YOU THINK THIS IS THE END?
Ha! I DOUBT IT.
TRUE... BUT
A "HERO," HUH?

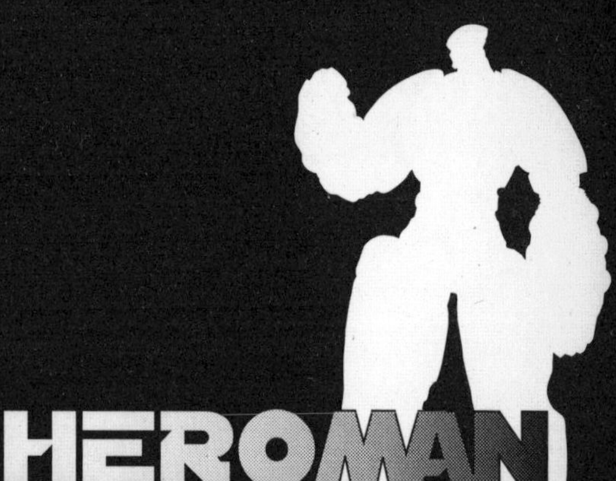
HEROMAN

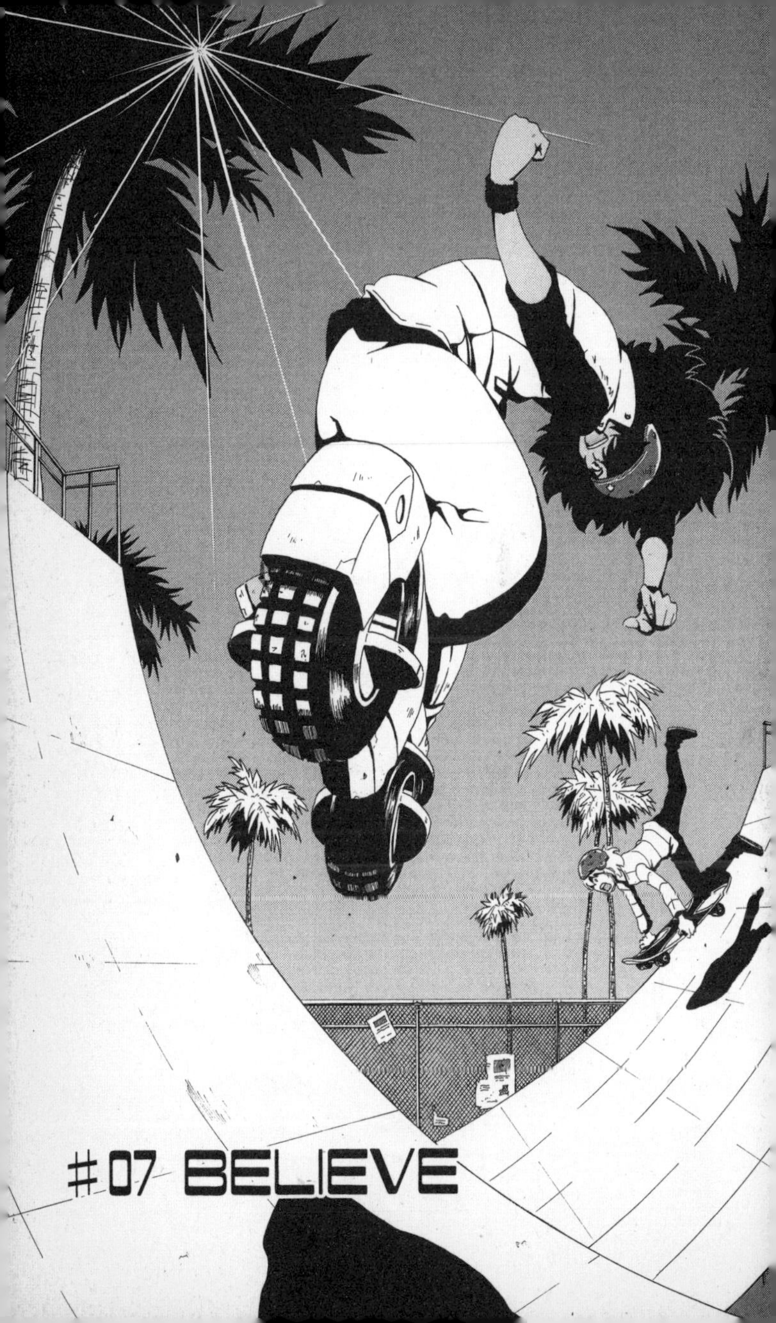

07 BELIEVE

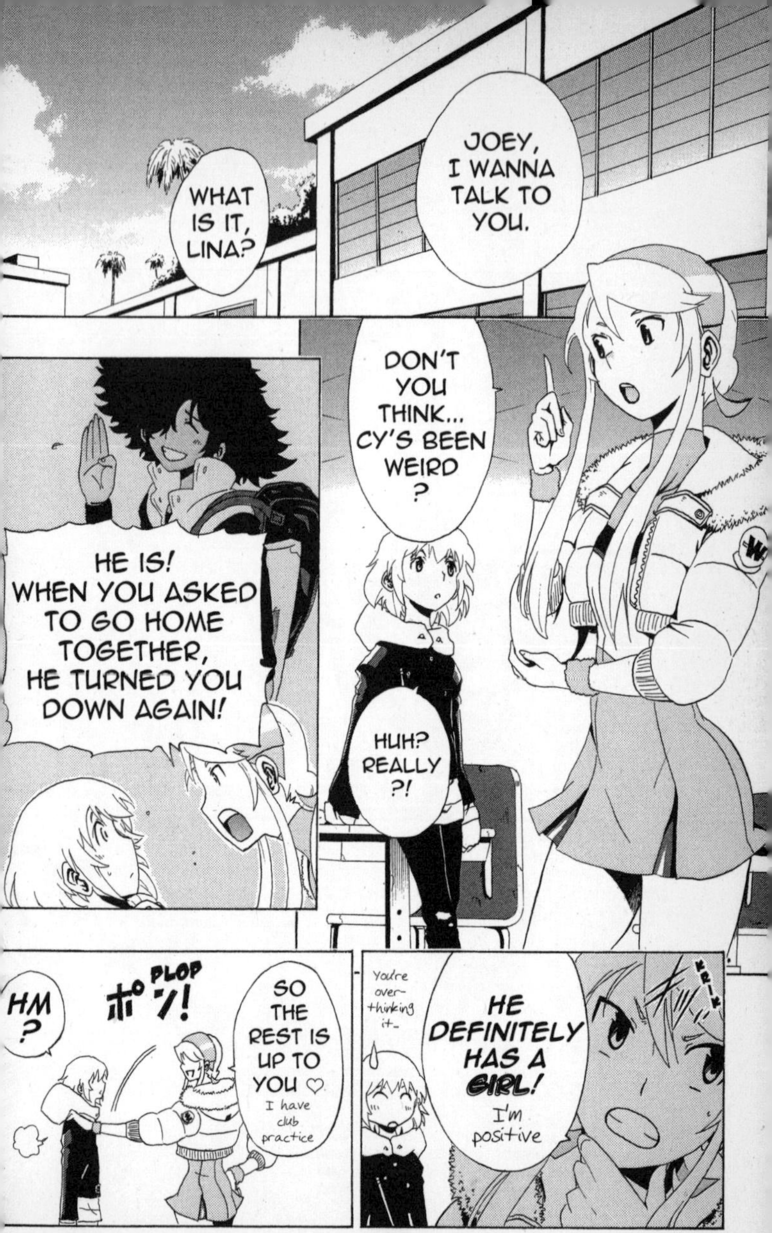
JOEY, I WANNA TALK TO YOU.
WHAT IS IT, LINA?
DON'T YOU THINK... CY'S BEEN WEIRD?
HUH? REALLY?!
HE IS! WHEN YOU ASKED TO GO HOME TOGETHER, HE TURNED YOU DOWN AGAIN!
KRIK
HE DEFINITELY HAS A GIRL!
I'm positive
You're over-thinking it...
SO THE REST IS UP TO YOU ♡
I have club practice
ポン! PLOP
HM?

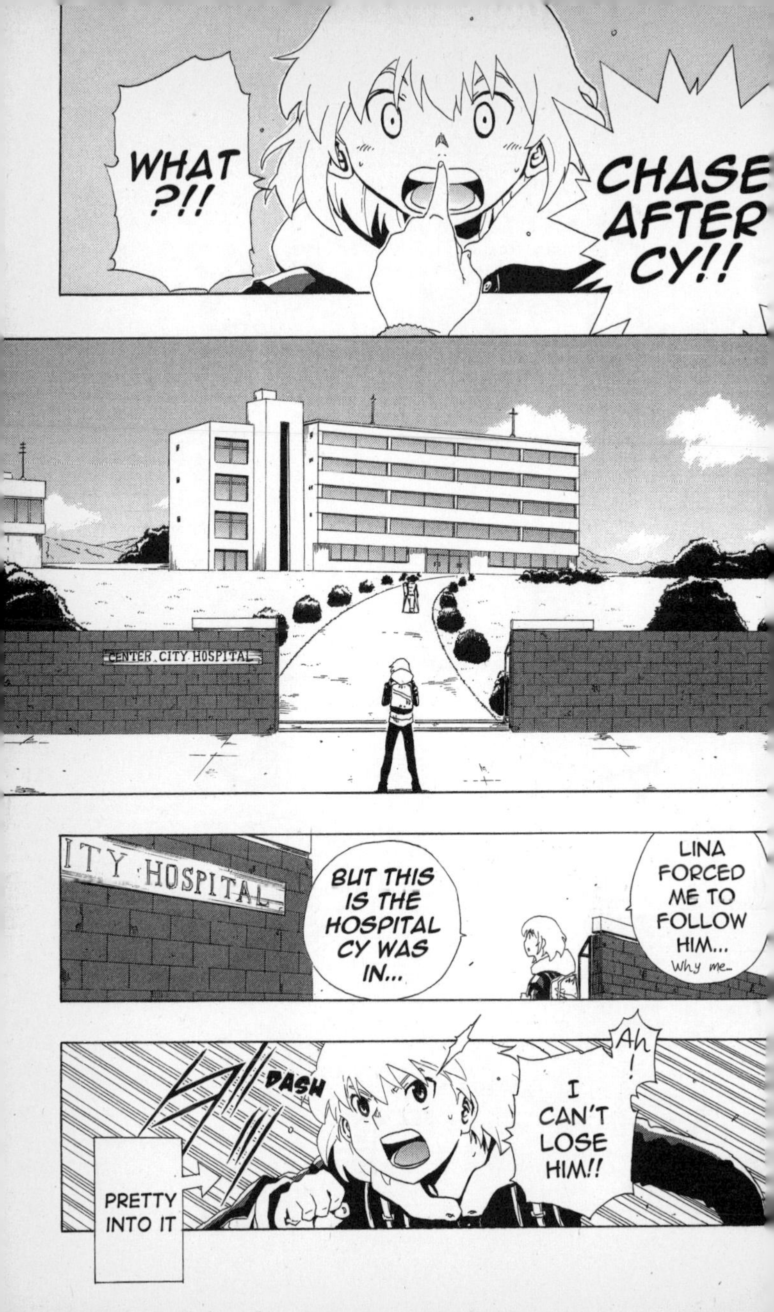
CHASE AFTER CY!!
WHAT ?!!
CENTER CITY HOSPITAL
LINA FORCED ME TO FOLLOW HIM...
Why me...
BUT THIS IS THE HOSPITAL CY WAS IN...
ITY HOSPITAL
Ah!
I CAN'T LOSE HIM!!
DASH
PRETTY INTO IT

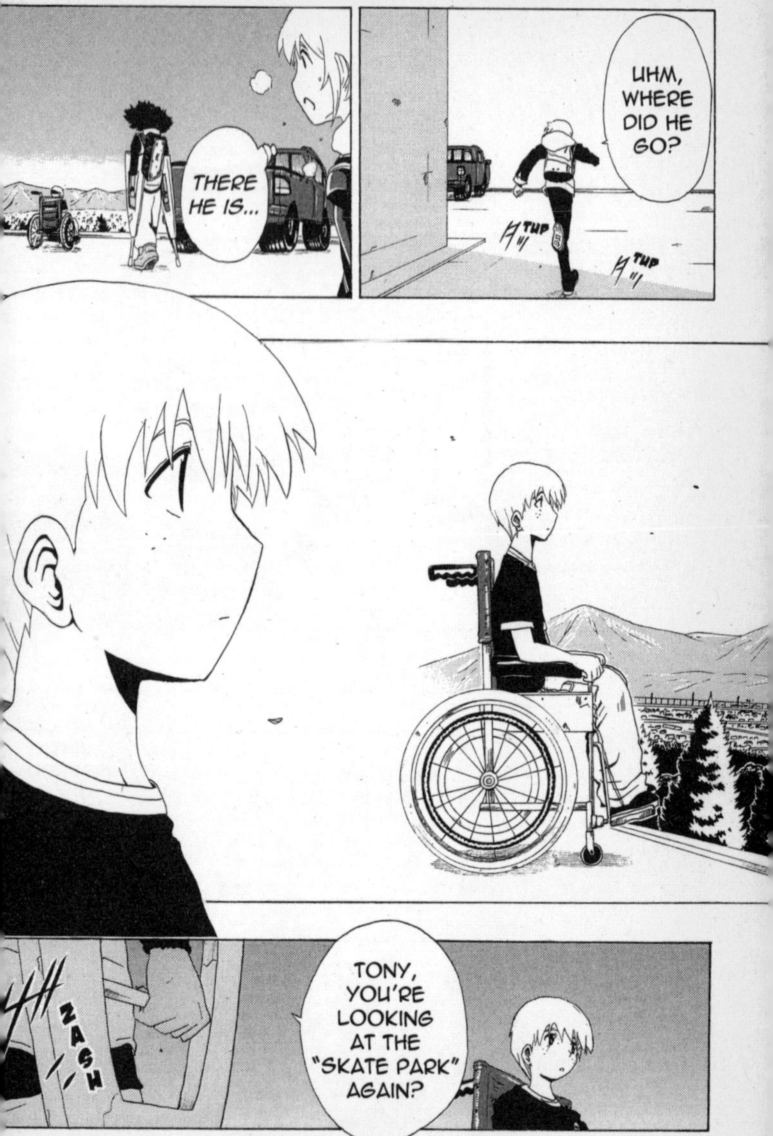
UHM, WHERE DID HE GO?
TUP
TUP
THERE HE IS...
TONY, YOU'RE LOOKING AT THE "SKATE PARK" AGAIN?
ZASH

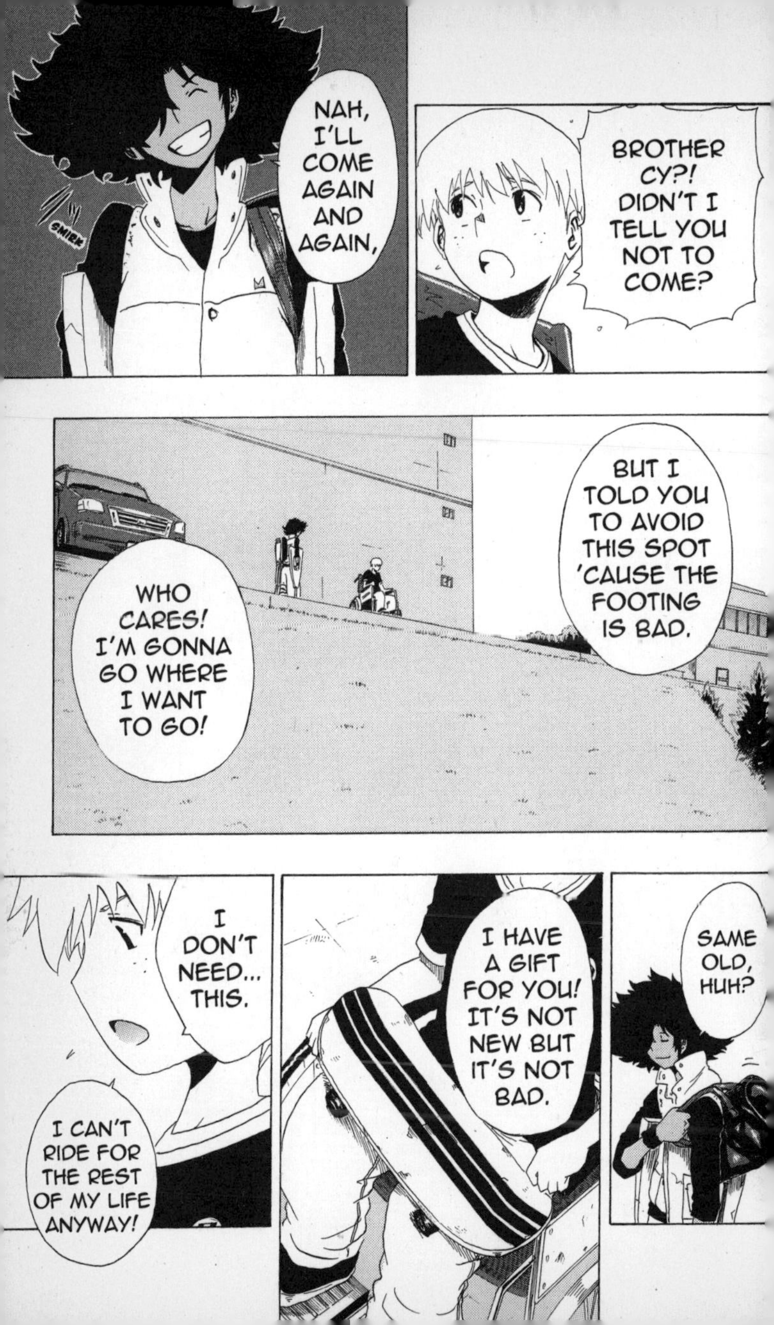
BROTHER CY?! DIDN'T I TELL YOU NOT TO COME?
NAH, I'LL COME AGAIN AND AGAIN,
SMIRK
BUT I TOLD YOU TO AVOID THIS SPOT 'CAUSE THE FOOTING IS BAD.
WHO CARES! I'M GONNA GO WHERE I WANT TO GO!
SAME OLD, HUH?
I HAVE A GIFT FOR YOU! IT'S NOT NEW BUT IT'S NOT BAD.
I DON'T NEED... THIS.
I CAN'T RIDE FOR THE REST OF MY LIFE ANYWAY!

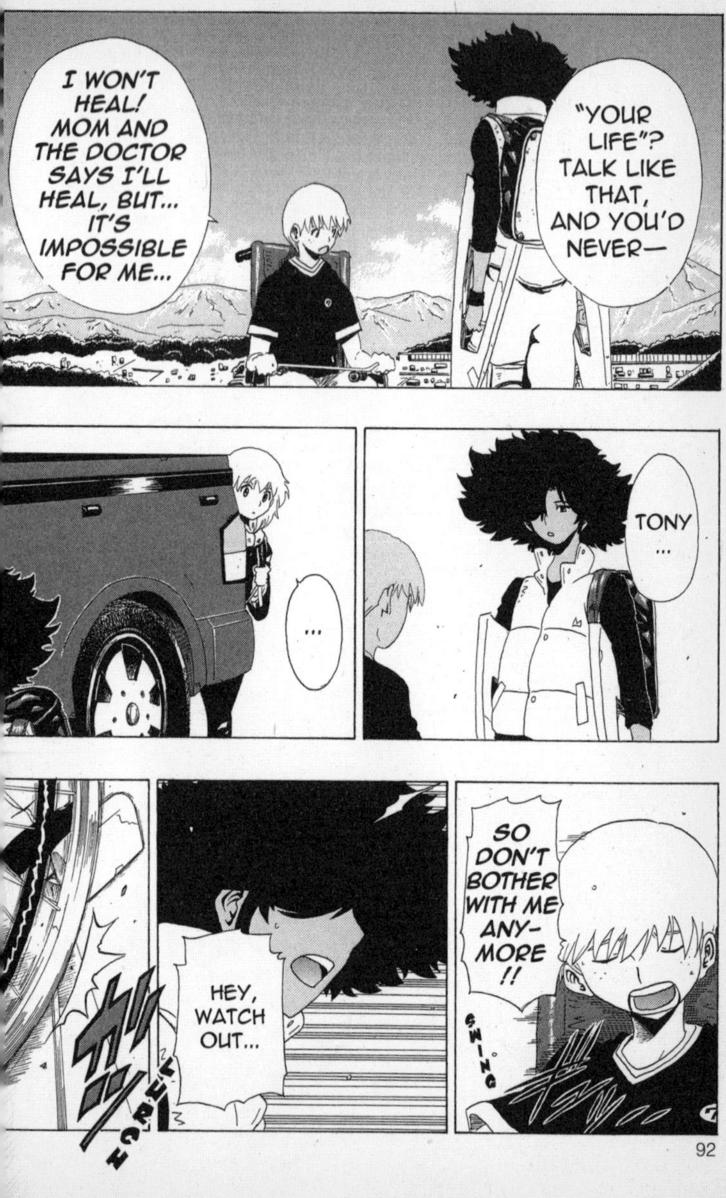
"YOUR LIFE"? TALK LIKE THAT, AND YOU'D NEVER—
I WON'T HEAL! MOM AND THE DOCTOR SAYS I'LL HEAL, BUT... IT'S IMPOSSIBLE FOR ME...
TONY ...
...
SO DON'T BOTHER WITH ME ANY-MORE !!
SWING
HEY, WATCH OUT...
LURCH

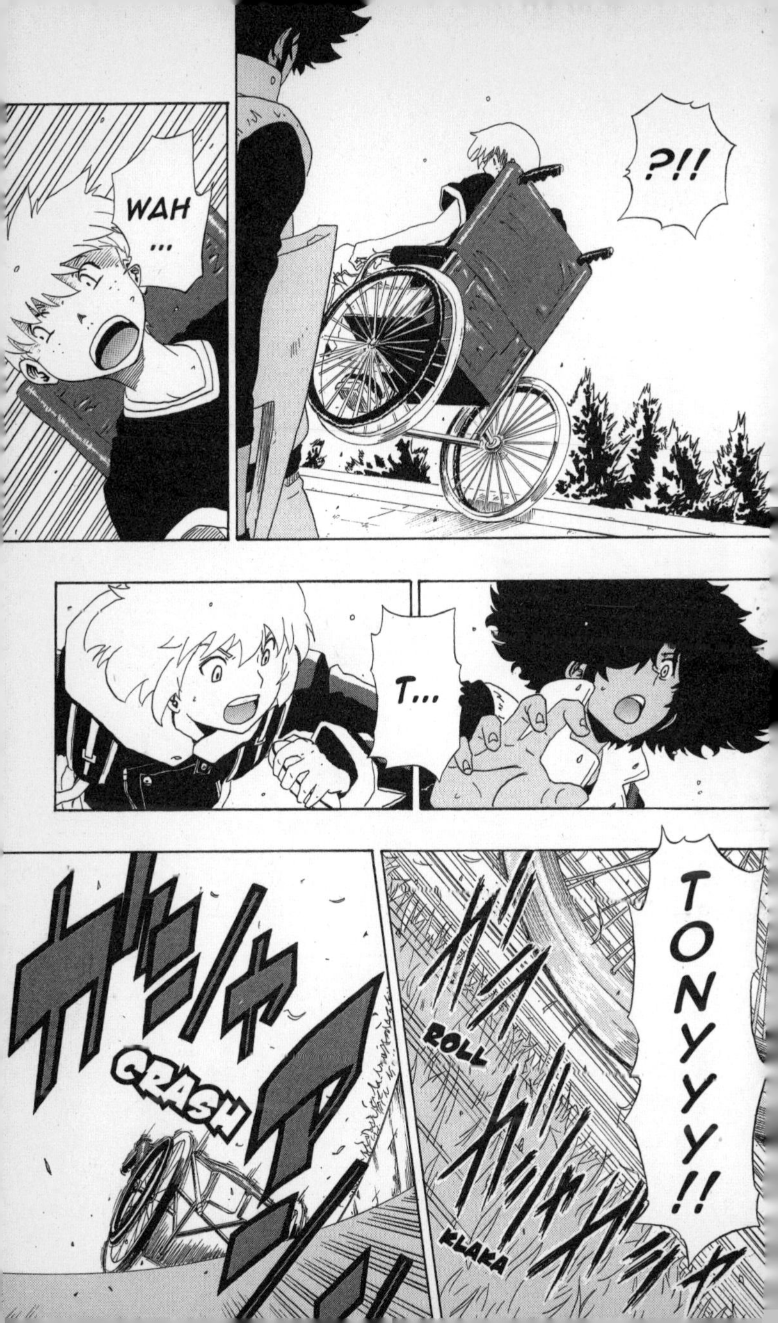
?!!
WAH ...
T...
TONYYY!!
ROLL
KLAKA
CRASH

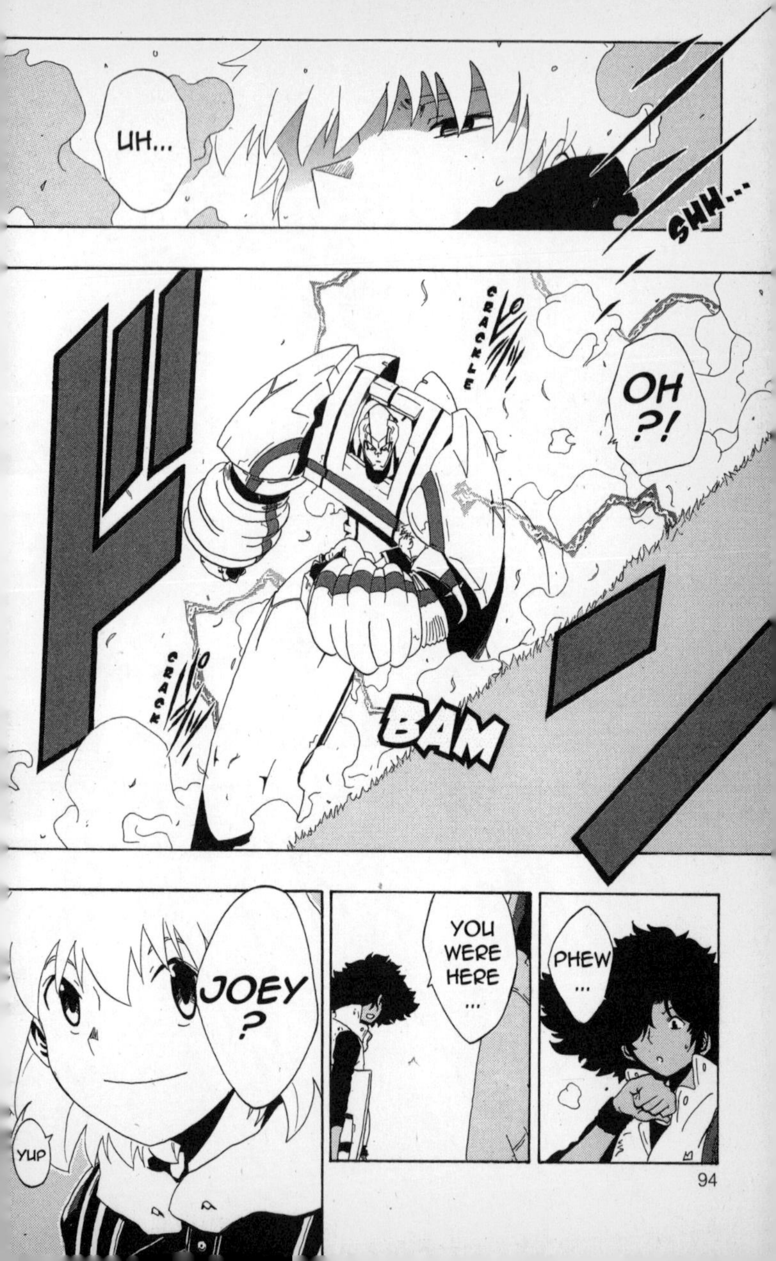
SHH...
UH...
OH ?!
CRACKLE
BAM
CRACK
PHEW ...
YOU WERE HERE ...
JOEY ?
YUP

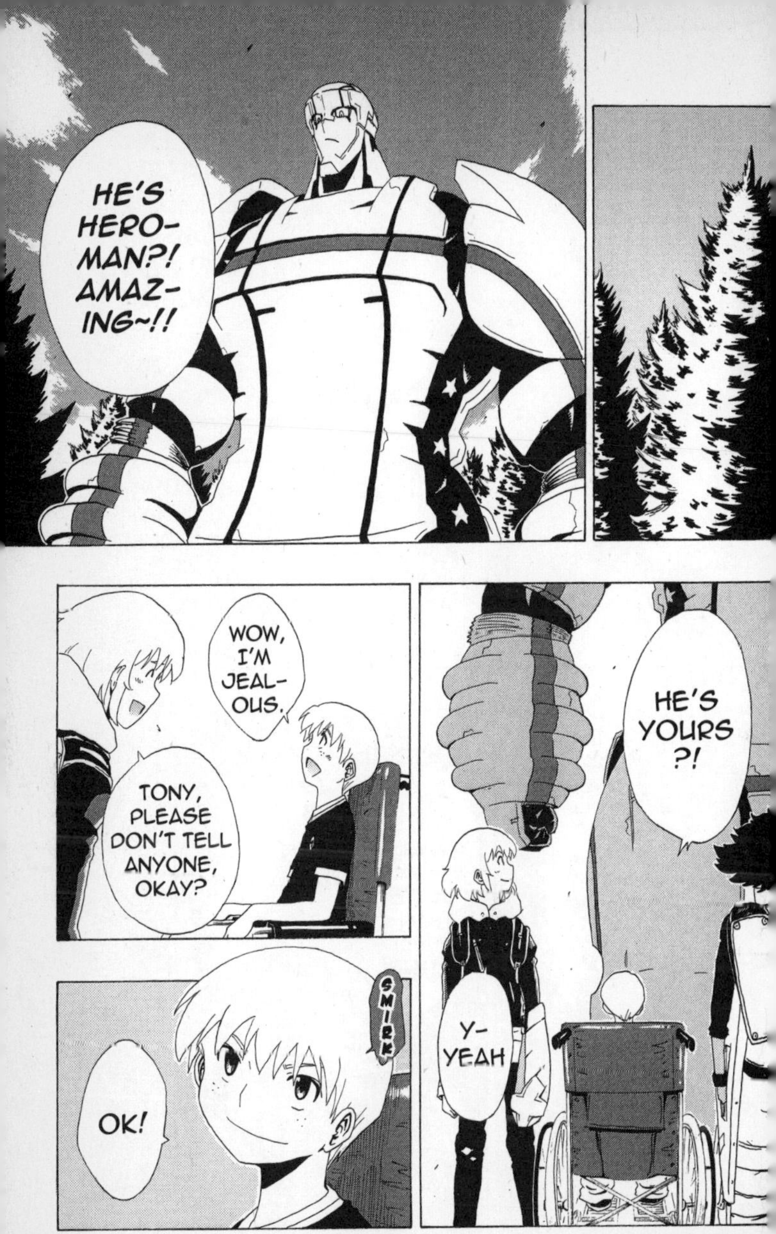
HE'S HERO-MAN?! AMAZ-ING~!!
HE'S YOURS ?!
Y-YEAH
WOW, I'M JEAL-OUS.
TONY, PLEASE DON'T TELL ANYONE, OKAY?
SMIRK
OK!

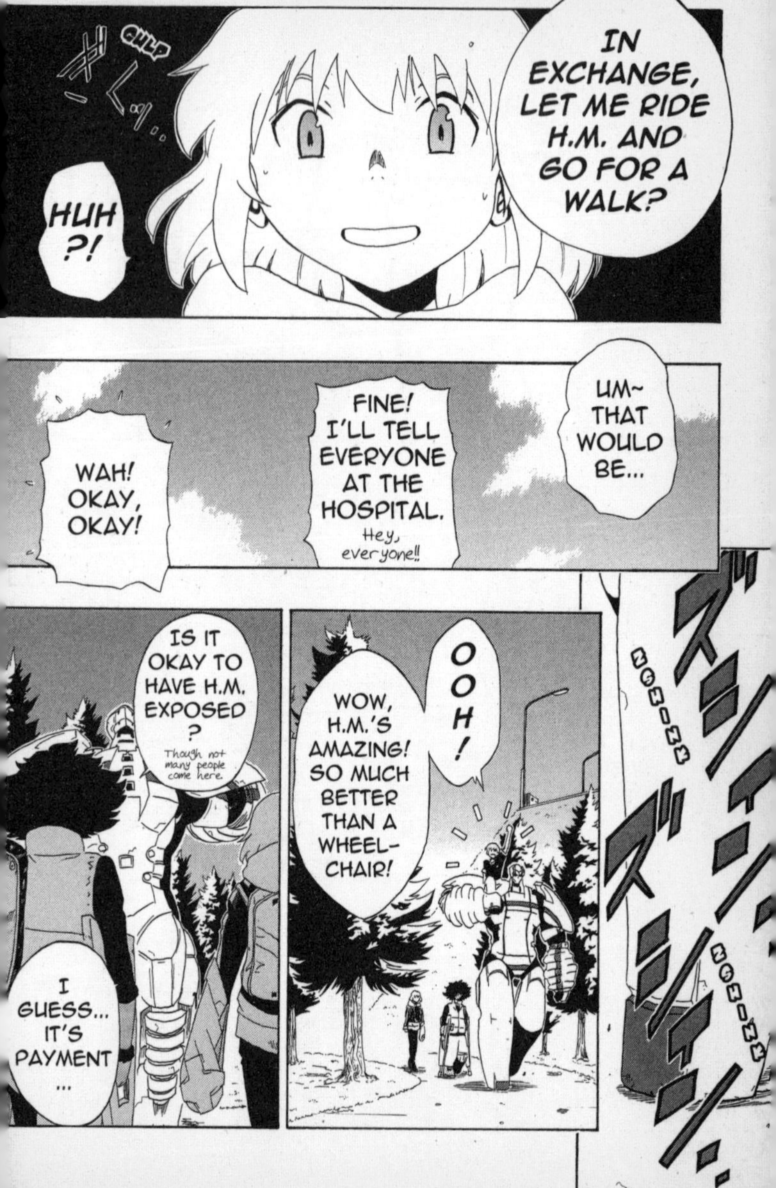
IN EXCHANGE, LET ME RIDE H.M. AND GO FOR A WALK?
GULP
HUH?!
UM~ THAT WOULD BE...
FINE! I'LL TELL EVERYONE AT THE HOSPITAL.
Hey, everyone!!
WAH! OKAY, OKAY!
ZSHINK
ZSHINK
OOH!
WOW, H.M.'S AMAZING! SO MUCH BETTER THAN A WHEEL-CHAIR!
IS IT OKAY TO HAVE H.M. EXPOSED?
Though not many people come here.
I GUESS... IT'S PAYMENT...

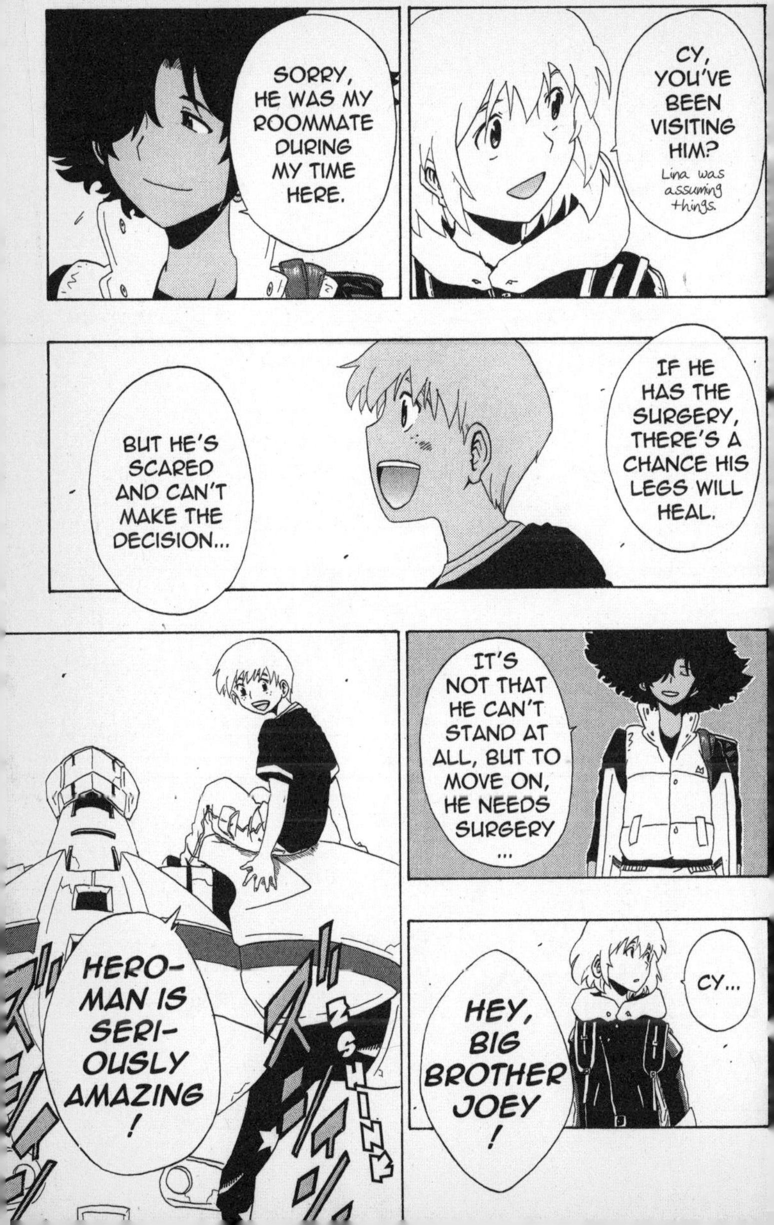

CY, YOU'VE BEEN VISITING HIM?
Lina was assuming things.
SORRY, HE WAS MY ROOMMATE DURING MY TIME HERE.
IF HE HAS THE SURGERY, THERE'S A CHANCE HIS LEGS WILL HEAL.
BUT HE'S SCARED AND CAN'T MAKE THE DECISION...
IT'S NOT THAT HE CAN'T STAND AT ALL, BUT TO MOVE ON, HE NEEDS SURGERY...
CY...
HEY, BIG BROTHER JOEY!
HERO-MAN IS SERIOUSLY AMAZING!
ZSHIINK

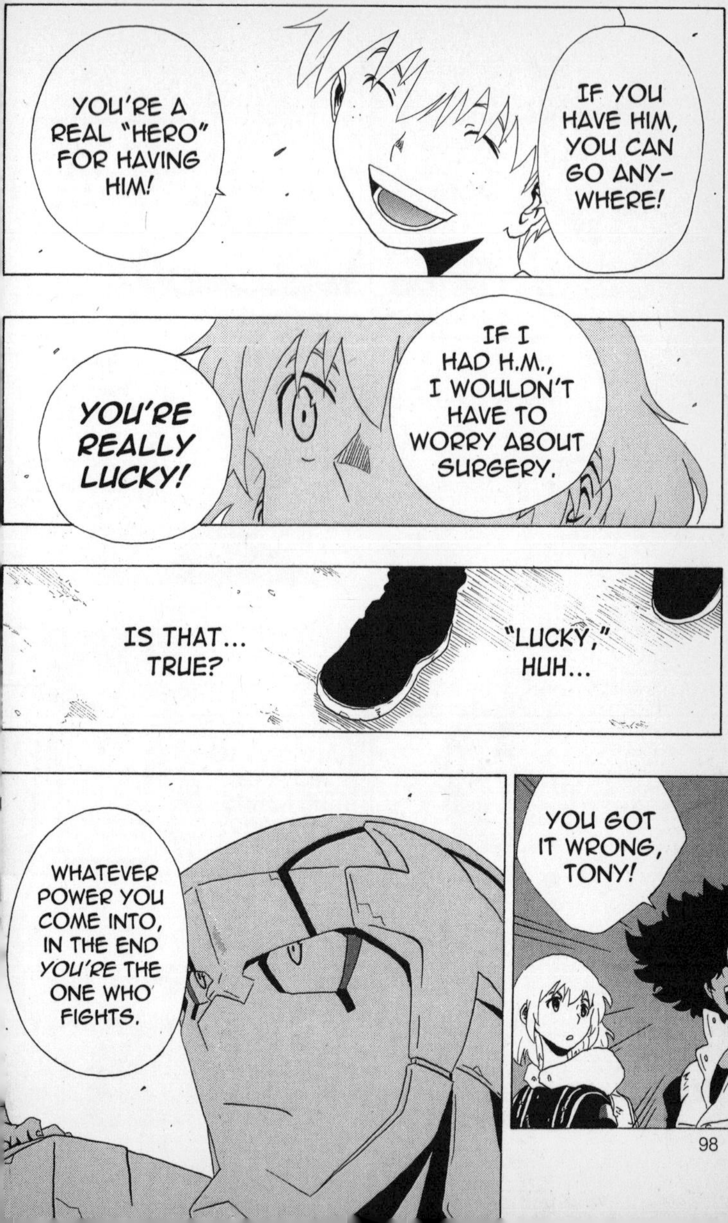
IF YOU HAVE HIM, YOU CAN GO ANY-WHERE!
YOU'RE A REAL "HERO" FOR HAVING HIM!
IF I HAD H.M., I WOULDN'T HAVE TO WORRY ABOUT SURGERY.
YOU'RE REALLY LUCKY!
"LUCKY," HUH...
IS THAT... TRUE?
YOU GOT IT WRONG, TONY!
WHATEVER POWER YOU COME INTO, IN THE END *YOU'RE* THE ONE WHO FIGHTS.

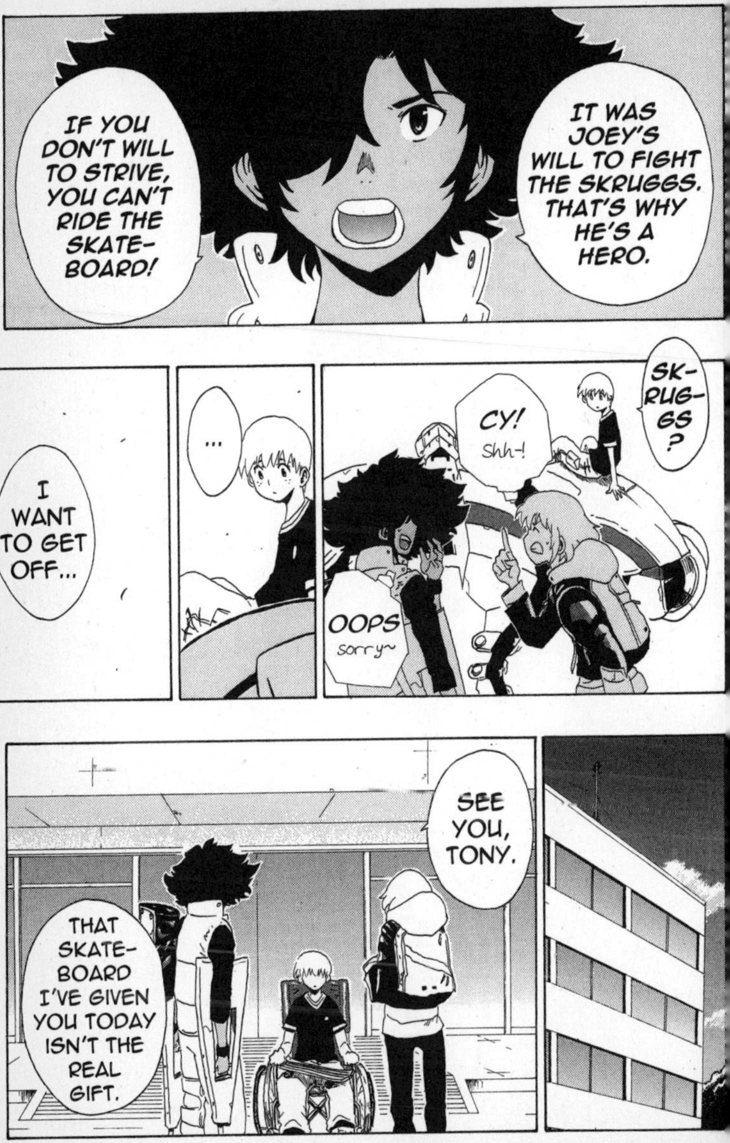
IT WAS JOEY'S WILL TO FIGHT THE SKRUGGS. THAT'S WHY HE'S A HERO.
IF YOU DON'T WILL TO STRIVE, YOU CAN'T RIDE THE SKATE-BOARD!
SK-RUG-GS?
CY!
Shh-!
OOPS
sorry~
...
I WANT TO GET OFF...
SEE YOU, TONY.
THAT SKATE-BOARD I'VE GIVEN YOU TODAY ISN'T THE REAL GIFT.

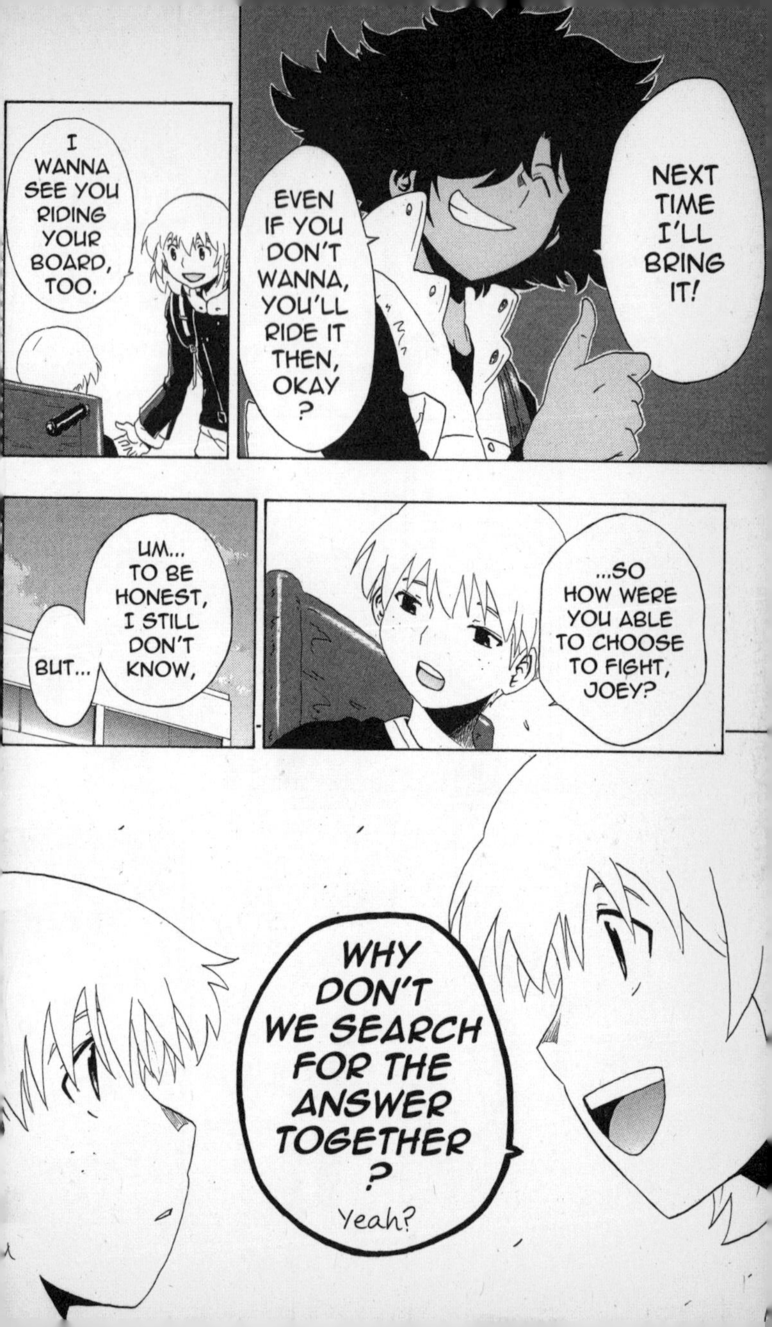
NEXT TIME I'LL BRING IT!
EVEN IF YOU DON'T WANNA, YOU'LL RIDE IT THEN, OKAY?
I WANNA SEE YOU RIDING YOUR BOARD, TOO.
...SO HOW WERE YOU ABLE TO CHOOSE TO FIGHT, JOEY?
UM... TO BE HONEST, I STILL DON'T KNOW,
BUT...
WHY DON'T WE SEARCH FOR THE ANSWER TOGETHER?
Yeah?

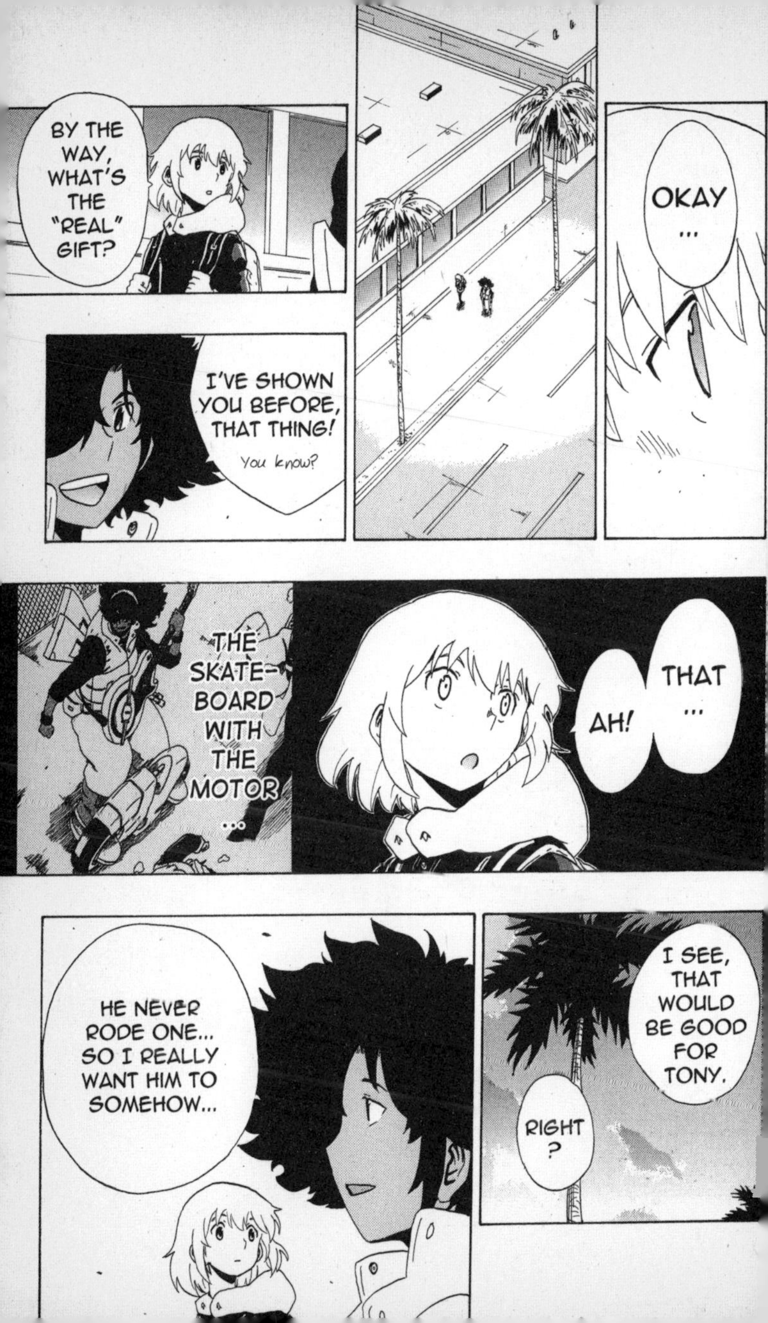
OKAY ...
BY THE WAY, WHAT'S THE "REAL" GIFT?
I'VE SHOWN YOU BEFORE, THAT THING!
You know?
THAT ...
AH!
THE SKATE-BOARD WITH THE MOTOR ...
I SEE, THAT WOULD BE GOOD FOR TONY.
RIGHT ?
HE NEVER RODE ONE... SO I REALLY WANT HIM TO SOMEHOW...

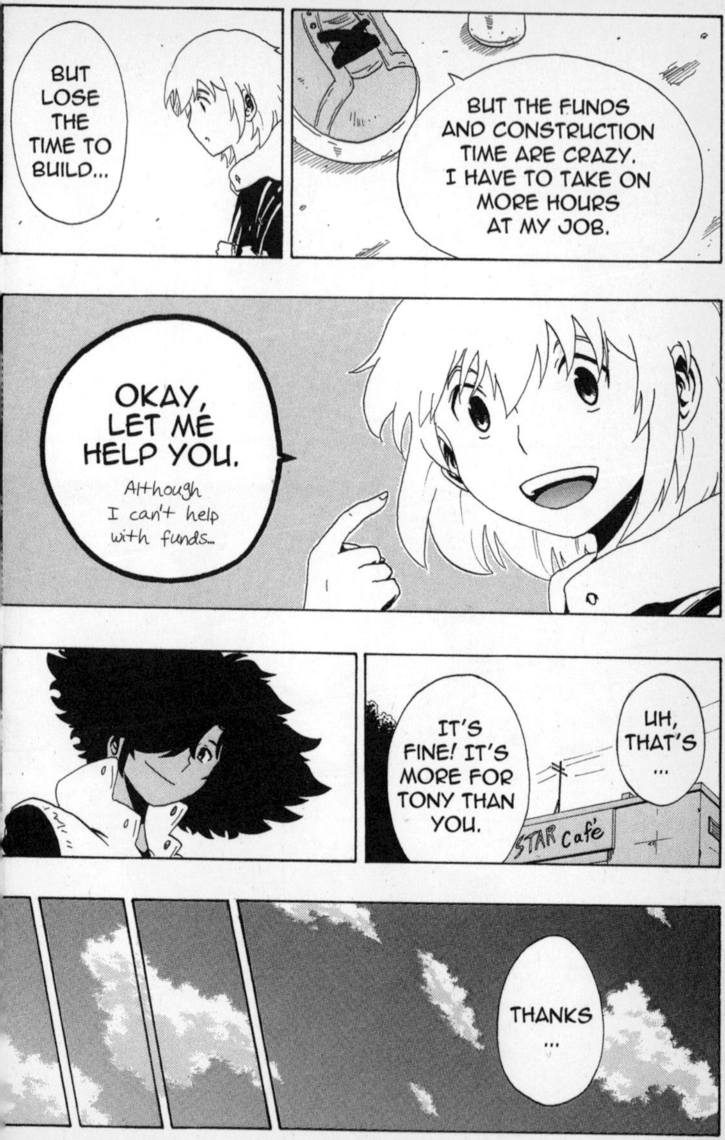
BUT THE FUNDS AND CONSTRUCTION TIME ARE CRAZY. I HAVE TO TAKE ON MORE HOURS AT MY JOB.
BUT LOSE THE TIME TO BUILD...
OKAY, LET ME HELP YOU.
Although I can't help with funds...
UH, THAT'S ...
IT'S FINE! IT'S MORE FOR TONY THAN YOU.
STAR Café
THANKS ...

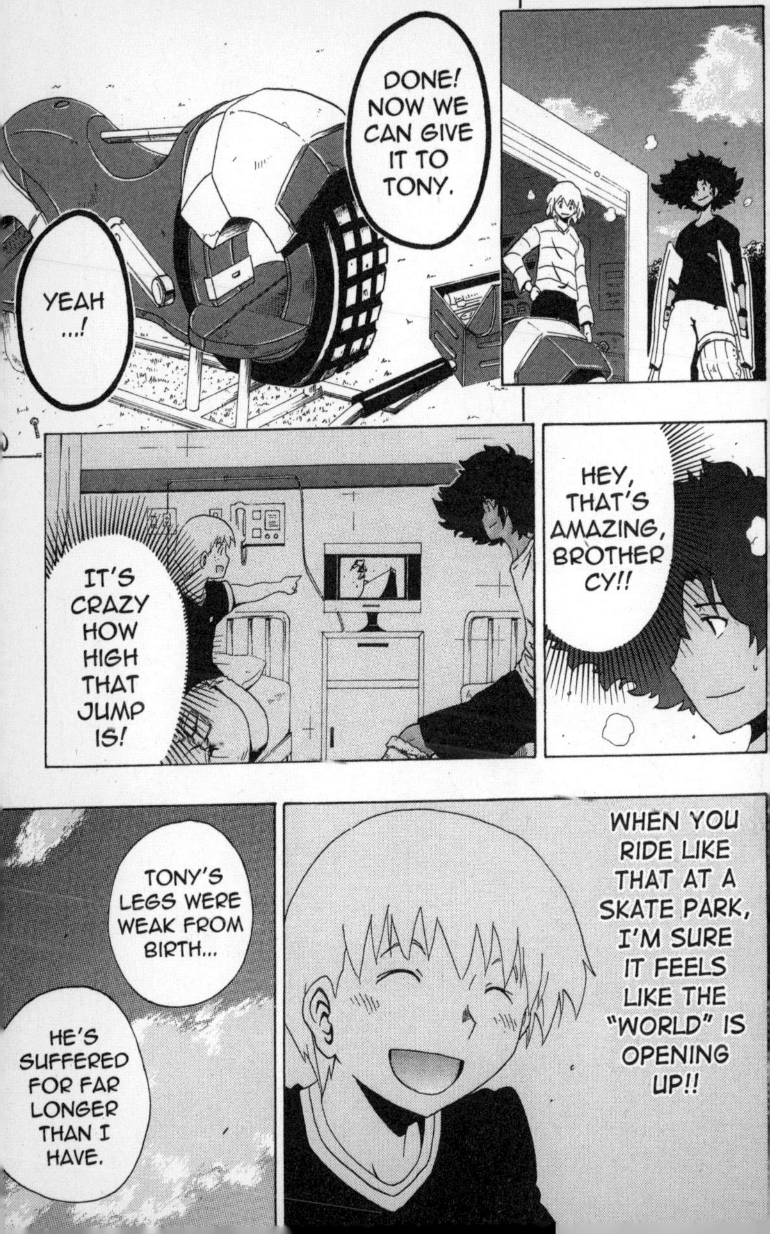
DONE! NOW WE CAN GIVE IT TO TONY.
YEAH ...!
HEY, THAT'S AMAZING, BROTHER CY!!
IT'S CRAZY HOW HIGH THAT JUMP IS!
WHEN YOU RIDE LIKE THAT AT A SKATE PARK, I'M SURE IT FEELS LIKE THE "WORLD" IS OPENING UP!!
TONY'S LEGS WERE WEAK FROM BIRTH...
HE'S SUFFERED FOR FAR LONGER THAN I HAVE.

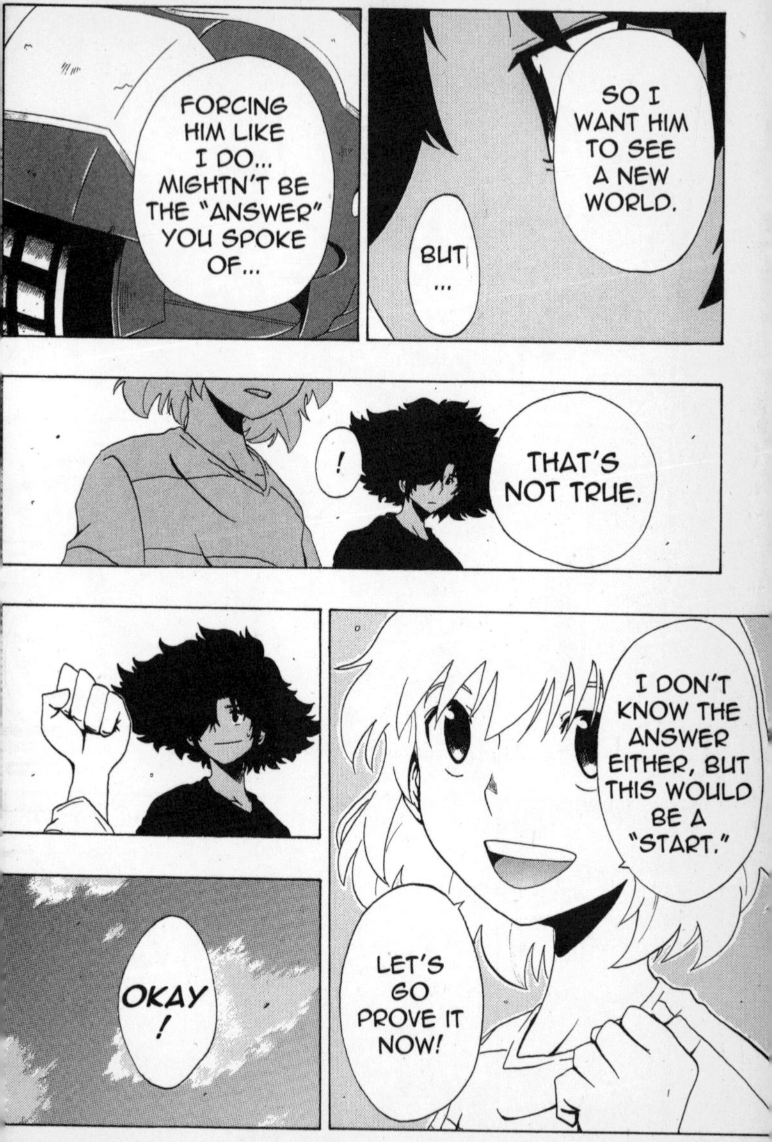
SO I WANT HIM TO SEE A NEW WORLD.
BUT ...
FORCING HIM LIKE I DO... MIGHTN'T BE THE "ANSWER" YOU SPOKE OF...
THAT'S NOT TRUE.
!
I DON'T KNOW THE ANSWER EITHER, BUT THIS WOULD BE A "START."
LET'S GO PROVE IT NOW!
OKAY!

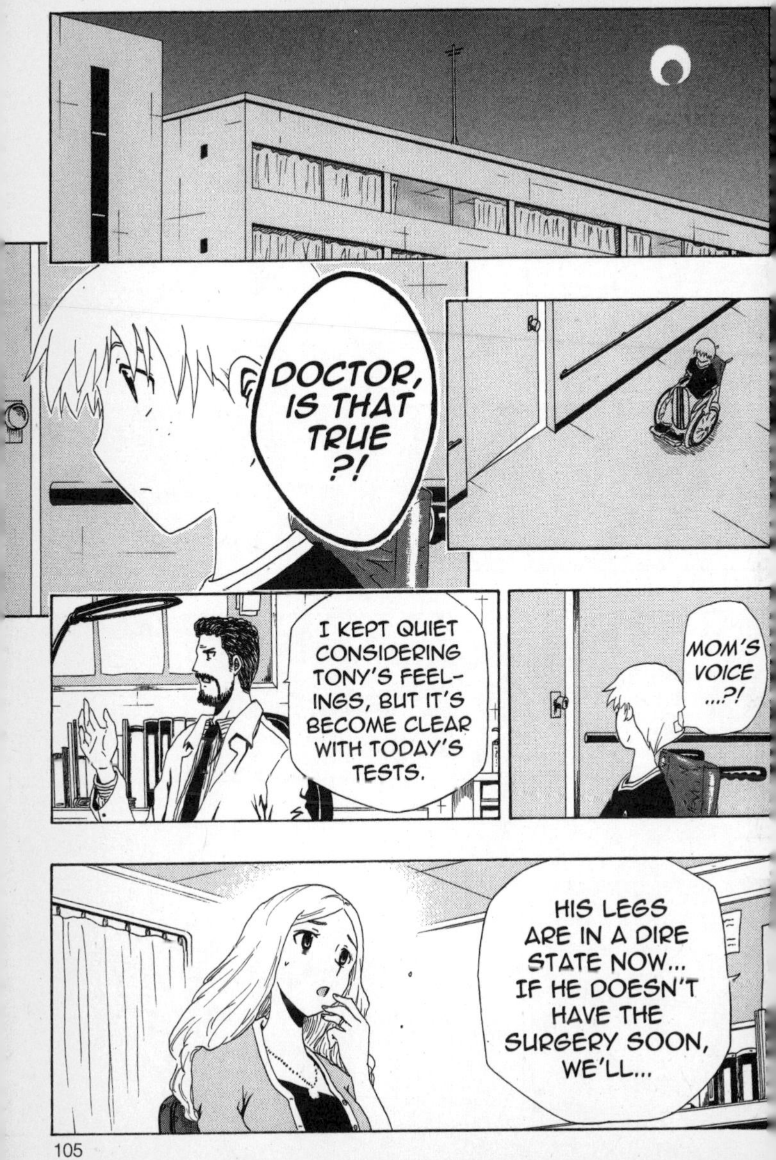
DOCTOR, IS THAT TRUE ?!
MOM'S VOICE ...?!
I KEPT QUIET CONSIDERING TONY'S FEEL- INGS, BUT IT'S BECOME CLEAR WITH TODAY'S TESTS.
HIS LEGS ARE IN A DIRE STATE NOW... IF HE DOESN'T HAVE THE SURGERY SOON, WE'LL...

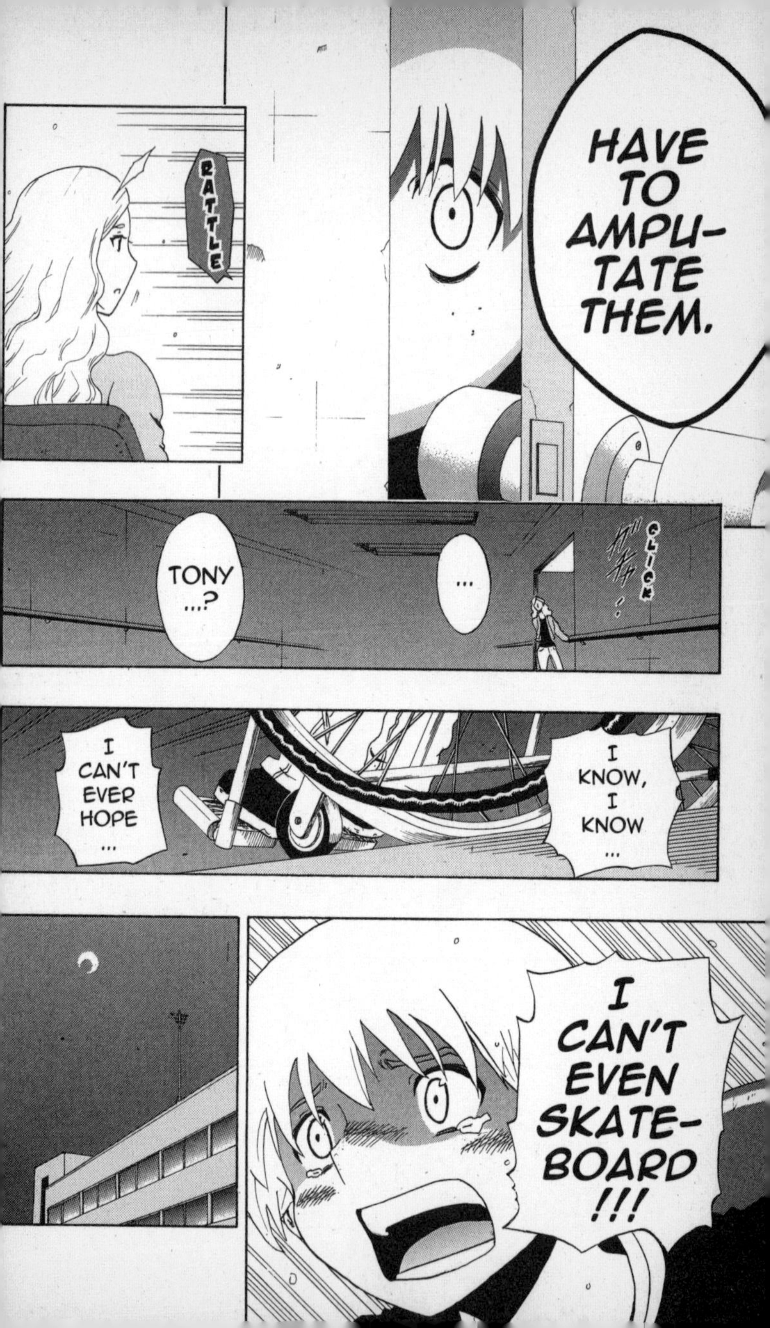

HAVE TO AMPU-TATE THEM.
RATTLE
CLICK
...
TONY ...?
I KNOW, I KNOW ...
I CAN'T EVER HOPE ...
I CAN'T EVEN SKATE-BOARD!!!

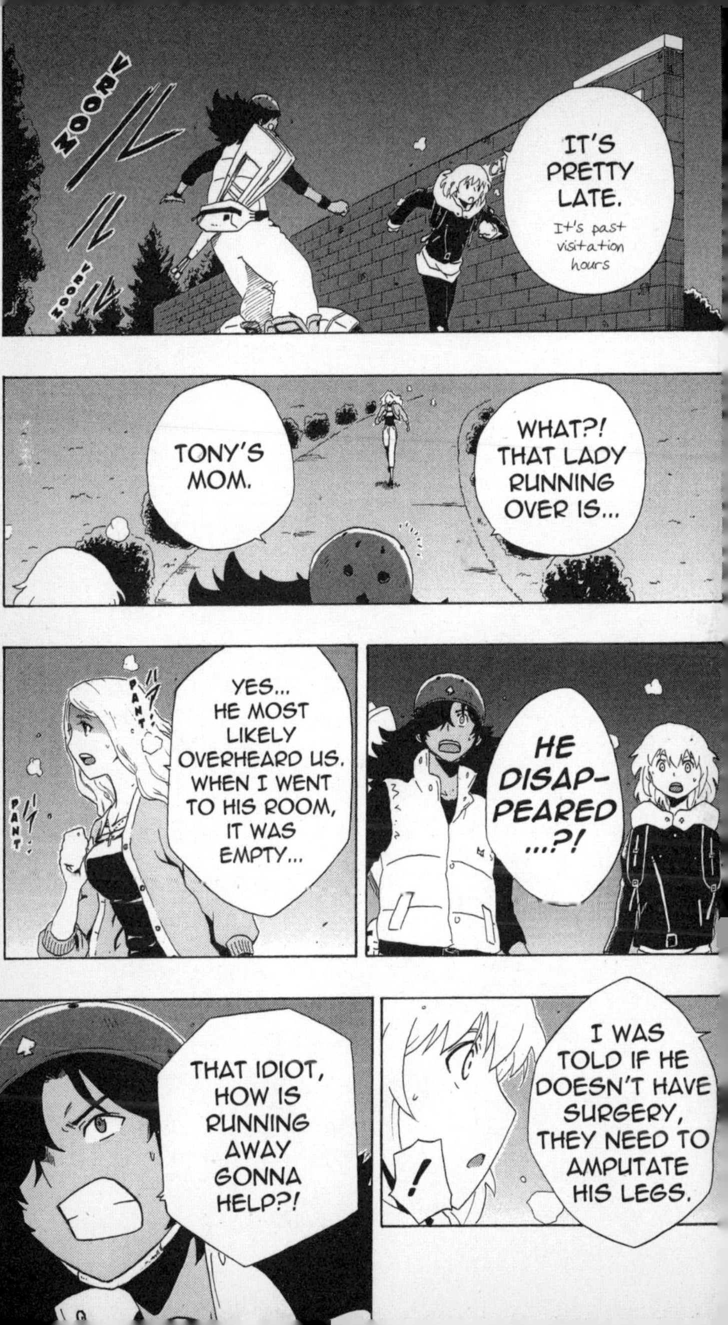
IT'S PRETTY LATE.
It's past visitation hours
WHAT?! THAT LADY RUNNING OVER IS...
TONY'S MOM.
HE DISAP-PEARED ...?!
PANT
PANT
YES... HE MOST LIKELY OVERHEARD US. WHEN I WENT TO HIS ROOM, IT WAS EMPTY...
I WAS TOLD IF HE DOESN'T HAVE SURGERY, THEY NEED TO AMPUTATE HIS LEGS.
!
THAT IDIOT, HOW IS RUNNING AWAY GONNA HELP?!

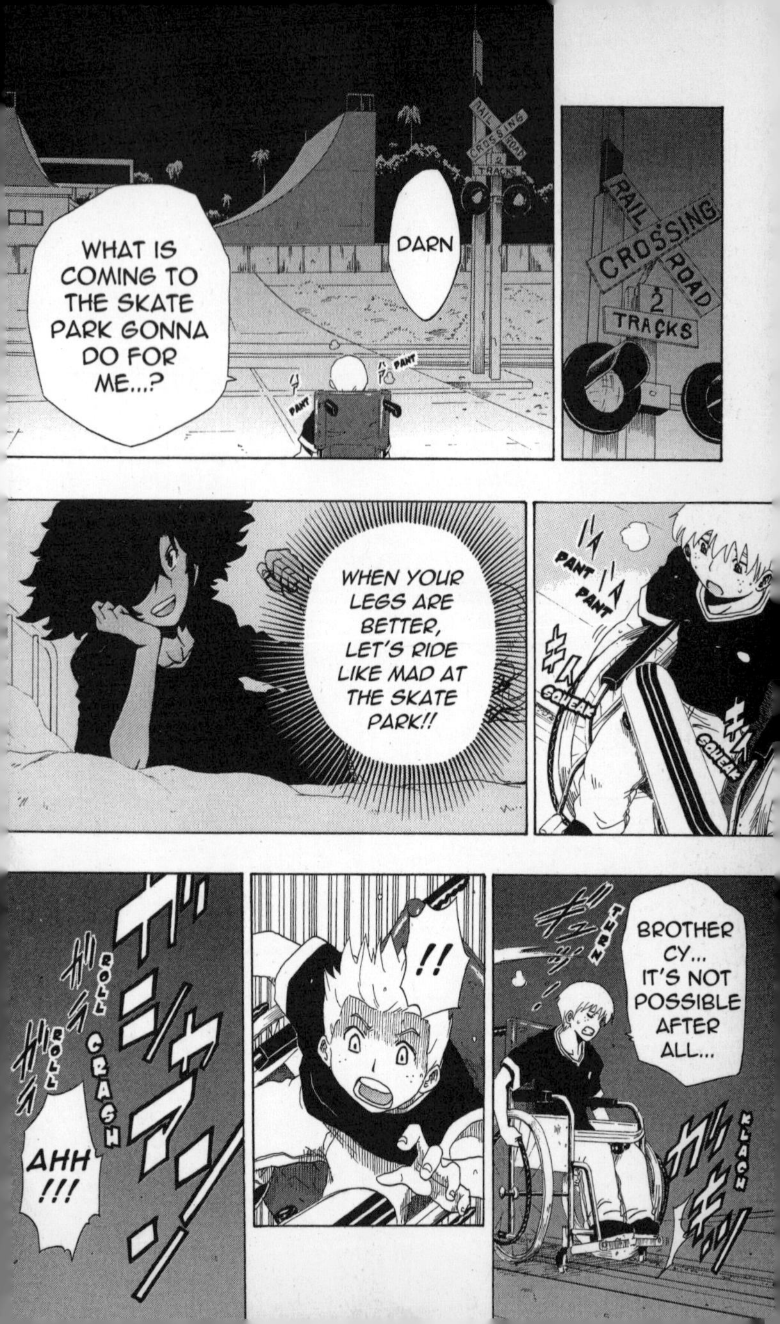
RAIL CROSSING ROAD
2
TRACKS
DARN
PANT
PANT
WHAT IS COMING TO THE SKATE PARK GONNA DO FOR ME...?
PANT
PANT
SQUEAK
SQUEAK
WHEN YOUR LEGS ARE BETTER, LET'S RIDE LIKE MAD AT THE SKATE PARK!!
BROTHER CY... IT'S NOT POSSIBLE AFTER ALL...
TURN
KLACH
!!
ROLL
ROLL
CRASH
AHH!!!

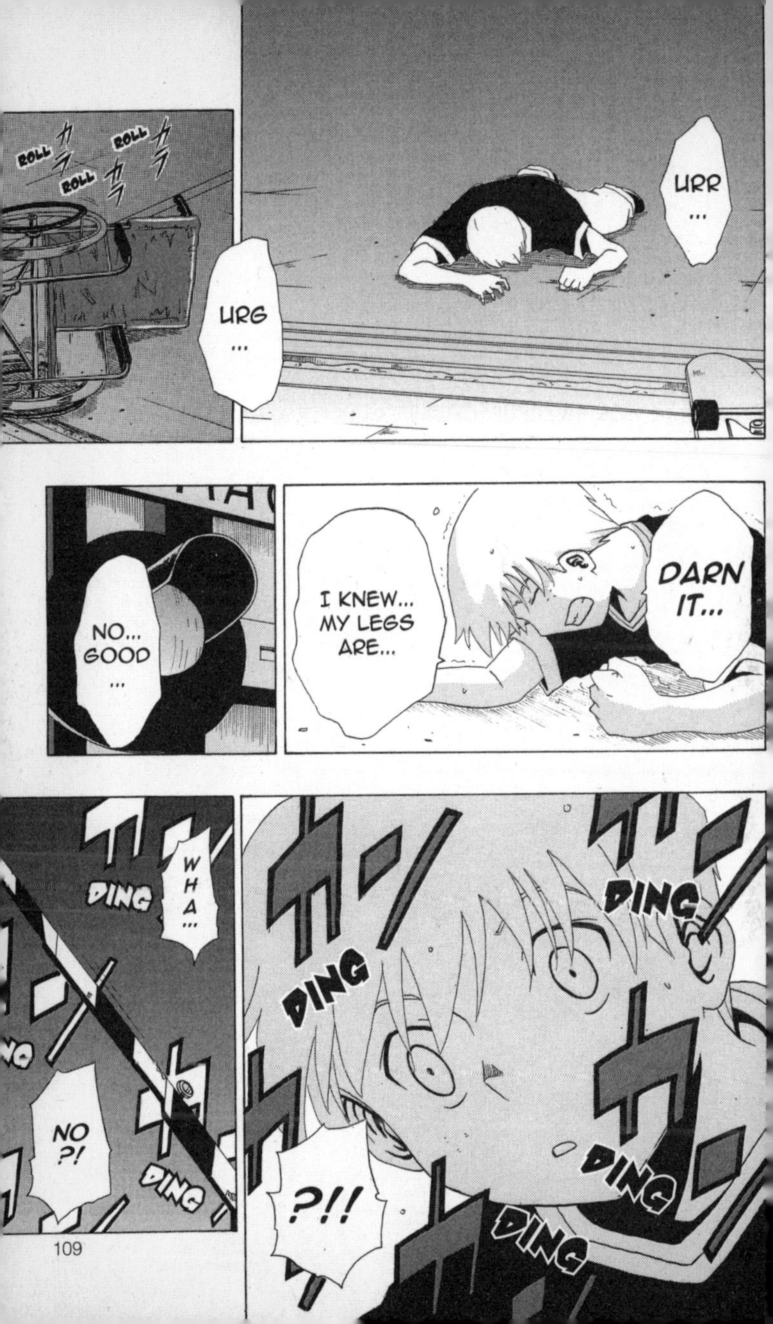
URR ...
URG ...
ROLL
カラ
ROLL
カラ
ROLL
カラ
DARN IT...
I KNEW... MY LEGS ARE...
NO... GOOD ...
DING
DING
DING
DING
DING
?!!
WHA...
DING
NO ?!
DING

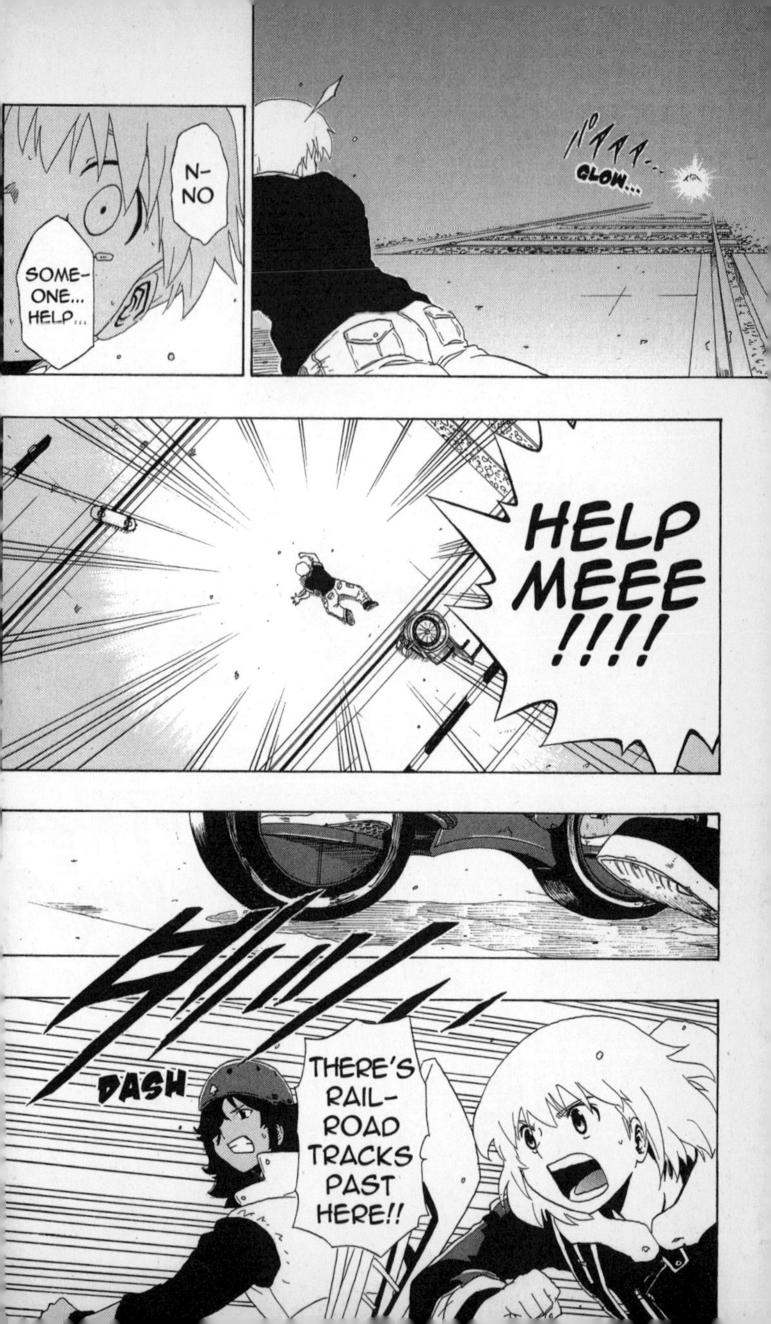
パァァァ...
GLOW...
N-NO
SOME-ONE... HELP...
HELP MEEE !!!!
DASH
THERE'S RAIL-ROAD TRACKS PAST HERE!!

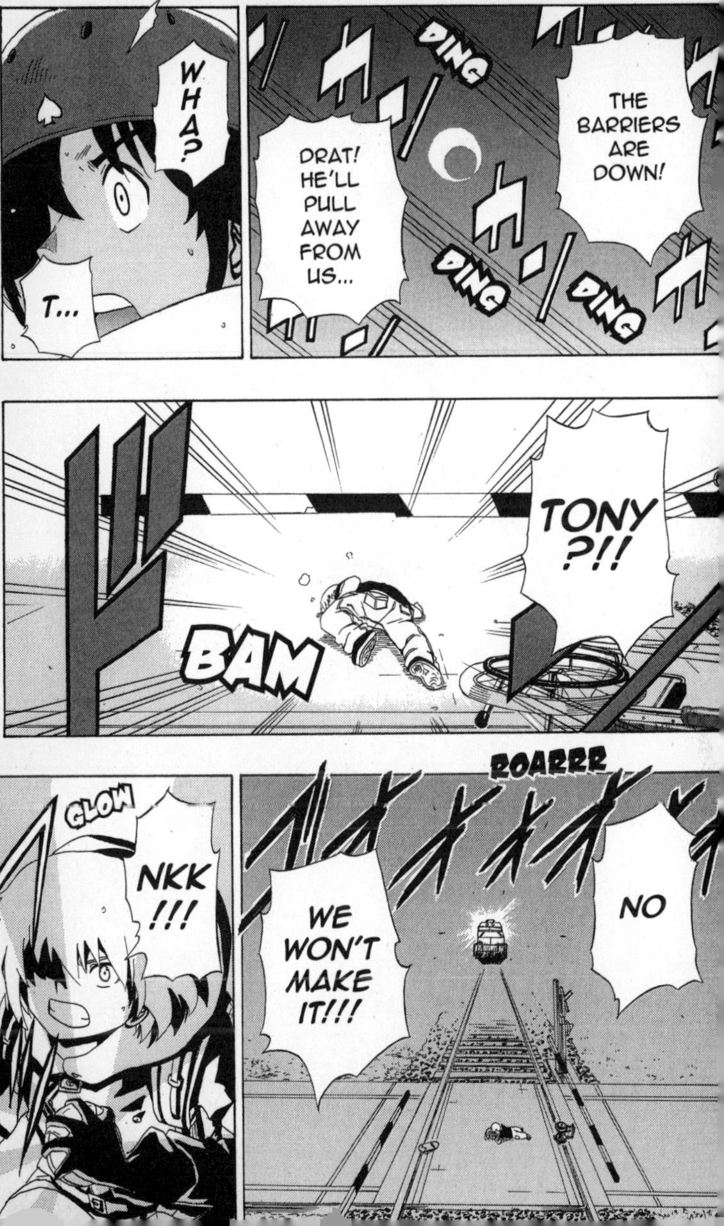
DING
DING
DING
THE BARRIERS ARE DOWN!
DRAT! HE'LL PULL AWAY FROM US...
WHA?
T...
TONY?!!
BAM
ROARRR
NO
WE WON'T MAKE IT!!!
GLOW
NKK!!!

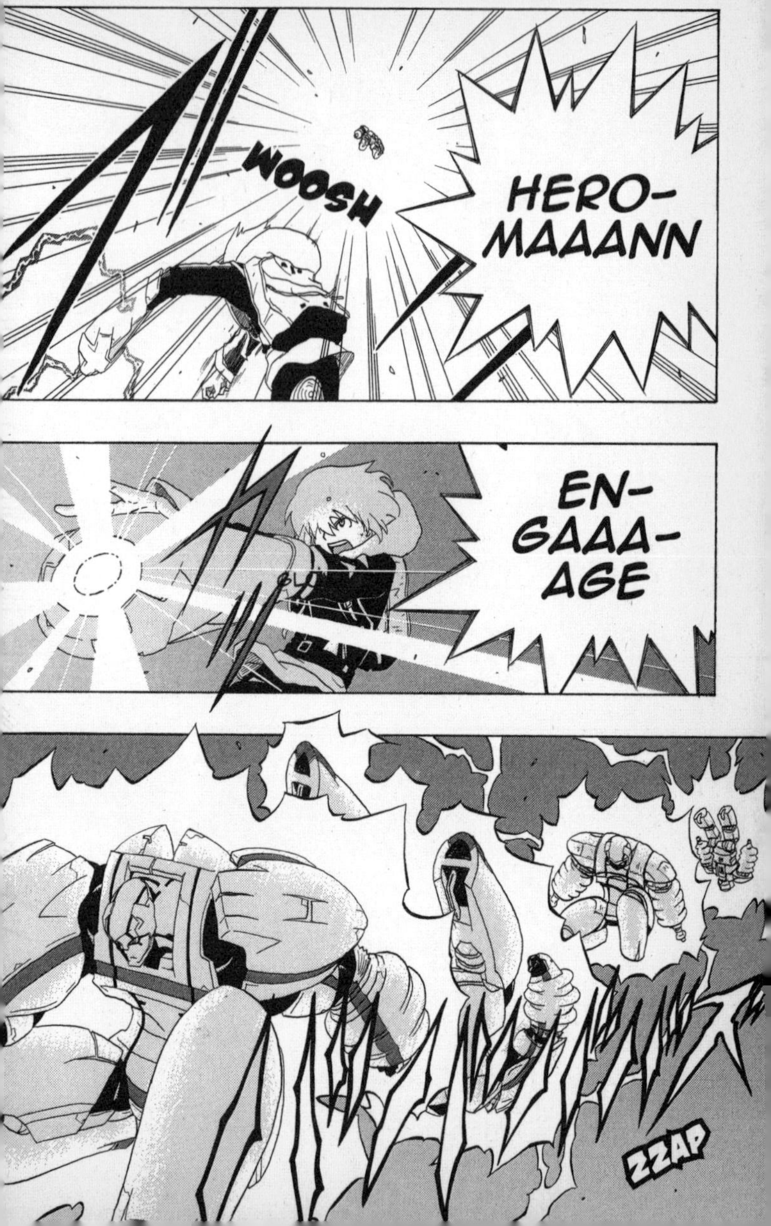
HERO-
MAAANN
WOOSH
EN-
GAAA-
AGE
ZZAP

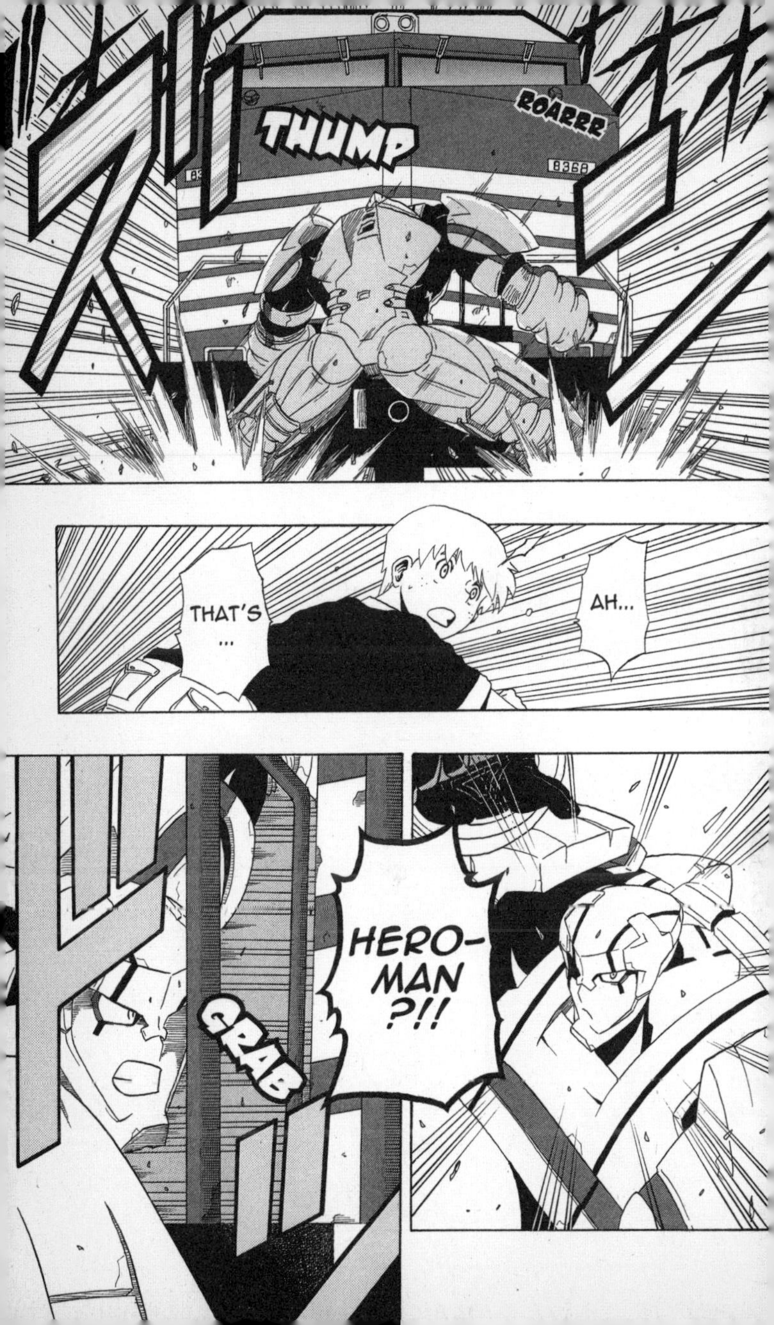
ROARRR
THUMP
AH...
THAT'S ...
HERO-MAN ?!!
GRAB

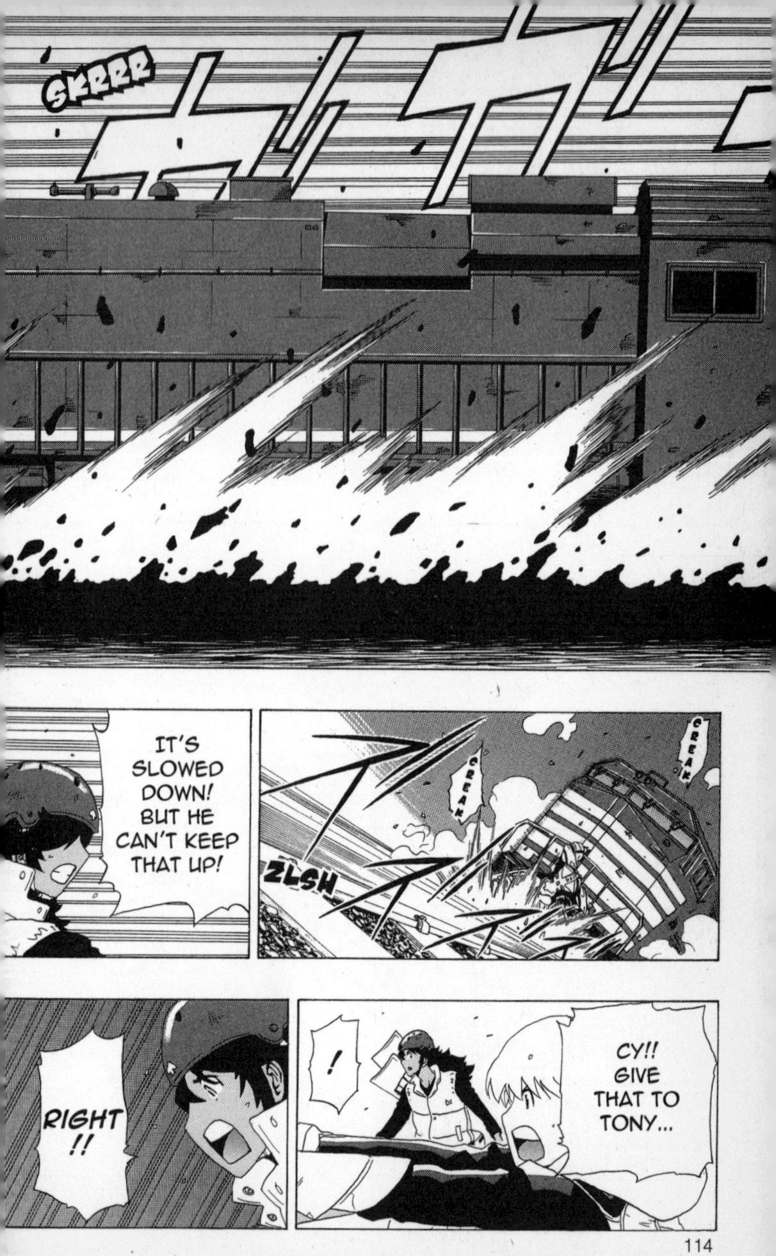
SKRRR
CREAK
CREAK
ZLSH
IT'S SLOWED DOWN! BUT HE CAN'T KEEP THAT UP!
CY!! GIVE THAT TO TONY...
!
RIGHT!!

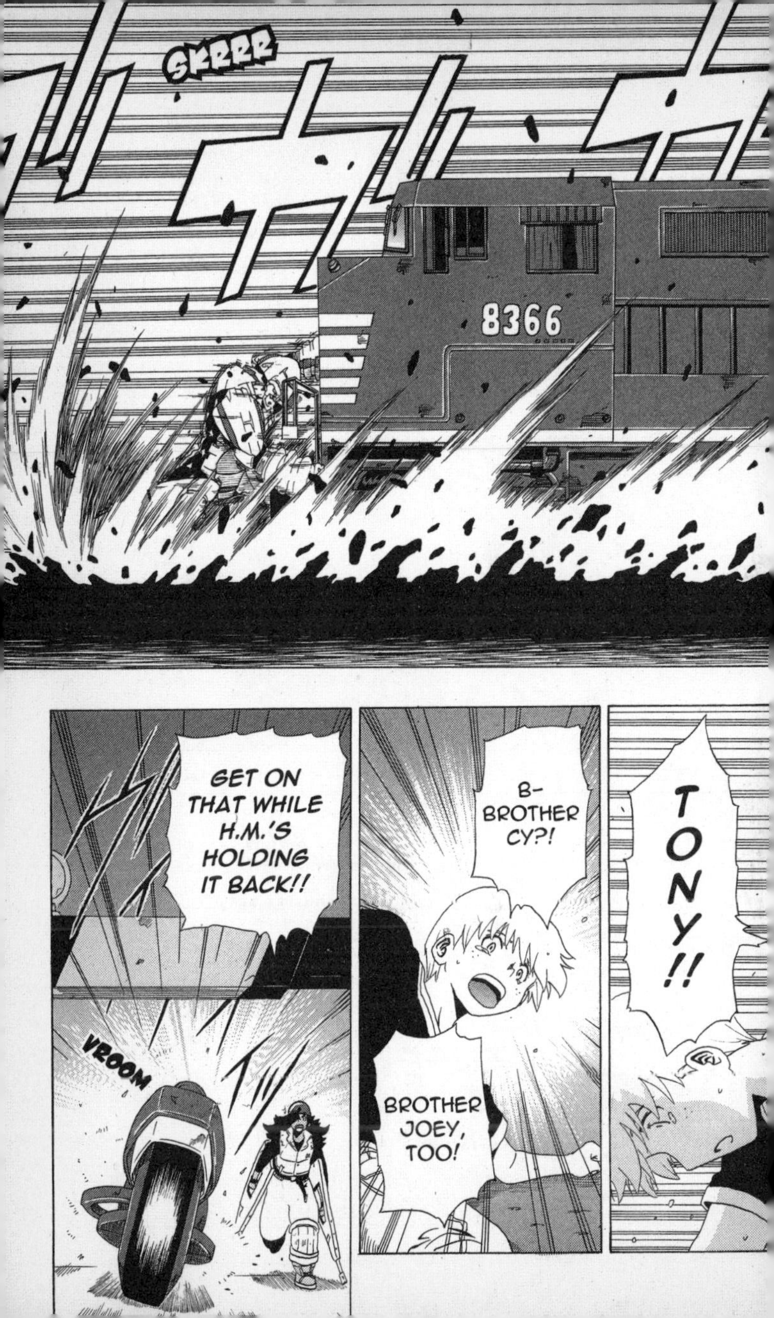
SKRRR
TONY!!
B-BROTHER CY?!
BROTHER JOEY, TOO!
GET ON THAT WHILE H.M.'S HOLDING IT BACK!!
VROOM

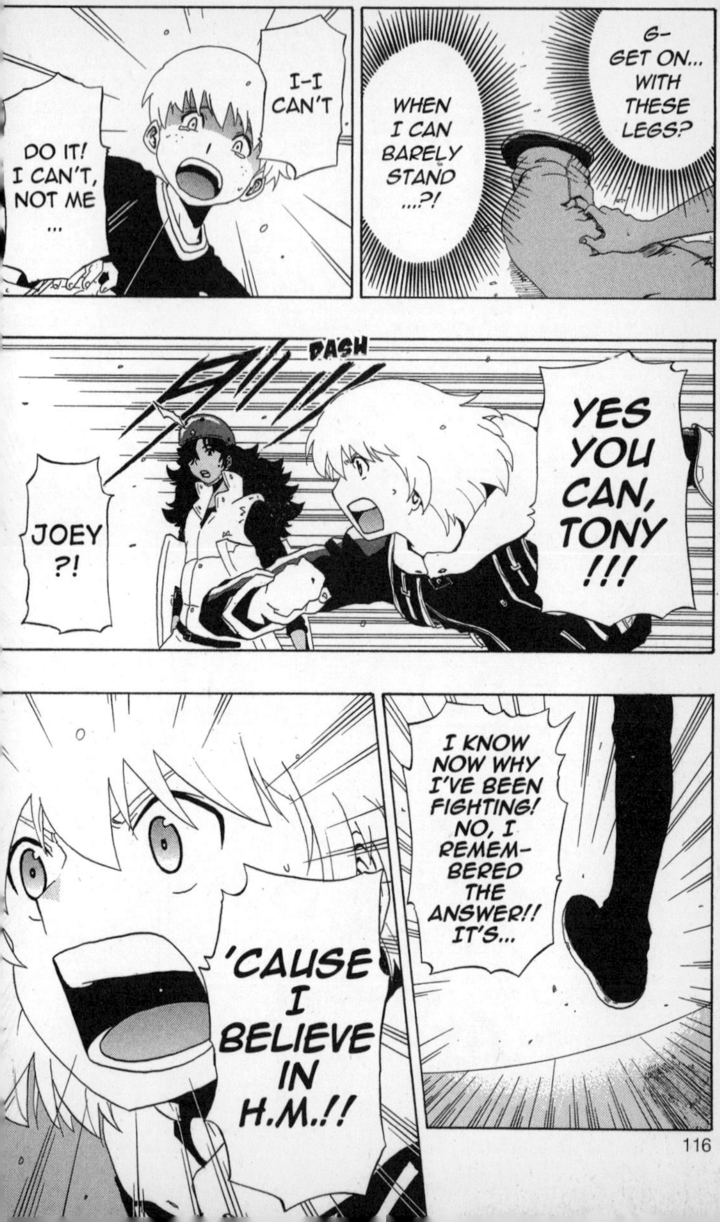
G- GET ON... WITH THESE LEGS?
WHEN I CAN BARELY STAND ...?!
I-I CAN'T
DO IT! I CAN'T, NOT ME ...
DASH
YES YOU CAN, TONY!!!
JOEY ?!
I KNOW NOW WHY I'VE BEEN FIGHTING! NO, I REMEMBERED THE ANSWER!! IT'S...
'CAUSE I BELIEVE IN H.M.!!

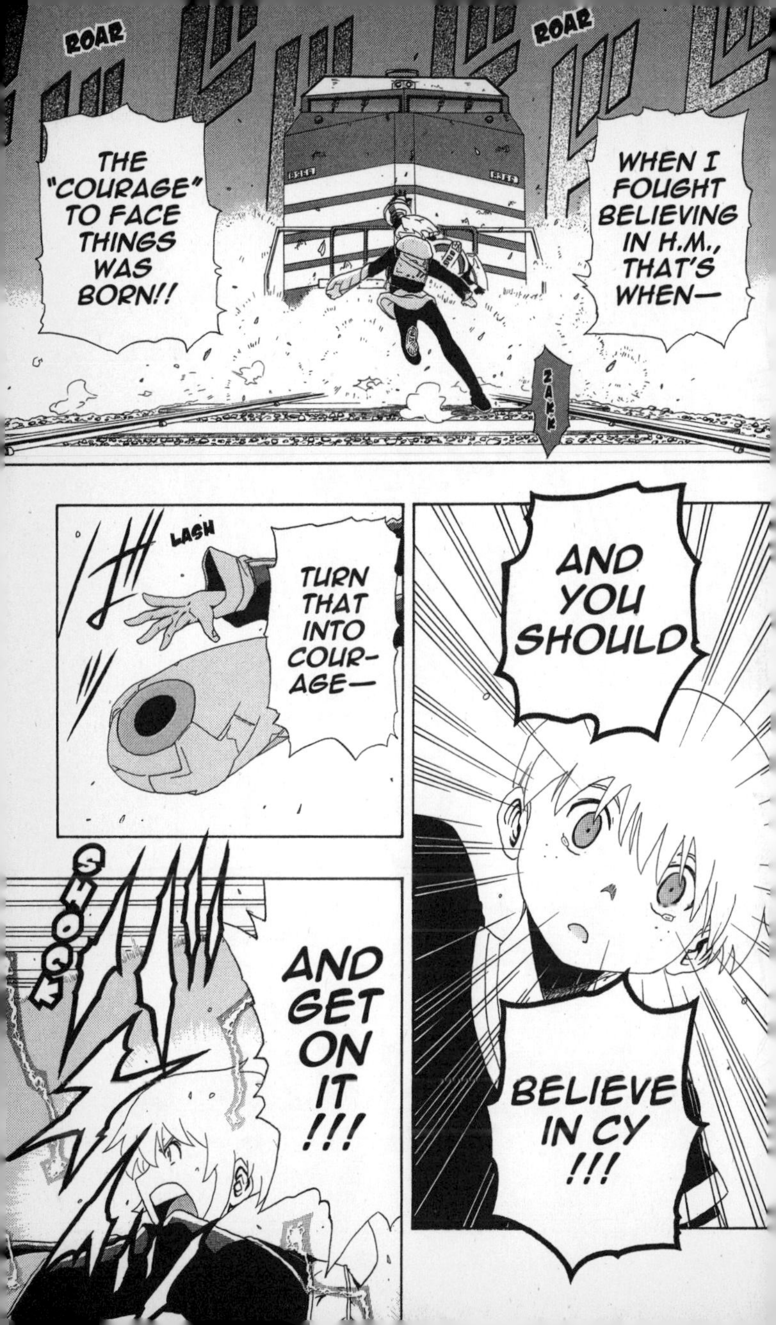
ROAR
WHEN I FOUGHT BELIEVING IN H.M., THAT'S WHEN—
ROAR
THE "COURAGE" TO FACE THINGS WAS BORN!!
ZAKK
AND YOU SHOULD
BELIEVE IN CY !!!
TURN THAT INTO COUR-AGE—
LASH
AND GET ON IT !!!
SHOCK

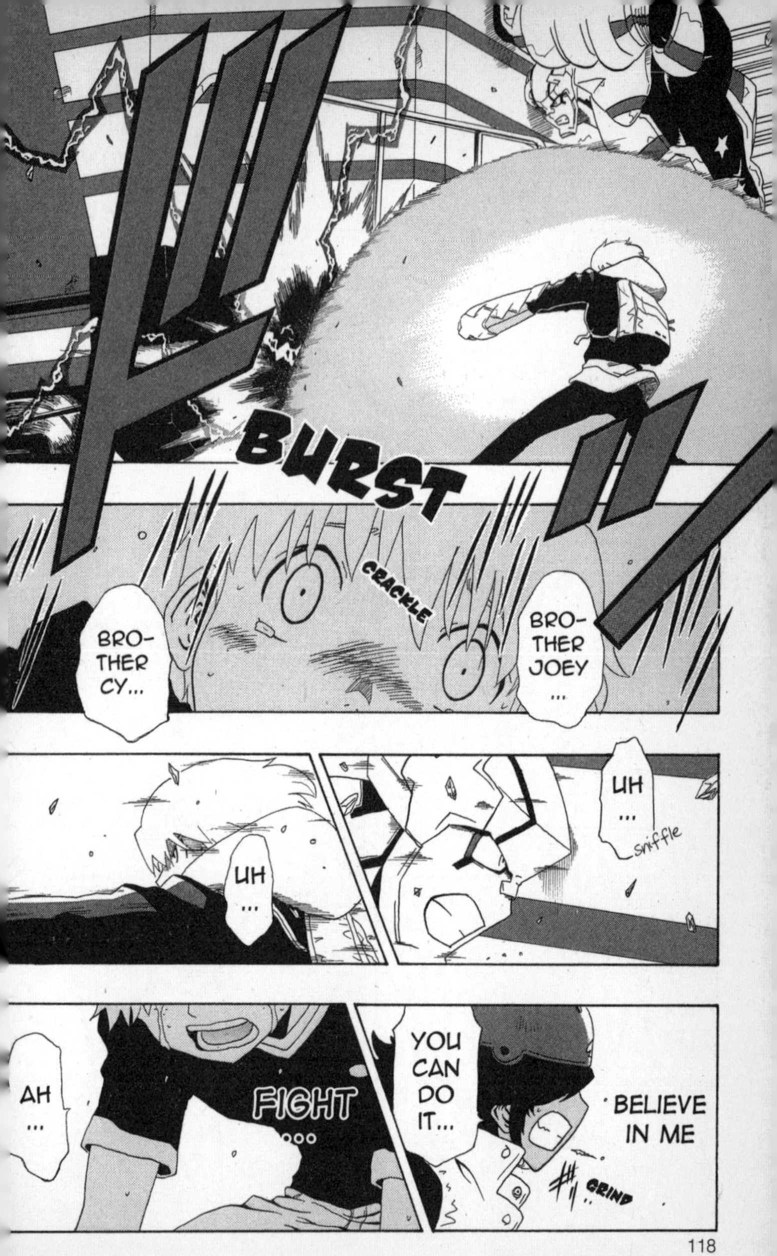
BURST
BRO-THER JOEY...
CRACKLE
BRO-THER CY...
UH...
sniffle
UH...
BELIEVE IN ME
GRIND
YOU CAN DO IT...
FIGHT...
AH...

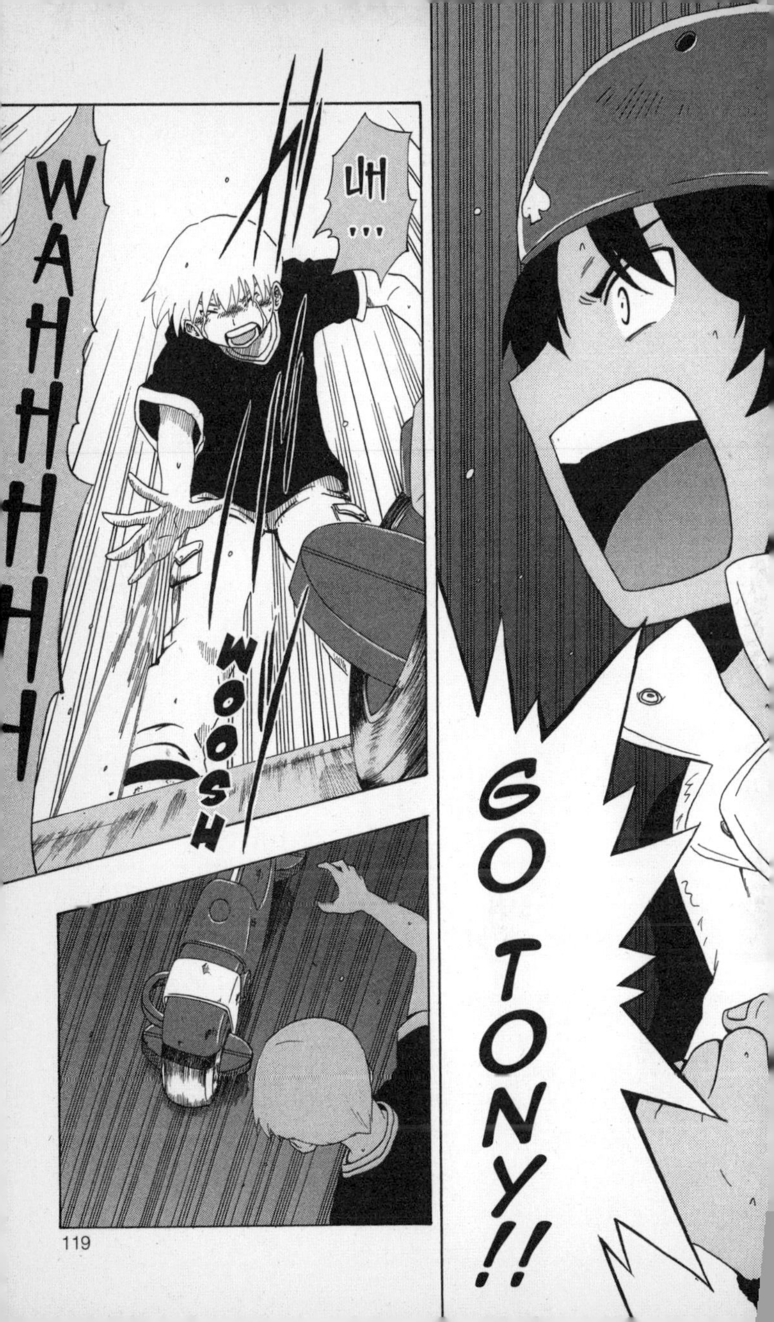
GO TONY!!
WAHHHHHH
UH ...
WOOOSH

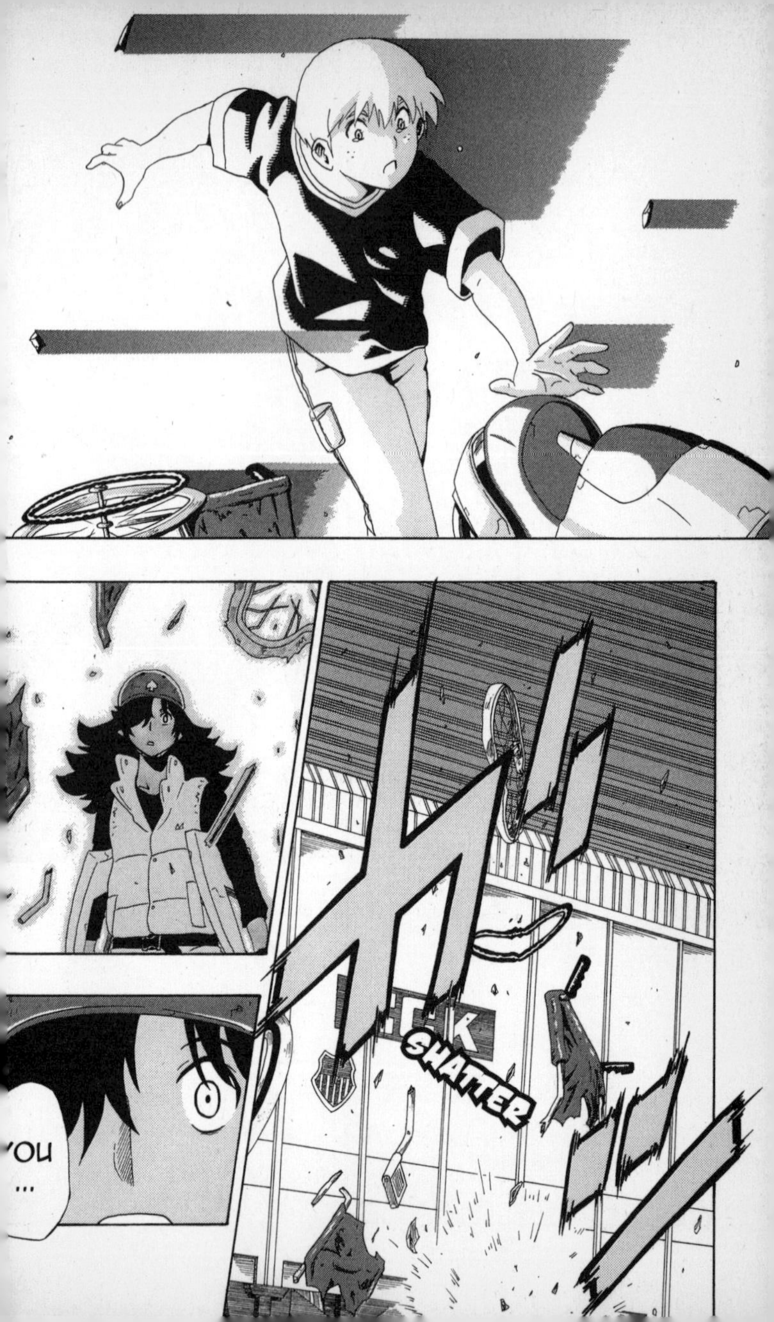
SHATTER
YOU ...

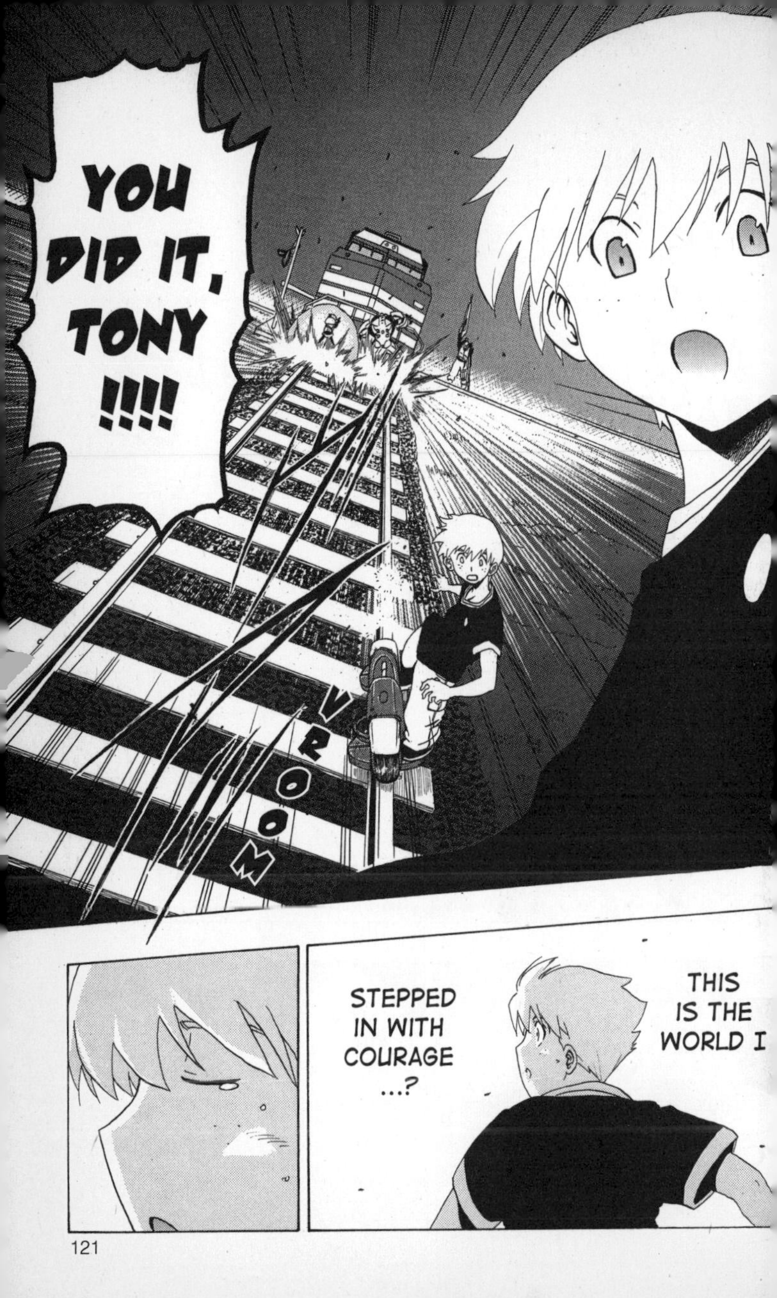
YOU DID IT, TONY !!!!
VROOOM
THIS IS THE WORLD I
STEPPED IN WITH COURAGE ...?

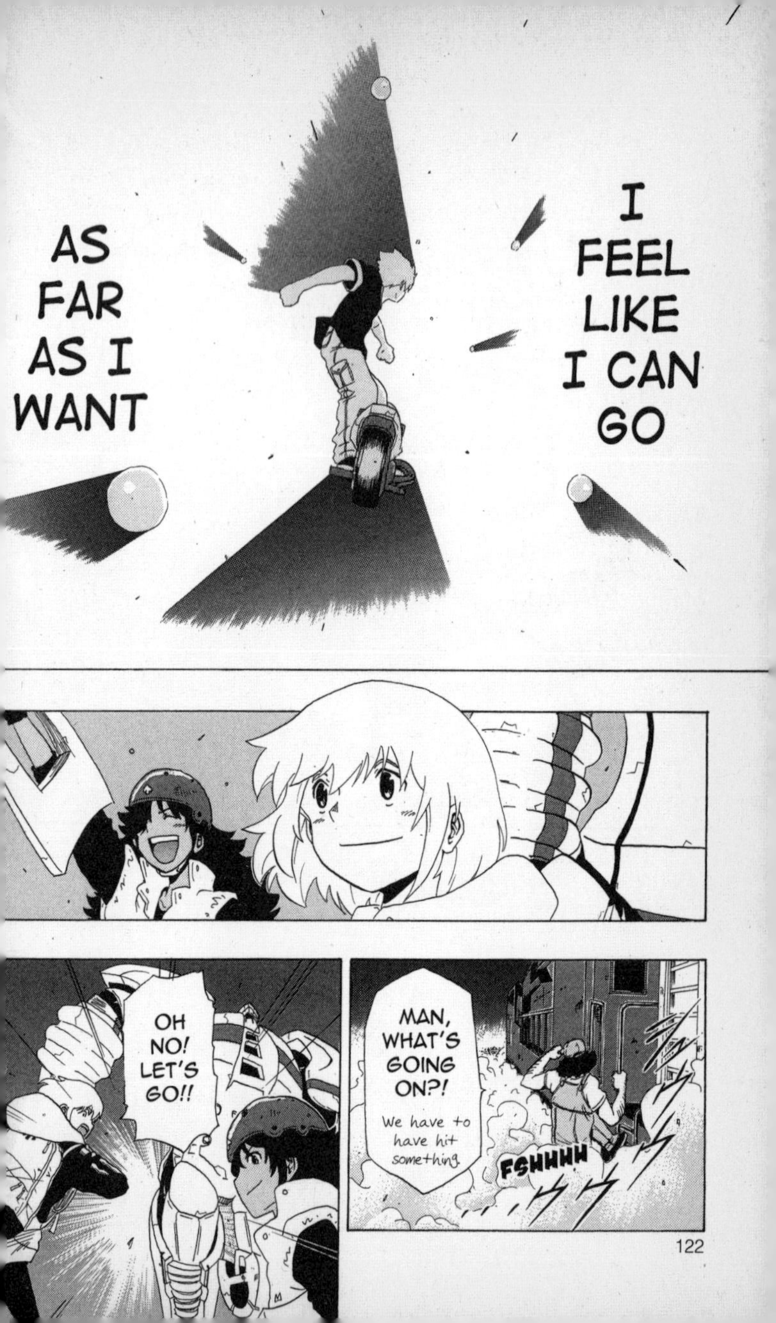
I FEEL LIKE I CAN GO
AS FAR AS I WANT
MAN, WHAT'S GOING ON?!
We have to have hit something.
FSHHHH
OH NO! LET'S GO!!

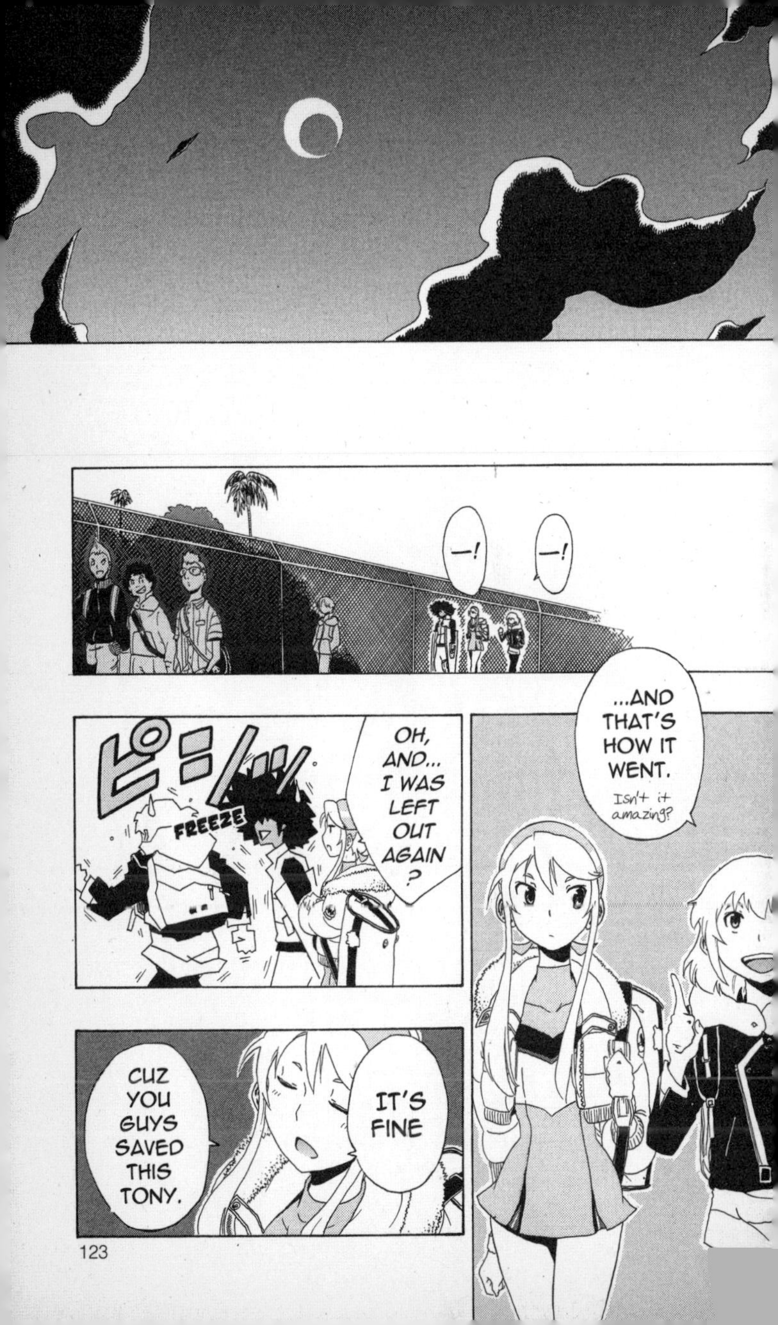
—!
—!
...AND THAT'S HOW IT WENT.
Isn't it amazing?
FREEZE
OH, AND... I WAS LEFT OUT AGAIN?
IT'S FINE
CUZ YOU GUYS SAVED THIS TONY.

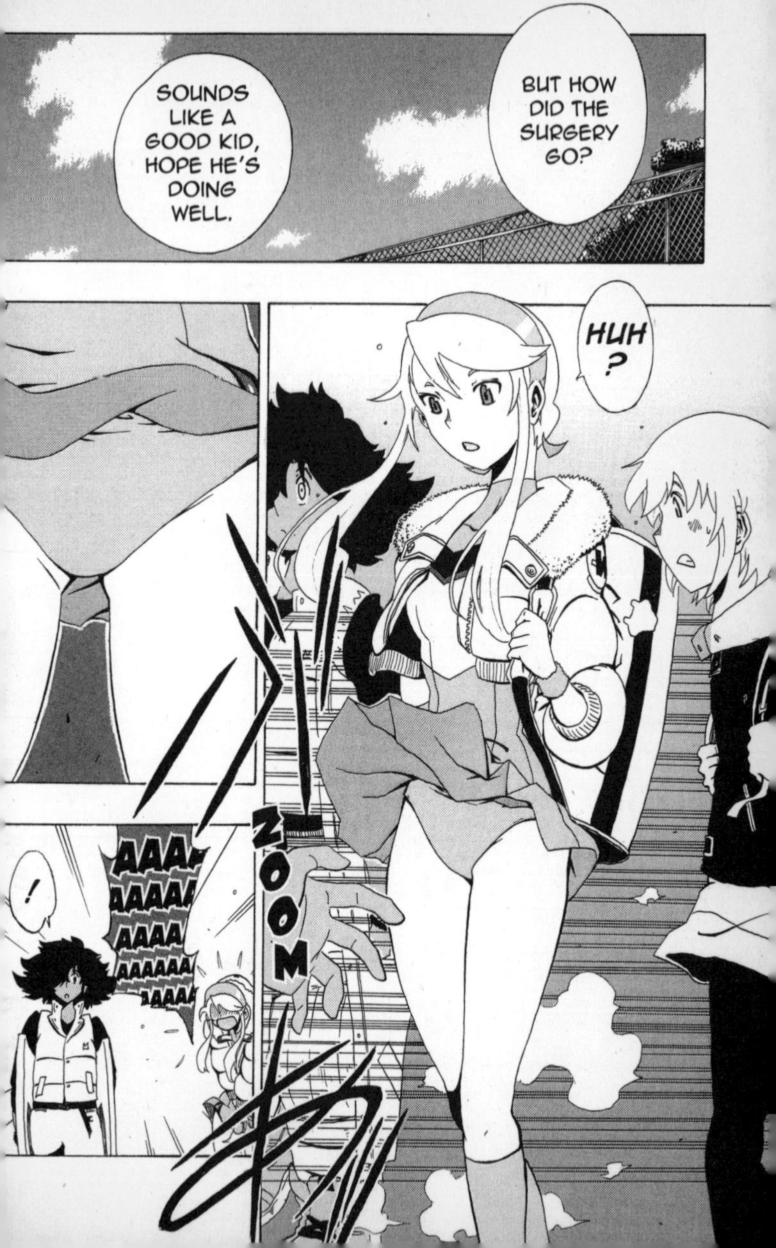
BUT HOW DID THE SURGERY GO?
SOUNDS LIKE A GOOD KID, HOPE HE'S DOING WELL.
HUH ?
ZOOM
AAAA AAAAA AAAA AAAAAA AAAA
!

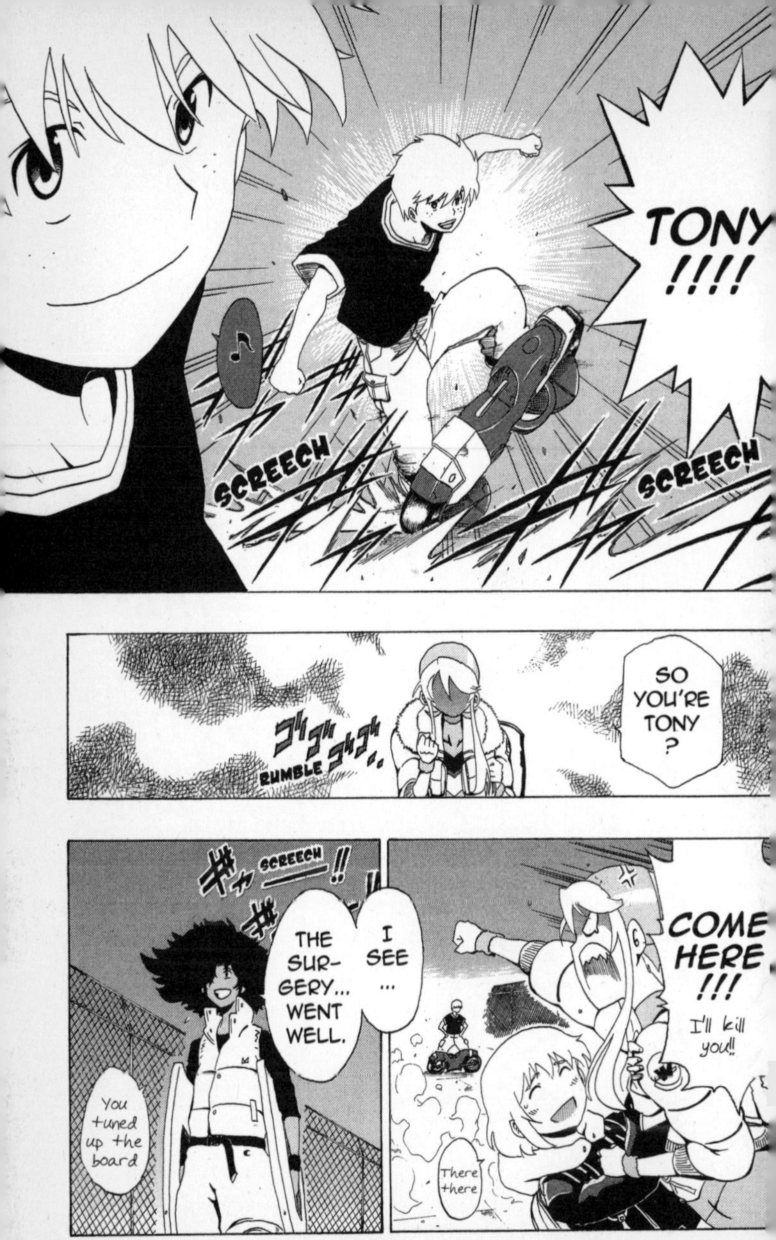
TONY!!!!
SCREECH
SCREECH
SO YOU'RE TONY?
RUMBLE
COME HERE!!!
I'll kill you!!
There there
SCREECH!!
I SEE...
THE SURGERY... WENT WELL.
You tuned up the board

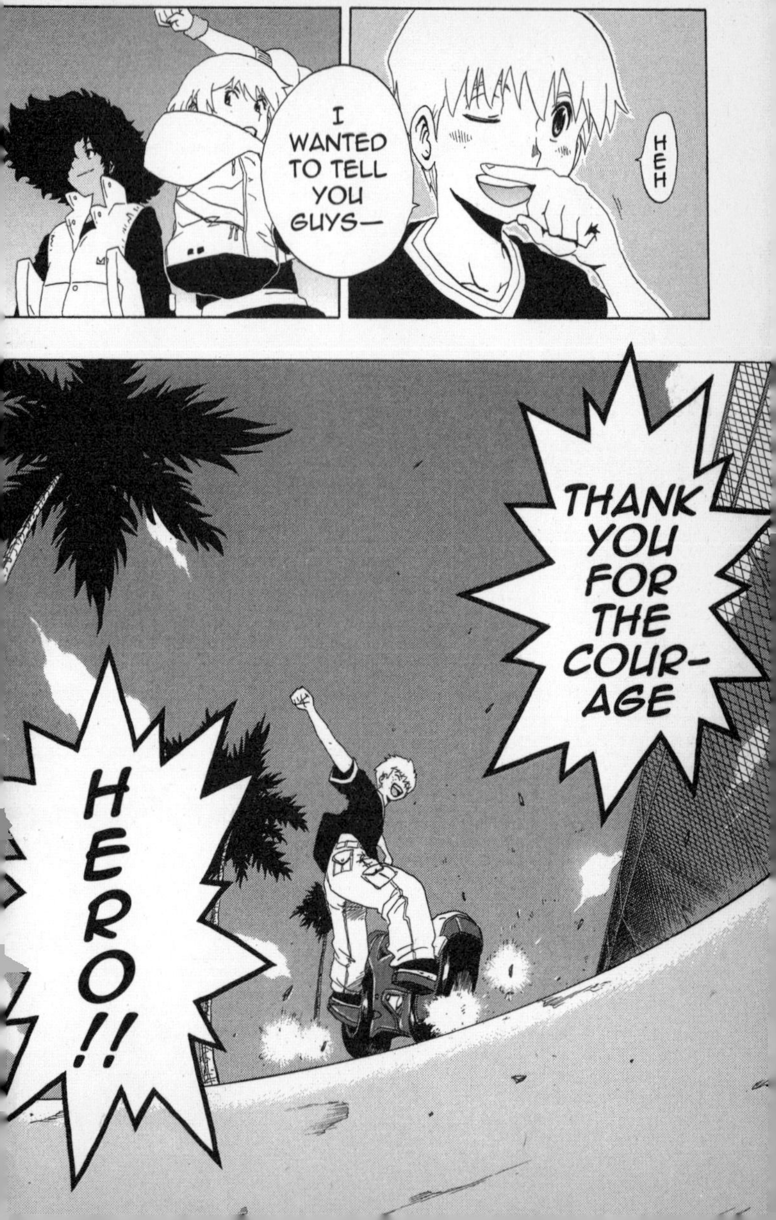
HEH
I WANTED TO TELL YOU GUYS—
THANK YOU FOR THE COUR-AGE
HERO!!

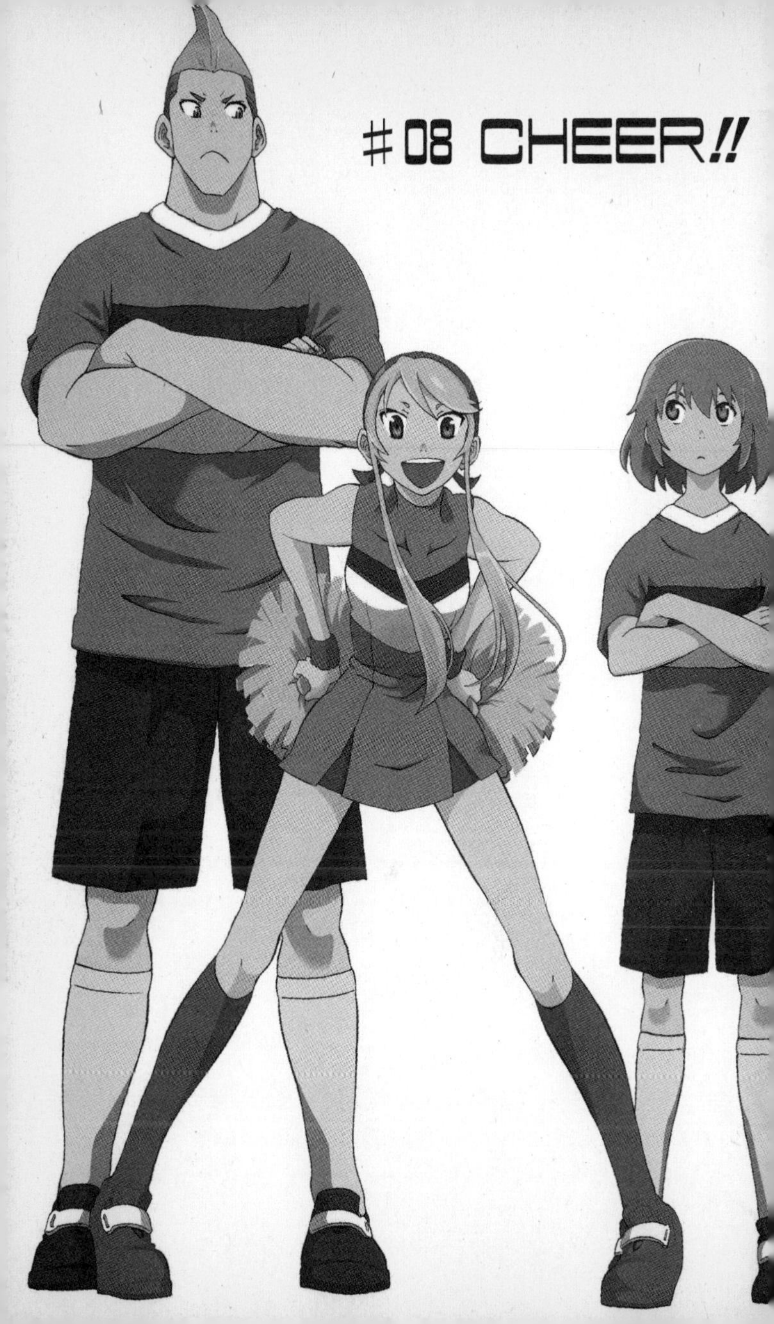
#08 CHEER!!

HEROMAN

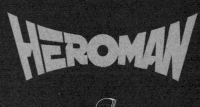

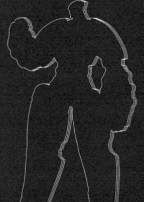

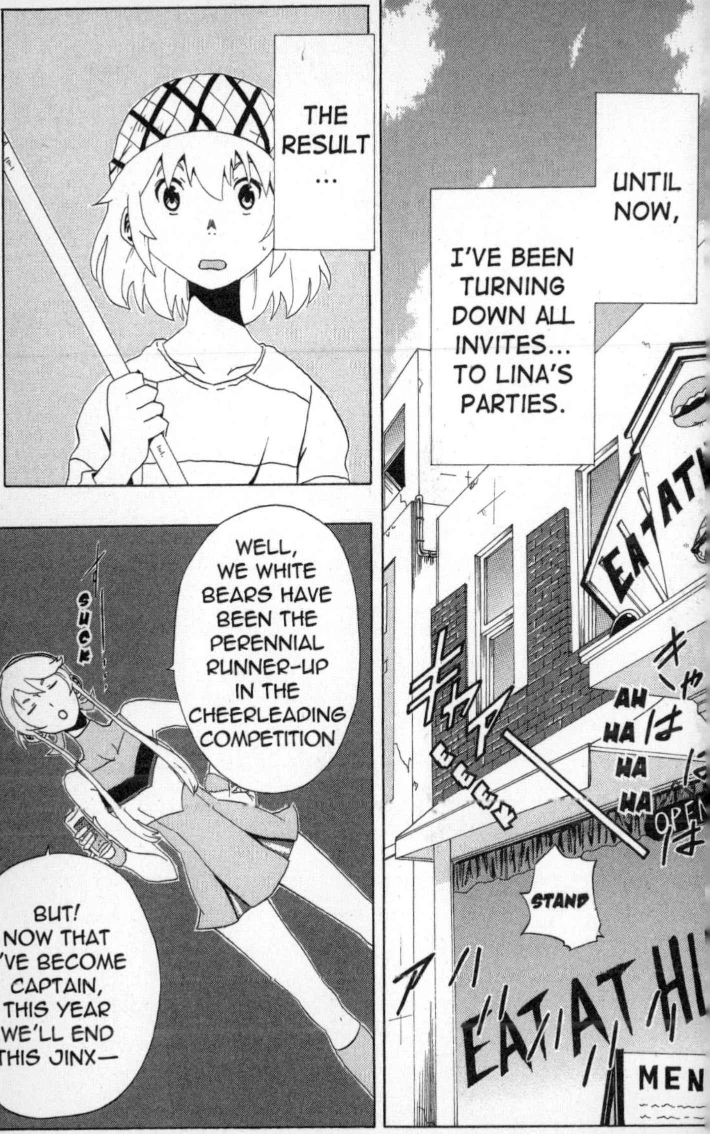
UNTIL NOW,
I'VE BEEN TURNING DOWN ALL INVITES... TO LINA'S PARTIES.
EEEK
AH HA HA HA
STAND
THE RESULT ...
WELL, WE WHITE BEARS HAVE BEEN THE PERENNIAL RUNNER-UP IN THE CHEERLEADING COMPETITION
SUCK
BUT! NOW THAT I'VE BECOME CAPTAIN, THIS YEAR WE'LL END THIS JINX—

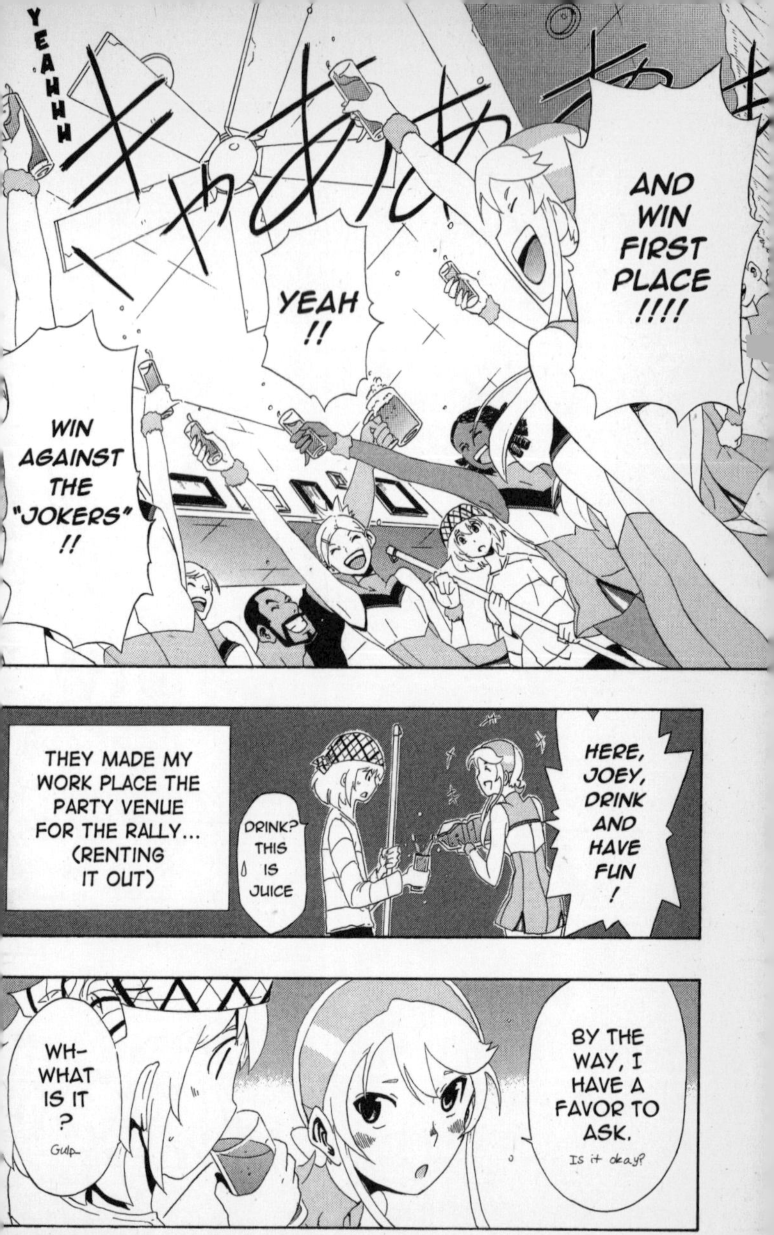
AND WIN FIRST PLACE !!!!
YEAH !!
YEAHHH
WIN AGAINST THE "JOKERS" !!
HERE, JOEY, DRINK AND HAVE FUN !
DRINK? THIS IS JUICE
THEY MADE MY WORK PLACE THE PARTY VENUE FOR THE RALLY... (RENTING IT OUT)
BY THE WAY, I HAVE A FAVOR TO ASK.
Is it okay?
WH-WHAT IS IT ?
Gulp

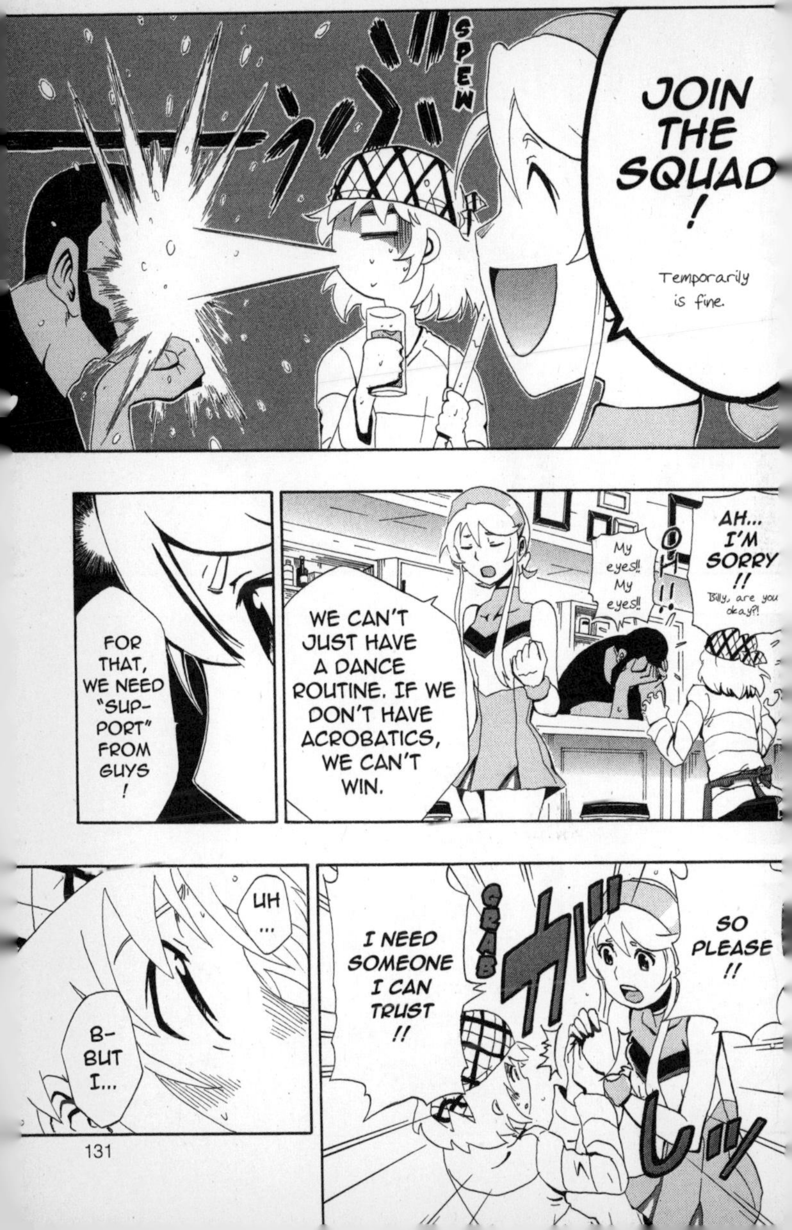
JOIN THE SQUAD!
Temporarily is fine.
SPEW
AH... I'M SORRY!!
Billy, are you okay?!
My eyes!! My eyes!!
WE CAN'T JUST HAVE A DANCE ROUTINE. IF WE DON'T HAVE ACROBATICS, WE CAN'T WIN.
FOR THAT, WE NEED "SUP-PORT" FROM GUYS!
SO PLEASE!!
GRAB
I NEED SOMEONE I CAN TRUST!!
UH...
B-BUT I...

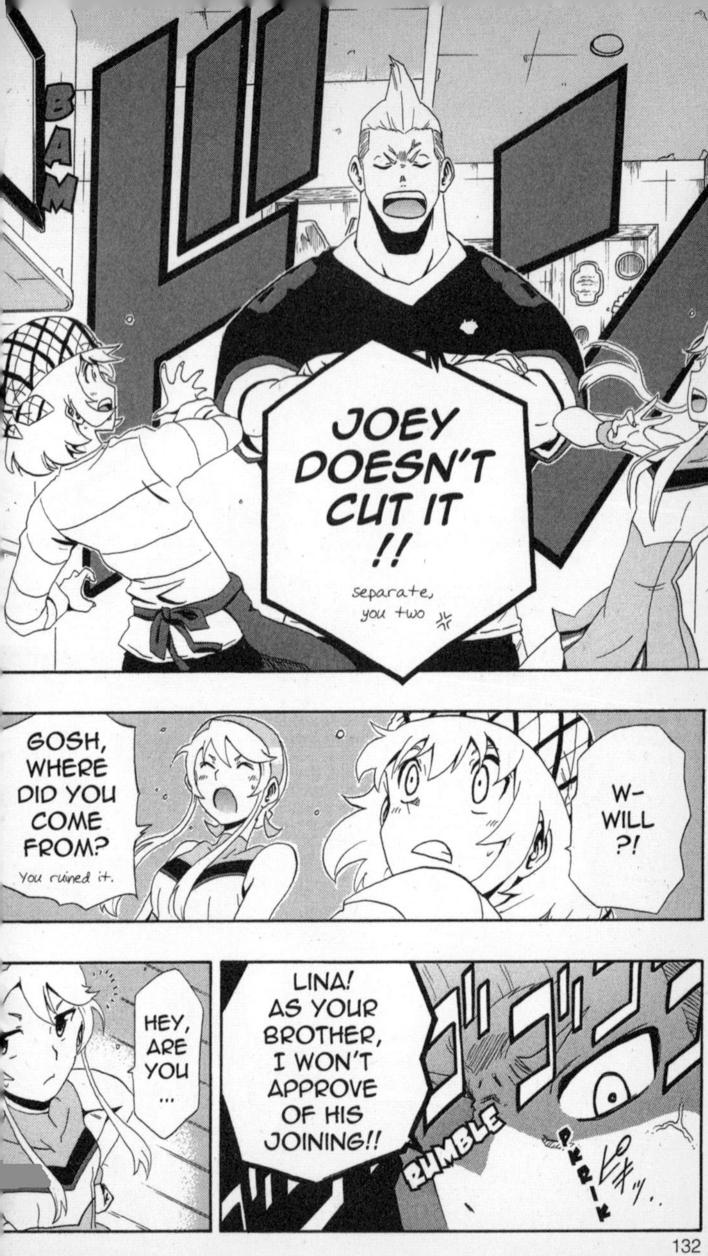
BAM
JOEY DOESN'T CUT IT !!
separate, you two
W-WILL ?!
GOSH, WHERE DID YOU COME FROM?
You ruined it.
LINA! AS YOUR BROTHER, I WON'T APPROVE OF HIS JOINING!!
RUMBLE
PKRIK
HEY, ARE YOU ...

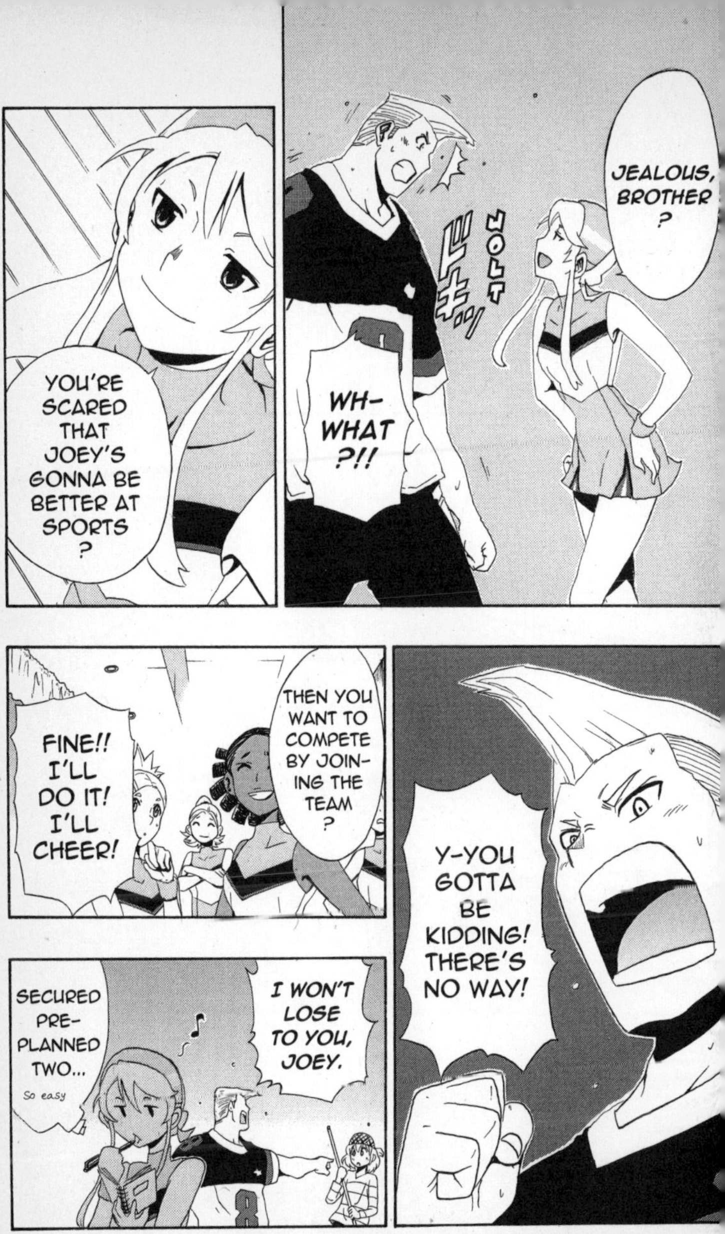
JEALOUS, BROTHER?
JOLT
WH-WHAT?!!
YOU'RE SCARED THAT JOEY'S GONNA BE BETTER AT SPORTS?
Y-YOU GOTTA BE KIDDING! THERE'S NO WAY!
THEN YOU WANT TO COMPETE BY JOIN-ING THE TEAM?
FINE!! I'LL DO IT! I'LL CHEER!
I WON'T LOSE TO YOU, JOEY.
SECURED PRE-PLANNED TWO...
So easy

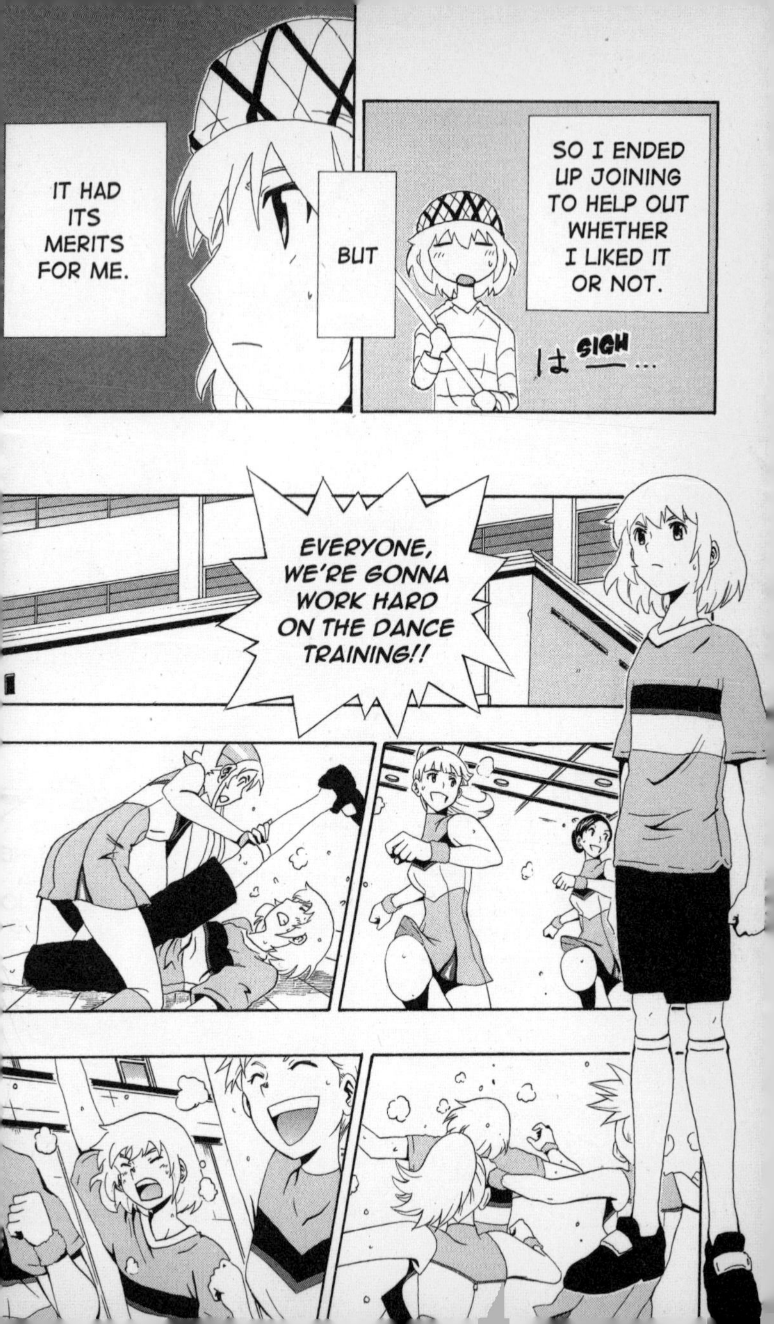
SO I ENDED UP JOINING TO HELP OUT WHETHER I LIKED IT OR NOT.
は SIGH ...
BUT
IT HAD ITS MERITS FOR ME.
EVERYONE, WE'RE GONNA WORK HARD ON THE DANCE TRAINING!!

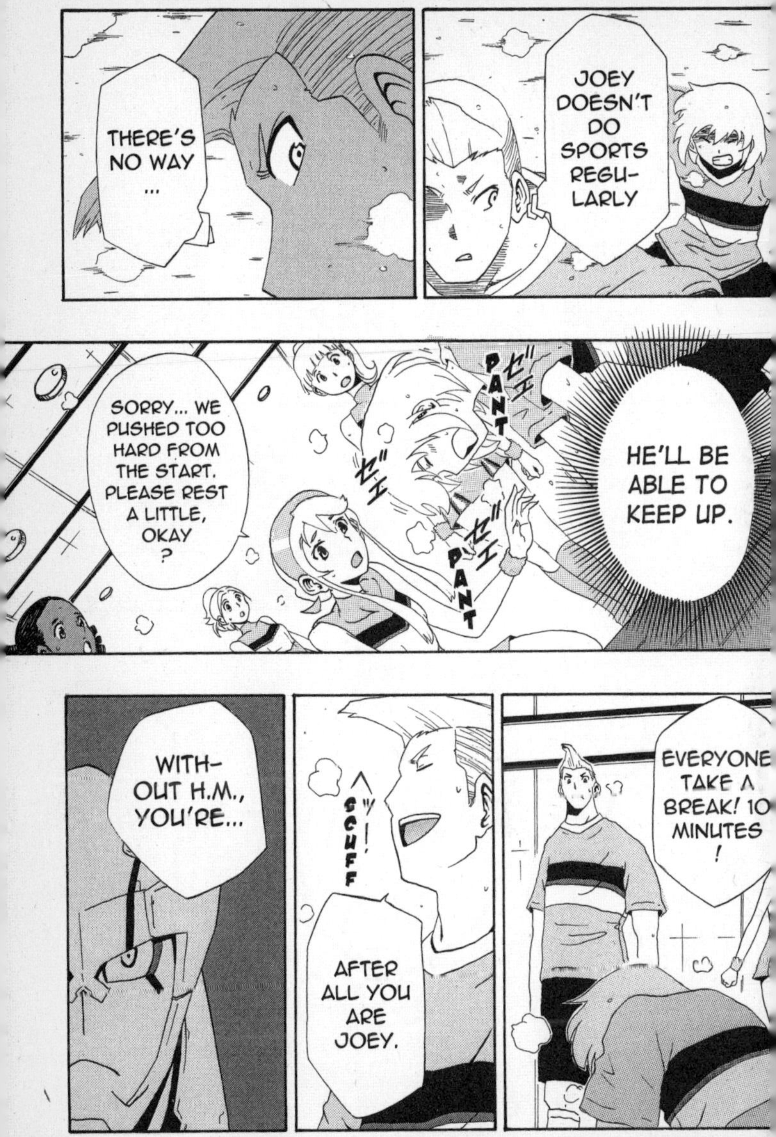
JOEY DOESN'T DO SPORTS REGU-LARLY
THERE'S NO WAY ...
HE'LL BE ABLE TO KEEP UP.
ゼェ PANT
ゼェ
ゼェ PANT
SORRY... WE PUSHED TOO HARD FROM THE START. PLEASE REST A LITTLE, OKAY?
EVERYONE TAKE A BREAK! 10 MINUTES!
SCUFF
AFTER ALL YOU ARE JOEY.
WITH-OUT H.M., YOU'RE...

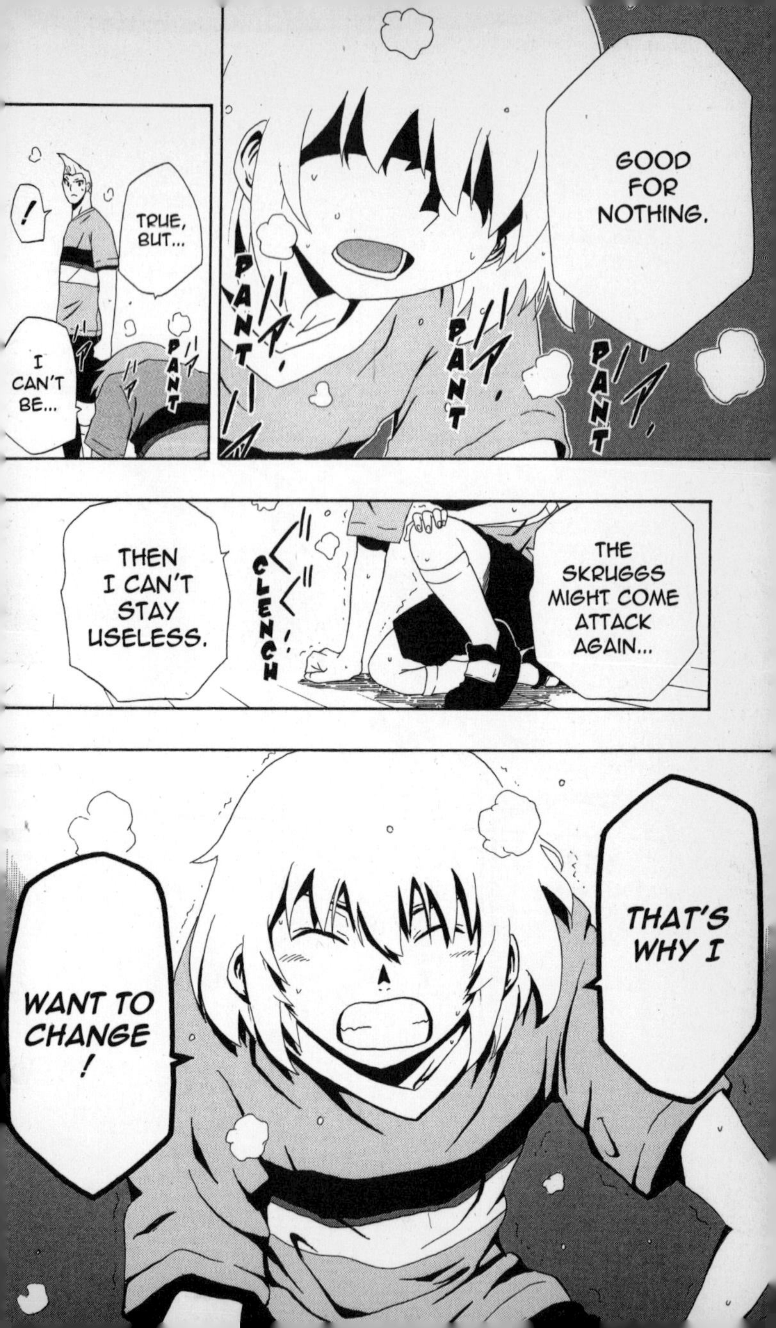
GOOD FOR NOTHING.
PANT
PANT
PANT
TRUE, BUT...
!
I CAN'T BE...
PANT
THE SKRUGGS MIGHT COME ATTACK AGAIN...
CLENCH
THEN I CAN'T STAY USELESS.
THAT'S WHY I
WANT TO CHANGE!

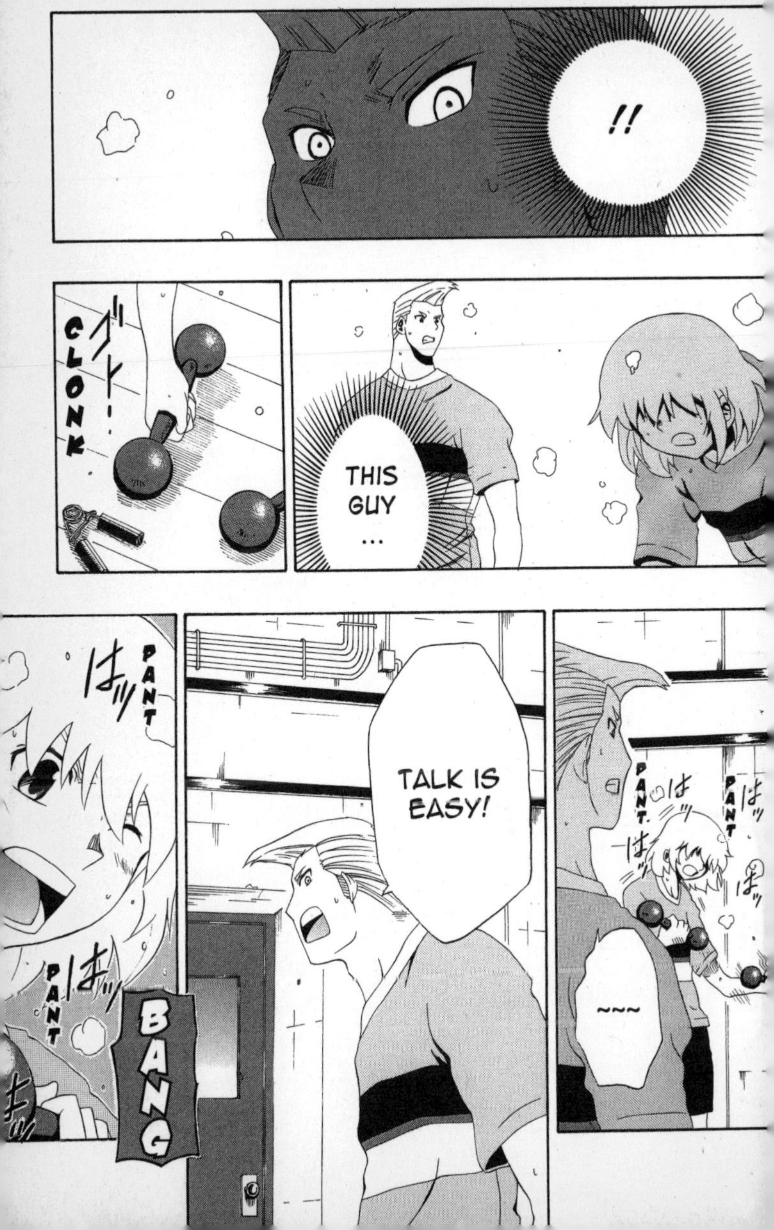
!!
THIS GUY ...
CLONK
PANT
PANT
~~~
TALK IS EASY!
PANT
PANT
BANG
~~~

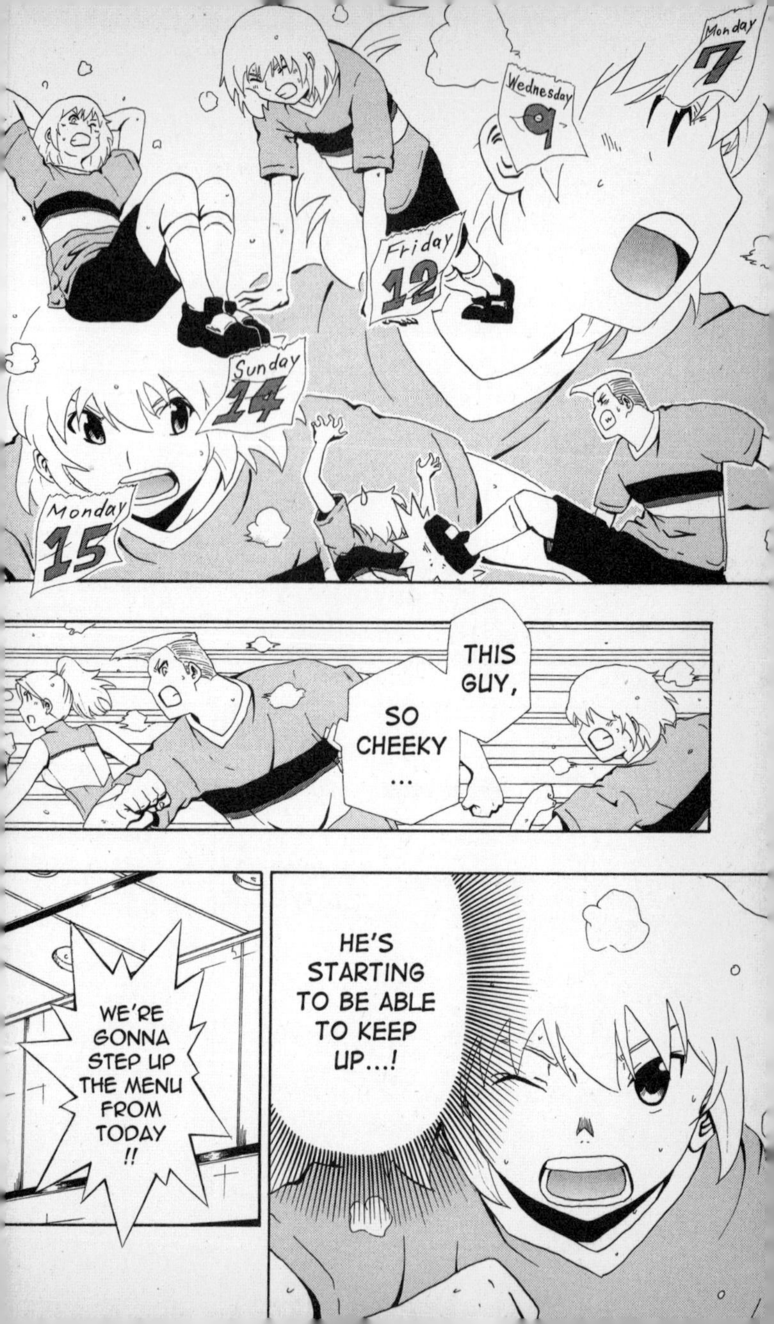
Monday 7
Wednesday 9
Friday 12
Sunday 14
Monday 15
THIS GUY,
SO CHEEKY ...
HE'S STARTING TO BE ABLE TO KEEP UP...!
WE'RE GONNA STEP UP THE MENU FROM TODAY !!

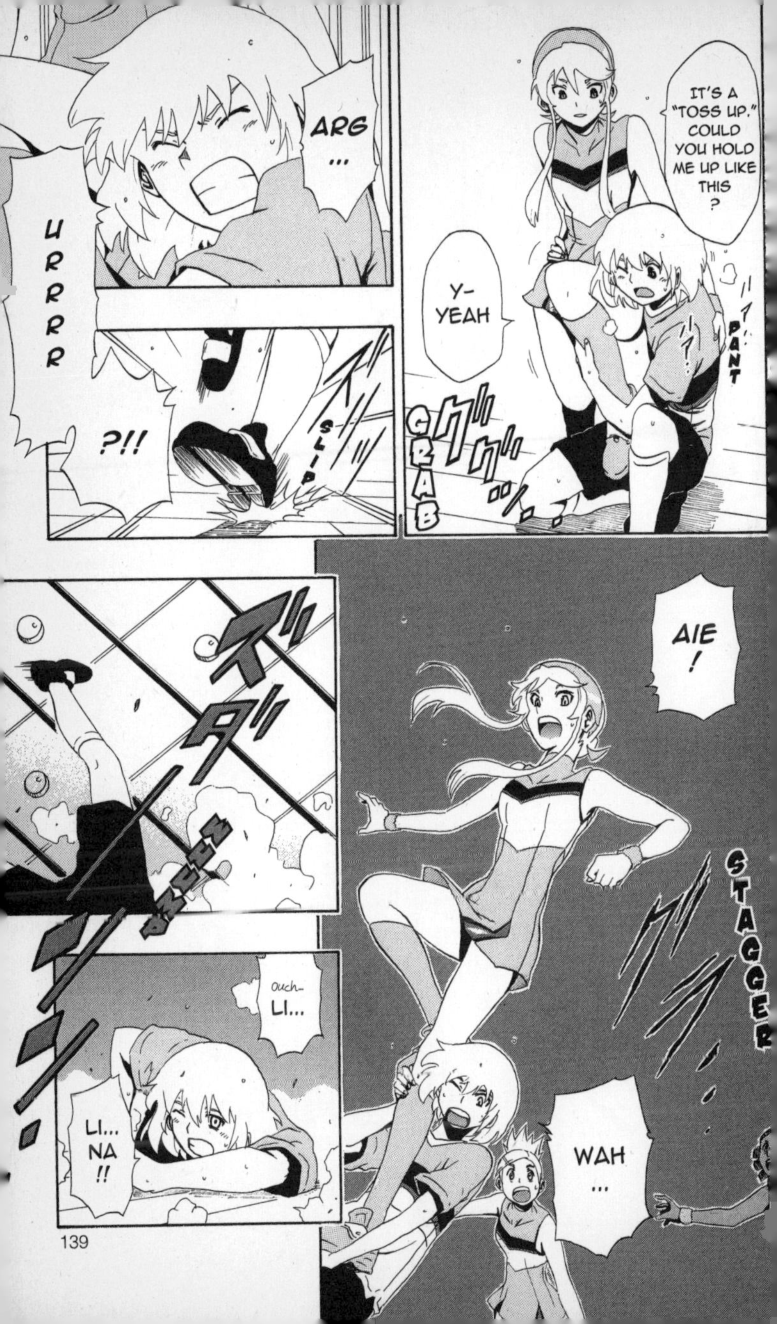
IT'S A "TOSS UP." COULD YOU HOLD ME UP LIKE THIS ?
PANT
Y-YEAH
GRAB
ARG ...
URRRR
?!!
SLIP
AIE !
STAGGER
WAH ...
WHUMP
ouch... LI...
LI... NA !!

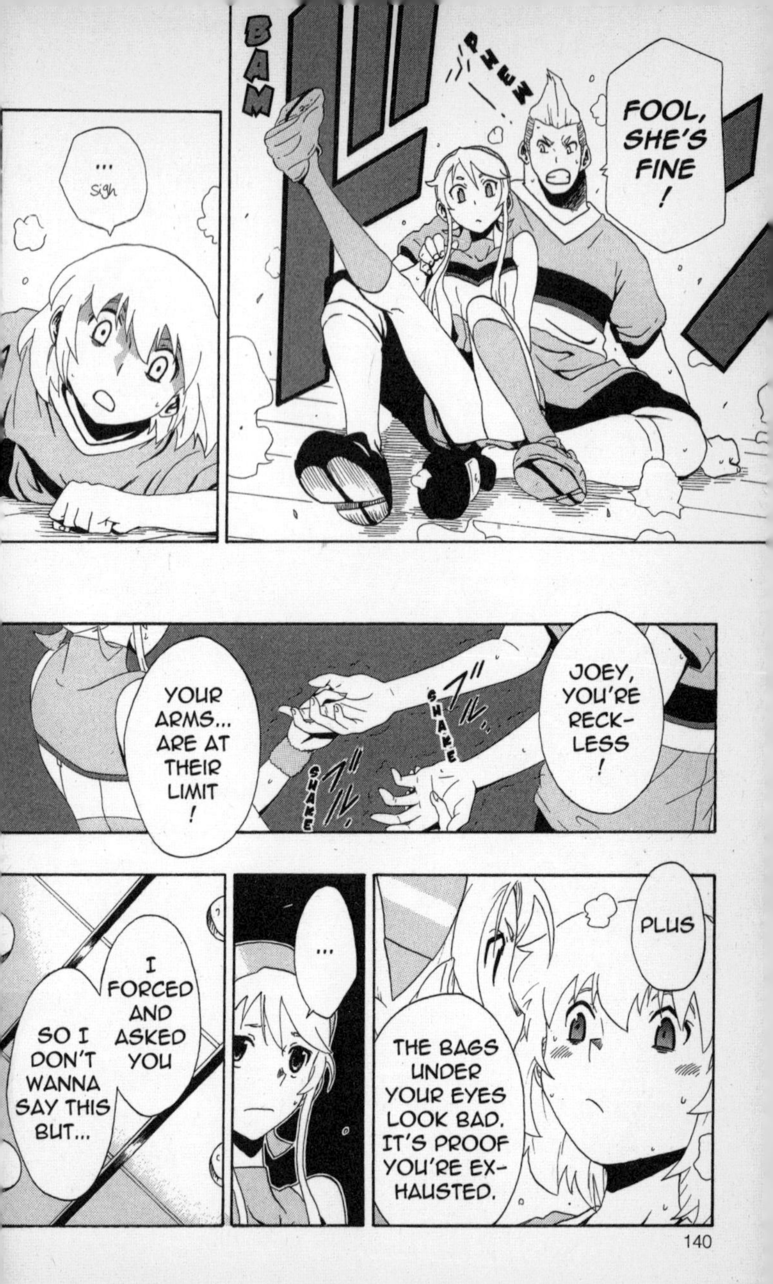
BAM
PHEW
FOOL, SHE'S FINE!
... Sigh
JOEY, YOU'RE RECK-LESS!
SHAKE
SHAKE
YOUR ARMS... ARE AT THEIR LIMIT!
PLUS
THE BAGS UNDER YOUR EYES LOOK BAD. IT'S PROOF YOU'RE EX-HAUSTED.
...
I FORCED AND ASKED YOU
SO I DON'T WANNA SAY THIS BUT...

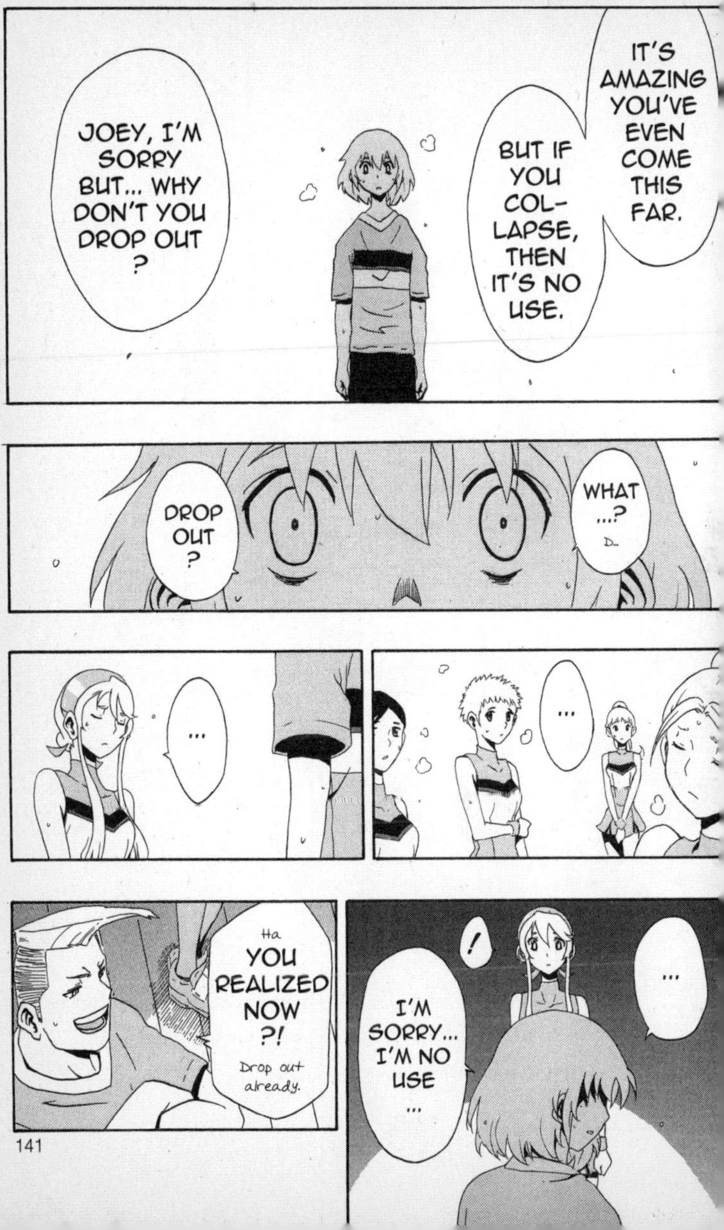
IT'S AMAZING YOU'VE EVEN COME THIS FAR.
BUT IF YOU COL-LAPSE, THEN IT'S NO USE.
JOEY, I'M SORRY BUT... WHY DON'T YOU DROP OUT ?
WHAT ...?
D...
DROP OUT ?
...
...
...
!
I'M SORRY... I'M NO USE ...
Ha
YOU REALIZED NOW ?!
Drop out already.

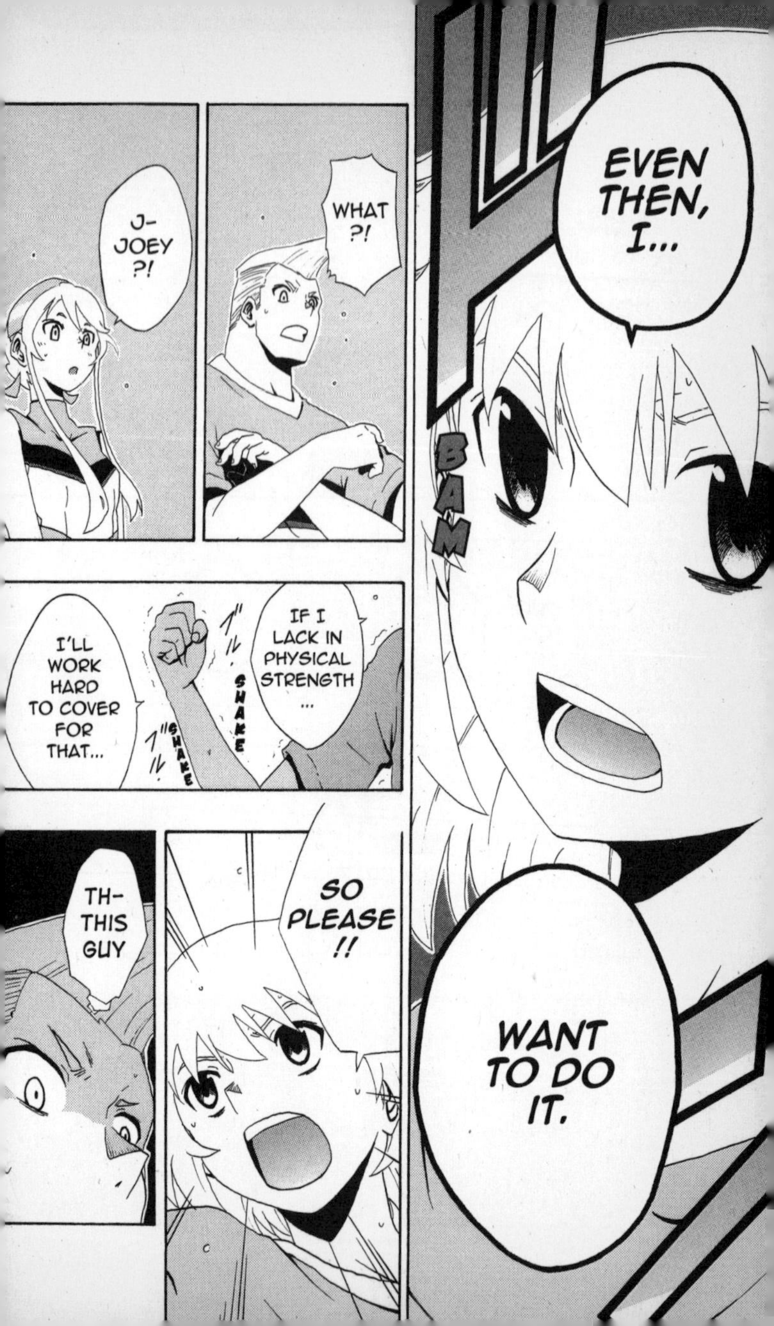
EVEN THEN, I...
BAM
WANT TO DO IT.
WHAT?!
J-JOEY?!
IF I LACK IN PHYSICAL STRENGTH...
SHAKE
SHAKE
I'LL WORK HARD TO COVER FOR THAT...
SO PLEASE!!
TH- THIS GUY

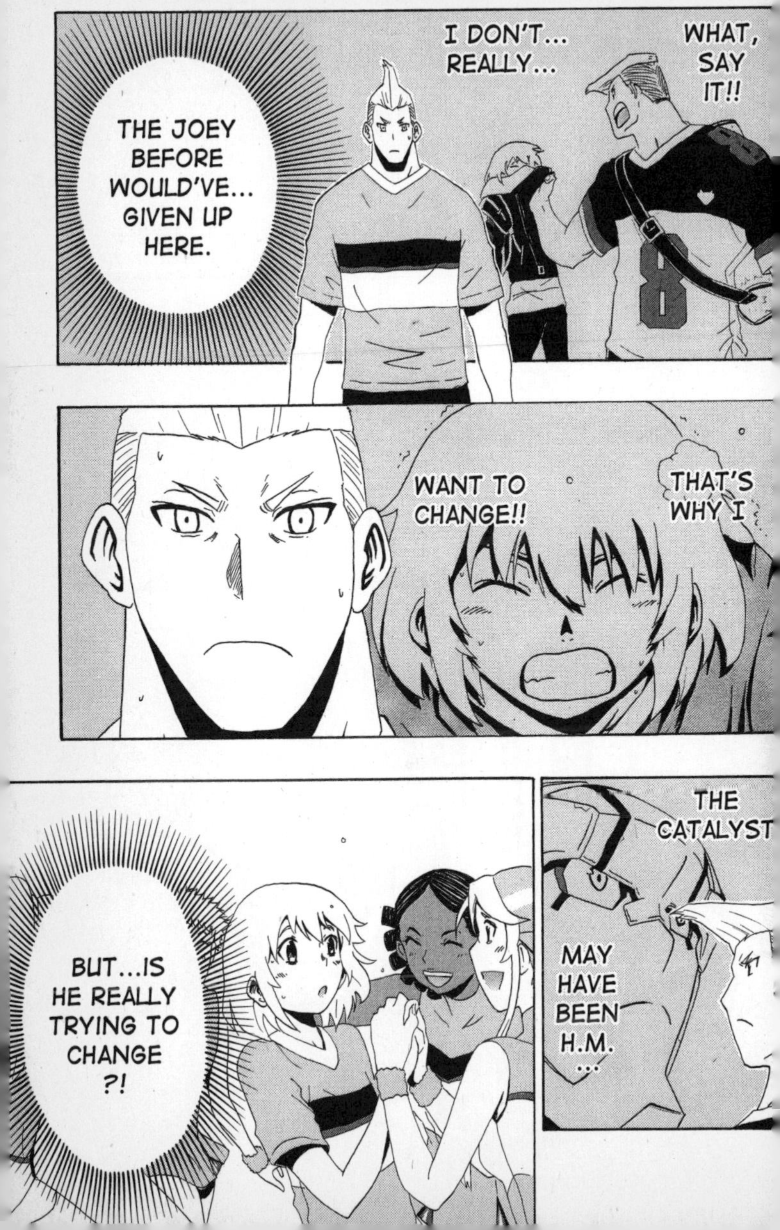
WHAT, SAY IT!!
I DON'T... REALLY...
THE JOEY BEFORE WOULD'VE... GIVEN UP HERE.
THAT'S WHY I
WANT TO CHANGE!!
THE CATALYST
MAY HAVE BEEN H.M. ...
BUT...IS HE REALLY TRYING TO CHANGE ?!

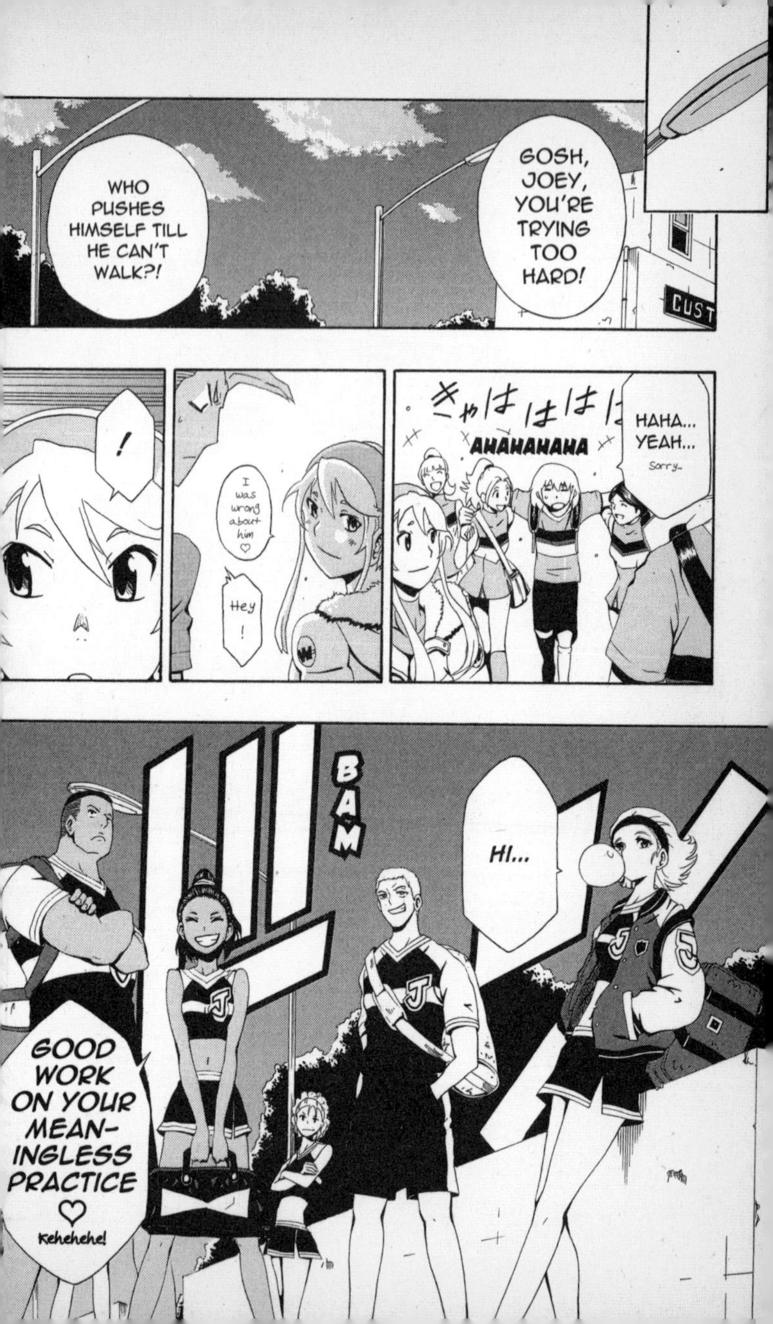

GOSH, JOEY, YOU'RE TRYING TOO HARD!
CUST
WHO PUSHES HIMSELF TILL HE CAN'T WALK?!
きゃははははは
AHAHAHAHA
HAHA... YEAH...
Sorry~
I was wrong about him ♡
Hey!
!
BAM
HI...
GOOD WORK ON YOUR MEAN-INGLESS PRACTICE ♡
Kehehehe!

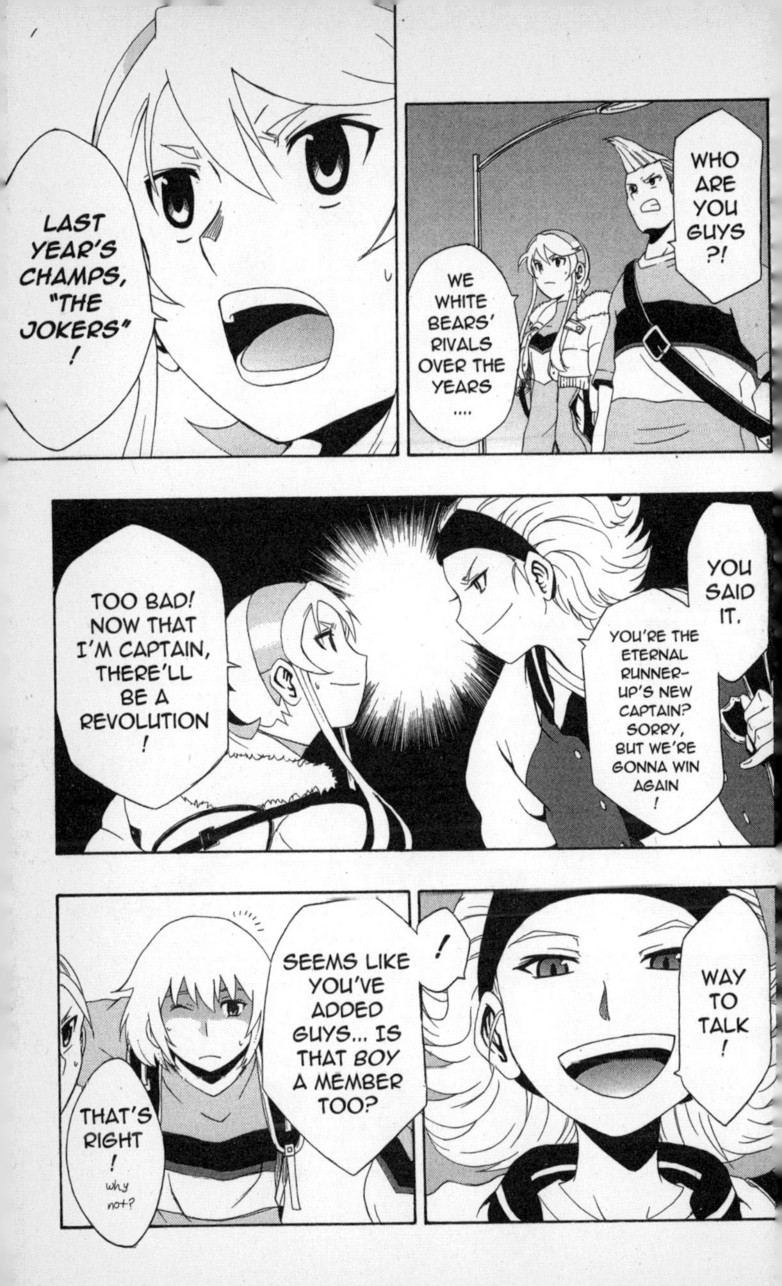

WHO ARE YOU GUYS?!
WE WHITE BEARS' RIVALS OVER THE YEARS....
LAST YEAR'S CHAMPS, "THE JOKERS"!
YOU SAID IT.
YOU'RE THE ETERNAL RUNNER-UP'S NEW CAPTAIN? SORRY, BUT WE'RE GONNA WIN AGAIN!
TOO BAD! NOW THAT I'M CAPTAIN, THERE'LL BE A REVOLUTION!
WAY TO TALK!
!
SEEMS LIKE YOU'VE ADDED GUYS... IS THAT *BOY* A MEMBER TOO?
THAT'S RIGHT! why not?

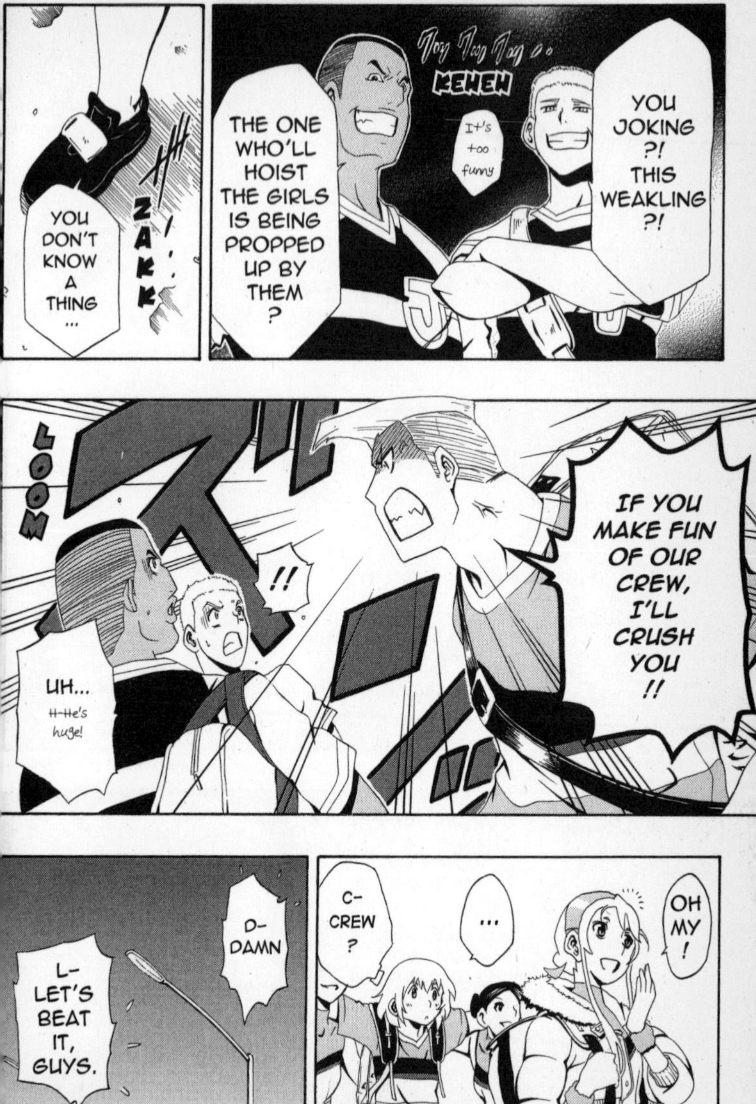
KEHEH
YOU JOKING?! THIS WEAKLING?!
It's too funny
THE ONE WHO'LL HOIST THE GIRLS IS BEING PROPPED UP BY THEM?
ZAKK
YOU DON'T KNOW A THING...
IF YOU MAKE FUN OF OUR CREW, I'LL CRUSH YOU!!
!!
UH... H-He's huge!
LOOM
OH MY!
...
C-CREW?
D-DAMN
L-LET'S BEAT IT, GUYS.

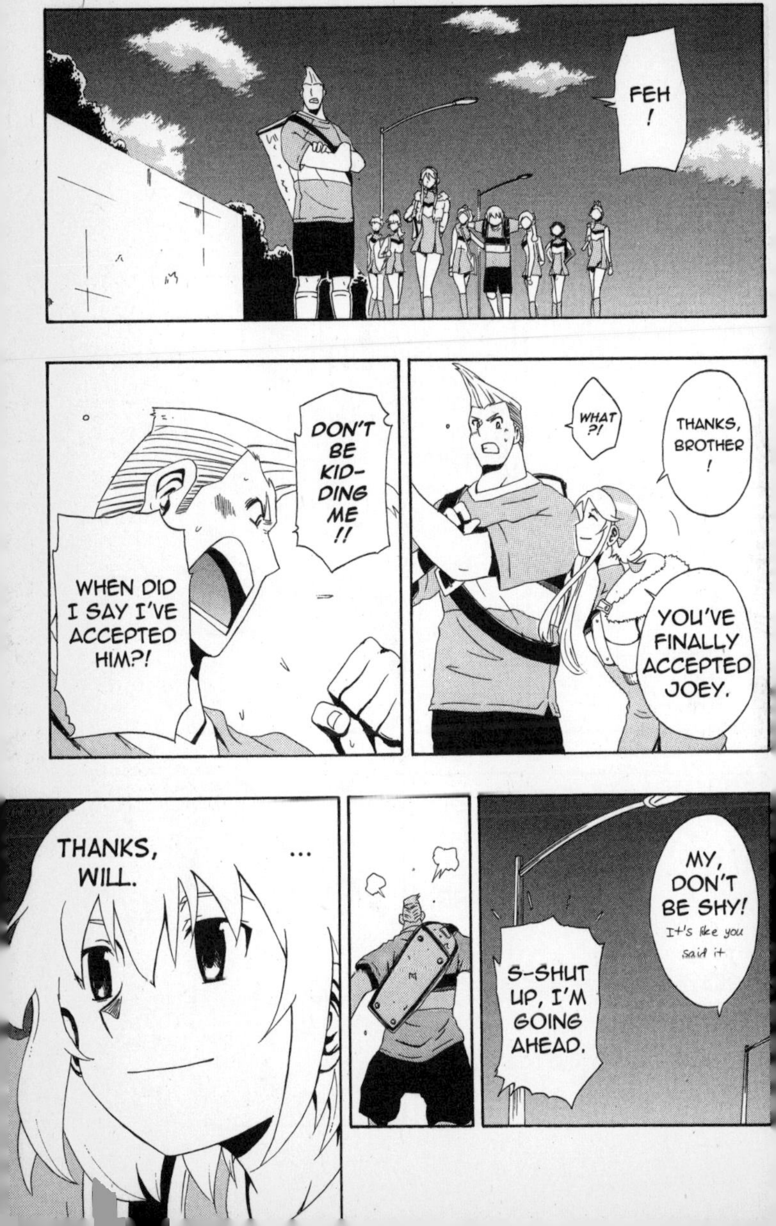
FEH!
THANKS, BROTHER!
YOU'VE FINALLY ACCEPTED JOEY.
WHAT?!
DON'T BE KID-DING ME!!
WHEN DID I SAY I'VE ACCEPTED HIM?!
MY, DON'T BE SHY!
It's like you said it
S-SHUT UP, I'M GOING AHEAD.
...
THANKS, WILL.

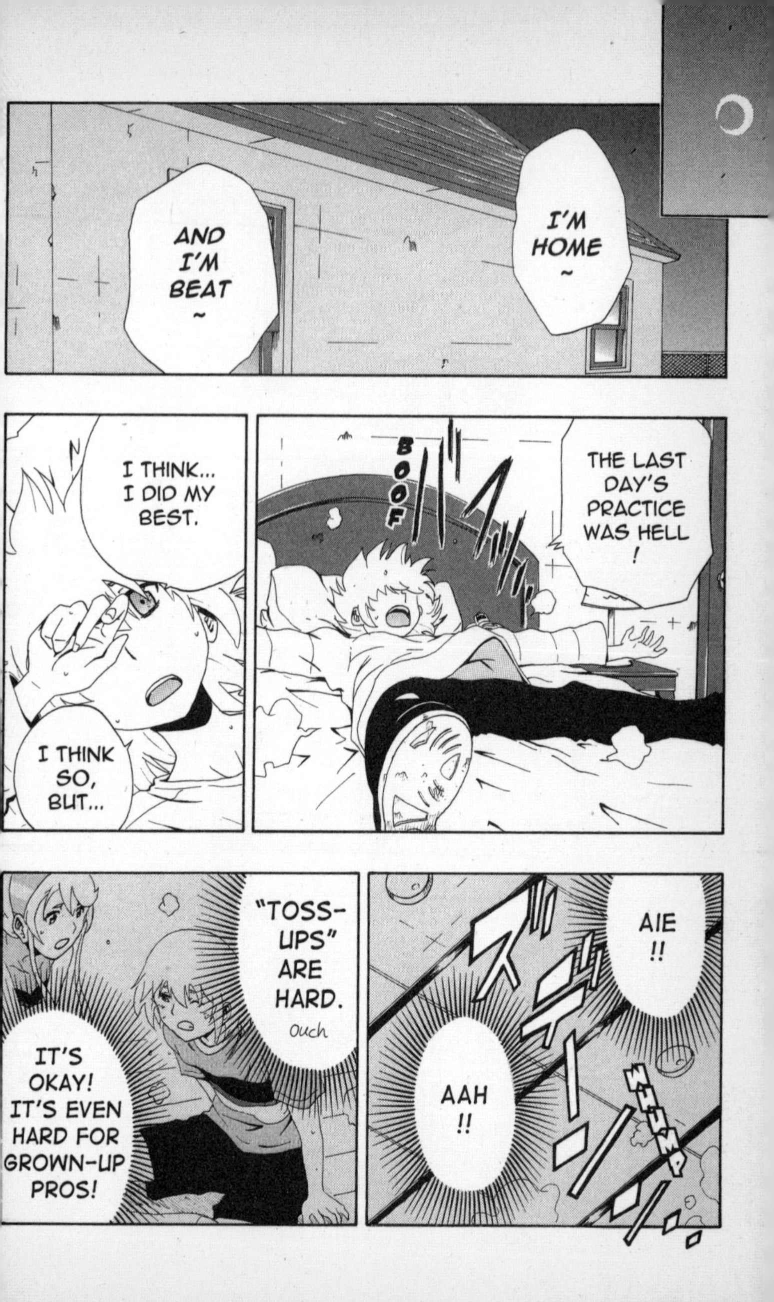
I'M HOME ~
AND I'M BEAT ~
BOOF
THE LAST DAY'S PRACTICE WAS HELL !
I THINK... I DID MY BEST.
I THINK SO, BUT...
AIE !!
AAH !!
WHUMP
"TOSS-UPS" ARE HARD.
ouch
IT'S OKAY! IT'S EVEN HARD FOR GROWN-UP PROS!

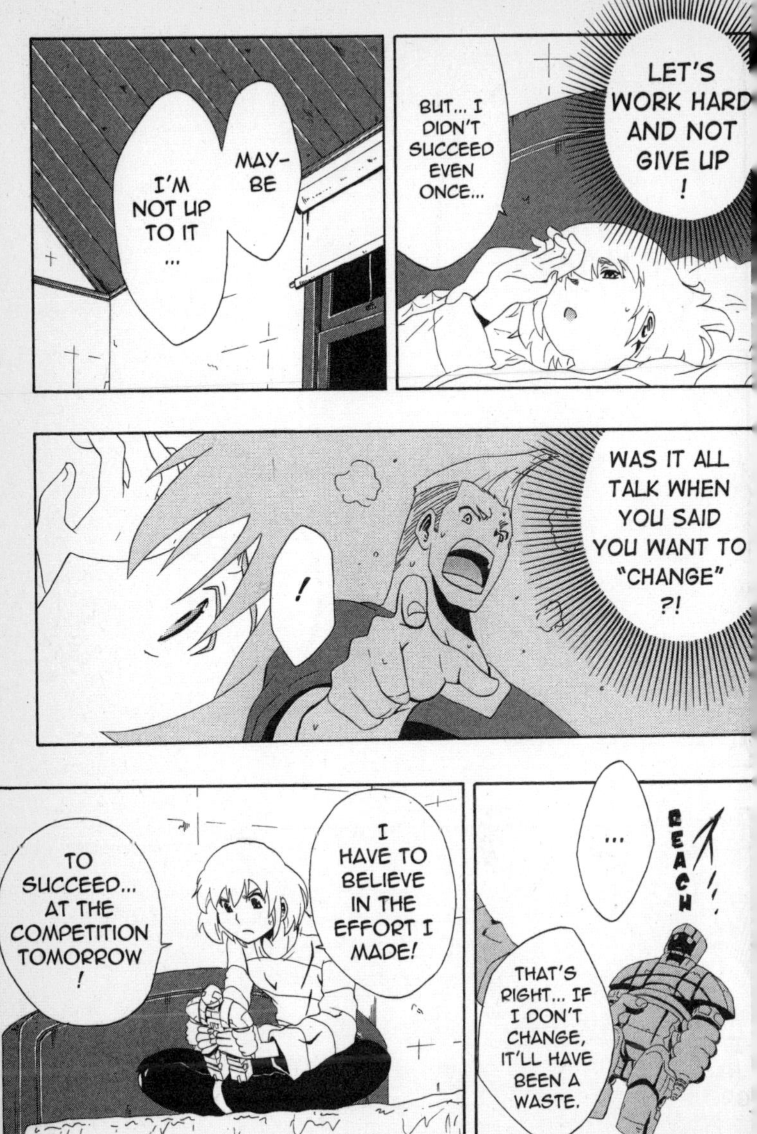
LET'S WORK HARD AND NOT GIVE UP !
BUT... I DIDN'T SUCCEED EVEN ONCE...
MAY-BE
I'M NOT UP TO IT ...
WAS IT ALL TALK WHEN YOU SAID YOU WANT TO "CHANGE" ?!
!
...
REACH
THAT'S RIGHT... IF I DON'T CHANGE, IT'LL HAVE BEEN A WASTE.
I HAVE TO BELIEVE IN THE EFFORT I MADE!
TO SUCCEED... AT THE COMPETITION TOMORROW !

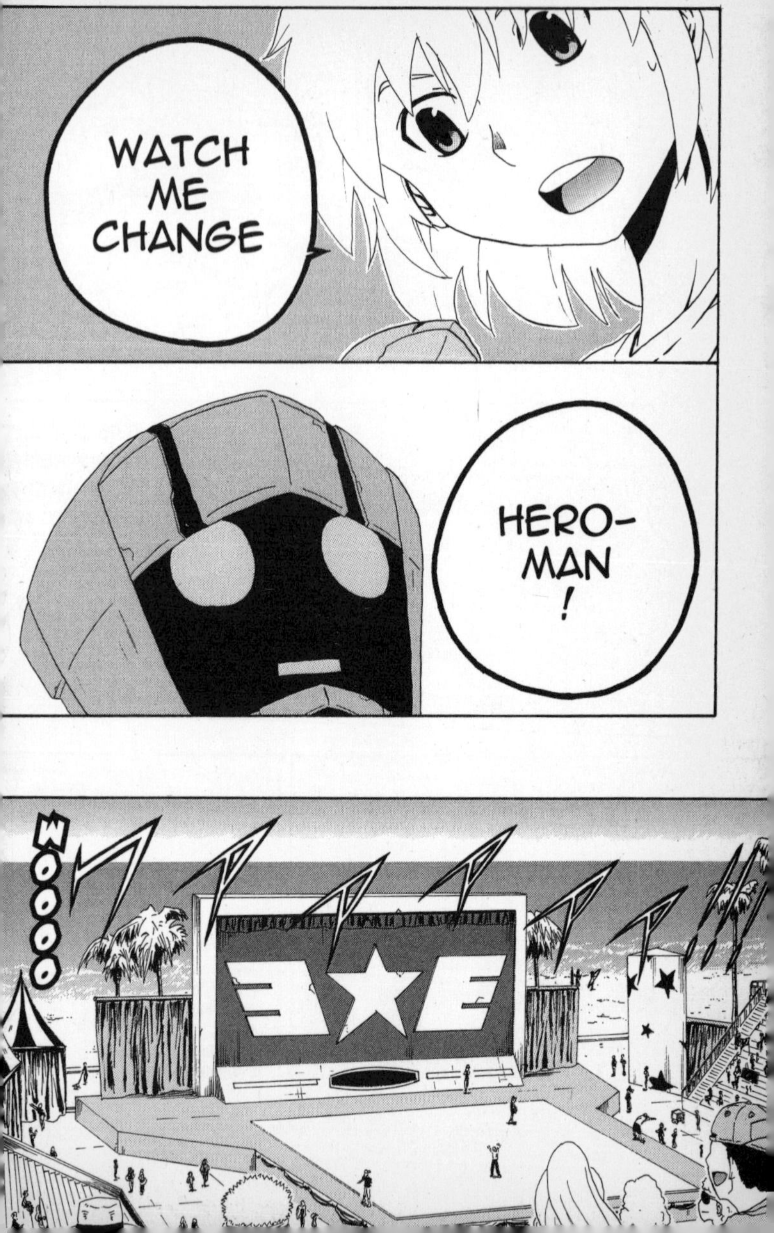
WATCH ME CHANGE
HERO-MAN!
WOOOOO

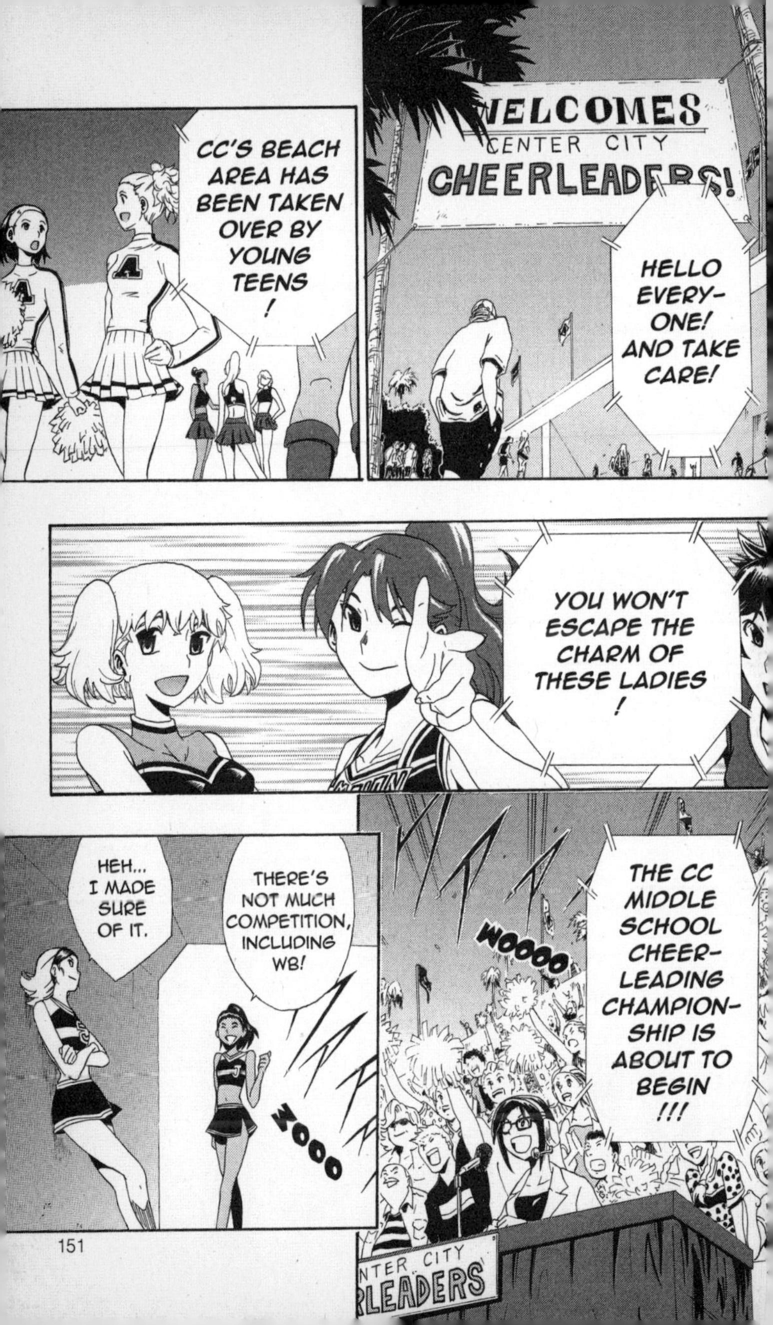
WELCOMES
CENTER CITY
CHEERLEADERS!
HELLO EVERY-ONE! AND TAKE CARE!
CC'S BEACH AREA HAS BEEN TAKEN OVER BY YOUNG TEENS !
YOU WON'T ESCAPE THE CHARM OF THESE LADIES !
THE CC MIDDLE SCHOOL CHEER-LEADING CHAMPION-SHIP IS ABOUT TO BEGIN !!!
WOOOO
NTER CITY
RLEADERS
THERE'S NOT MUCH COMPETITION, INCLUDING WB!
HEH... I MADE SURE OF IT.
WOOO

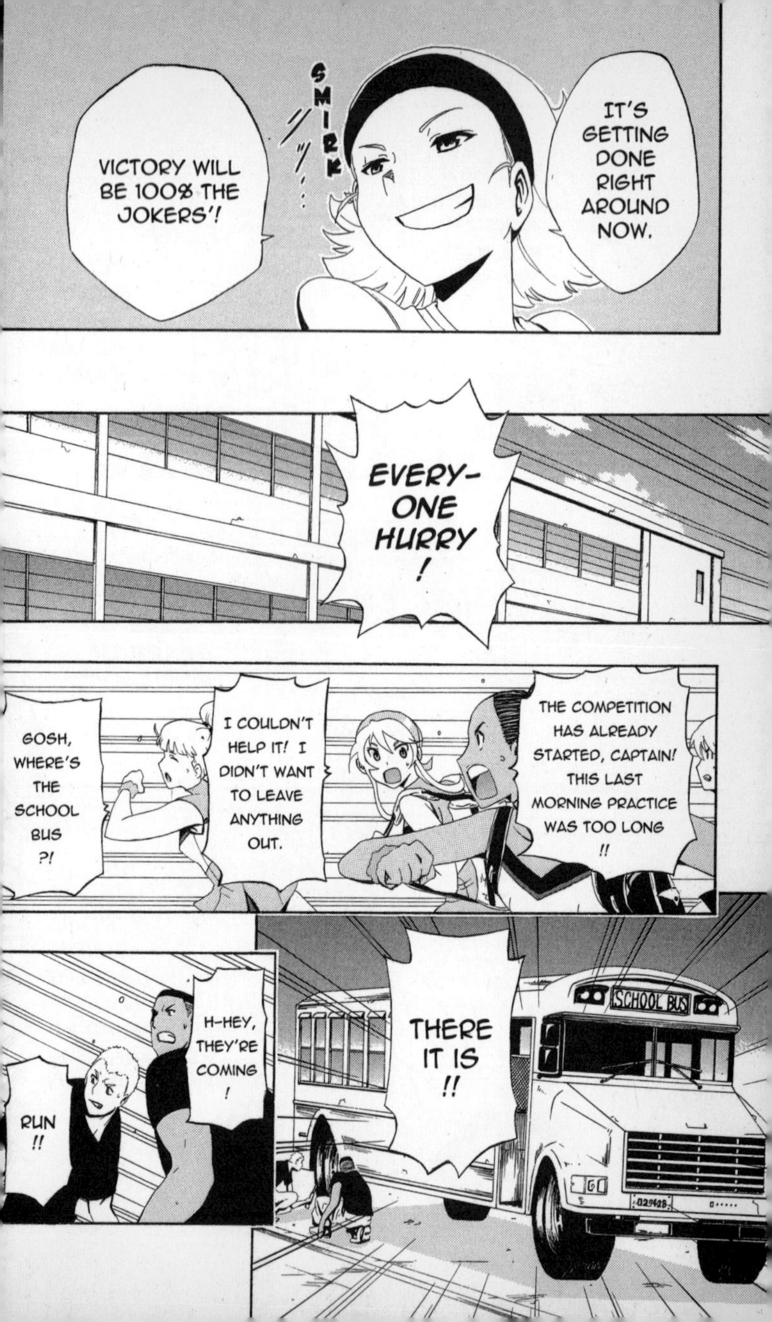
IT'S GETTING DONE RIGHT AROUND NOW.
SMIRK
VICTORY WILL BE 100% THE JOKERS'!
EVERY-ONE HURRY!
THE COMPETITION HAS ALREADY STARTED, CAPTAIN! THIS LAST MORNING PRACTICE WAS TOO LONG!!
I COULDN'T HELP IT! I DIDN'T WANT TO LEAVE ANYTHING OUT.
GOSH, WHERE'S THE SCHOOL BUS?!
THERE IT IS!!
SCHOOL BUS
H-HEY, THEY'RE COMING!
RUN!!

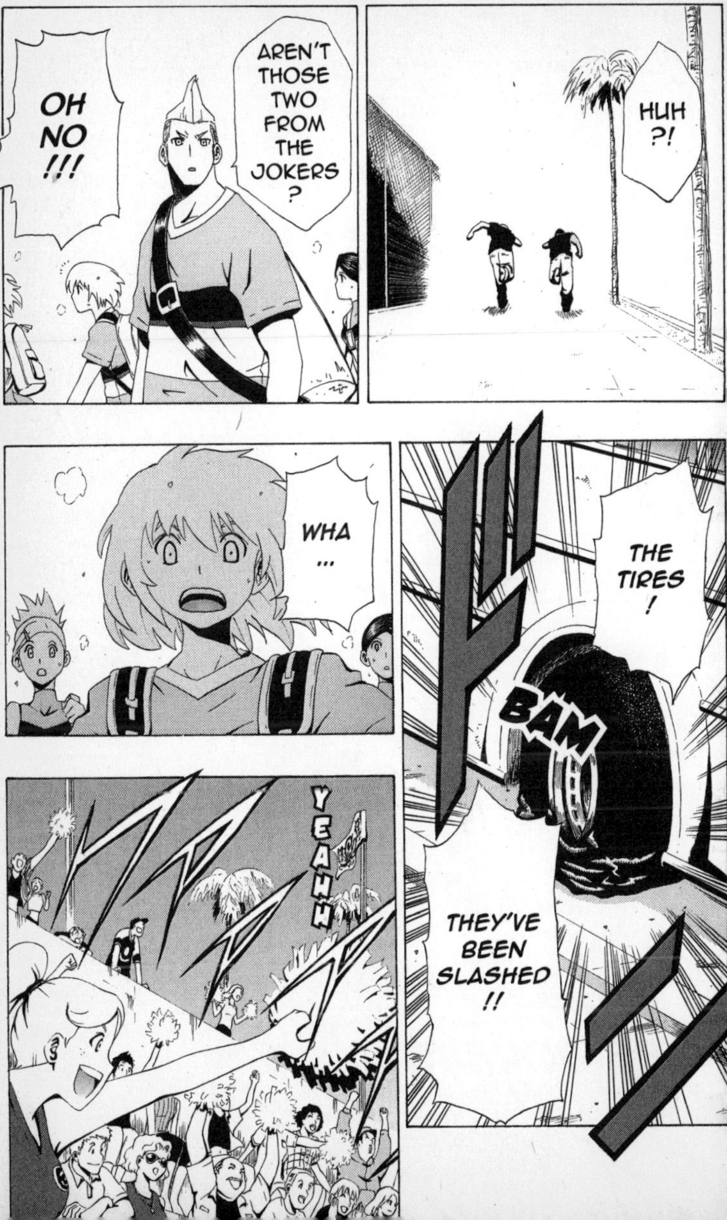
HUH ?!
AREN'T THOSE TWO FROM THE JOKERS ?
OH NO !!!
THE TIRES !
BAM
THEY'VE BEEN SLASHED !!
WHA ...
YEAHH

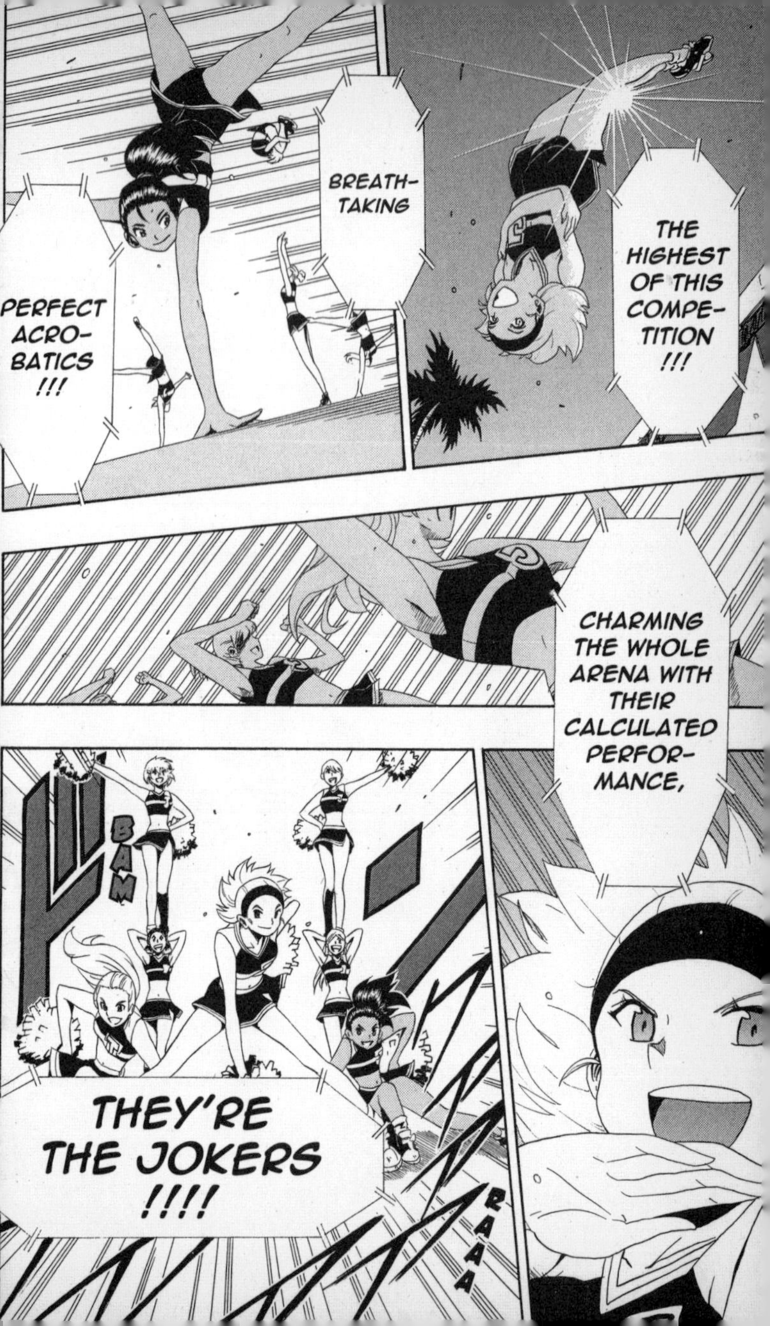
THE HIGHEST OF THIS COMPETITION !!!
BREATH-TAKING
PERFECT ACROBATICS !!!
CHARMING THE WHOLE ARENA WITH THEIR CALCULATED PERFORMANCE,
RAAAA
BAM
THEY'RE THE JOKERS !!!!

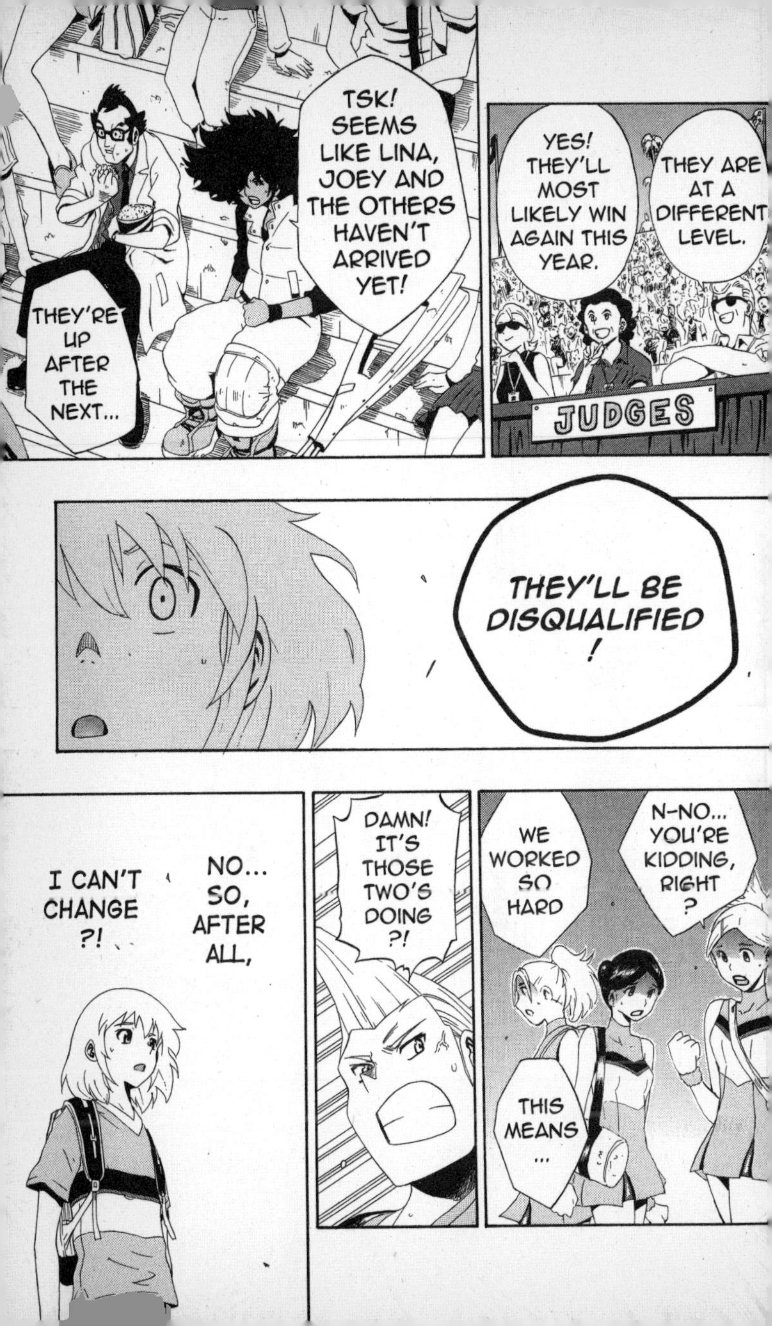
THEY ARE AT A DIFFERENT LEVEL.
YES! THEY'LL MOST LIKELY WIN AGAIN THIS YEAR.
JUDGES
TSK! SEEMS LIKE LINA, JOEY AND THE OTHERS HAVEN'T ARRIVED YET!
THEY'RE UP AFTER THE NEXT...
THEY'LL BE DISQUALIFIED!
N-NO... YOU'RE KIDDING, RIGHT?
WE WORKED SO HARD
THIS MEANS ...
DAMN! IT'S THOSE TWO'S DOING?!
NO... SO, AFTER ALL,
I CAN'T CHANGE?!

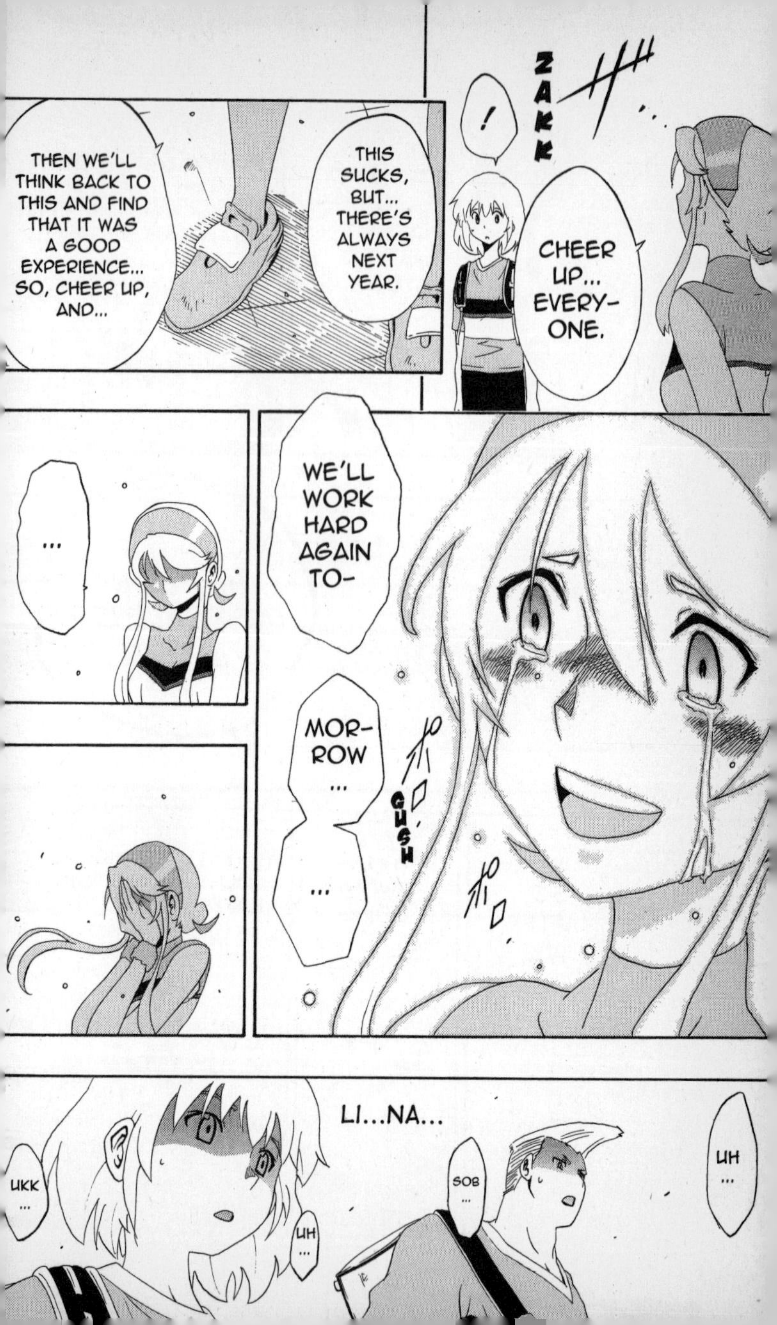
ZAKK
!
CHEER UP... EVERY-ONE.
THIS SUCKS, BUT... THERE'S ALWAYS NEXT YEAR.
THEN WE'LL THINK BACK TO THIS AND FIND THAT IT WAS A GOOD EXPERIENCE... SO, CHEER UP, AND...
WE'LL WORK HARD AGAIN TO-
MOR-ROW...
...
GUSH
...
UH...
SOB...
LI...NA...
UH...
UKK...

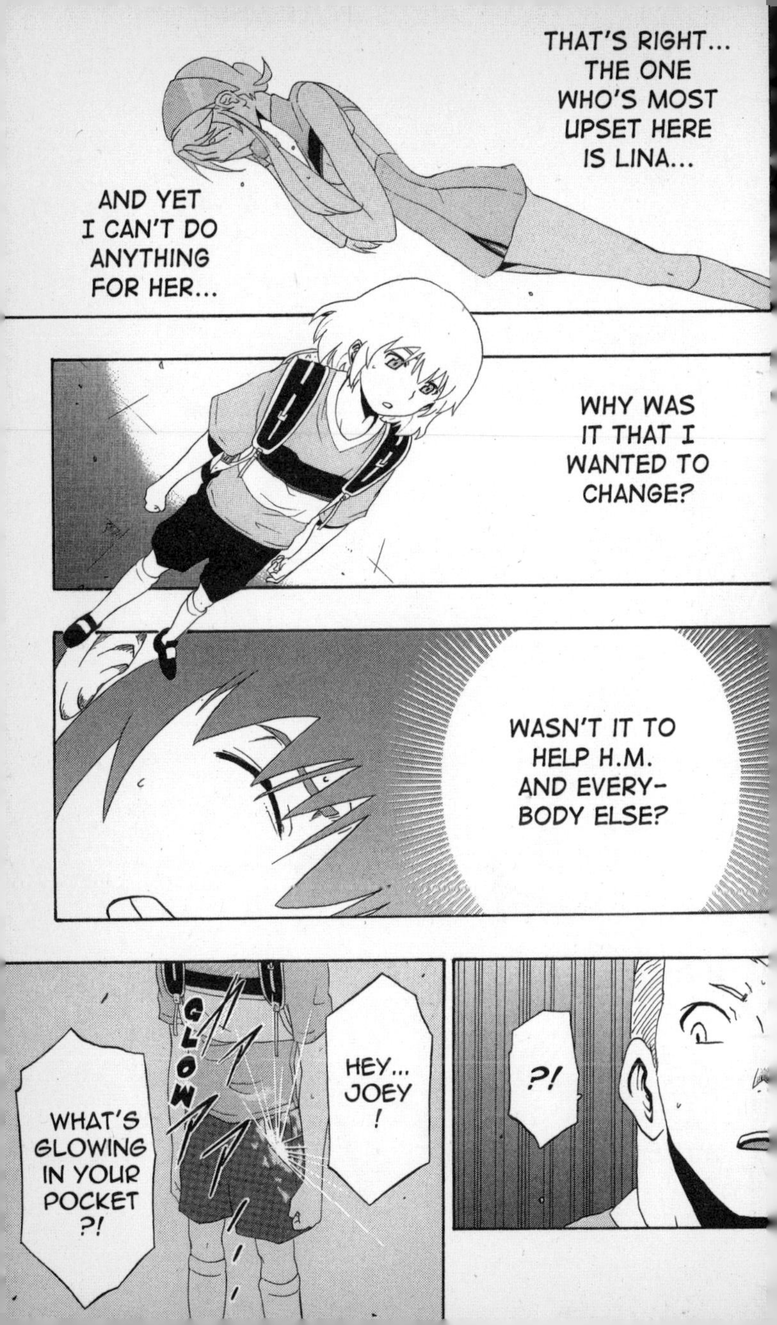
THAT'S RIGHT... THE ONE WHO'S MOST UPSET HERE IS LINA...
AND YET I CAN'T DO ANYTHING FOR HER...
WHY WAS IT THAT I WANTED TO CHANGE?
WASN'T IT TO HELP H.M. AND EVERY-BODY ELSE?
?!
HEY... JOEY!
GLOW
WHAT'S GLOWING IN YOUR POCKET ?!

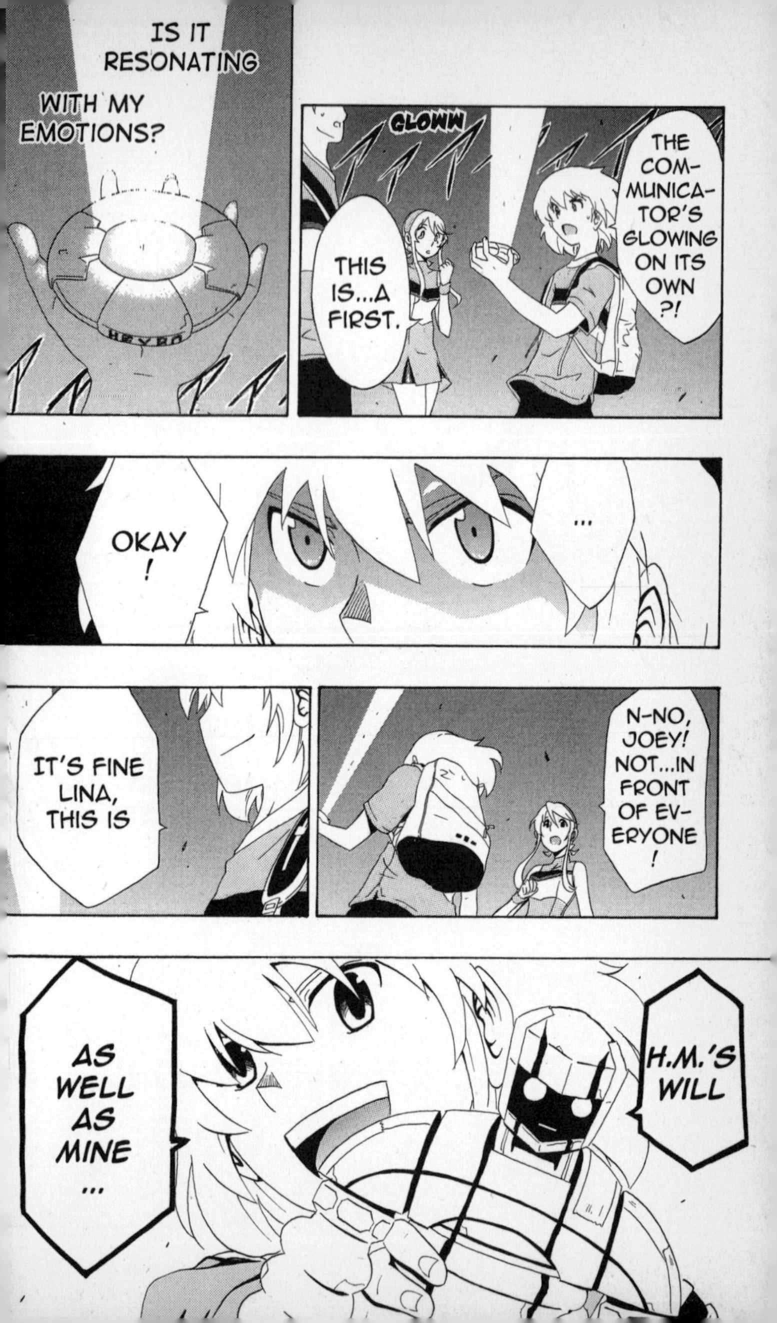
GLOWW
THE COMMUNICATOR'S GLOWING ON ITS OWN?!
THIS IS...A FIRST.
IS IT RESONATING
WITH MY EMOTIONS?
...
OKAY!
N-NO, JOEY! NOT...IN FRONT OF EVERYONE!
IT'S FINE LINA, THIS IS
H.M.'S WILL
AS WELL AS MINE...

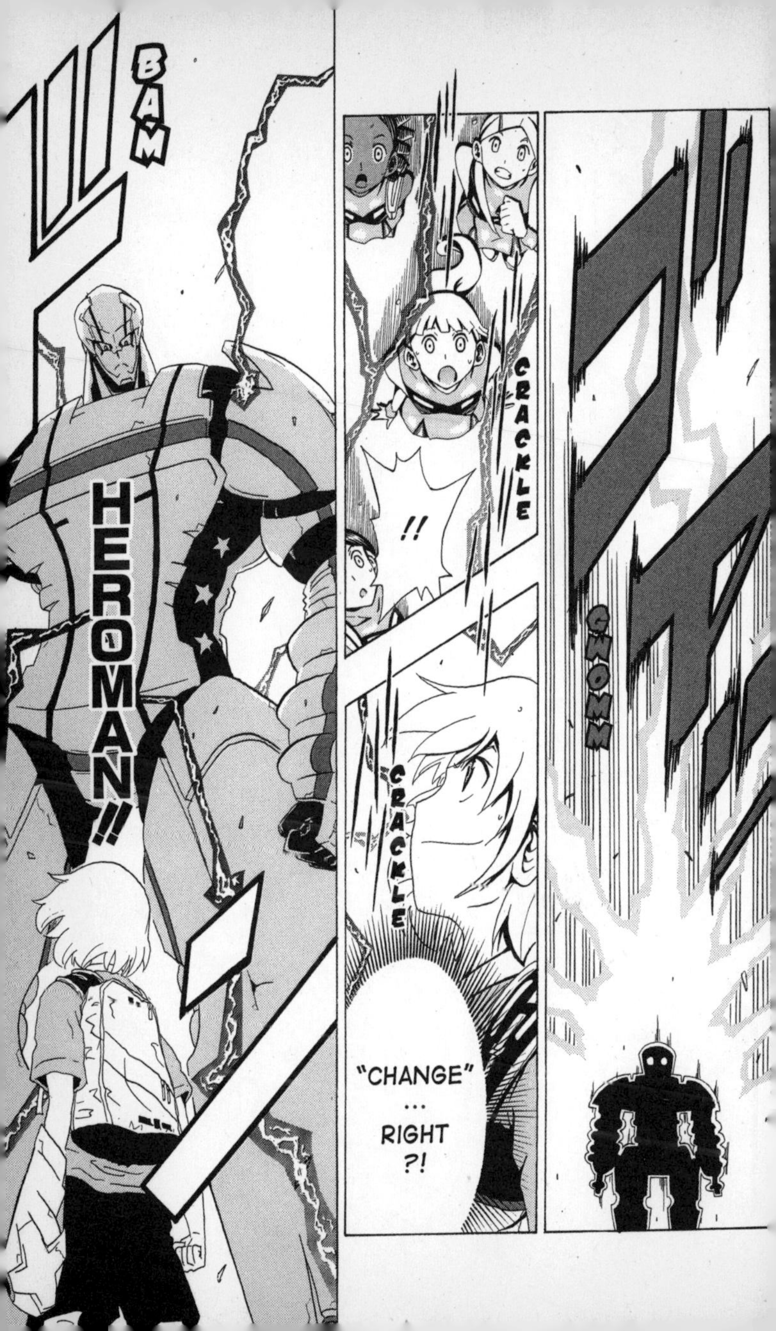

GWOMM
CRACKLE
!!
CRACKLE
"CHANGE" ... RIGHT ?!
BAM
HEROMAN!!

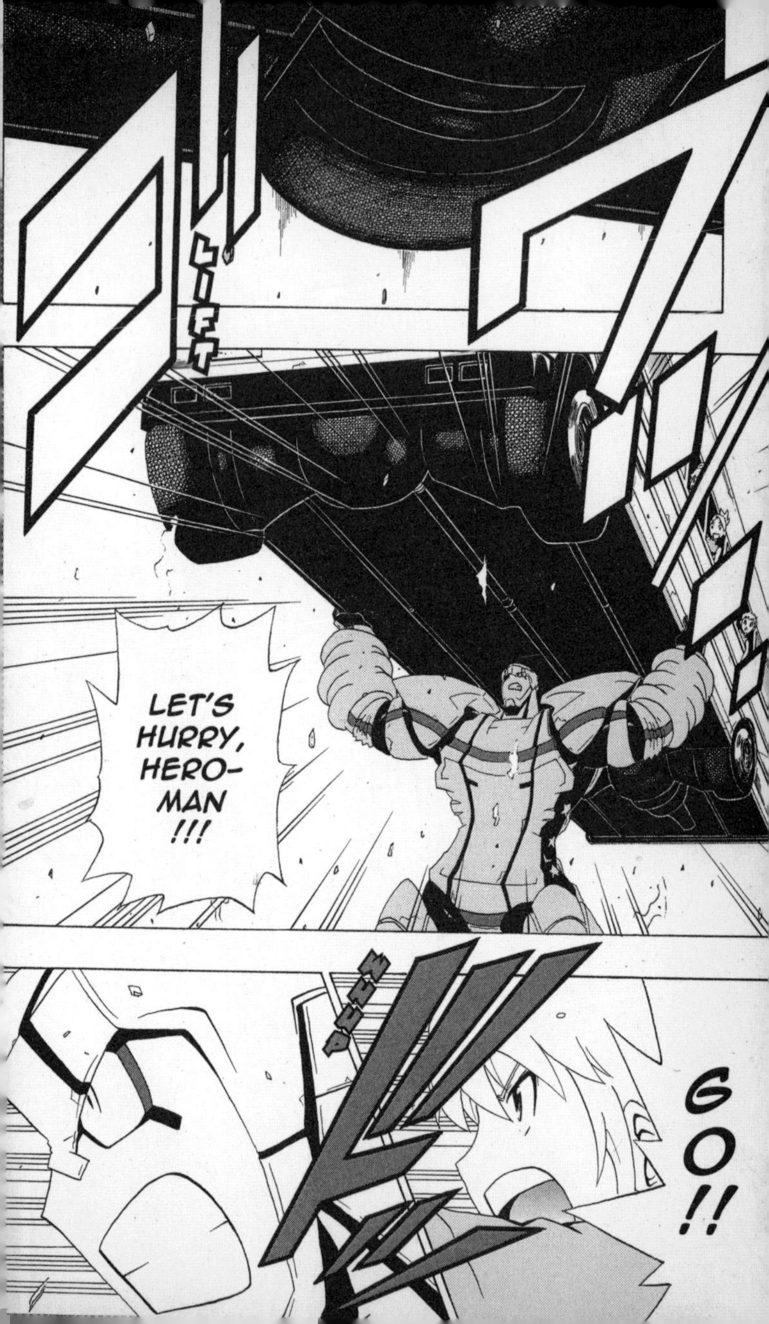
LIFT
LET'S HURRY, HERO-MAN !!!
WHUP
GO!!

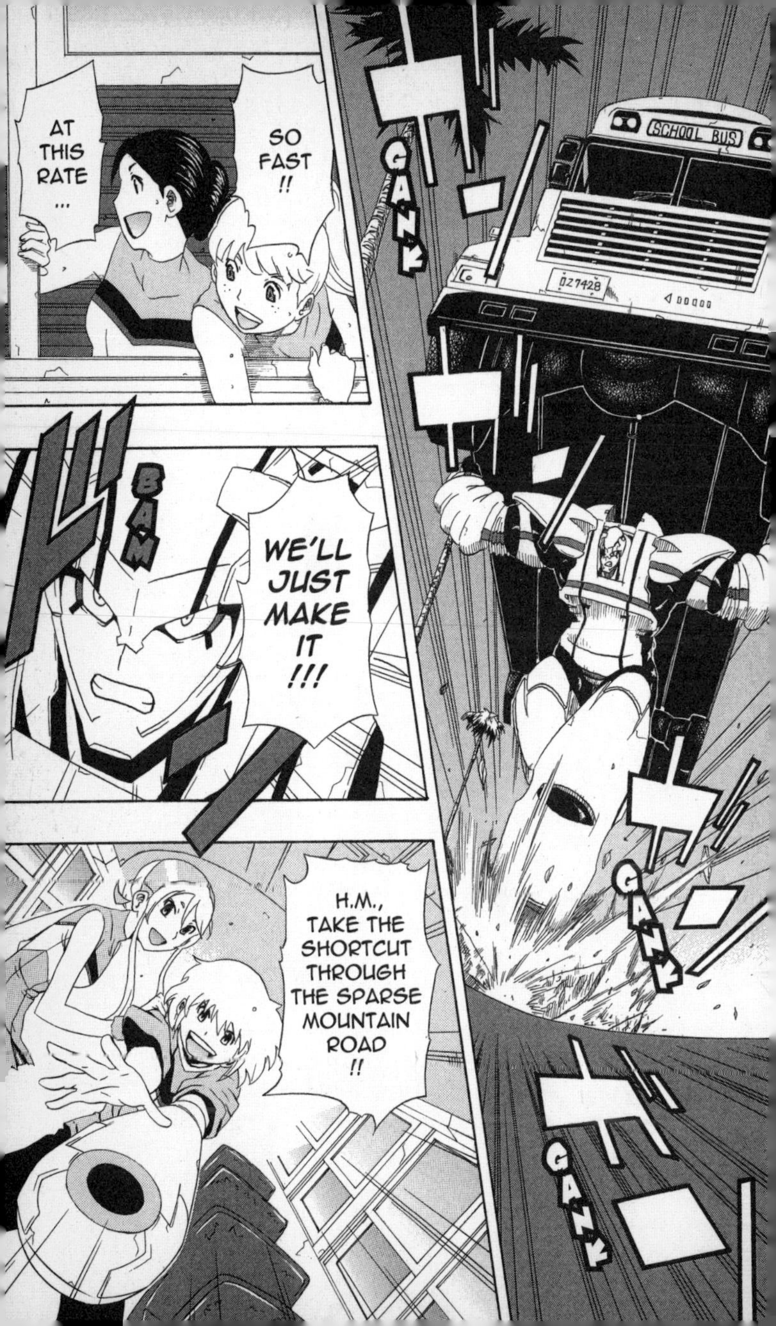
SCHOOL BUS
DZ7428
GANK
GANK
GANK
SO FAST !!
AT THIS RATE ...
WE'LL JUST MAKE IT !!!
BAM
H.M., TAKE THE SHORTCUT THROUGH THE SPARSE MOUNTAIN ROAD !!

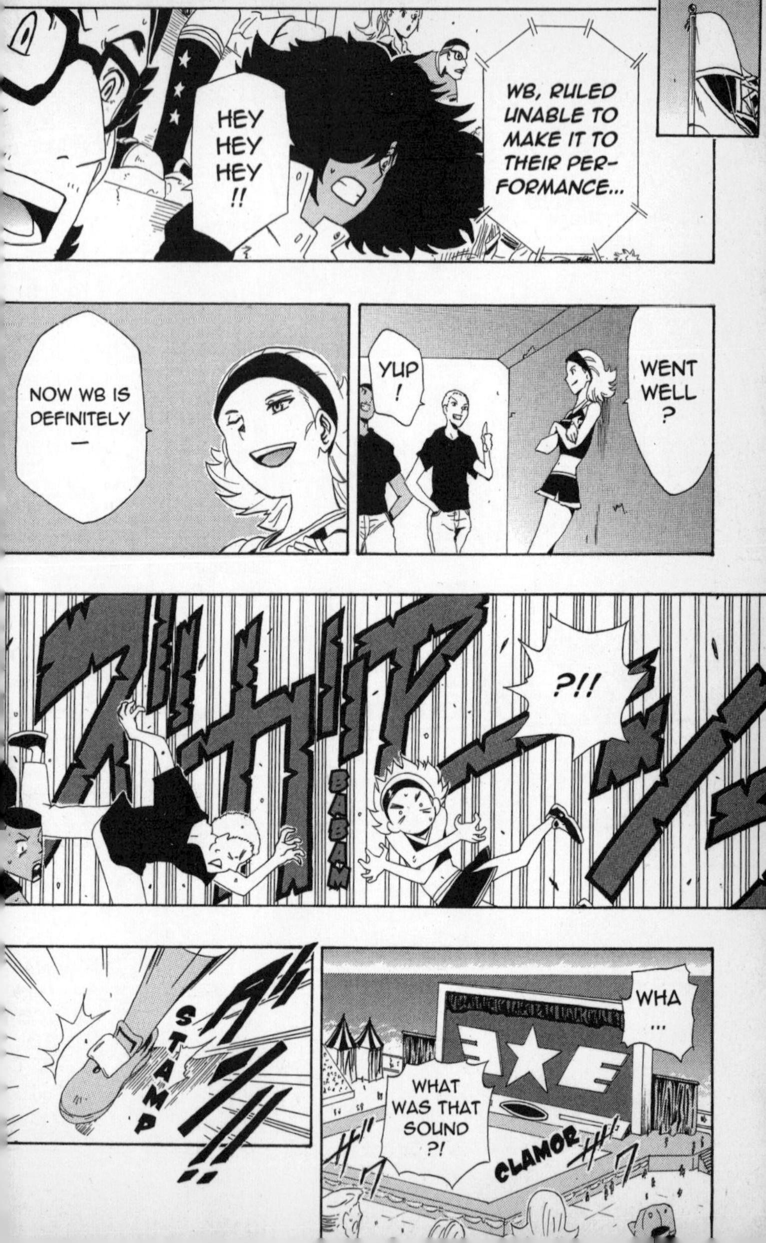
WB, RULED UNABLE TO MAKE IT TO THEIR PER-FORMANCE...
HEY HEY HEY !!
WENT WELL ?
YUP !
NOW WB IS DEFINITELY —
?!!
BABAM
WHA ...
WHAT WAS THAT SOUND ?!
CLAMOR
STAMP

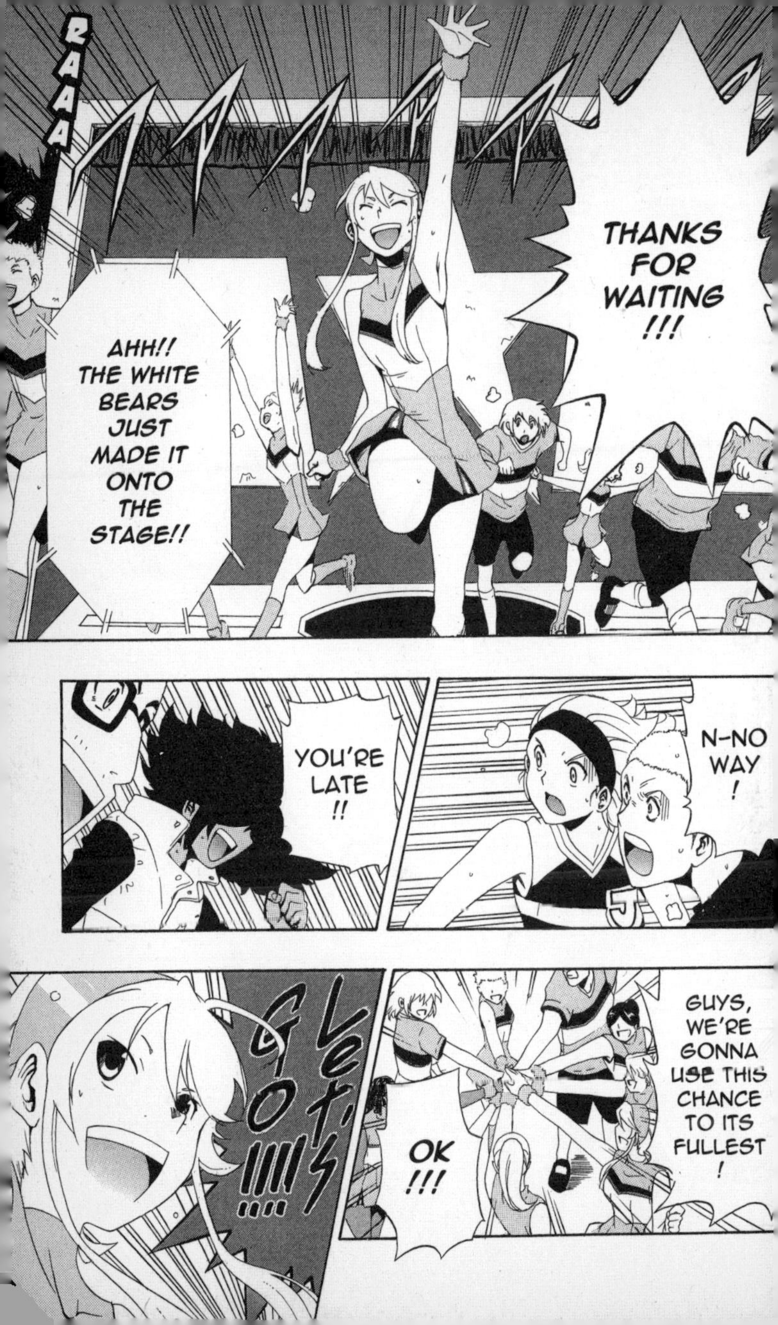
RAAAA
THANKS FOR WAITING !!!
AHH!! THE WHITE BEARS JUST MADE IT ONTO THE STAGE!!
N-NO WAY !
YOU'RE LATE !!
GUYS, WE'RE GONNA USE THIS CHANCE TO ITS FULLEST !
OK !!!
LET'S GO!!!!!!

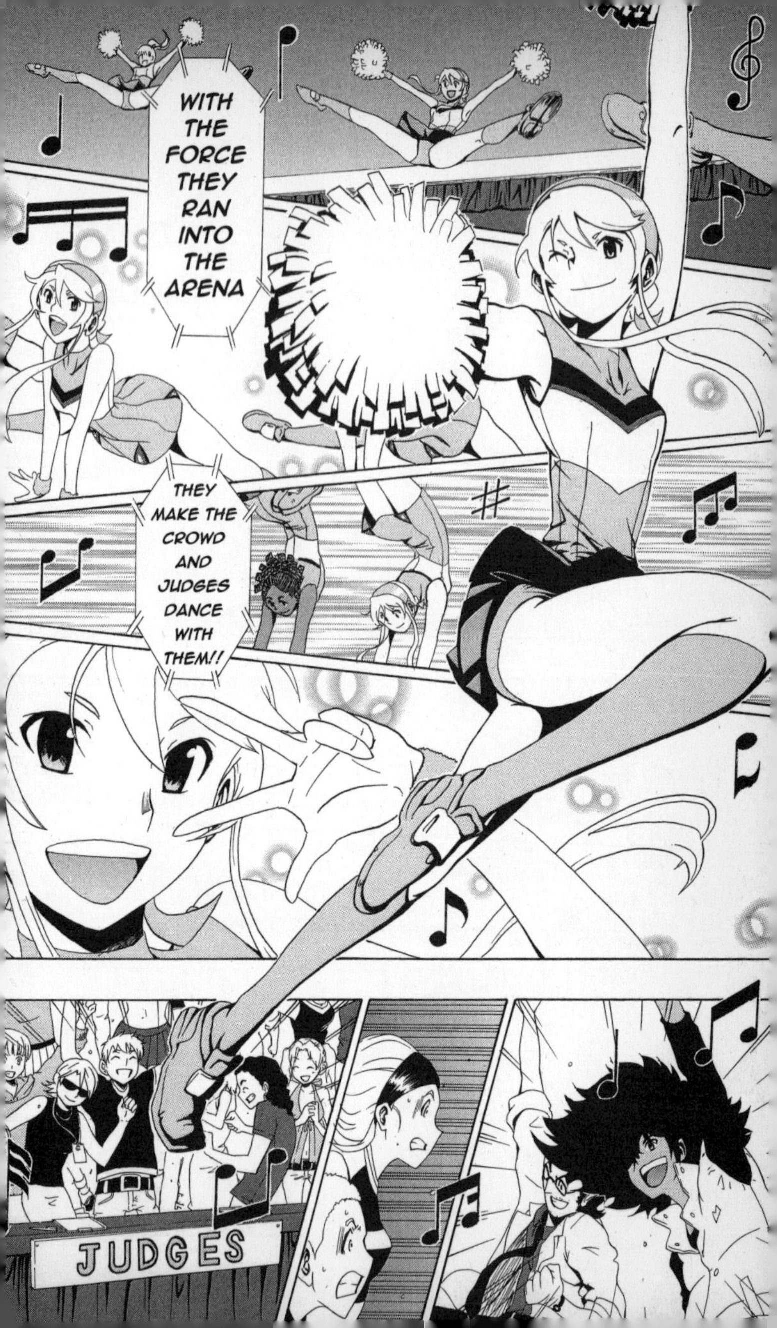
WITH THE FORCE THEY RAN INTO THE ARENA
THEY MAKE THE CROWD AND JUDGES DANCE WITH THEM!!
JUDGES

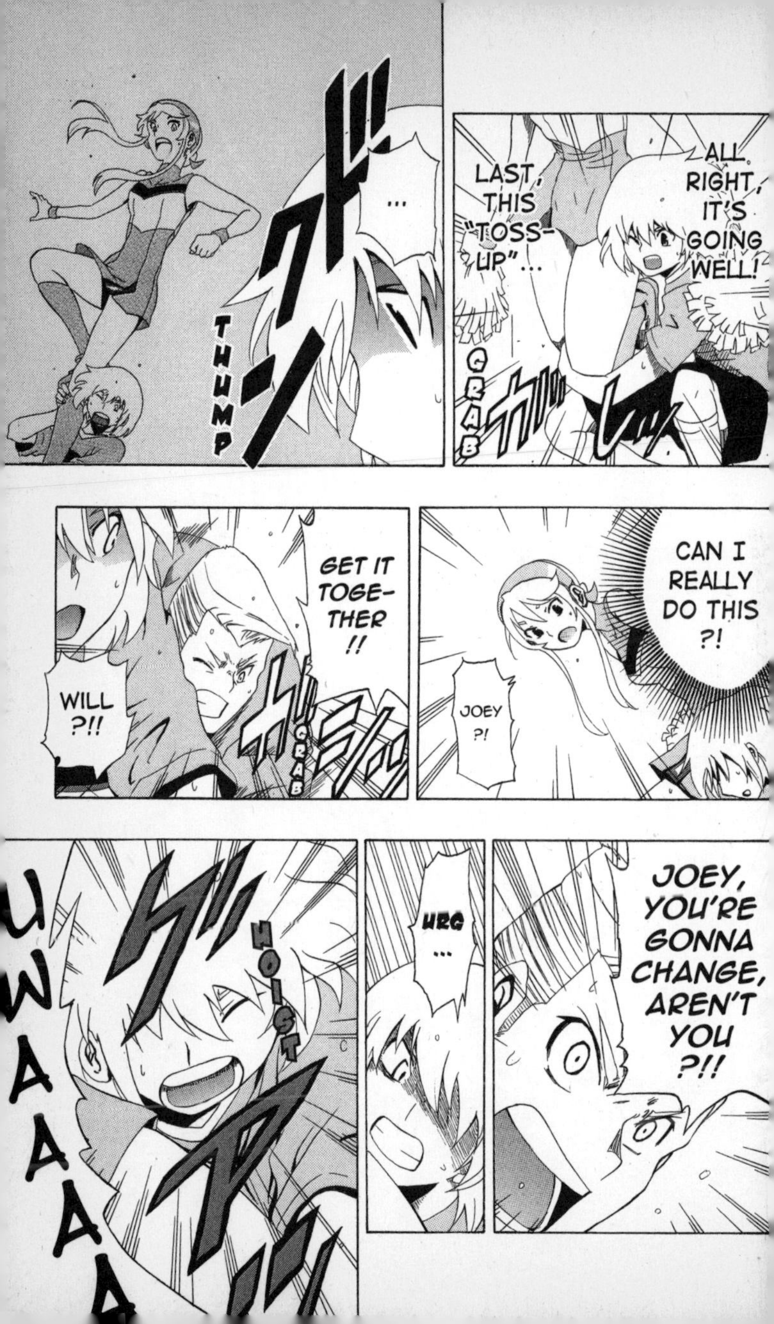
ALL RIGHT, IT'S GOING WELL!
LAST, THIS "TOSS-UP"...
GRAB
...
THUMP
CAN I REALLY DO THIS ?!
JOEY ?!
GET IT TOGE-THER !!
GRAB
WILL ?!!
JOEY, YOU'RE GONNA CHANGE, AREN'T YOU ?!!
URG ...
HOIST
UWAAAA

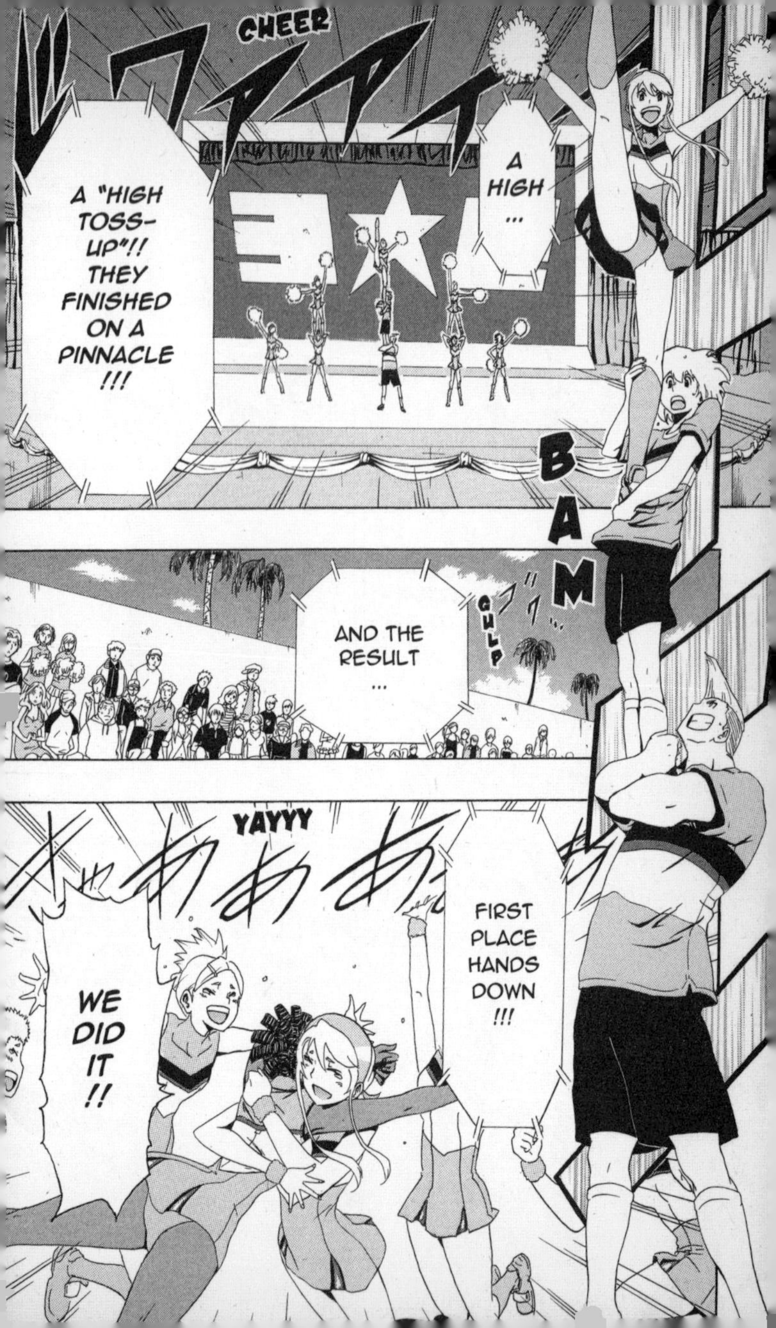
CHEER
A HIGH ...
A "HIGH TOSS-UP"!! THEY FINISHED ON A PINNACLE !!!
BAM
GULP
AND THE RESULT ...
YAYYY
FIRST PLACE HANDS DOWN !!!
WE DID IT !!

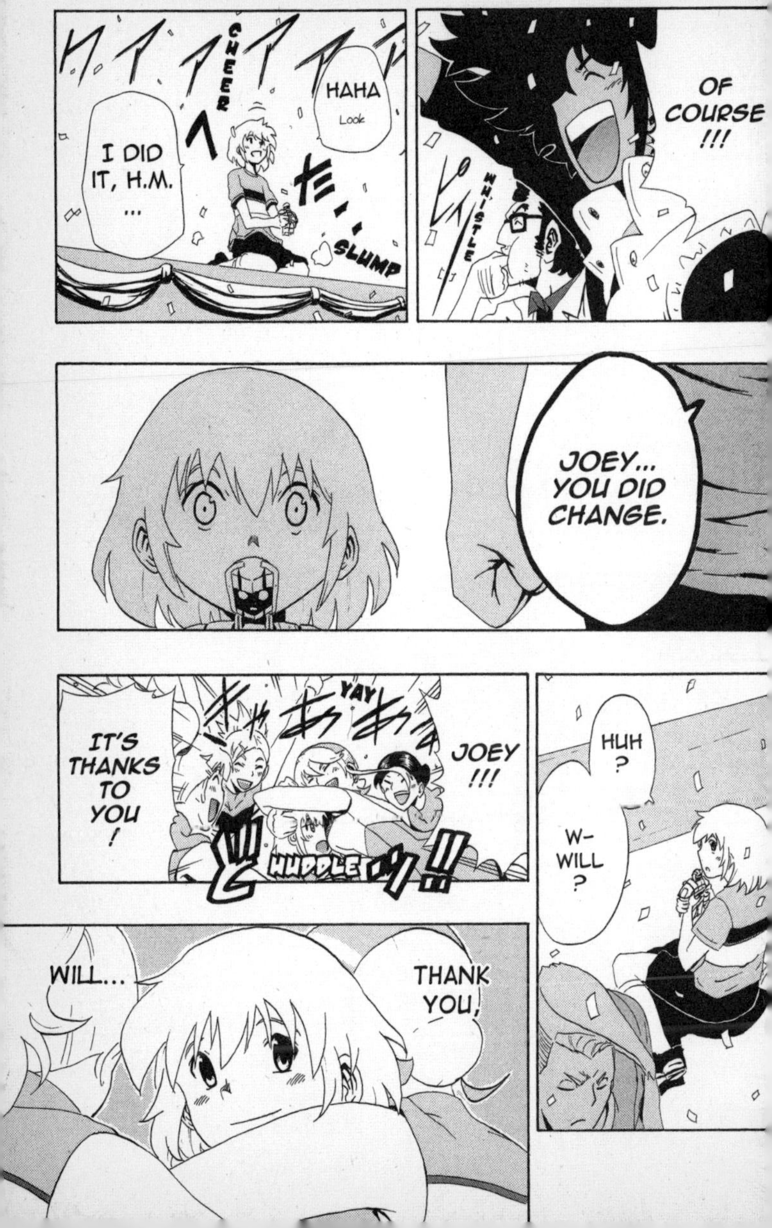
OF COURSE !!!
WHISTLE
CHEER
HAHA
Look
I DID IT, H.M. ...
SLUMP
JOEY... YOU DID CHANGE.
HUH ?
W-WILL ?
YAY
JOEY !!!
IT'S THANKS TO YOU !
HUDDLE
THANK YOU!
WILL...

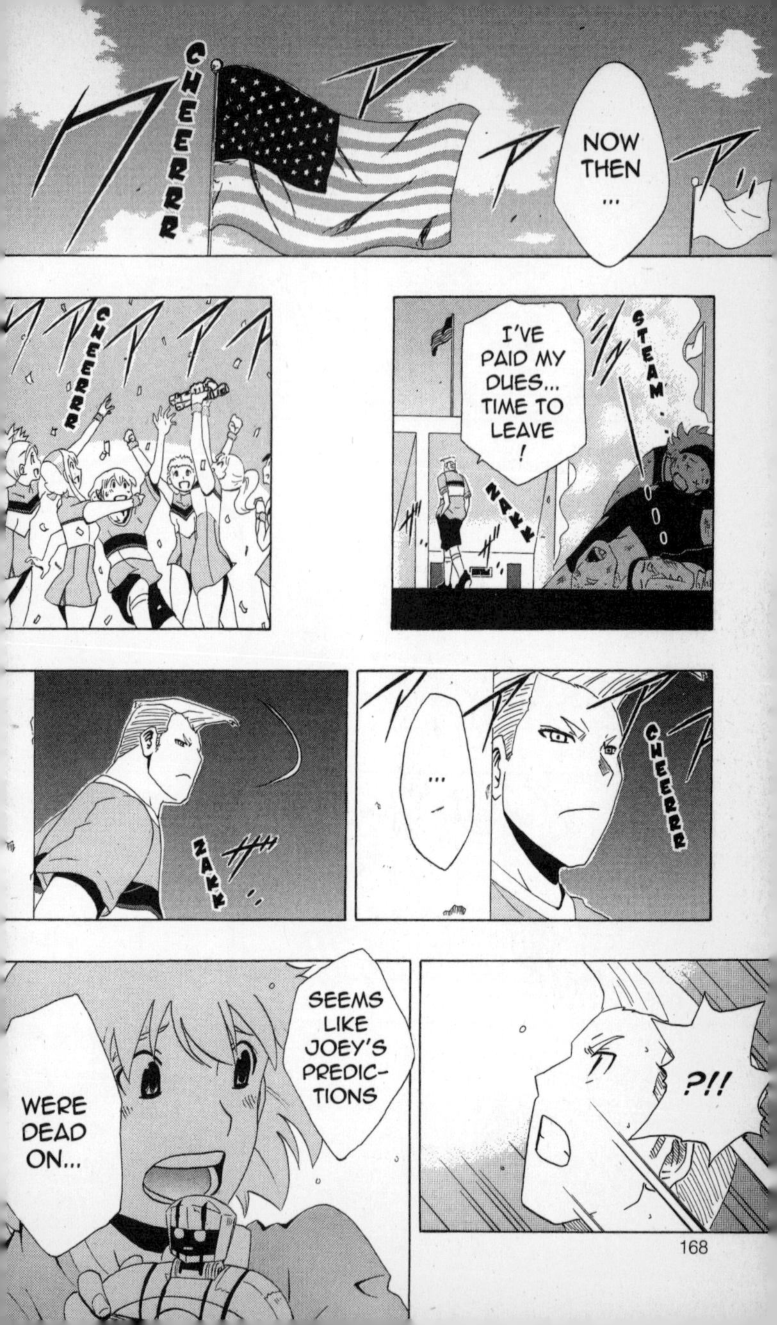
NOW THEN ...
CHEERRR
STEAM
I'VE PAID MY DUES... TIME TO LEAVE!
ZAKK
CHEERRR
CHEERRR
...
ZAKK
?!!
SEEMS LIKE JOEY'S PREDICTIONS
WERE DEAD ON...

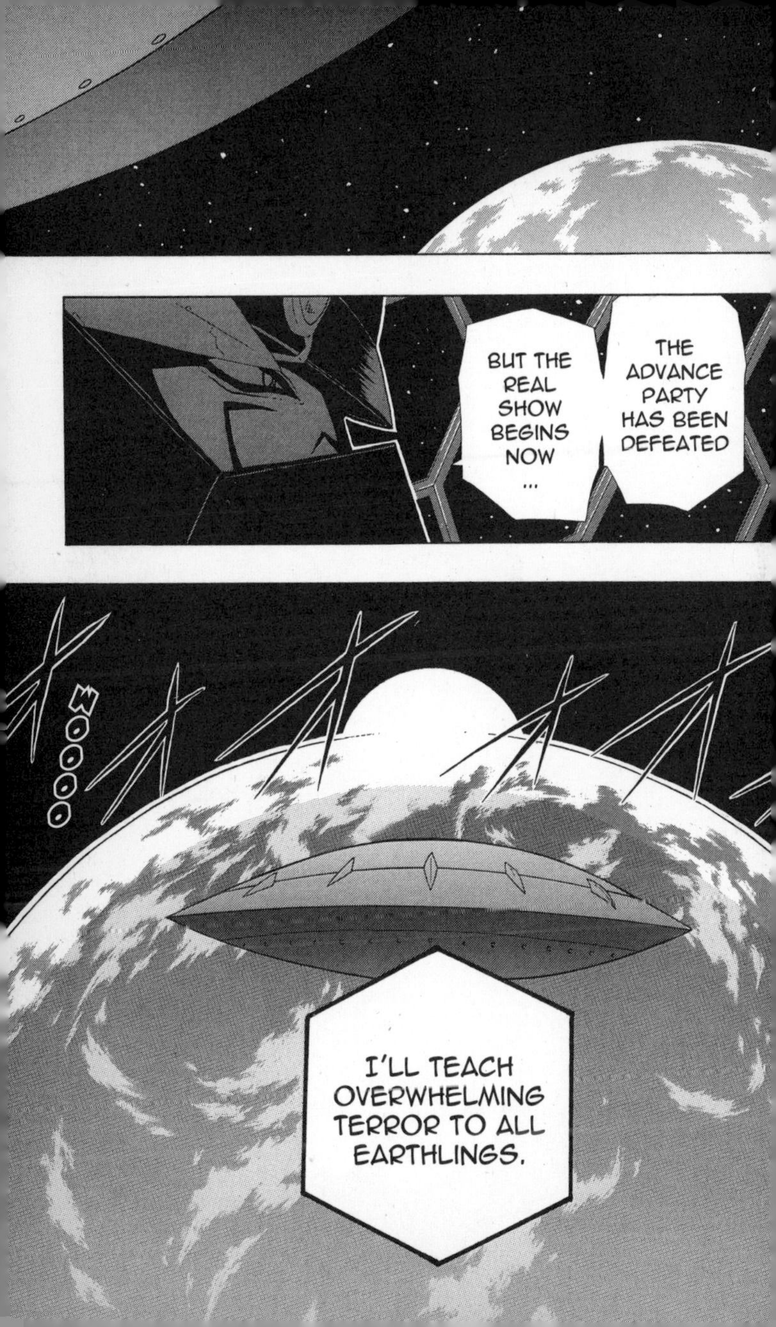
THE ADVANCE PARTY HAS BEEN DEFEATED
BUT THE REAL SHOW BEGINS NOW ...
WOOOOOO
I'LL TEACH OVERWHELMING TERROR TO ALL EARTHLINGS.

HEROMAN

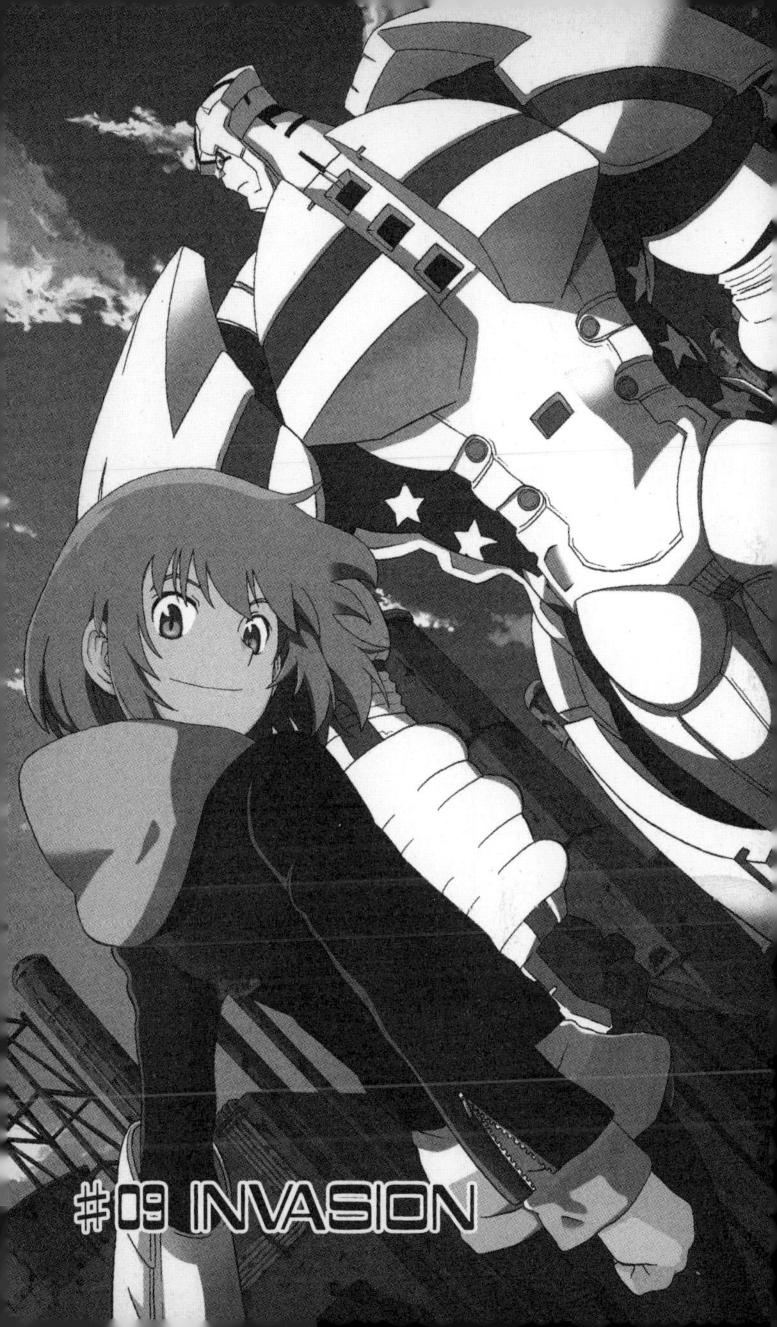
#09 INVASION

—HERO MAN·2—

〈STAFF〉

YUKI SUZUKI

MASATO YOSHIOKA

CHITOSHI AOKI

AYA OTA

HIROSHI IWASAKI

KAZUNORI KUWAHARA

〈SPECIAL THANKS〉

HITOSHI NANBA

SHIGETO KOYAMA

SHINGO TAKEBA

NAOKI AMANO

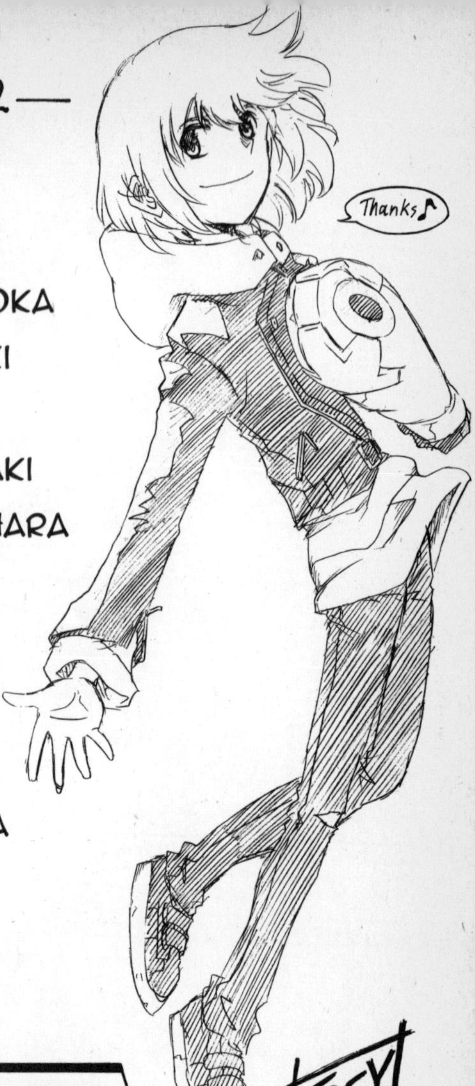
Thanks♪
JOEY
TAMON.

TO BE CONTINUED

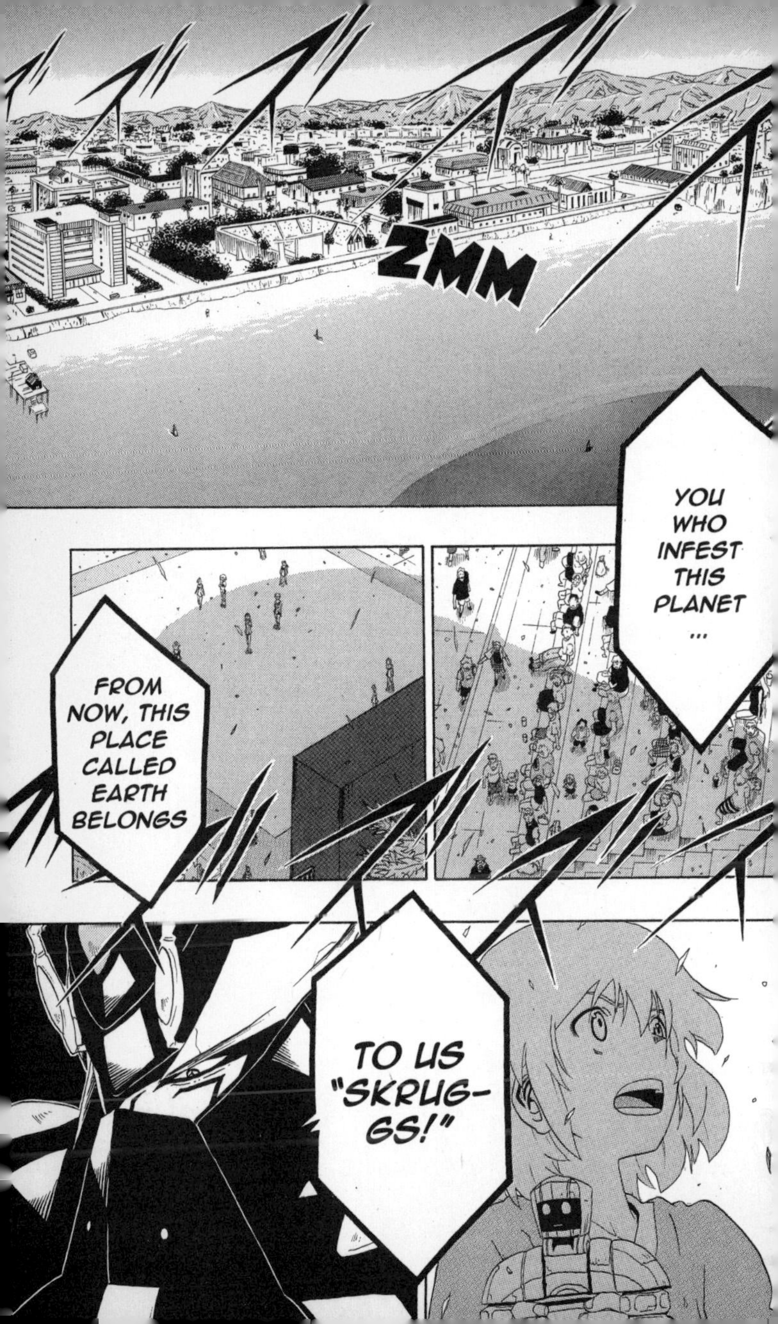
ZMM
YOU WHO INFEST THIS PLANET ...
FROM NOW, THIS PLACE CALLED EARTH BELONGS
TO US "SKRUG-GS!"

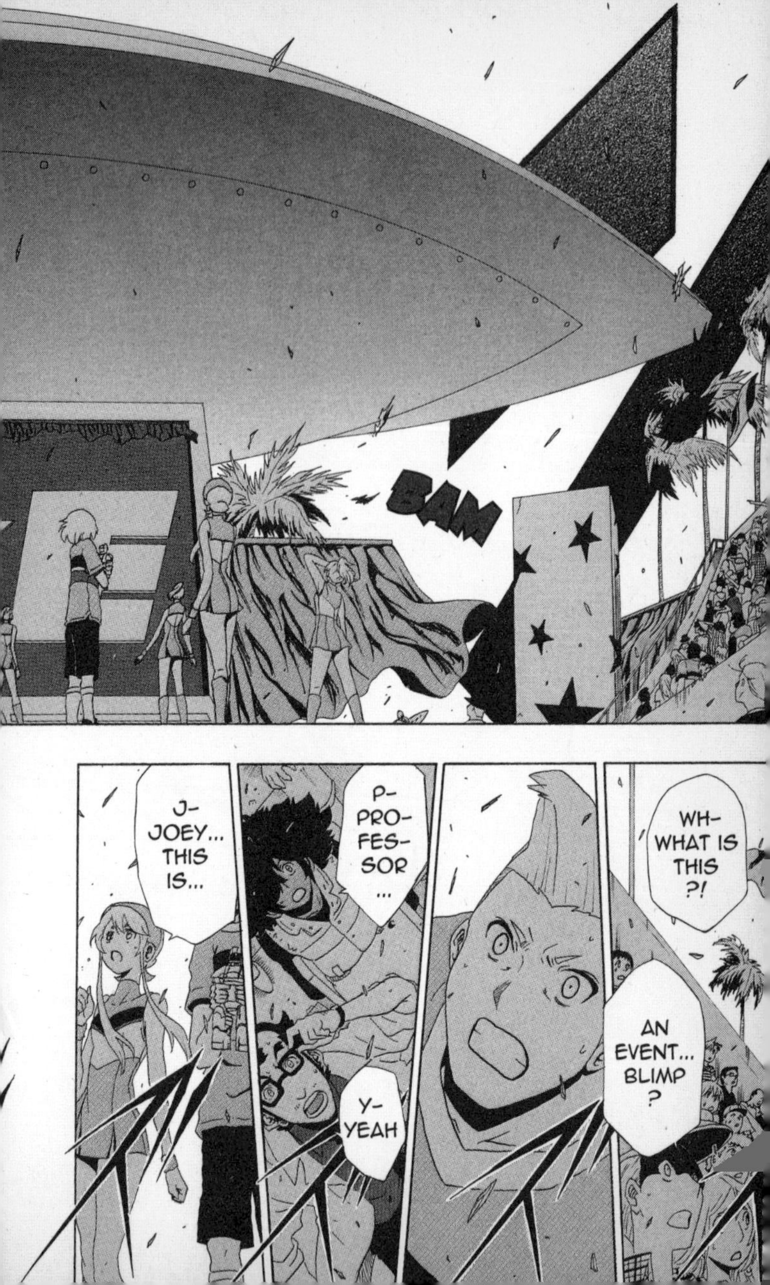
BAM
WH- WHAT IS THIS ?!
AN EVENT... BLIMP ?
P- PRO- FES- SOR ...
Y- YEAH
J- JOEY... THIS IS...

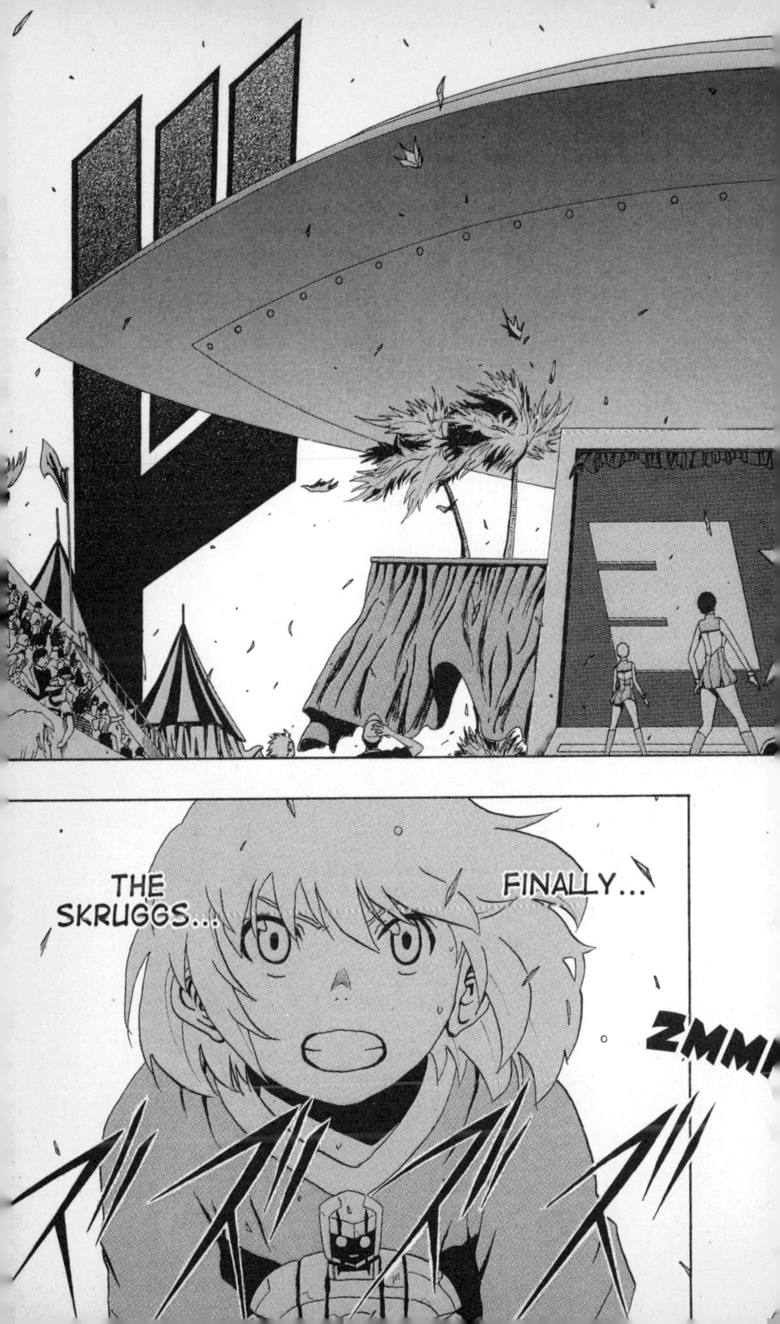
FINALLY...
THE SKRUGGS...
ZMM

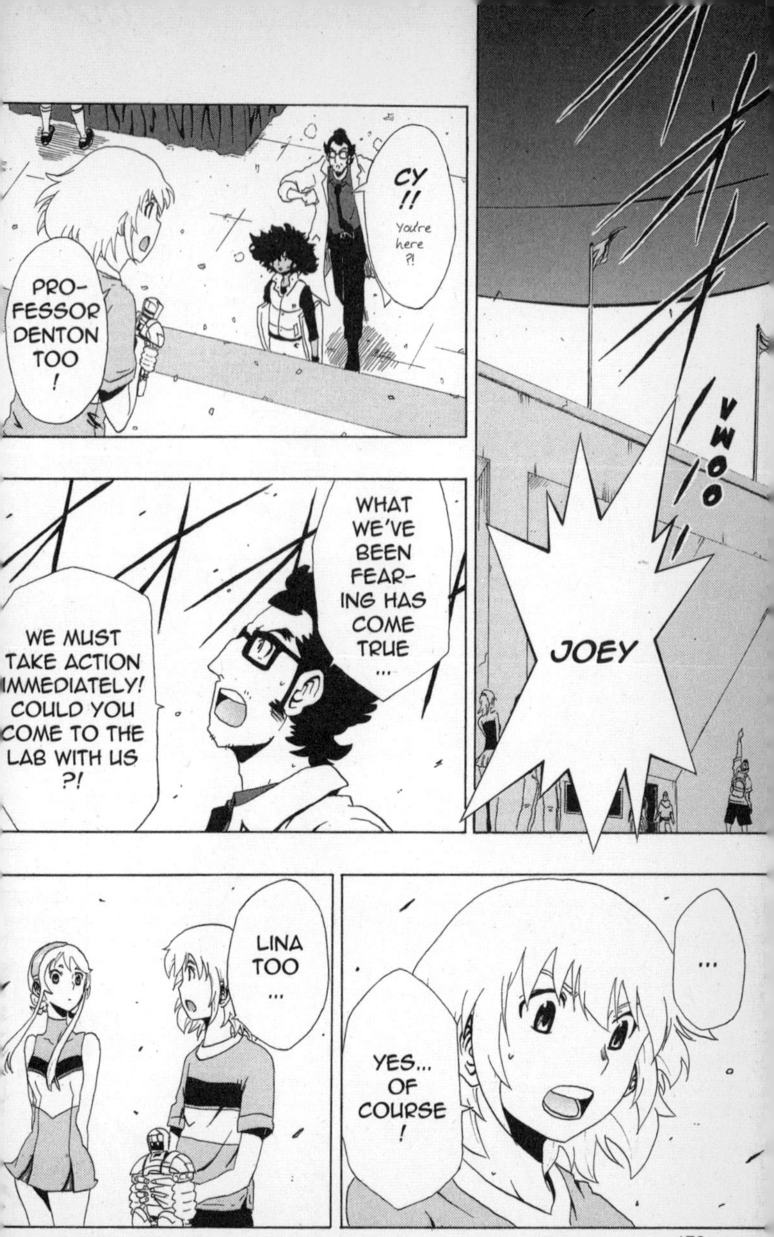
VWOO
JOEY
CY!! You're here?!
PROFESSOR DENTON TOO!
WHAT WE'VE BEEN FEARING HAS COME TRUE...
WE MUST TAKE ACTION IMMEDIATELY! COULD YOU COME TO THE LAB WITH US?!
...
YES... OF COURSE!
LINA TOO...

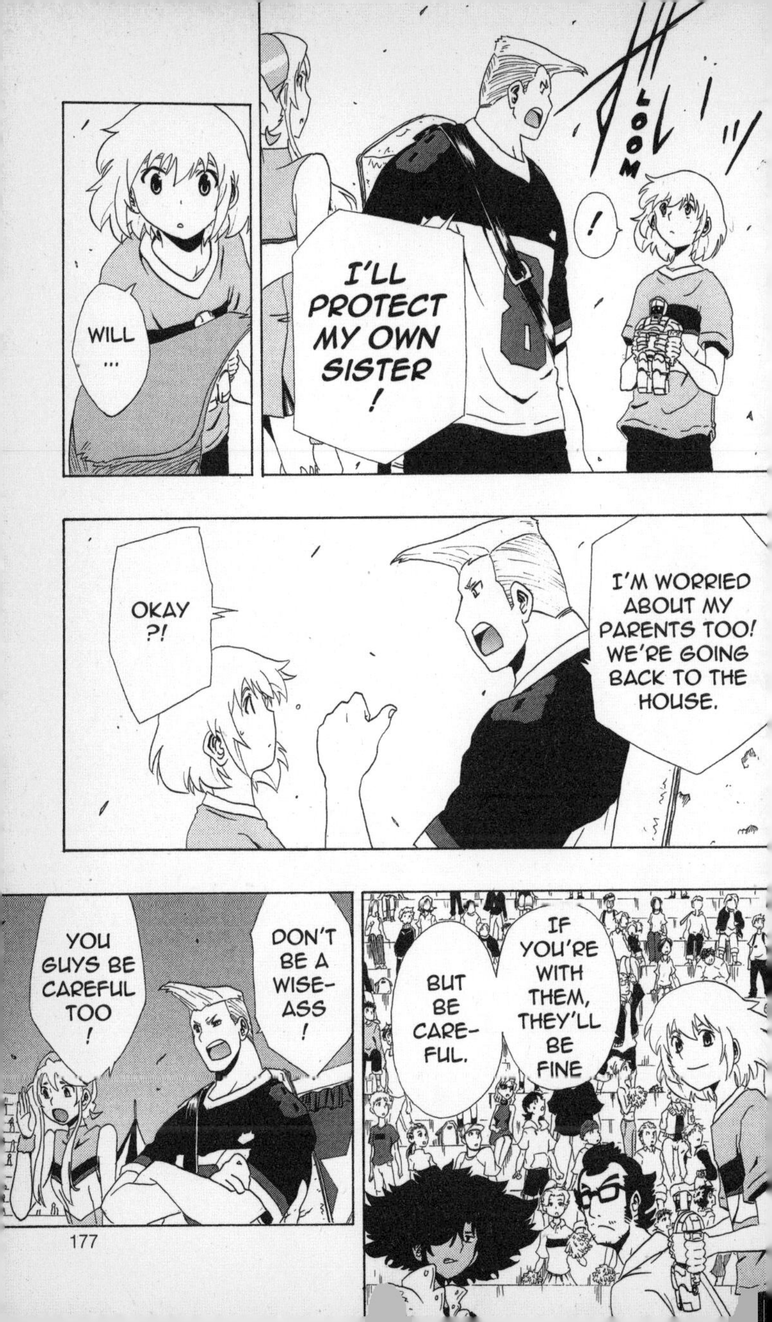
LOOM
!
I'LL PROTECT MY OWN SISTER!
WILL...
I'M WORRIED ABOUT MY PARENTS TOO! WE'RE GOING BACK TO THE HOUSE.
OKAY?!
IF YOU'RE WITH THEM, THEY'LL BE FINE
BUT BE CAREFUL.
DON'T BE A WISE-ASS!
YOU GUYS BE CAREFUL TOO!

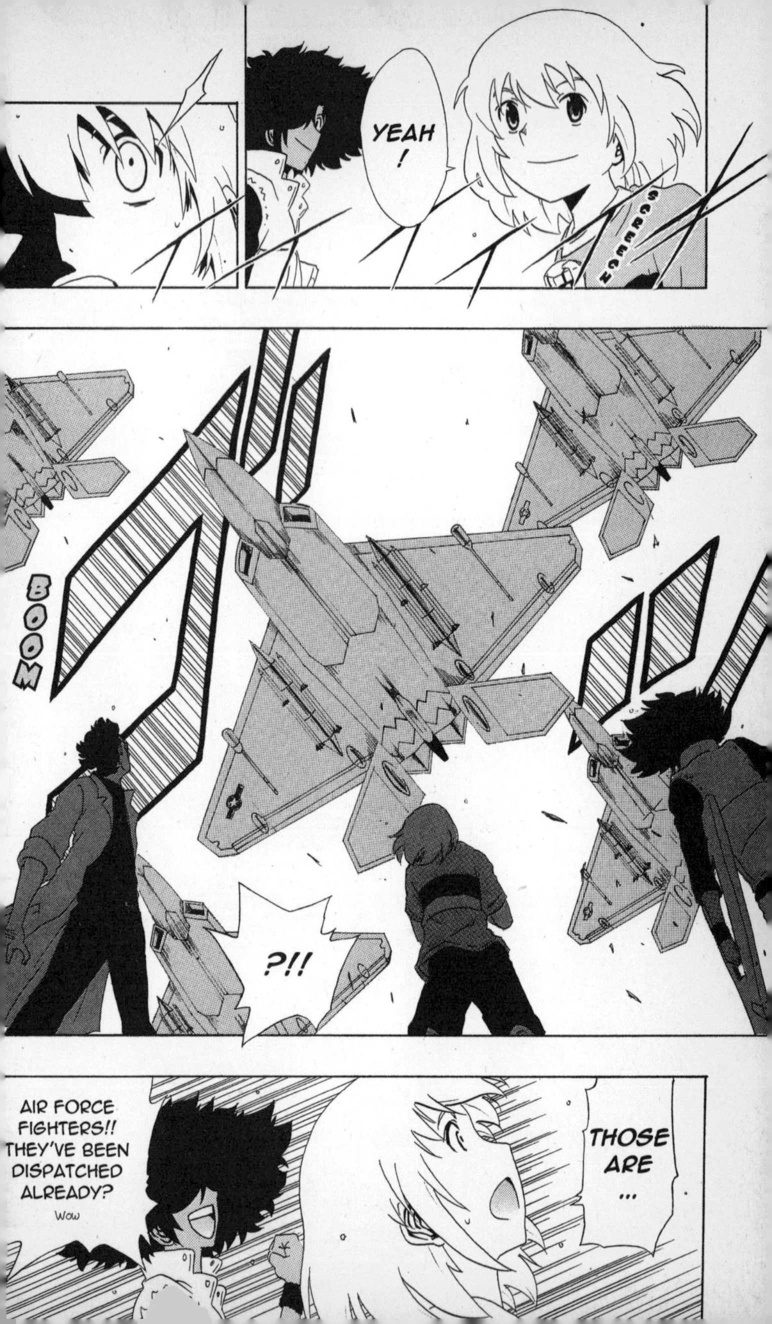
YEAH!
SCREEECH
BOOM
?!!
THOSE ARE ...
AIR FORCE FIGHTERS!! THEY'VE BEEN DISPATCHED ALREADY?
WOW

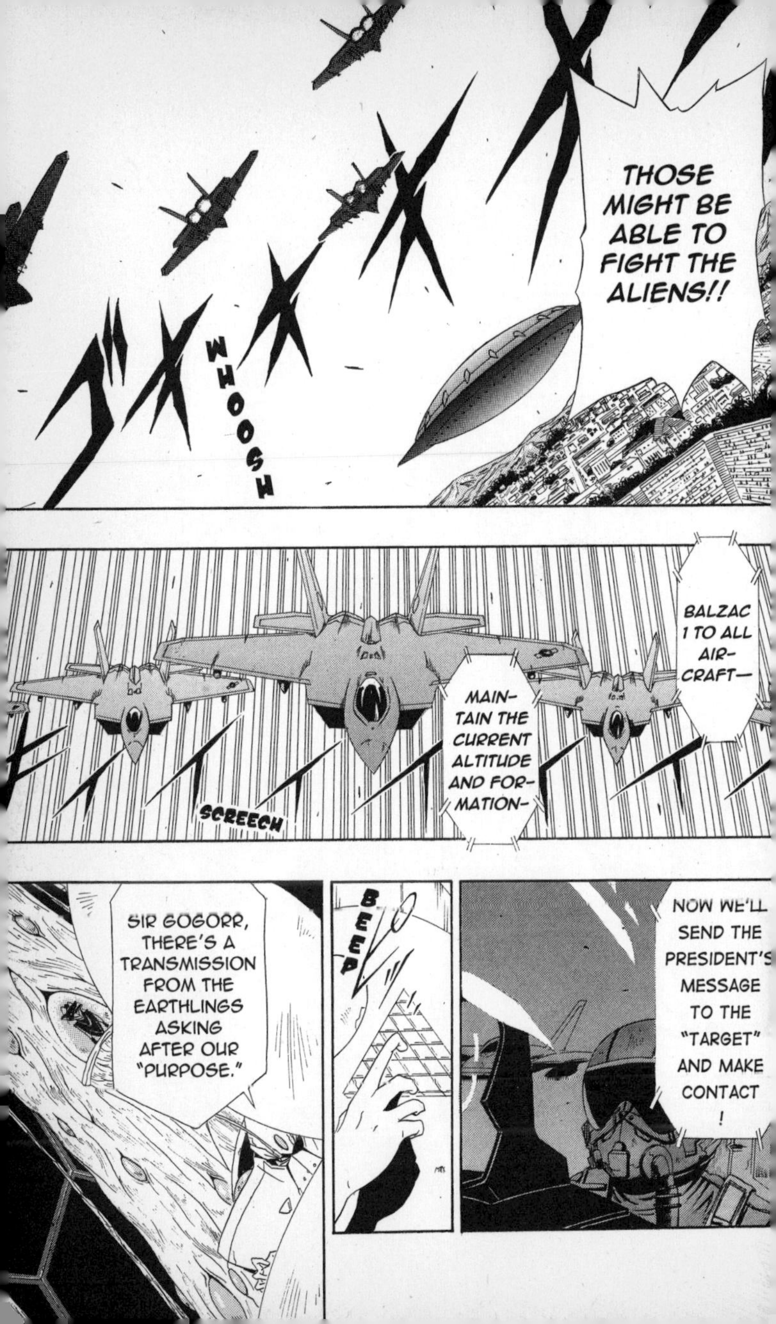
THOSE MIGHT BE ABLE TO FIGHT THE ALIENS!!
WHOOSH
BALZAC 1 TO ALL AIR-CRAFT—
MAIN-TAIN THE CURRENT ALTITUDE AND FOR-MATION-
SCREECH
NOW WE'LL SEND THE PRESIDENT'S MESSAGE TO THE "TARGET" AND MAKE CONTACT!
BEEP
SIR GOGORR, THERE'S A TRANSMISSION FROM THE EARTHLINGS ASKING AFTER OUR "PURPOSE."

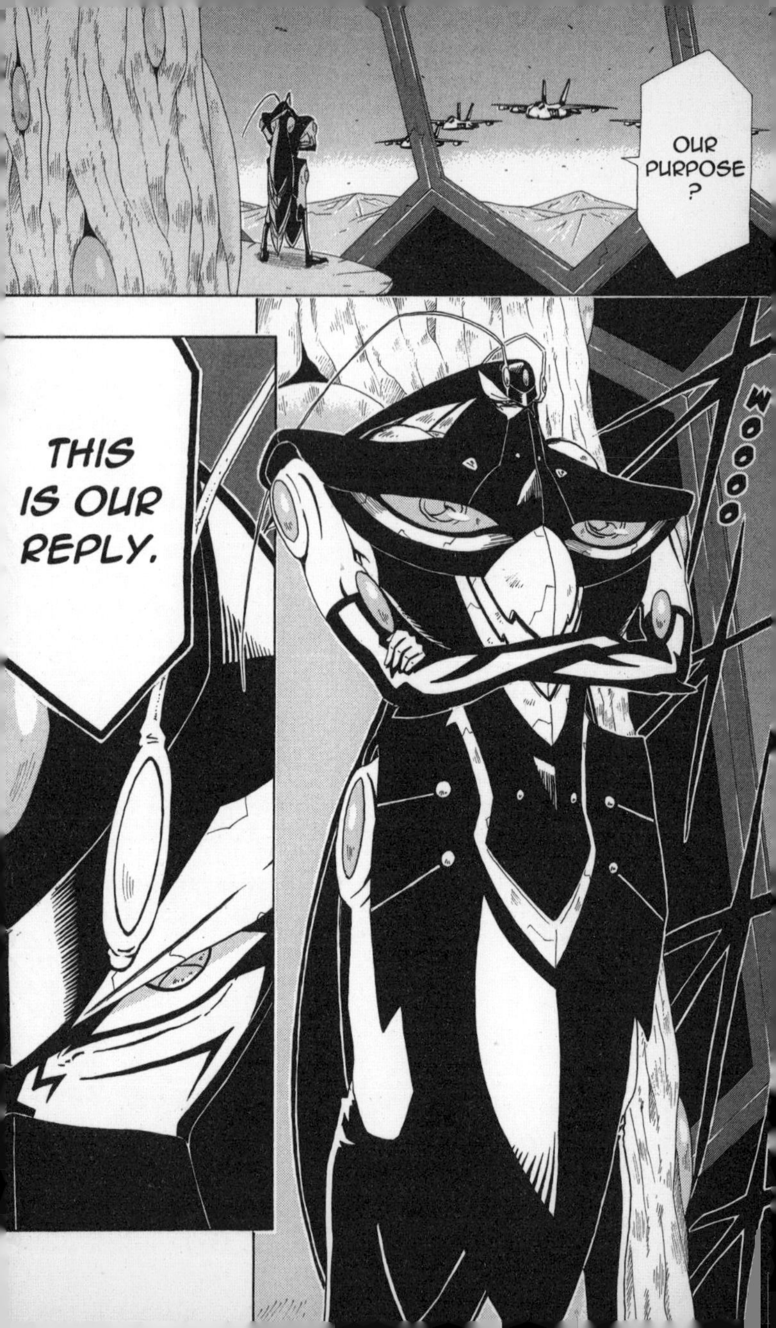

OUR PURPOSE?
WOOOOO
THIS IS OUR REPLY.

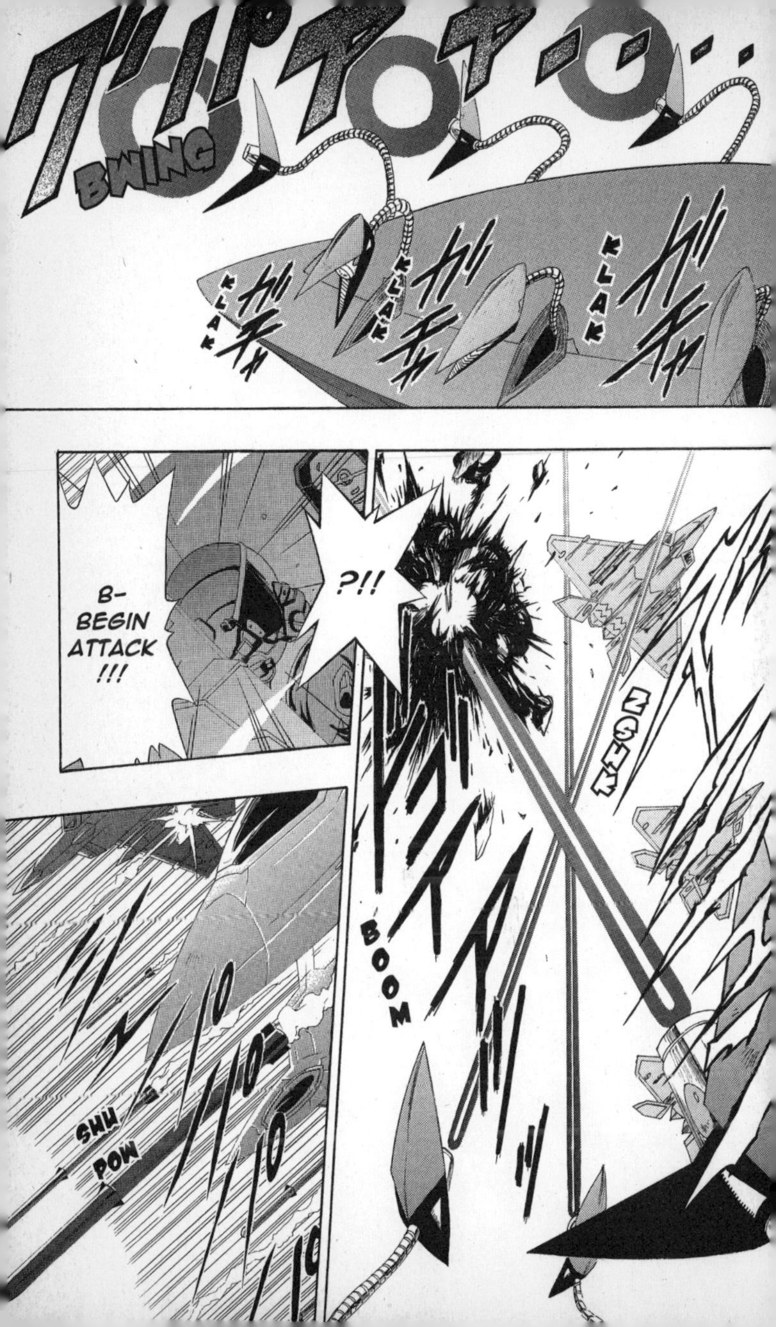
BWING
KLAK
KLAK
KLAK
?!!
ZSHK
BOOM
B- BEGIN ATTACK !!!
SHU
POW

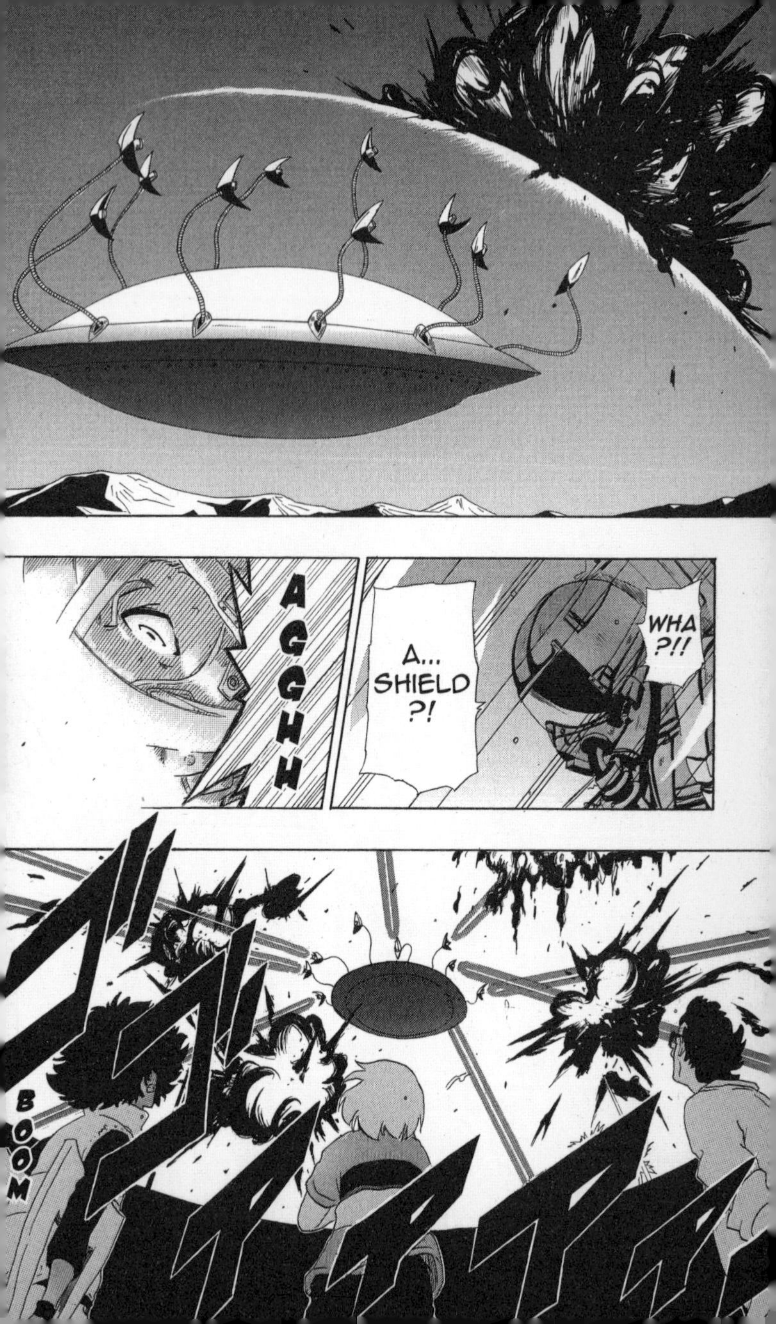
WHA ?!!
A... SHIELD ?!
AGGHH
BOOM

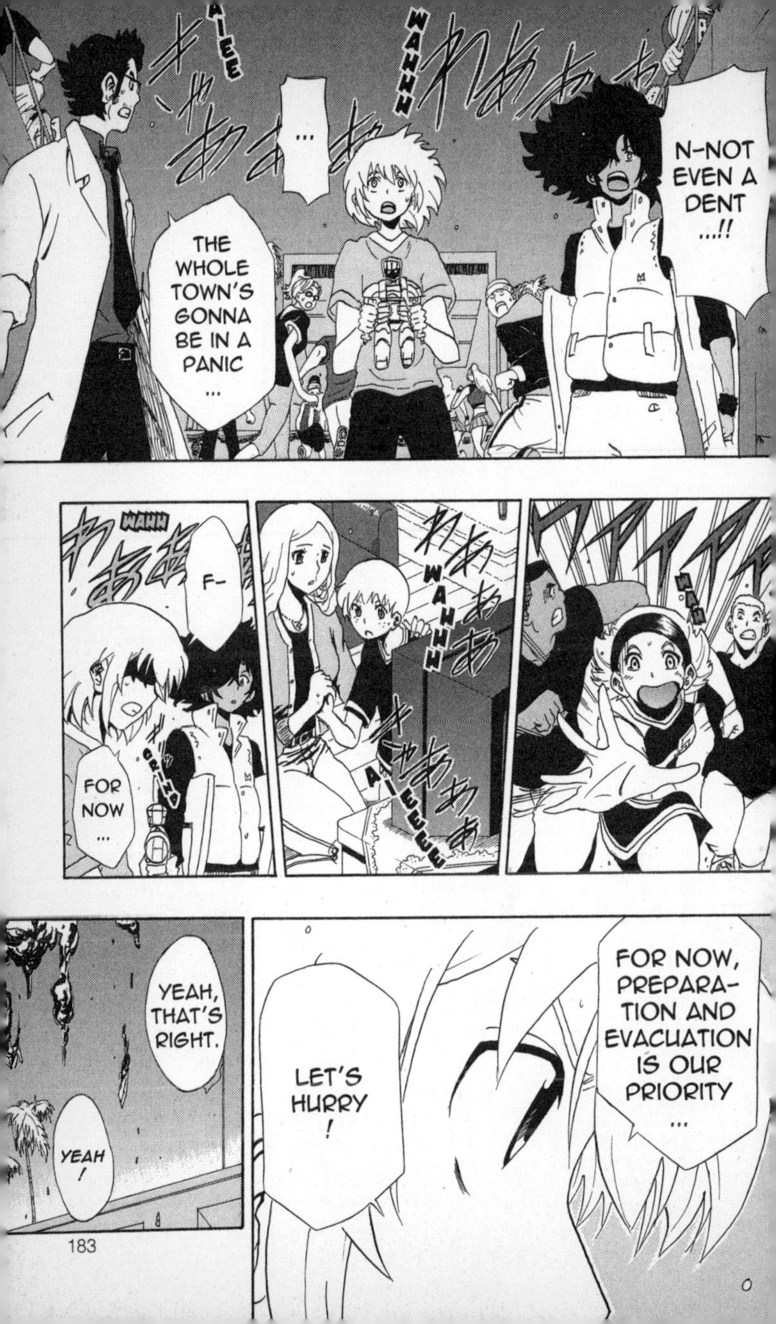
N-NOT EVEN A DENT ...!!
WAHHH
AIEE
...
THE WHOLE TOWN'S GONNA BE IN A PANIC ...
WAH
WAHHH
AIEEEEE
WAHH
F-
GRIP
FOR NOW ...
FOR NOW, PREPARATION AND EVACUATION IS OUR PRIORITY ...
LET'S HURRY !
YEAH, THAT'S RIGHT.
YEAH !

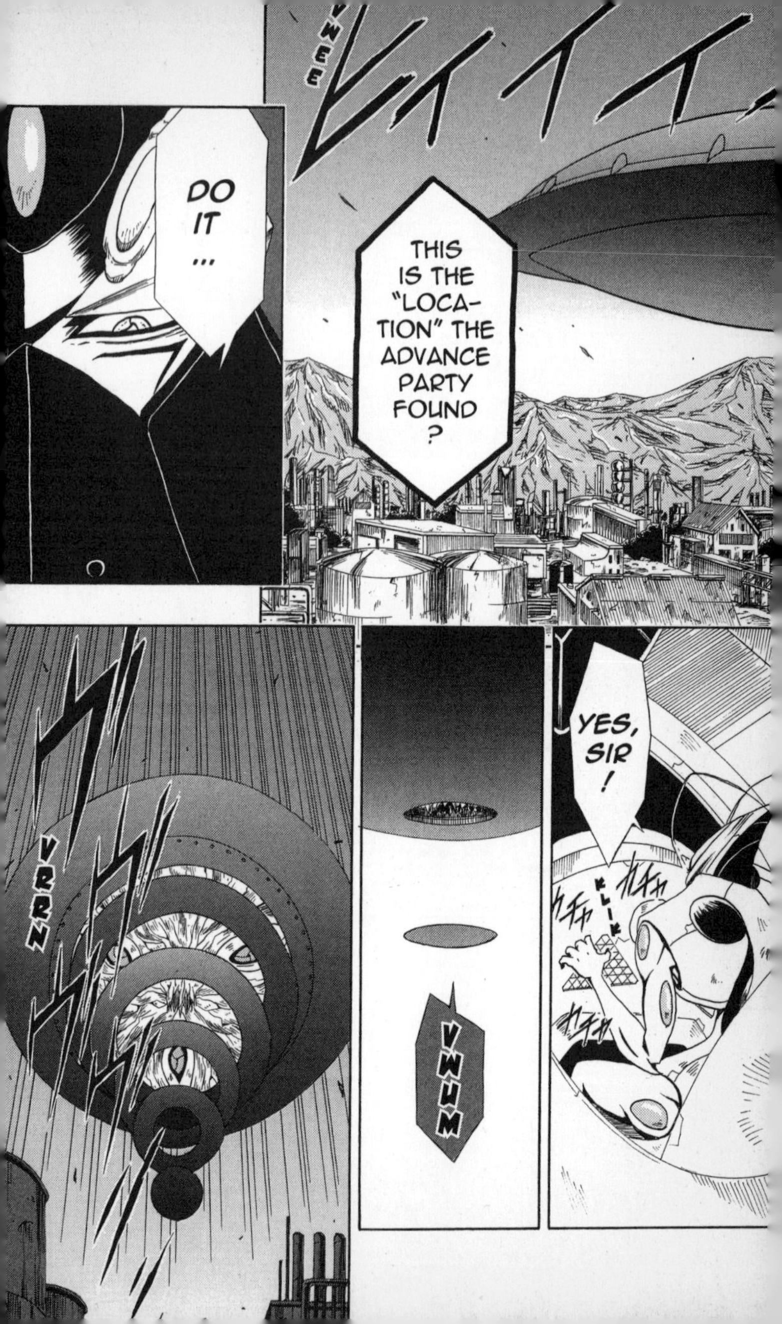
VWEEE
THIS IS THE "LOCATION" THE ADVANCE PARTY FOUND?
DO IT...
YES, SIR!
VWUM
VRRN

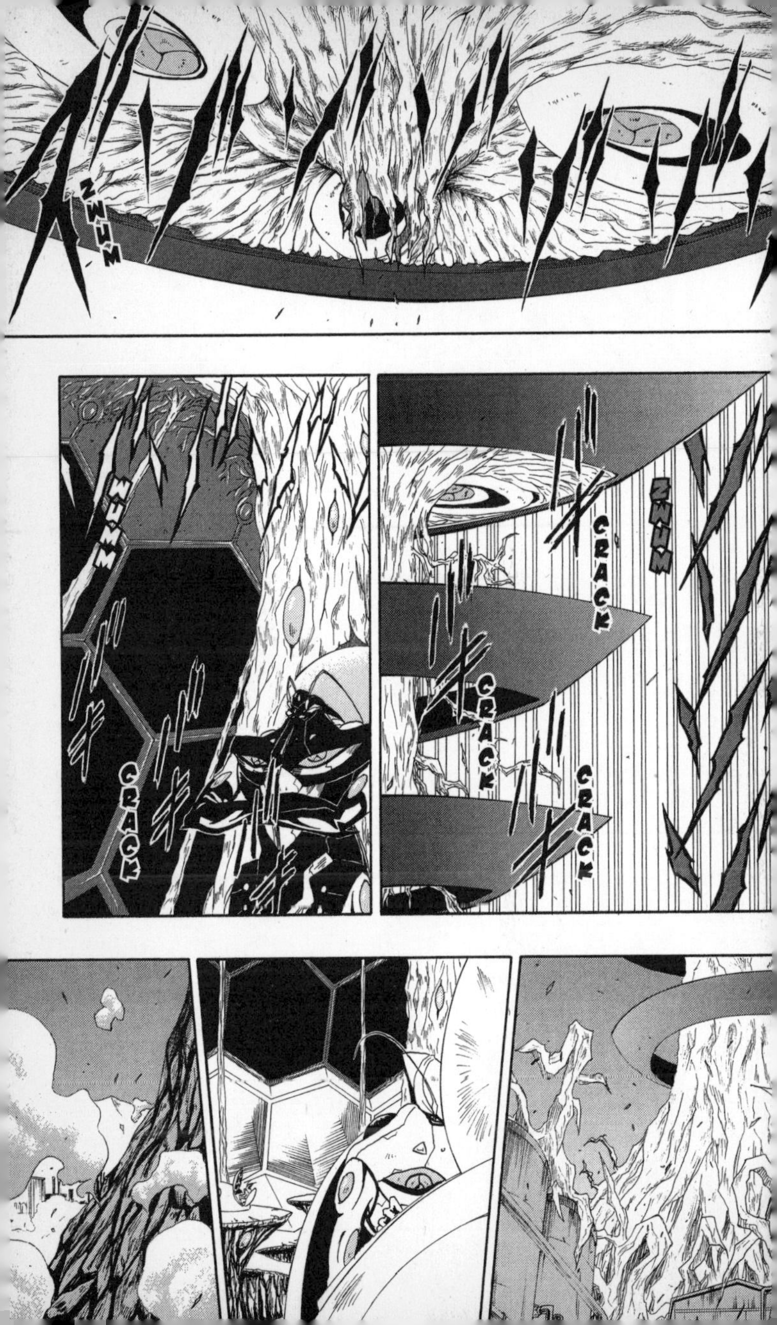
ZWUM
ZWUM
CRACK
CRACK
CRACK
WUMM
CRACK

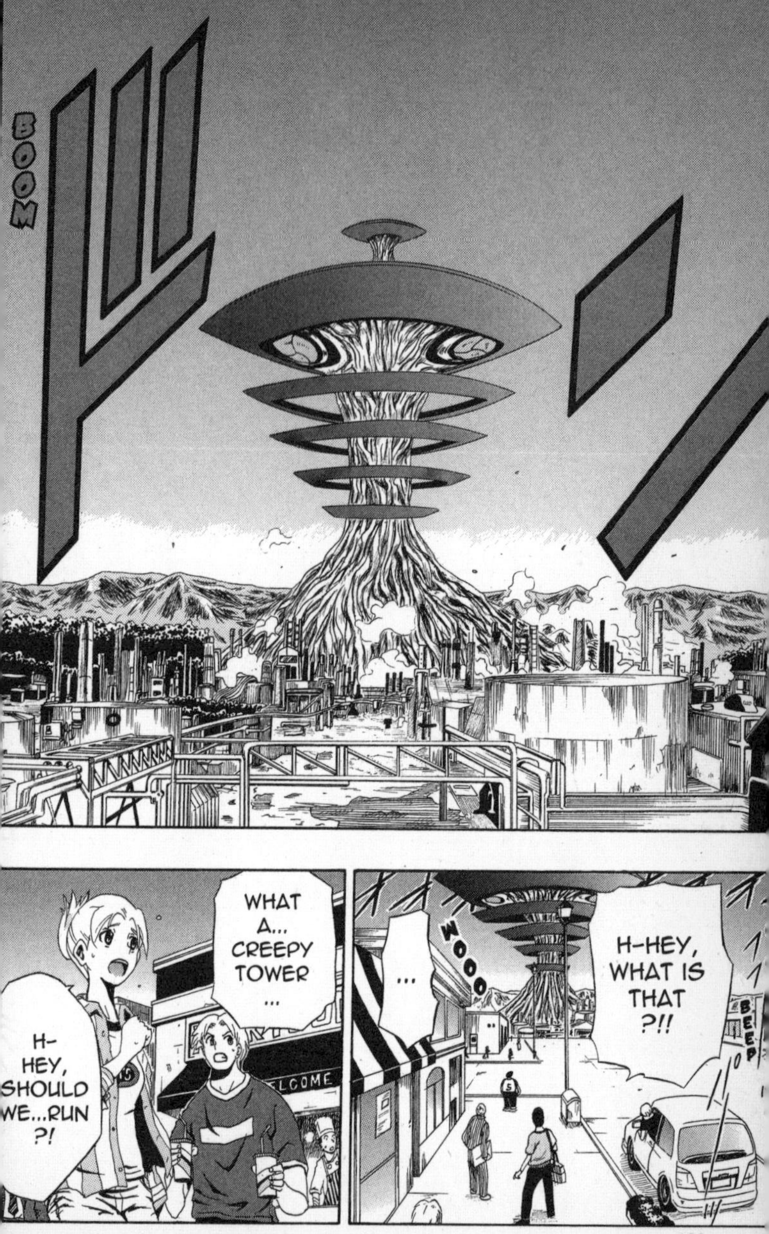
BOOM
H-HEY, WHAT IS THAT ?!!
WOOO
...
BEEP
WHAT A... CREEPY TOWER ...
H- HEY, SHOULD WE...RUN ?!

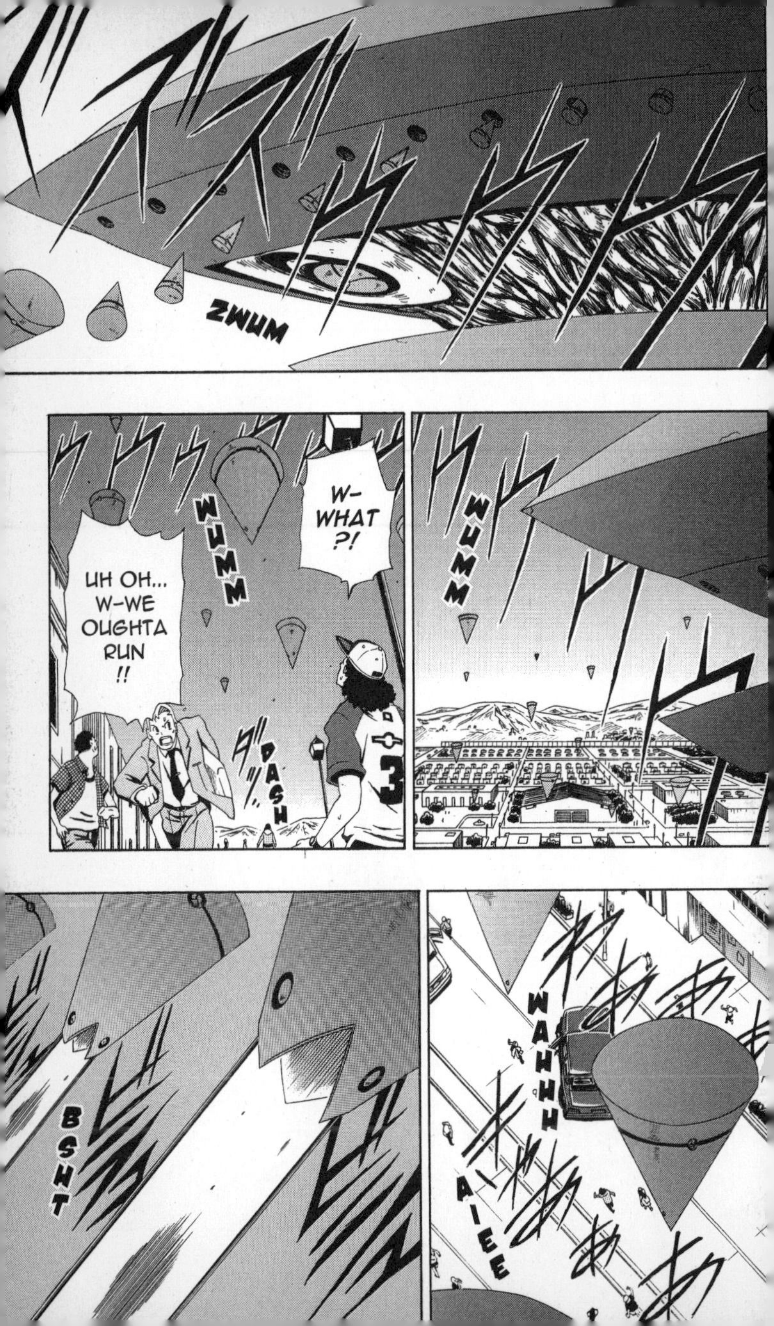
ZWUM
WUMM
W-WHAT ?!
WUMM
UH OH... W-WE OUGHTA RUN !!
DASH
WAHHH
AIEEE
BSHT

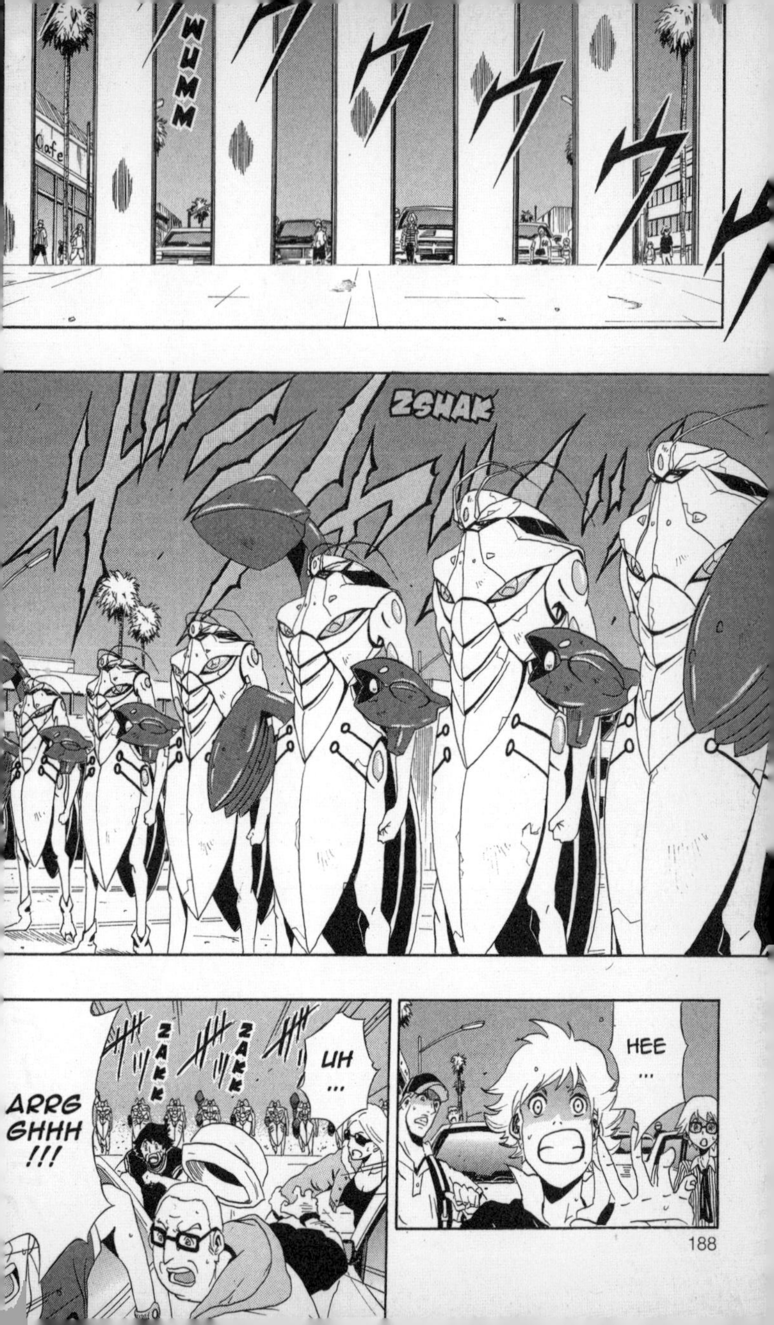
WUMM
ZSHAK
HEE ...
UH ...
ZAKK
ZAKK
ARRGGHHH!!!

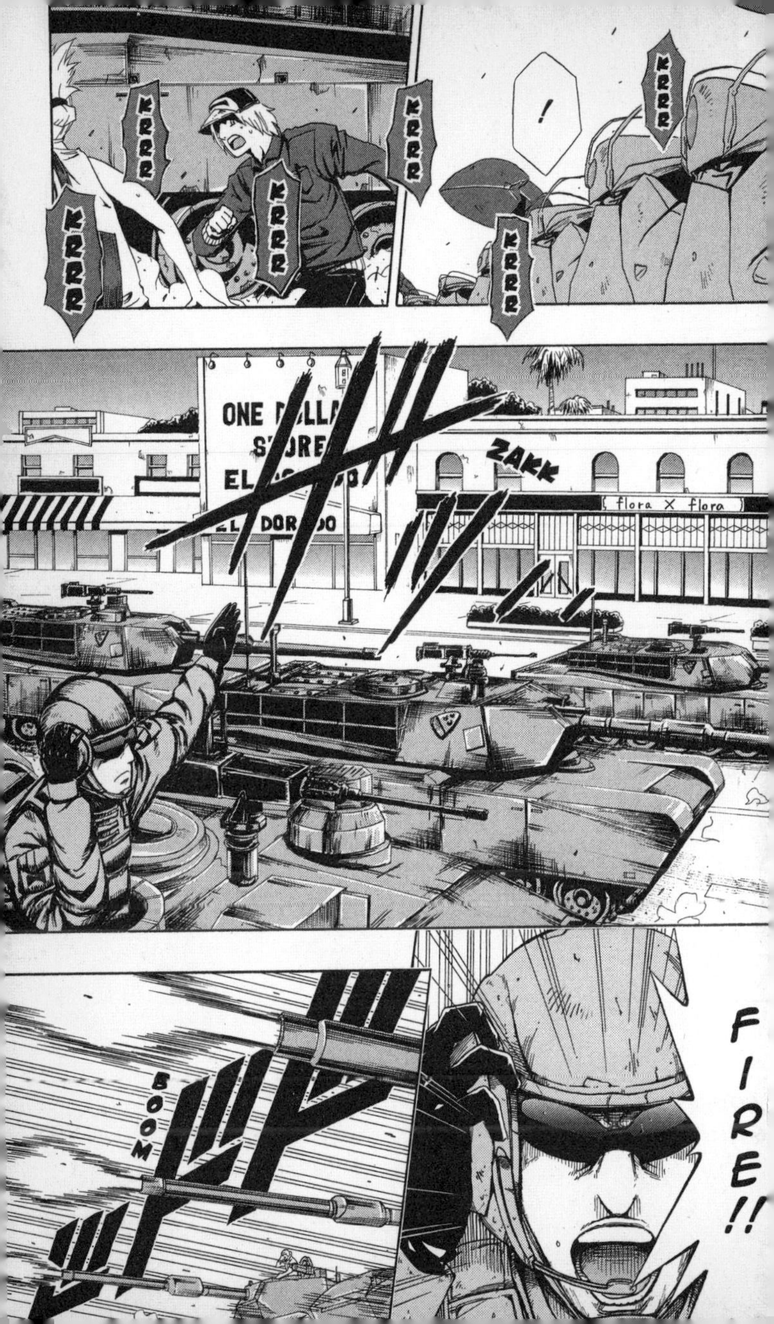
!
KRRR
KRRR
KRRR
KRRR
KRRR
KRRR
ZAKK
flora X flora
FIRE!!
BOOM

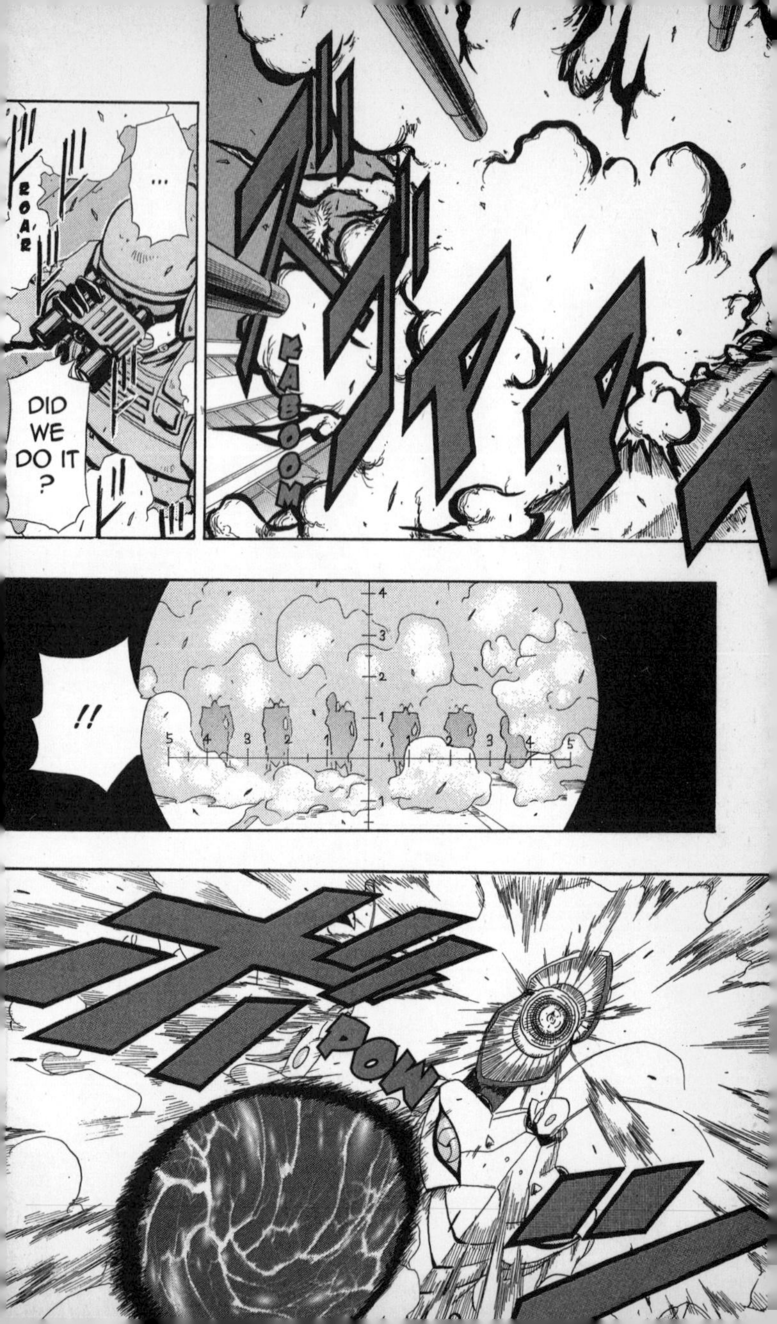
KABOOM
ROAR
...
DID WE DO IT?
!!
POW

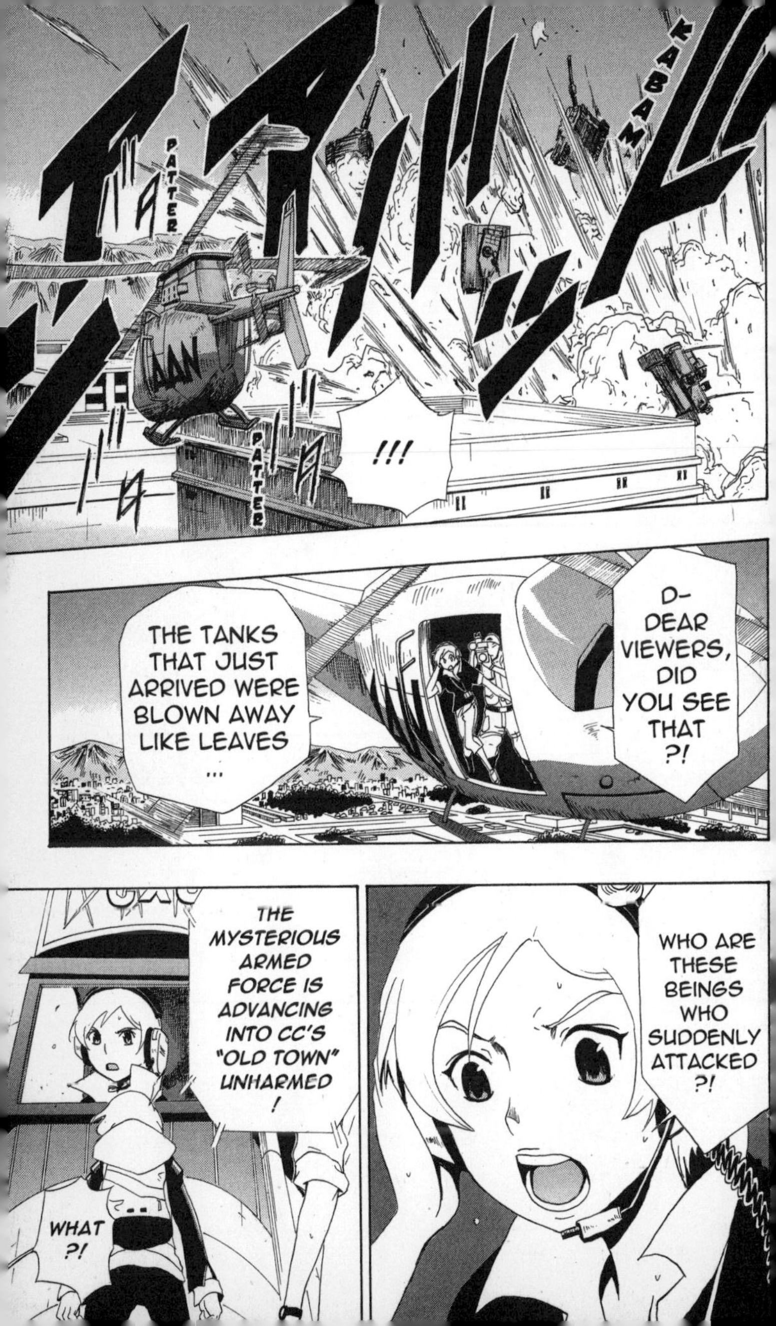
KABAM
!!!
PATTER
PATTER
D-DEAR VIEWERS, DID YOU SEE THAT?!
THE TANKS THAT JUST ARRIVED WERE BLOWN AWAY LIKE LEAVES ...
WHO ARE THESE BEINGS WHO SUDDENLY ATTACKED?!
THE MYSTERIOUS ARMED FORCE IS ADVANCING INTO CC'S "OLD TOWN" UNHARMED!
WHAT?!

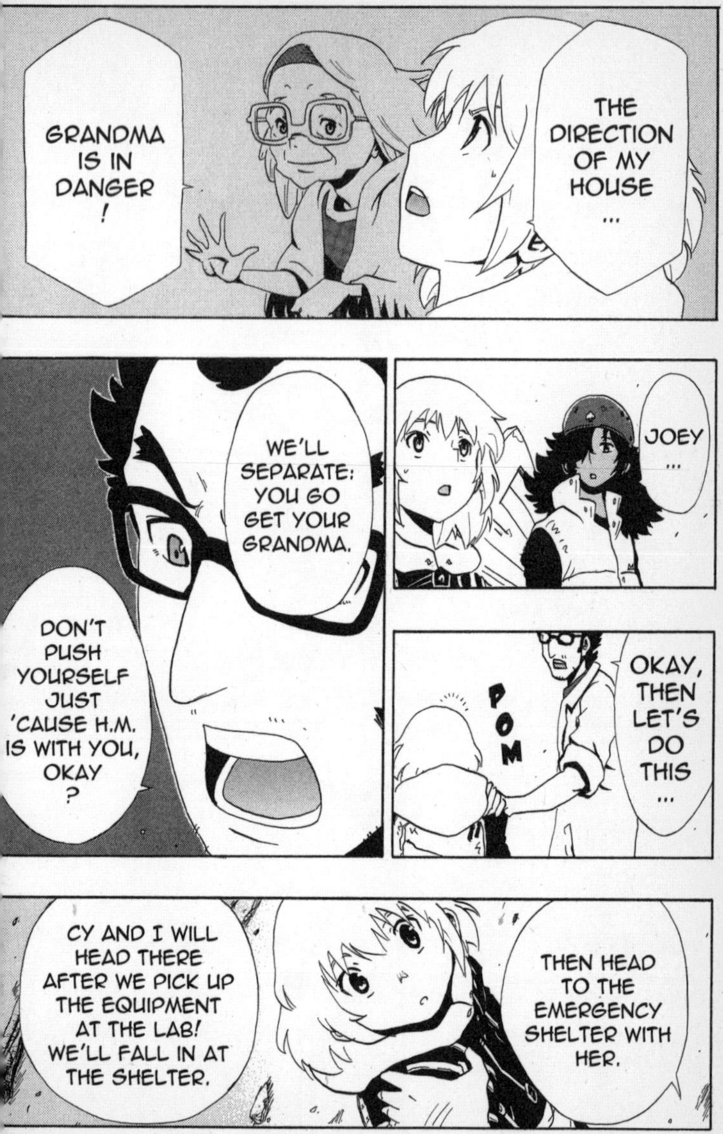
THE DIRECTION OF MY HOUSE ...
GRANDMA IS IN DANGER!
JOEY ...
OKAY, THEN LET'S DO THIS ...
POM
WE'LL SEPARATE: YOU GO GET YOUR GRANDMA.
DON'T PUSH YOURSELF JUST 'CAUSE H.M. IS WITH YOU, OKAY?
THEN HEAD TO THE EMERGENCY SHELTER WITH HER.
CY AND I WILL HEAD THERE AFTER WE PICK UP THE EQUIPMENT AT THE LAB! WE'LL FALL IN AT THE SHELTER.

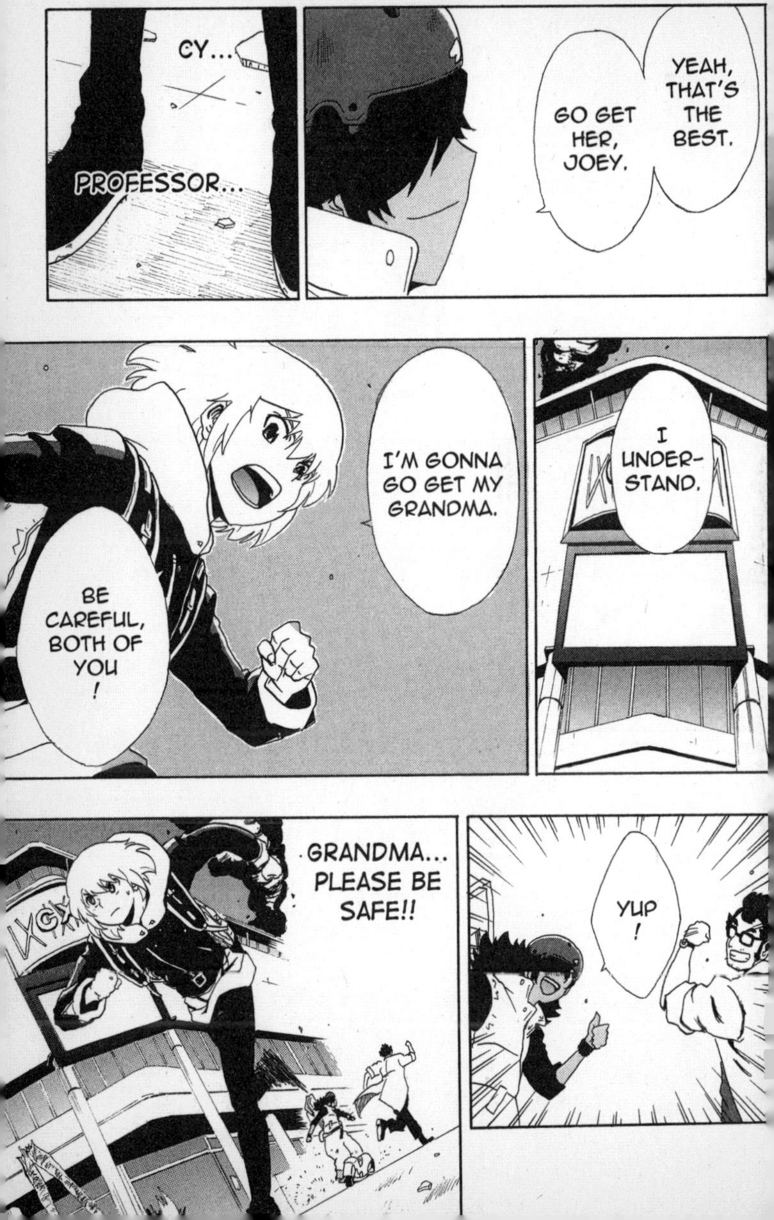
YEAH, THAT'S THE BEST.
GO GET HER, JOEY.
CY...
PROFESSOR...
I UNDER-STAND.
I'M GONNA GO GET MY GRANDMA.
BE CAREFUL, BOTH OF YOU!
YUP!
GRANDMA... PLEASE BE SAFE!!

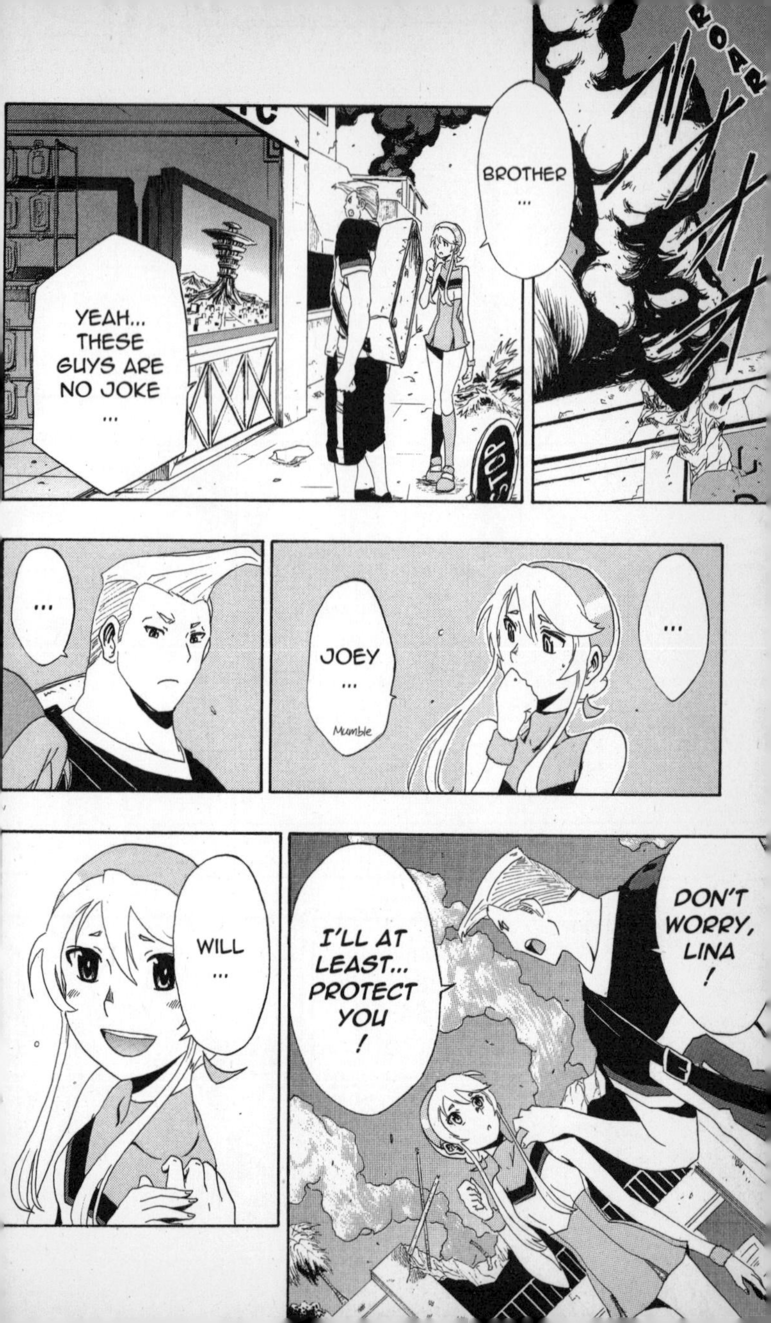
ROAR
BROTHER...
YEAH... THESE GUYS ARE NO JOKE...
...
JOEY... Mumble
...
DON'T WORRY, LINA!
I'LL AT LEAST... PROTECT YOU!
WILL...

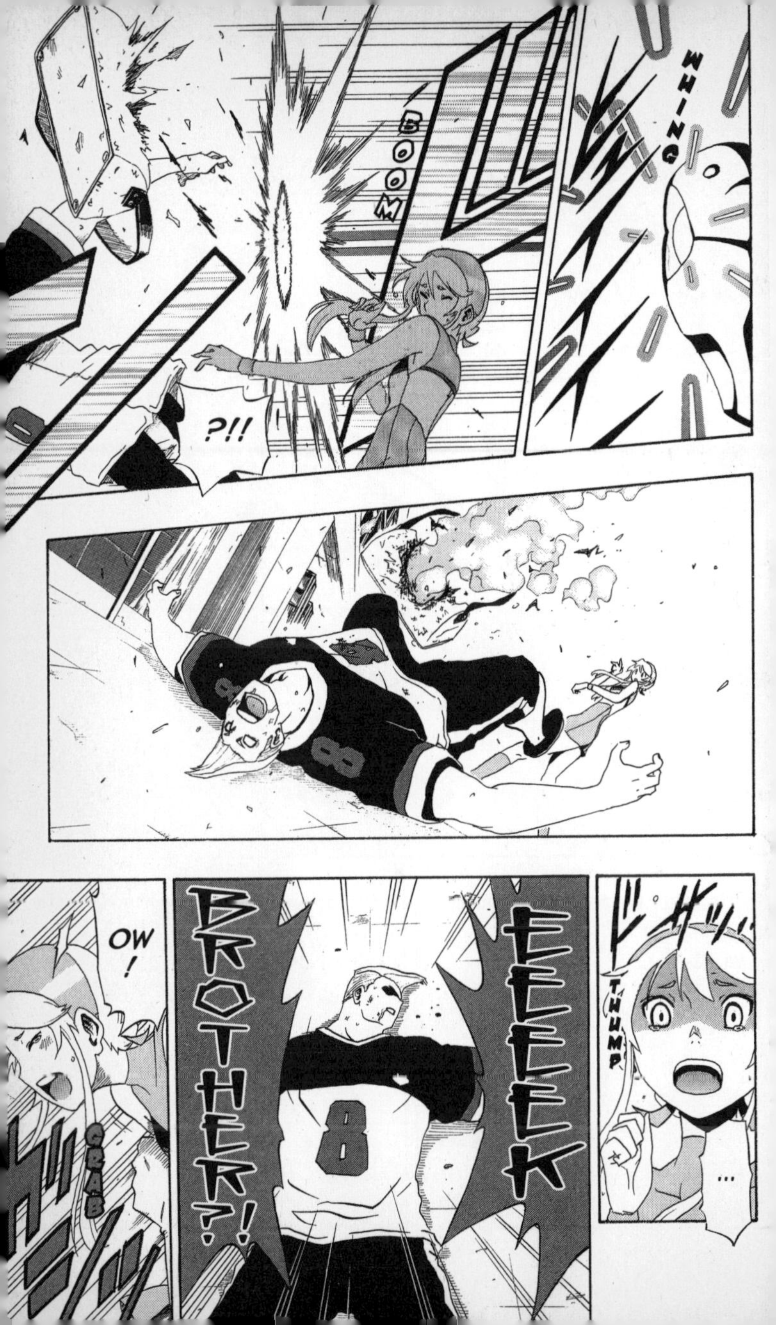
WHING
BOOM
?!!
THUMP
...
EEEEK
BROTHER?!
OW!
GRAB

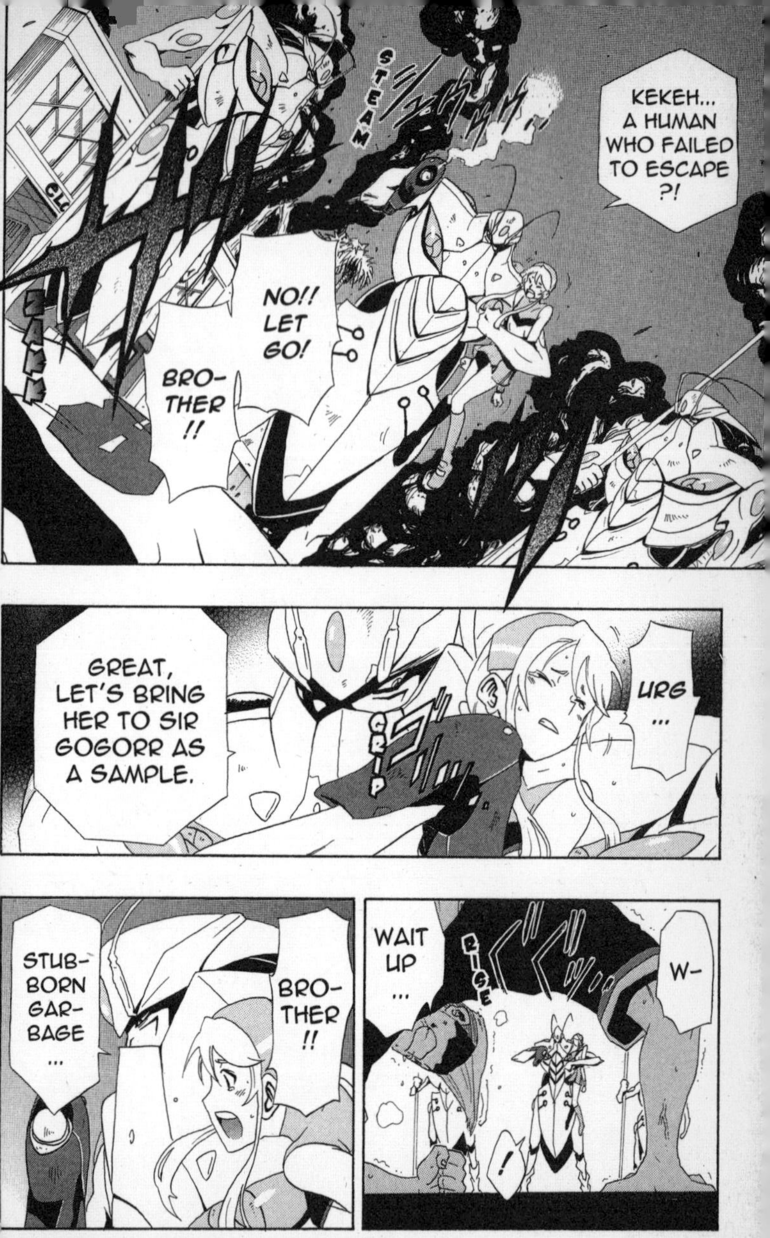
KEKEH... A HUMAN WHO FAILED TO ESCAPE ?!
STEAM
NO!! LET GO!
BRO-THER !!
URG ...
GRIP
GREAT, LET'S BRING HER TO SIR GOGORR AS A SAMPLE.
W-
RISE
WAIT UP ...
!
BRO-THER !!
STUB-BORN GAR-BAGE ...

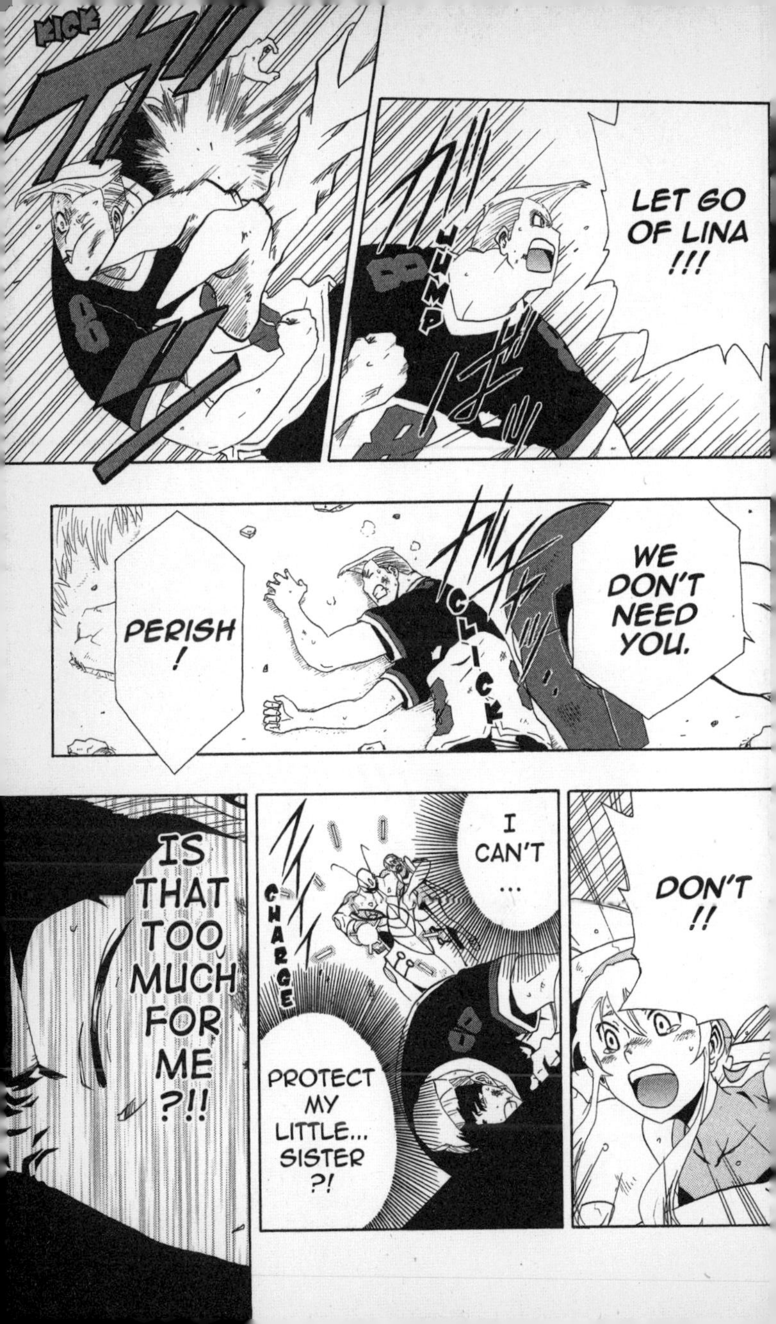
LET GO OF LINA !!!
JUMP
KICK
WE DON'T NEED YOU.
CLICK
PERISH!
DON'T !!
I CAN'T ...
CHARGE
PROTECT MY LITTLE... SISTER ?!
IS THAT TOO MUCH FOR ME ?!!

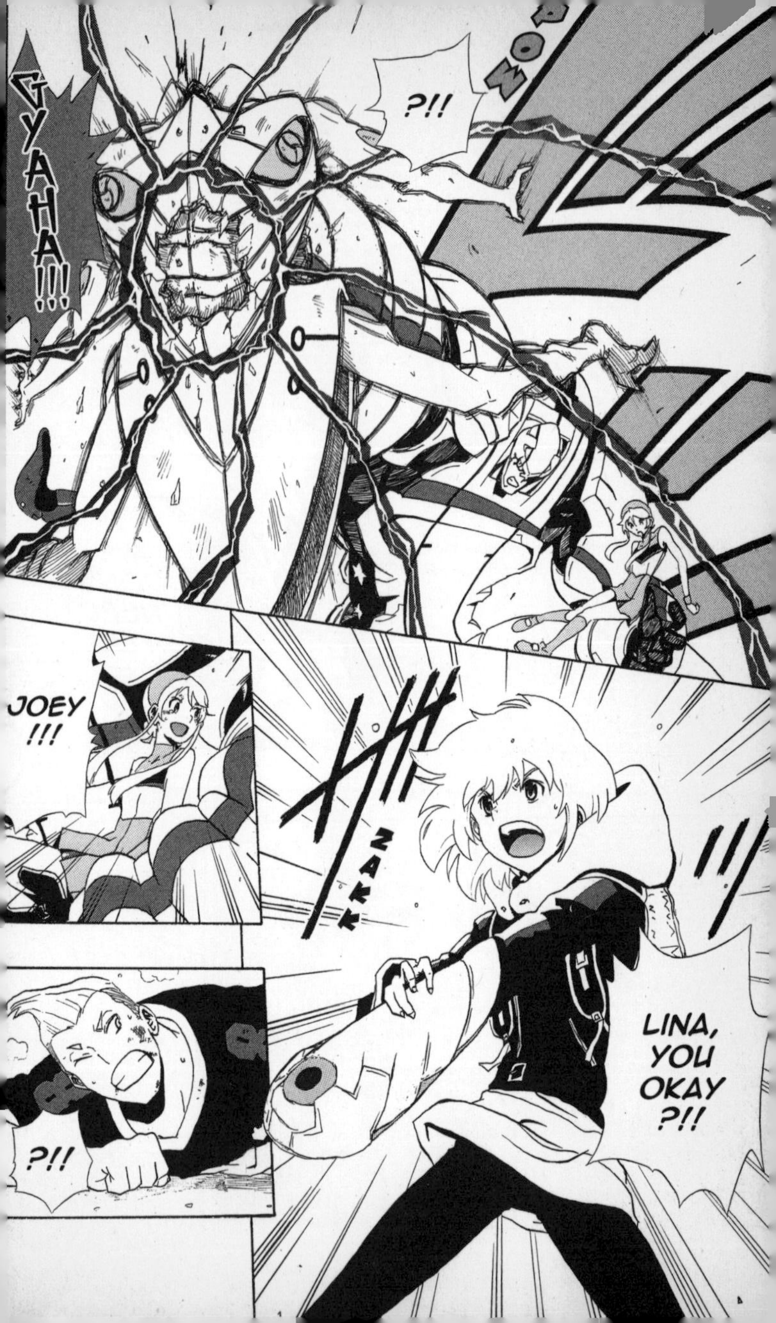
POW
?!!
GYAHA!!!
ZAKK
LINA, YOU OKAY ?!!
JOEY !!!
?!!

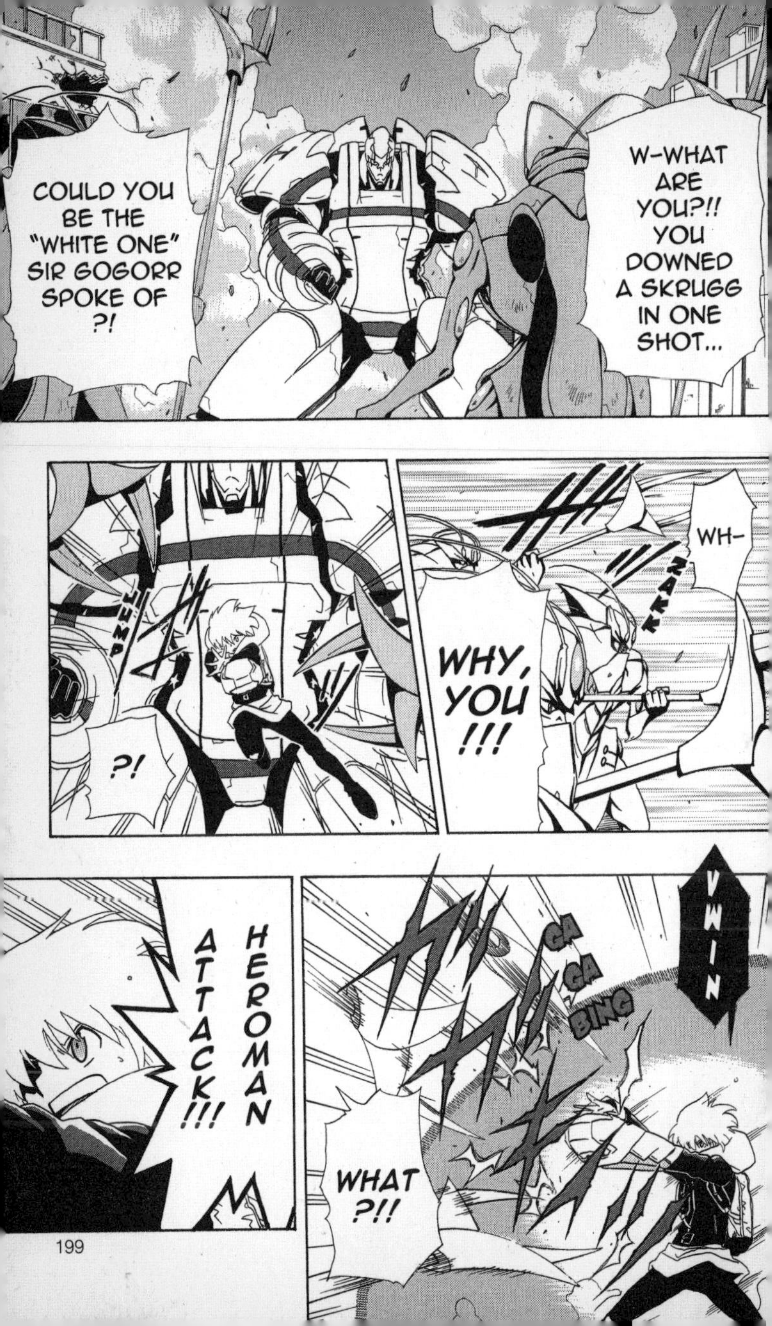
W-WHAT ARE YOU?!! YOU DOWNED A SKRUGG IN ONE SHOT...
COULD YOU BE THE "WHITE ONE" SIR GOGORR SPOKE OF ?!
WH-
ZAKK
WHY, YOU !!!
JUMP
?!
VWIN
GA GA BING
WHAT ?!!
HEROMAN ATTACK!!!

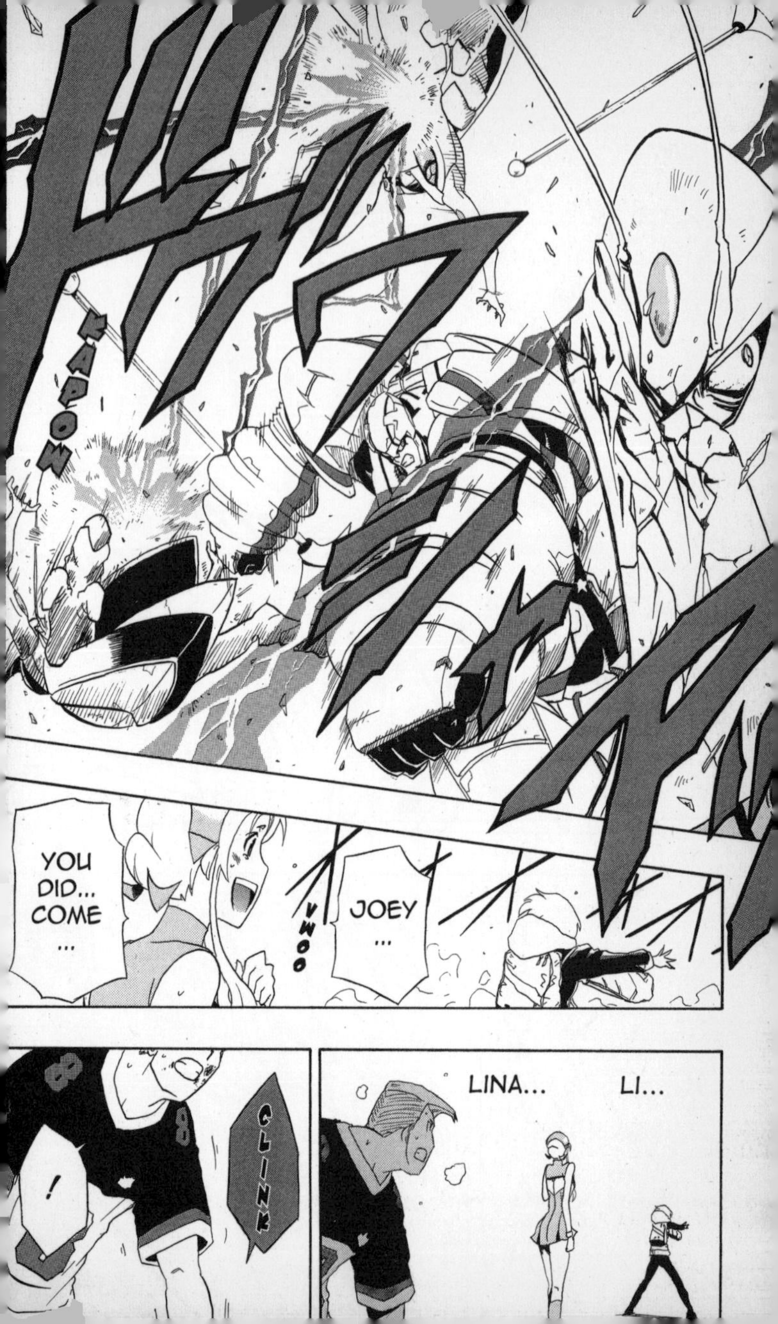
KAPOW
JOEY ...
VWOO
YOU DID... COME ...
LI...
LINA...
CLINK
!

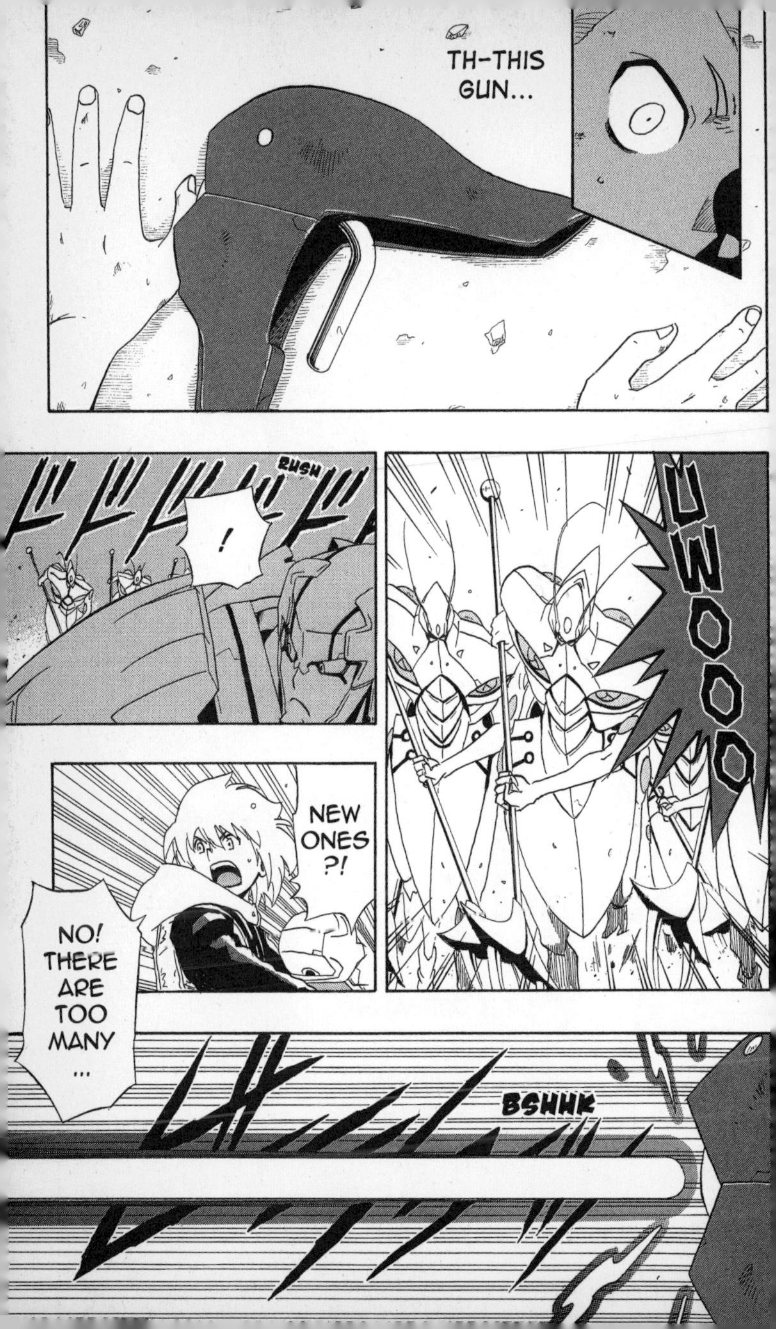
TH-THIS GUN...
UWOOOO
RUSH
!
NEW ONES ?!
NO! THERE ARE TOO MANY ...
BSHHK

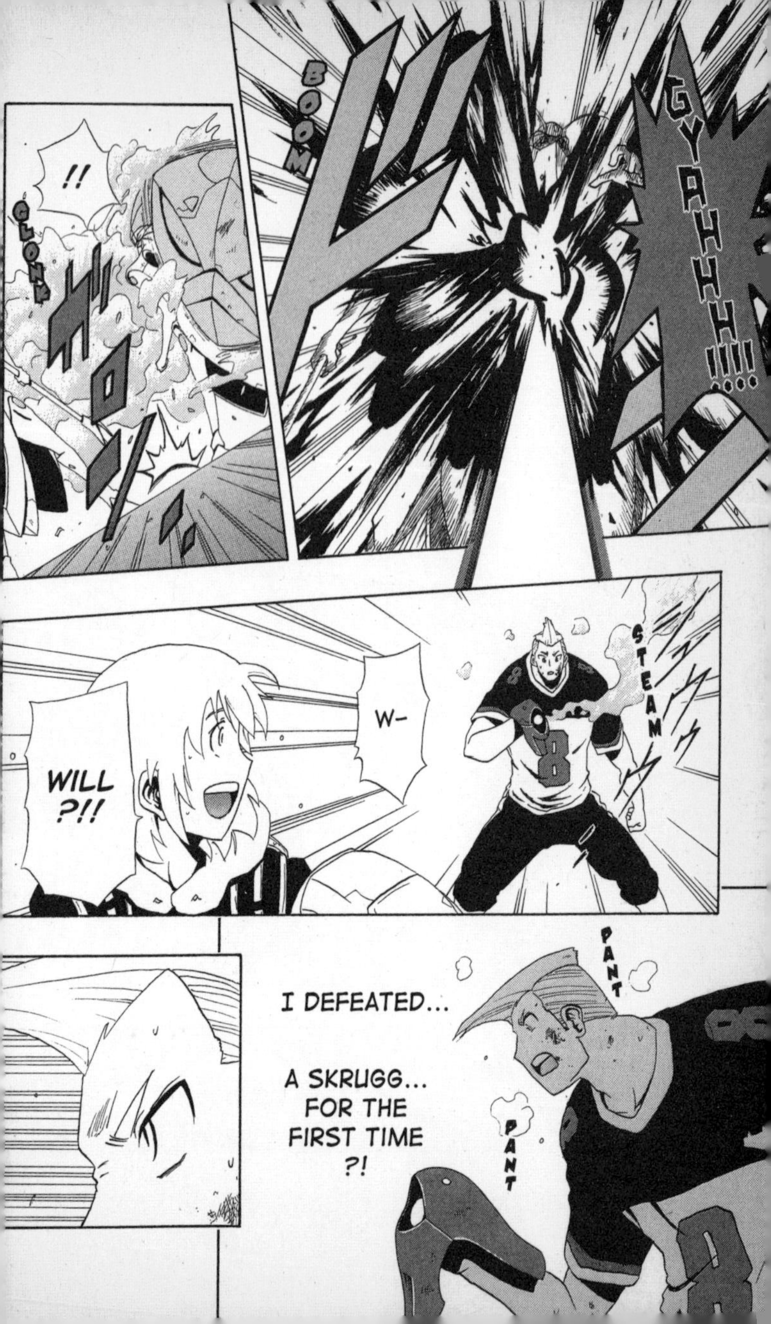

GYAHHH!!!...
BOOM
!!
GLONK
STEAM
W-
WILL ?!!
PANT
I DEFEATED...
A SKRUGG... FOR THE FIRST TIME ?!
PANT

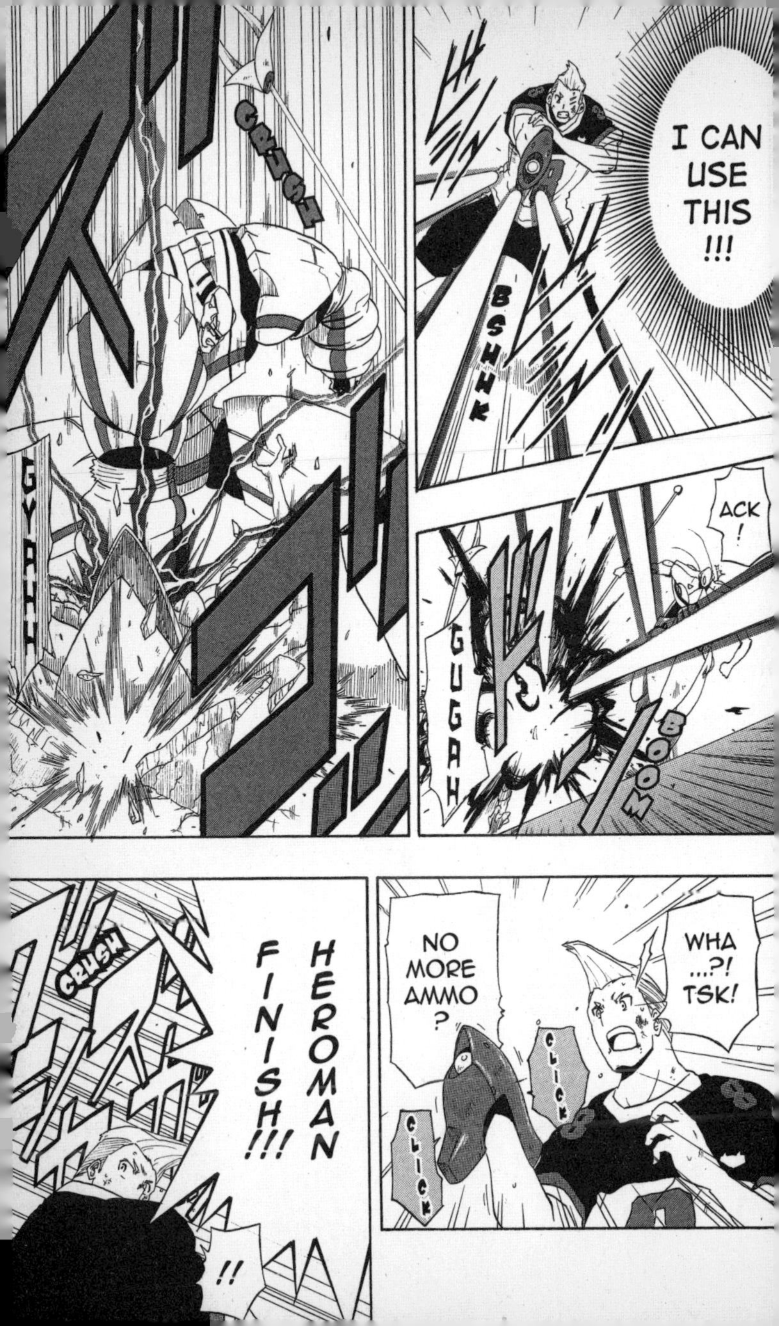
I CAN USE THIS !!!
BSHHHK
ACK!
GUGAH
BOOM
CRUSH
GYAHH
WHA ...?! TSK!
NO MORE AMMO?
CLICK
CLICK
HEROMAN
FINISH!!!
CRUSH
!!

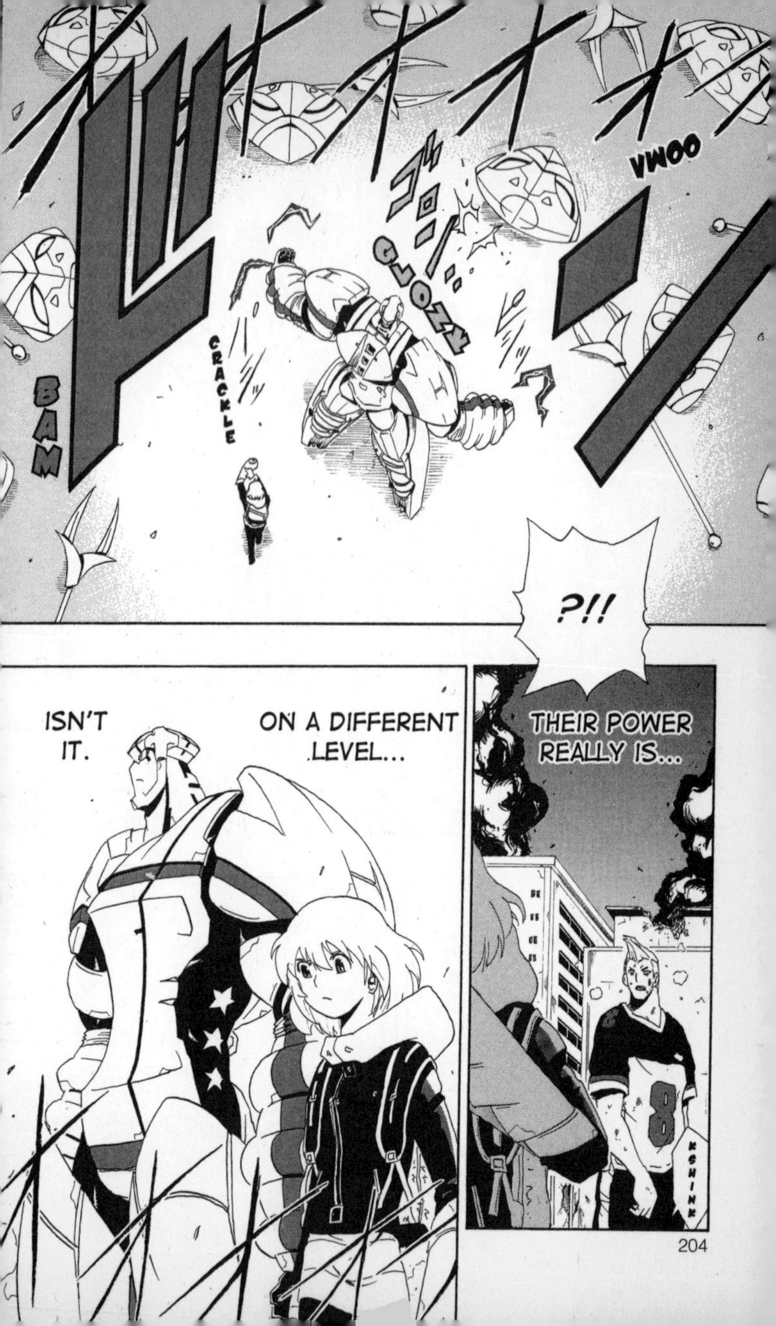
VWOO
GLONK
CRACKLE
BAM
?!!
THEIR POWER REALLY IS...
KSHINK
ON A DIFFERENT LEVEL...
ISN'T IT.

...

JOEY

!!

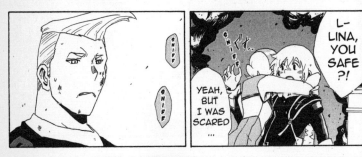

SNIFF

SNIFF

L-LINA, YOU SAFE ?!

YEAH, BUT I WAS SCARED ...

AS I AM NOW, I...

I'M SORRY... LINA.

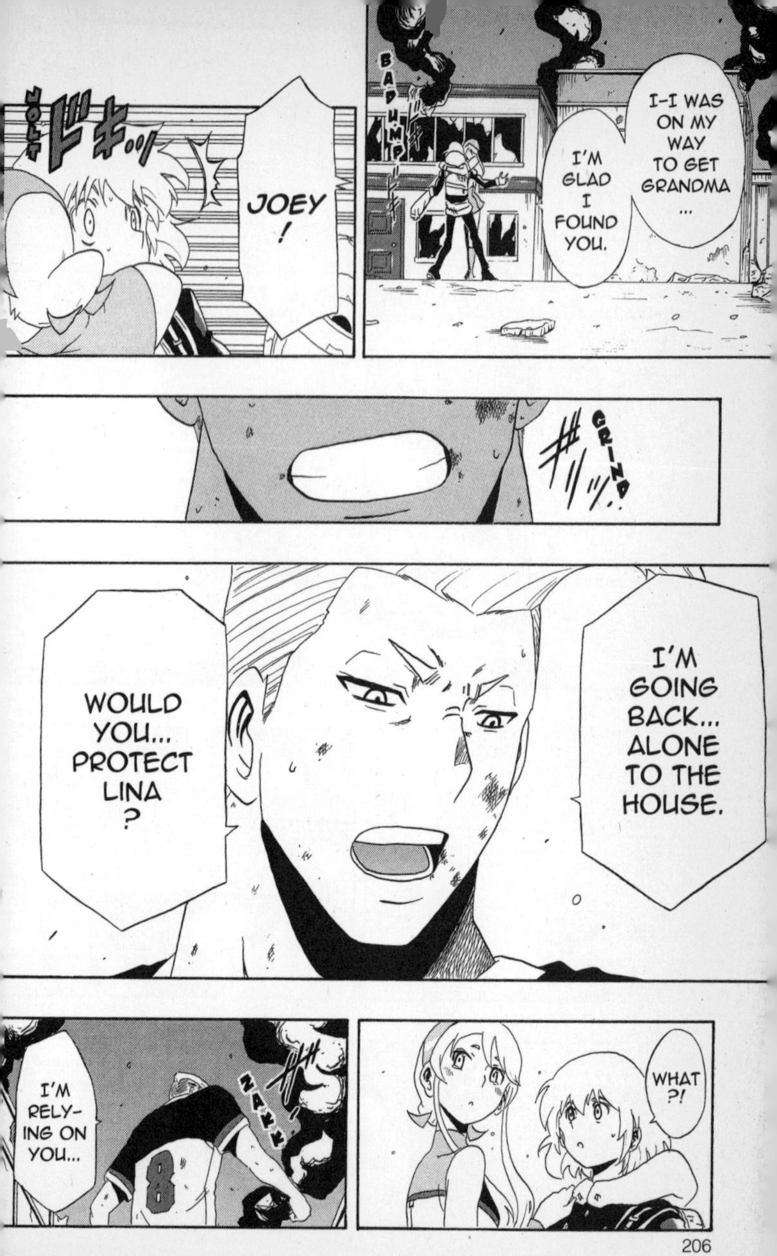
I-I WAS ON MY WAY TO GET GRANDMA ...
I'M GLAD I FOUND YOU.
BADUMP
JOEY!
JOLT
ドキッ
GRIND
I'M GOING BACK... ALONE TO THE HOUSE.
WOULD YOU... PROTECT LINA?
WHAT?!
ZAKK
I'M RELYING ON YOU...

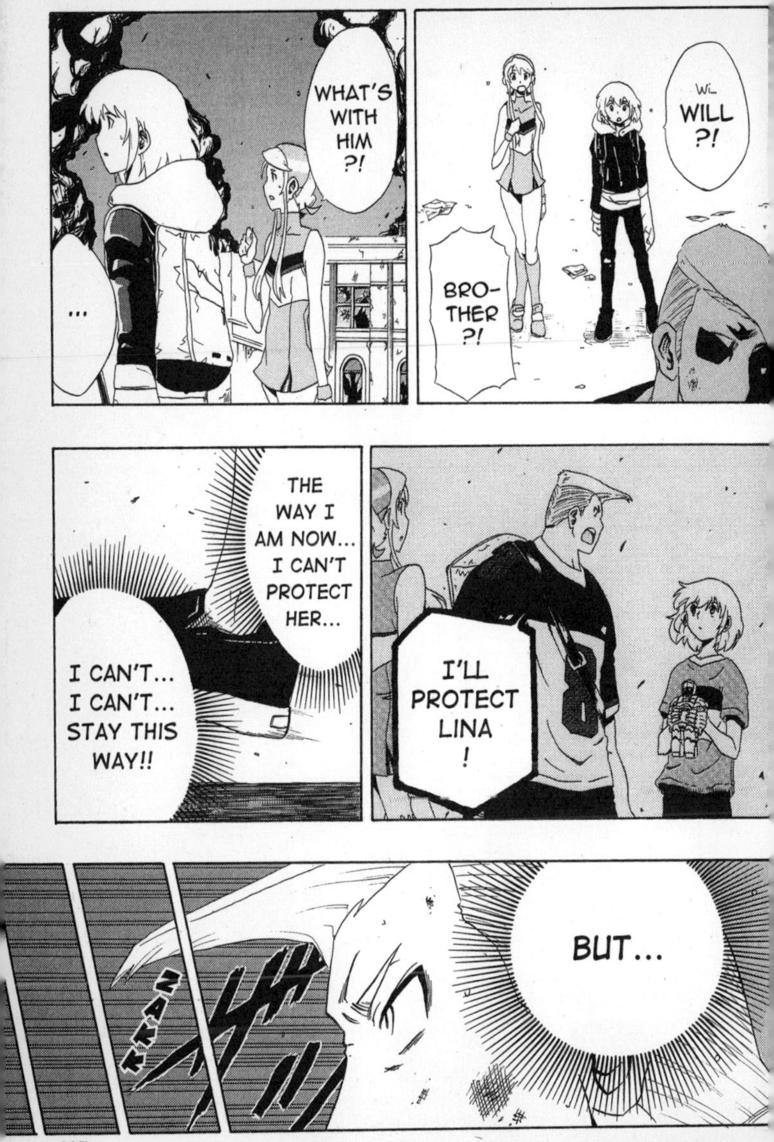
Wi... WILL?!
BROTHER?!
WHAT'S WITH HIM?!
...
I'LL PROTECT LINA!
THE WAY I AM NOW... I CAN'T PROTECT HER...
I CAN'T... I CAN'T... STAY THIS WAY!!
BUT...
ZAKK

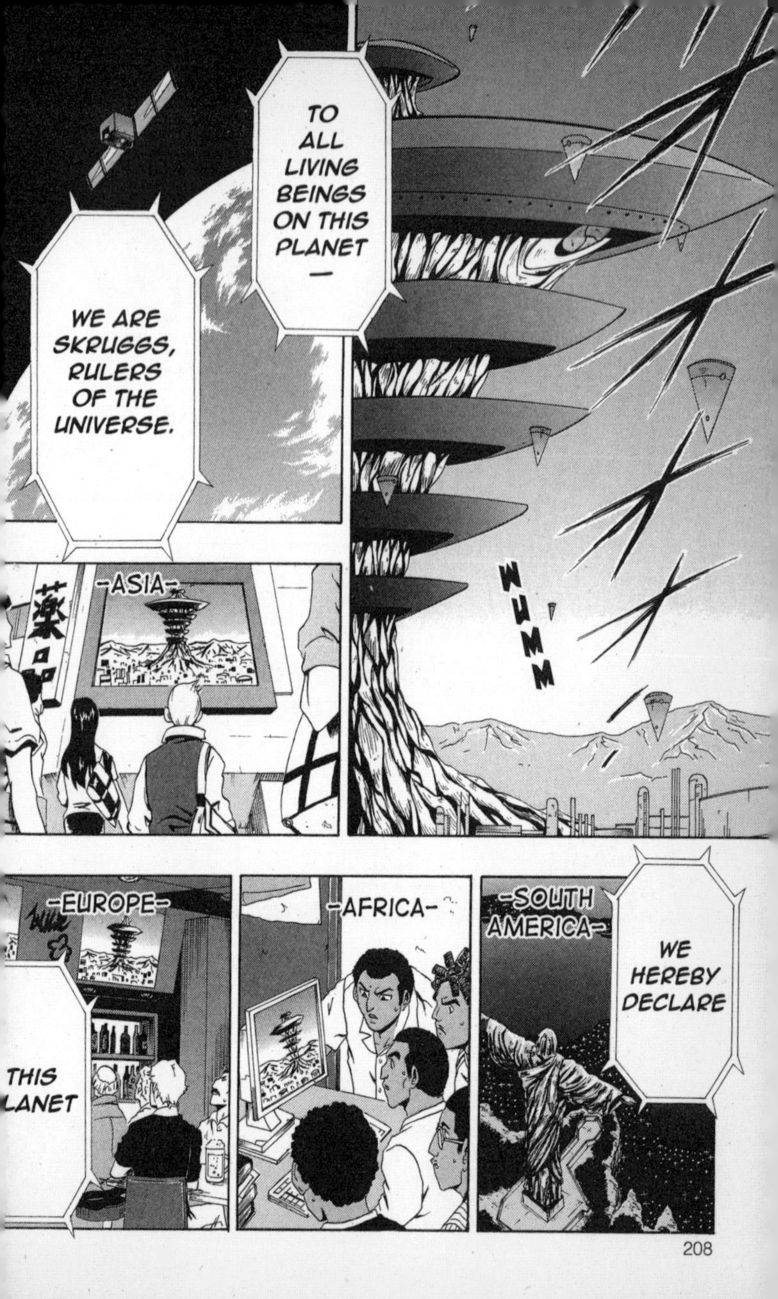
TO ALL LIVING BEINGS ON THIS PLANET —
WUMM
WE ARE SKRUGGS, RULERS OF THE UNIVERSE.
-ASIA-
-SOUTH AMERICA-
WE HEREBY DECLARE
-AFRICA-
-EUROPE-
THIS LANET

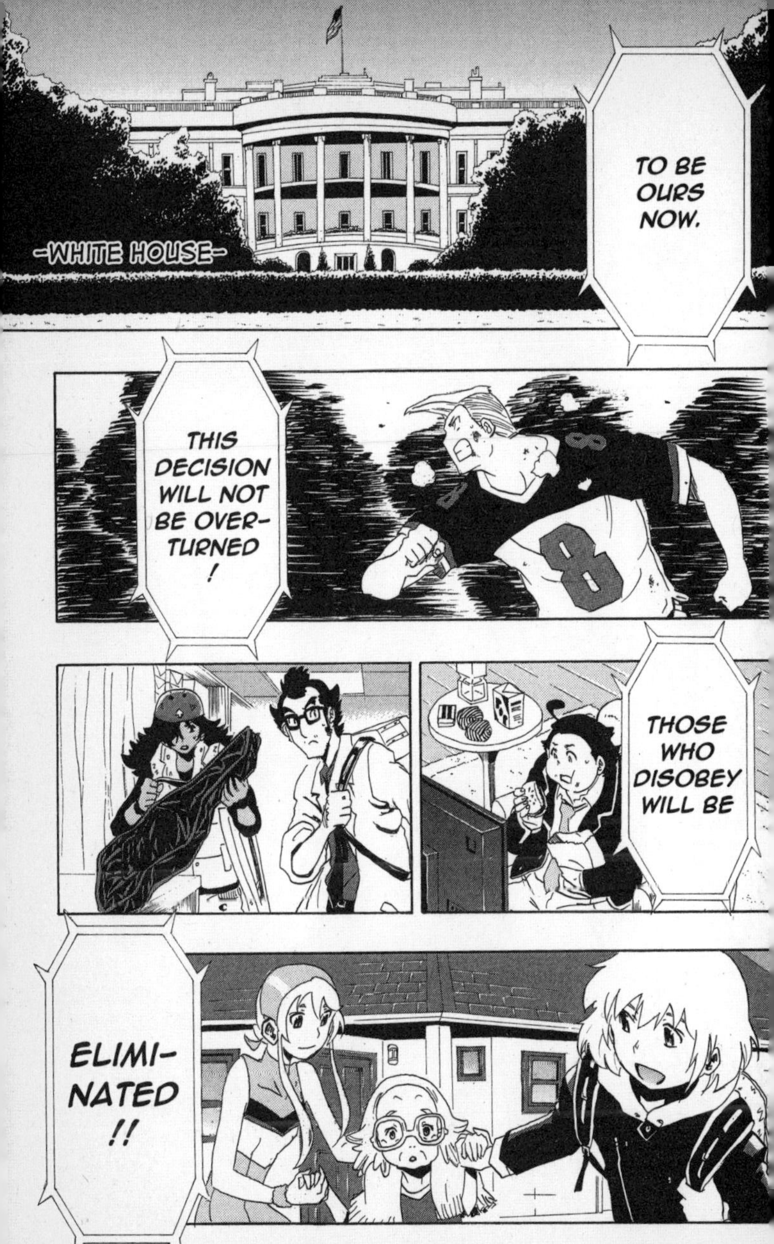
TO BE OURS NOW.
-WHITE HOUSE-
THIS DECISION WILL NOT BE OVER-TURNED!
THOSE WHO DISOBEY WILL BE
ELIMI-NATED!!

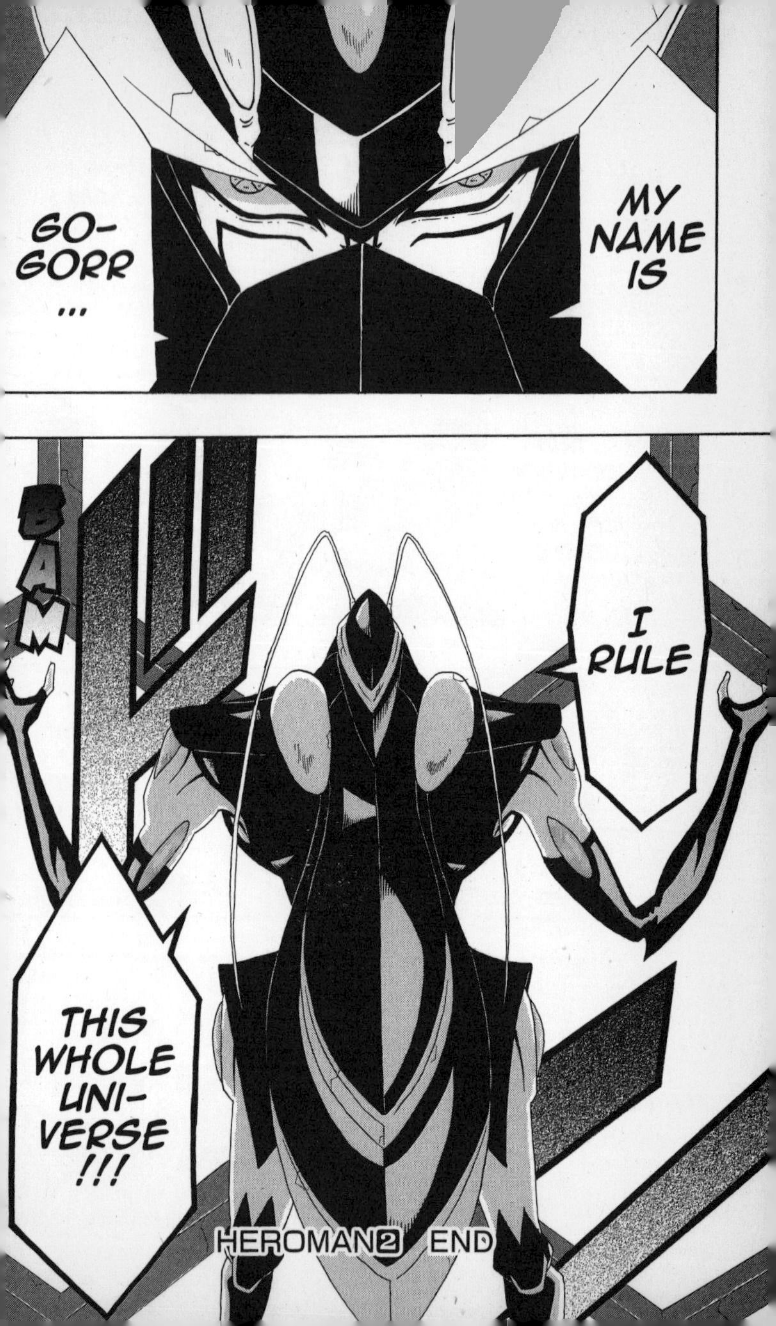
MY NAME IS
GO-GORR ...
I RULE
BAM
THIS WHOLE UNI-VERSE!!!
HEROMAN2 END

VOLUME 3
COMING THIS
FEBRUARY!

It's clearly a comedy, but when it takes a turn into drama, it doesn't feel un-natural. *14 Days in Shonan* looks like one of those series that can be brutally funny when it wants to be."
—*Comics Alliance*

I loved it… The most surprising thing about *14 Days in Shonan* is its ability to address serious social problems without devolving into an Afterschool special." —*The Manga Critic*

Suffice to say, the first chapter grabbed me almost immediately. It was the same *Great Teacher Onizuka* humor I remember, and most importantly, I re-acted the same to it as I had when I was stuck in my college dorm on those long Syracuse winter nights." —*Japanator*

Established fans will definitely get more out of it, but there's enough fun here to 'open the doors of all hearts,' as Onizuka himself would put it." —*Otaku USA*

GTO
GREAT TEACHER ONIZUKA
14 DAYS in SHONAN
by TORU FUJISAWA

Completed only last year, this new arc in the saga of the most badass teacher ever requires no prior schooling in the fran-hise to move you (when you aren't laughing your head off).

VOLUMES 1 TO 6 AVAILABLE NOW!
200 pages, $10.95 each

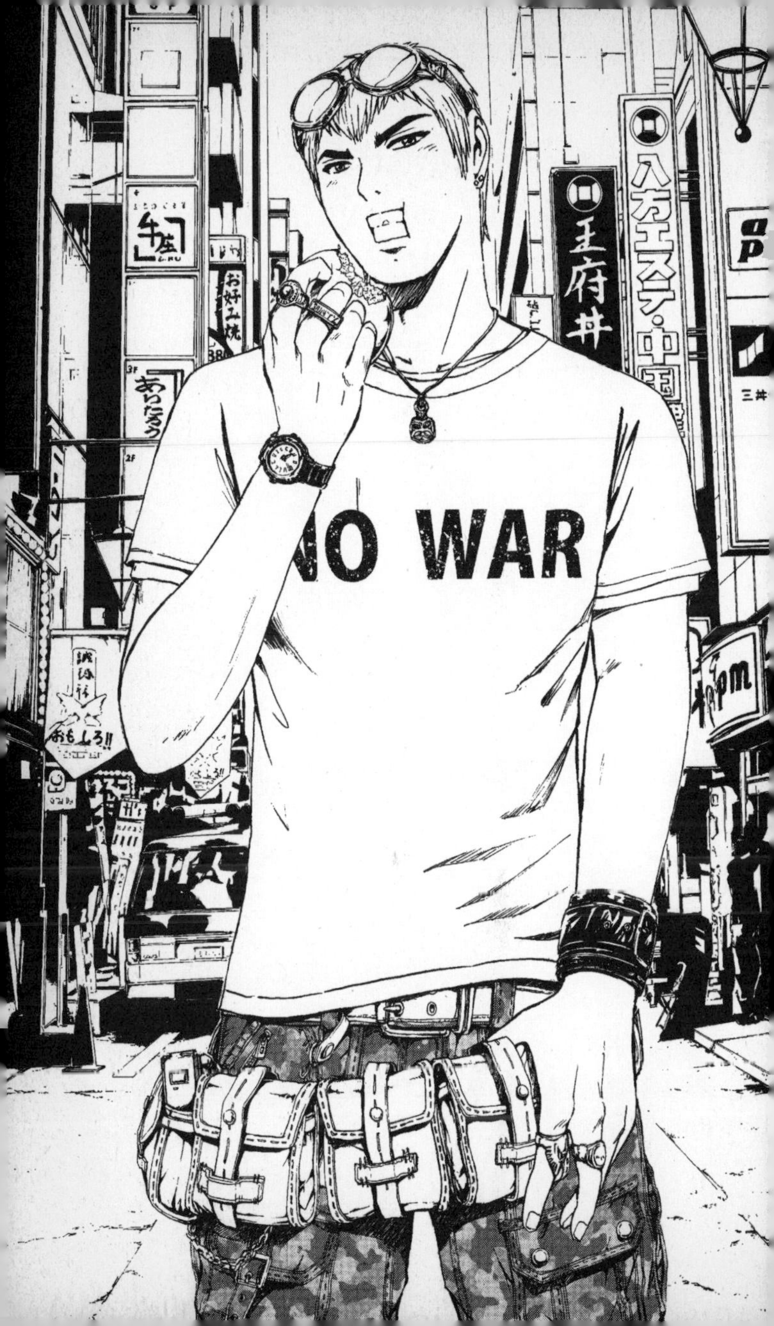
NO WAR

HEROMAN

Heroman, volume 2

Translation: Midori Maejima
Production: Taylor Esposito
           Nicole Dochych
           Daniela Yamada
           Jeremy Khan

First published in Japan in 2010 by SQUARE ENIX CO., LTD.
English translation rights arranged with SQUARE ENIX CO., LTD. and Vertical, Inc.
through Tuttle-Mori Agency, Inc.

Translation provided by Vertical, Inc., 2012
Published by Vertical, Inc., New York

Originally published in Japanese as *HEROMAN 2* by Square Enix Co., Ltd.
First serialized in *Gekkan Shounen GanGan*, 2009-2011

This is a work of fiction.

ISBN: 978-1-935654-59-9

Manufactured in Canada

First Edition

Vertical, Inc.
451 Park Avenue South
7th Floor
New York, NY 10016
www.vertical-inc.com

WRONG WAY

Japanese books, including manga like this one,
are meant to be read from right to left.
So the front cover is actually the back cover, and vice versa.
To read this book, please flip it over
and start in the top right-hand corner.
Read the panels, and the bubbles in the panels,
from right to left,
then drop down to the next row and repeat.
It may make you dizzy at first, but forcing your brain to
do things backwards makes you smarter in the long run.
We swear.